THE EIGHTIETH ANNUAL MEETING OF THE AMERICAN ACADEMY OF POLITICAL AND SOCIAL SCIENCE

APRIL 9 AND 10, 1976
THE BENJAMIN FRANKLIN HOTEL
PHILADELPHIA, PENNSYLVANIA

For several days prior to the Annual Meeting the Academy will have held a Bicentennial Conference on the United States Constitution. Principal participants from that Conference will address each session of the Annual Meeting on the topic

BICENTENNIAL CONFERENCE ON THE CONSTITUTION:
A REPORT TO THE ACADEMY

Approximately 1,000 persons will be in attendence sometime during the two days of sessions, representing a wide variety of cultural, civic and scientific organizations.

Members are cordially invited to attend and will automatically receive full information.

- Proceedings of the 80th Annual Meeting will be published as the July issue of THE ANNALS.

- FOR DETAILS WRITE TO: THE AMERICAN ACADEMY OF POLITICAL AND SOCIAL SCIENCE • BUSINESS OFFICE • 3937 CHESTNUT STREET, PHILADELPHIA, PENNSYLVANIA 19104

VOLUME 423   JANUARY 1976

THE ANNALS

of The American Academy *of* Political
and Social Science

RICHARD D. LAMBERT, *Editor*
ALAN W. HESTON, *Assistant Editor*

CRIME AND JUSTICE IN AMERICA:
1776–1976

Special Editor of This Volume

GRAEME R. NEWMAN
Professor
School of Criminal Justice
State University of New York
at Albany
Albany, New York

PHILADELPHIA

Library of Congress Catalog Card Number 75-36472

DOROTHY ANN HOFFMAN, *Copy Editor*

JOANNE S. SMITH, *Book Review Copy Editor*

International Standard Book Numbers (ISBN)

ISBN 0-87761-197-1, vol. 423, 1976; paper—$4.00

ISBN 0-87761-196-3, vol. 423, 1976; cloth—$5.00

Issued bimonthly by The American Academy of Political and Social Science at 3937 Chestnut St., Philadelphia, Pennsylvania 19104. Cost per year: $15.00 paperbound; $20.00 clothbound. Add $1.50 to above rates for membership outside U.S.A. Second-class postage paid at Philadelphia and at additional mailing offices.

Editorial and Business Offices, 3937 Chestnut Street, Philadelphia, Pennsylvania 19104.

CONTENTS

iii

BOOK DEPARTMENT   PAGE

INTERNATIONAL RELATIONS

AFRICA, ASIA AND LATIN AMERICA

EUROPE

CONTENTS

PREFACE

We conduct our lives on the basis of many realities. Some of these realities depend on the flimsiest assumptions—such as the assumption of expecting consistent and predictable behaviors in social relationships. Other realities border on the delusional—such as the working hypothesis that one will always be here tomorrow. But generally, realities are a mixture of both extremes—of certainty and uncertainty, of myth and fact.

The cultural context of crime is no exception. Although probably everyone has been "victimized" to some degree or another by crime—ranging from the imposition of higher retail prices because of shoplifting to a direct victimization in a mugging—the reality of crime varies with one's closeness to or remoteness from it. Our scientific knowledge of crime can only be secondhand—we must rely on officials' reports, victims' reports, or self-admissions. In this sense, crime achieves a kind of phantom nature and is therefore highly susceptible to imaginary interpretations.

But the treatment of crime in America has not been so much imaginary as visionary. The American republic was founded upon a vision, and Americans have remained idealists and visionaries ever since. It is often argued that America has sacrificed its ideals for material growth. Of course, this is patently false. Its very ideal has been material growth, and by world standards it has achieved a very high level. America's poor are a long way from the poorest in the world. Cynics would observe that idealists, like Don Quixote, invariably come to grief. And indeed, it would seem that Americans have paid a price for their idealism. Crime has kept well in step with each social reform and each increase in material wealth.

Has the time come for an about-face? As academic research and theory have more and more emphasized the "unreal" qualities of crime—its "social construction," its "dark figure" (the underworld?)—the people and the government have insisted upon its "realities," especially of being cheated, raped, or mugged.

There can be no simple answers. Let the government act upon these realities as it must. A people and its leaders generate their own myths. This is the stuff on which a national culture is built. Crime is not created by these myths, but rather it is given its meaning by them. Indeed, crime may alter its outward forms as the patterns of culture change; hence, the specific increases in female crime. But crime is endemic to every kind of complex society. One may therefore argue that crime is not only "not bad" but even ordinary, so that an idealism which seeks to eradicate crime is indeed misplaced, even romantic.

To celebrate our 200th year of crime, I have tried to bring together a number of papers which (1) trace some historical origins of crime and justice in America; (2) examine some cultural expressions of crime through fact, fiction, and policy; and (3) are themselves representative of the cultural context of crime. Some of the papers attempt to destroy myths; others to comprehend them. Still others try to break out of the visionary mold and plead for rationality. We have on our hands, Wilkins says, a "mad, bad, sick" confusion. The colossal complexity of the concept of crime cannot be doubted, and its role in the mythical foundations of national culture has yet to be apprehended. Perhaps if we can rid ourselves of this confusing moralism about crime, we will be able to go forward with clear heads and protect ourselves.

GRAEME R. NEWMAN

Criminal Violence in America:
The First Hundred Years

By ROGER LANE

ABSTRACT: America has long been notorious for its violence, but illegitimate criminal violence has received relatively little attention. *Vigilantism* is the best known of the
specifically American forms of social violence. Woven deeply
into our history, bound up in the westward movement, the
gun culture, and slavery, vigilantism in its wider sense was
an important form of political expression. Mob violence
reached its apogee in the North before the Civil War, but continued to flourish in the South and West through 1876 and gave
the whole nation a heritage of direct action in the name of
justice. *Gunfighting* has been less important in our actual
history, but very significant in our national imagination. The
gunfighting mystique, and our fascination with it, has contributed heavily to our tradition of violence. *Urban riot and
crime* are new fields of study, drawing heavily on interdisciplinary methods. Recent work on the city of Philadelphia,
for example, may be used in several ways. The nature of
collective violence reveals something about the city's own
polity and, in connection with other studies of individual
violence, something about social and economic stages of
development. In brief, all sorts of street violence decreased
with the Industrial Revolution, and the Centennial City was
quieter than any earlier.

---

*Roger Lane is Professor of History at Haverford College, Educated at Yale and
Harvard Universities, he is the author of a book on the police of nineteenth-century
Boston and of a number of articles, largely on the history of crime. He has also
contributed to the President's Commission on the Causes and Prevention of
Violence.*

1

B Y THE time of its first centennial, in 1876, the United States had already earned its persisting reputation as the most violent society in the Western world. Born in revolution, still battling its Indian population, the nation was just then recovering from civil war. All this is familiar; sanctioned violence, formal warfare, has been the stuff of history since Thucydides. But about ordinary unsanctioned criminal violence, for which this country is equally noted, much less is known.[1]

The problems are obvious. Criminal activity is by nature difficult to reconstruct with accuracy, and historians must deal with scanty sources in some areas and with encrusted popular delusions in others. As a result, the existing scholarship is often tentative and limited primarily to three areas. The first area deals with aspects of lawlessness closely related to the major political concerns of the first American century. The second also deals with distinctive and often colorful American phenomena. The last and most recent deals with urban crime and riot in an attempt to understand the process of social and economic development. All three are united at least by the conviction that, if a society truly gets the violence it deserves, then the nature and extent of that violence may do much to illuminate the character of that society.

VIGILANTISM: THE PEOPLE ARE THE LAW

The great themes of American history, from the beginnings through the Civil War, have involved the often paradoxical relationships among freedom, democracy, slavery, and the frontier. The association of these elements has its origin deep in the colonial past. Slavery, in its peculiarly American form, was in part a product of the same seventeenth-century need for manpower which did much to elevate the condition of free labor. Southern fears of black insurrection, too, as well as life in the wilderness, contributed to that widespread familiarity with firearms which contributed to victory in the Revolution. The United States was, in fact, born a "gun culture," its self-image institutionalized in the Second Amendment and justified by an ideology which associated freedom with armed self-defense, as at Bunker Hill.[2] And from this point of view, the most significant of the American forms of violence is, in its wider sense, vigilantism. At once crime and reaction to crime, product originally of the southern frontier, vigilantism came to be associated with a democratic ideology which proved truly double-edged to those concerned with social and political stability.[3]

1. One provocative essay, largely dealing with political violence, is Hofstadter's introduction to Richard Hofstadter and Michael Wallace, eds., *American Violence: A Documentary History* (New York: Vintage Books, 1971). Despite many recent books, the best historical collection remains Hugh Davis Graham and Ted Robert Gurr, eds., *Violence in America: Historical and Comparative Perspectives: A Report to the National Commission on the Causes and Prevention of Violence, June 1969* (New York: New American Library Inc., 1969).

2. See Lee Kennett and James Laverne Anderson, *The Gun in America: The Origins of a National Dilemma* (Westport, Conn.: The Greenwood Press, 1975), chs. 1–3.

3. On "classic" vigilantism, see especially Richard Maxwell Brown, *The South Carolina Regulators* (Cambridge, Mass.: The Belknap Press, 1963); and R. M. Brown, "The American Vigilante Tradition," in *Violence in America*, ed. Davis and Gurr, pp. 144–218.

The conditions which produced the first Regulator Movement in South Carolina in the 1760s were replicated continually on later frontiers. Areas without effective agents of justice attracted not only lone bandits but also, sometimes, whole communities whose members defied the accepted traditions of the wider society. Activities such as counterfeiting, horse-thievery, and the stealing or recruitment of women and slaves offended the values of more respectable settlers. Upper-class concern typically resulted in formal organizations, complete with rules and officers, for the purpose of upholding order if not law. "Trials" of a sort were frequently held, with offenders sentenced to whipping or banishment. These groups often attracted dubious supporters, always involved dubious methods, and sometimes provoked a reaction among "moderators," real or pretended supporters of rule by law. But, in general, they served at least the purpose of cauterizing outlaw sanctuaries, part of the continual process by which orderly values were imposed on the wilderness.

This classic vigilantism moved, with an unaccountable leap of some decades, from South Carolina to the "Old West," from Tennessee to Illinois. It proved equally adaptable on the other side of the Mississippi, in such diverse environments as Texas and California, the mining camps of the mountain states, and, by 1876, the cattle country of the Great Plains. Everywhere there were abuses, and sometimes Regulator movements degenerated into factional bloodletting and small-scale civil wars. But most eastern conservatives held that the practice was useful. Foreign observers also— and scarcely an important visitor failed to comment—tended to feel that the ends justified these characteristically primitive American means.

Vigilantism, however, in the looser sense, was not confined to the frontier or practiced solely by men of substance who obeyed traditional rules. The special terminology, as well as the practice, had become, by the 1820s, nearly universal throughout the South and West. "Captain Stick" and "Squire Birch" were called in even where the law was firmly established. And the maturing ideology of the practice was based on a conveniently flexible belief in popular sovereignty—the idea that since law is ultimately derived from the majority, justice may be dispensed by the people directly.

Americans were quite conscious of the political importance of mob activity. The decade of agitation preceding the Revolution had popularized the use of tar and feathers, and the verb "to lynch" apparently owes its origins to the harassment of Tories in wartime Virginia.[4] These patriotic memories reinforced the many impulses which fueled riotous behavior throughout our early history. However, it was the period after 1830 in which mobbing enjoyed its heyday as a major form of political expression.[5] Historians are unable to agree on a single cause for this phenomenon, but it seems partly the result of the political intensity of what is loosely called the Jacksonian Era, together with a variety of real or imagined threats to American traditions.

While targets varied, the most

4. James Elbert Cutler, *Lynch-Law: An Investigation into the History of Lynching in the United States* (New York: Longmans, Green, 1905), p. 29.
5. Much of the history of mobs is inseparable from the general histories of the era; for more, see section three.

important were those which seemed to threaten the cherished values of liberty, equality, and traditional white Protestant domination. The Catholic and newly formed Mormon churches qualified on all of these grounds.[6] Both were hierarchical, mysterious organizations, governed without regard for popular democracy. Too, in a period of sexual restraint and anxiety, the unusual customs practiced by the Mormons and attributed, in many scatological works, to Catholic clergy, encouraged honest workingmen to project their own fantasies onto these alien religions.[7] The threat was further intensified by rapid growth. Catholicism grew with the great influx of Irish, particularly after the famine years of the 1840s. While neither so numerous nor so widespread, the Mormons were growing even faster and could dominate the areas around such settlements as Naovoo, Illinois, briefly the largest city in the state.

Serious trouble began in the notably riotous year of 1834, when a group of "truckmen" burnt a nunnery outside of Boston, simultaneously "liberating" and chastising the inhabitants, just as similar mobs had destroyed whorehouses in earlier years. The Mormons, later, were driven from Ohio to Missouri and thence to Illinois by hostile neighbors, until in 1844 the martyrdom of their leadership and the destruction of their city forced them into the western deserts. Attacks on the Irish meanwhile increased throughout the decade and into the next.

But the issues of race and slavery, and the freedom to discuss them, greatly overshadowed others as catalysts of popular disturbance. Again, the causes were manifold. The same Irish who suffered the attacks of nativists were often involved in bitter economic and residential competition with established blacks and joined in any assault on black neighborhoods. At the other end of the social scale, conservative businessmen led the mob which roughed up the abolitionist William Lloyd Garrison on the streets of Boston in 1835.[8] Men of affairs recognized that, unlike unpopular religious groups, the antislavery forces, while still tiny, posed a real and not imaginary threat to the nation. A breach with the South, by splitting the union, would disrupt a national prosperity built in considerable part upon the trade in cotton.

Other thoughtful men, however, were deeply troubled by the increasing tendency to breach the constitution in order to preserve it. Abraham Lincoln was one of many who condemned illegal direct action, explicitly associating the vigilantism of the South and West with antiabolitionist outbreaks in the north.[9] The fear that democracy would degenerate into anarchy was as old as Aristotle. But neither doubt nor protest stilled the accelerating course of mob violence. Most of it was perpetrated by those who wished at all costs to preserve the southern connection. But the antislavery men,

6. On Anti-Catholic Rioting, see Ray Allen Billington, *Protestant Crusade: A Study of the Origins of American Nationalism* (New York: MacMillan Co., 1938); on Mormons, see Thomas O'Dea, *The Mormons* (Chicago: University of Chicago Press, 1957).

7. David Brion Davis, "Intergroup Conflict," in *American History and the Social Sciences*, ed. Edward N. Saveth (Glencoe: The Free Press, 1964), pp. 175–189.

8. Roger Lane, *Policing the City: Boston, 1822–1855* (Cambridge, Mass.: Harvard University Press, 1967), pp. 29–30.

9. Benjamin Thomas, *Abraham Lincoln* (New York: Knopf, 1952), pp. 71–72.

too, could invoke the ideology of extremism in pursuit of liberty and call upon a Higher Law, legitimizing their own actions in the name of American principles. "Vigilance Committees," significantly named, were formed to frustrate the enforcement of the hated Fugitive Slave Act of 1850. One Boston mob, attempting to free a fugitive, Anthony Burns, murdered a man in 1854, and it took more than two thousand armed men to march Burns down State Street to the harbor and onto a ship for Richmond.[10]

No such differences of opinion troubled the white South. There, too, the years around 1830 seem to mark a turning point. Black insurrection had always been the most frightening of crimes for southerners. And while there had been no previous acts of overt rebellion in the history of the Republic, the 1831 Nat Turner Revolt in Virginia finally realized these fears by taking some fifty-seven white lives. Thereafter, fear of the consequences of lightened control, together with the increasing success of the cotton economy, contributed to the efficiency with which local antislavery sentiment was crushed. While the Turner incident remained unique, occasional attempts at black revenge or freedom were magnified many times by a tense white population easily swayed by rumor. Through the 1840s and 1850s a number of brutal lynchings and harassments of troublesome blacks and their alleged white accomplices effectively made the whole region, on this sensitive subject, a closed society.[11]

And while elected officials condoned and even encouraged these measures, the means of closure was not official suppression so much as lawless popular action.

The effect of the Civil War was to alter but not to end these manifestations of vigilantism. While mob activity abated in northern cities, western vigilantism seemed to grow in intensity as it crossed the Mississippi. More and larger organizations were formed, more victims claimed, fewer rules observed. By 1876 the verb "to lynch," which once had meant violence short of murder, had acquired its present definition, as rope and bullet succeeded whipping post and banishment.[12] To the South, meanwhile, the Era of Reconstruction gave new sanction to this and other illegal means of repression. Native whites reacted to black political power by denying its legitimacy. Reconstruction authority was defied and the traditional "order" upheld by private violence, once again in the name of popular sovereignty. All over the South, formal groups such as the Ku Klux Klan, as well as informal night riders, complemented political protest with a kind of guerilla warfare. By 1876 they had won; federal troops remained in only two states and would soon be gone entirely.

Slavery, then, had been ended, and the frontier was receding. But the country had not recovered from either. Both, combined with an ideology of popular rights which was common to all regions, contributed to a heritage in which the persecution of minorities and the lawless administration of "justice" were justified on the highest grounds of American tradition.

10. Lane, *Policing the City*, pp. 72–74, 90–92.

11. On southern mobs, see Clement V. Eaton, "Mob Violence in the Old South," *Mississippi Valley Historical Review*, vol. 29 (1942), pp. 351ff.

12. Cutler, *Lynch-Law*, p. 135.

THE GUNFIGHTER: THE INDIVIDUAL BEYOND THE LAW

If vigilantism was the most significant of the violent crimes associated with America, it was by no means the only one. Crowds at the Philadelphia Centennial still heard rumors of little Charlie Ross, from nearby Germantown, who had been abducted two years earlier in the first notorious kidnapping for ransom.[13] Just three years before, it seems, Floyd Hatfield's theft of Randolph McCoy's pigs had set off the country's most celebrated family feud.[14] But then as now, these and other famous cases of the era were overshadowed by the attention paid to western gunfighting.

Several elements contributed to the creation of the gunfighter as hero. Some were legal and historical, others technological, a few peculiar to the West. But none were as important as those popular traditions which virtually provided lines and stage directions for a long generation of violent characters who became, quite literally, legends in their own time.

Part of this fascination resulted from the fact that guns in America, associated from the first with liberty, became associated with honor as well. The custom of duelling, by the time of its late eighteenth-century importation into America, was a matter of pistols rather than swords.[15] And while the business fell out of favor in the northern states, in part because of the killing of Alexander Hamilton in 1804, it found a warmer atmosphere in the South. Indeed, when European enthusiasm also waned, as the nineteenth century took hold, the American South became the most enthusiastic stronghold of the custom.

By mid-century, however, the code duello had degenerated considerably from its aristocratic origins. While the gallants of Charleston still insisted upon a certain punctillio, it was impossible, in a society where all free men insisted upon their equality, to restrict the concept of honor to any elite. The inevitable democratization involved two related changes. One is that the weaponry was democratized as well, and bowie knives, shotguns, and finally six-shooters proved far more lethal than one-shot duelling pistols. The other, equally predictable, was that the definition of "duel" was stretched as far as the definition of "gentlemen." Duelling was almost universally illegal, even where it was most common. But when governors, senators, and presidents of the United States were all proudly involved, tradition decreed that this was a matter outside of the law. Since almost any homicidal brawl could be interpreted, in areas where men were routinely armed, as a matter either of self-defense or of honor, the participants were often beyond official justice, and local opinion grew not only tolerant but even romantic about the mystique of gunfighting.

Duelling declined in the older South as the Civil War and its aftermath perhaps absorbed most violent energies. But the gunfighter, together with the romanticized outlaw, continued to flourish in the Southwest and West. And most importantly, they flourished back East as well, in the pages of the popular

13. Dee Brown, *The Year of the Century: 1876* (New York: Charles Scribner's Sons, 1966), p. 263.

14. Hofstadter and Wallace, *American Violence*, p. 397.

15. On duelling, see William Oliver Stevens, *Pistols at Ten Paces: The Story of the Code of Honor in America* (Boston: Houghton Mifflin Co., 1940).

press. The process has not yet ended.

Recent historiography has, however, developed along lines opposed to popular tradition. One group of scholars has taken a hard second look at the reality behind the legends; the other has explored the formation and significance of the legends themselves.

The first group has served to demythologize much of western history. It remains true that "the actual administration of justice was not favorably regarded . . . on the frontier," a distrust both measured and fostered by such phenomena as low rates of conviction and wholesale pardons.[16] Much if not most lawless violence was directed at outgunned minorities, considered beyond the reach of legal protection— not only Indians and Mexicans but also Chinese and Mormons.[17] Almost no one was likely to be shot down in the classic one-on-one gun duel. Furthermore very few marshals or sheriffs were known as gunfighters. Even when, during the 1870s, lawmen such as Wild Bill Hickok patrolled the Kansas cowtowns, people were scarcely deafened by the roar of six-guns. One study has shown that during the fifteen-year heyday of the five leading towns, a total of only forty-five homicides was reported.[18] Drunken men did fight, as back East, over cards and women. But then as now, lawmen dealt largely with a tawdry parade of alcoholics, morals offenders, and petty thieves. "Small town law enforcement has actually changed very little in the West during the last century."[19]

Given all this, much of the recent interest in western history has centered on the way in which these unpromising materials were converted into the stuff of romance.

Part of the answer is simply a matter of technology and salesmanship. The invention of the rotary steampress enabled editors, after the 1840s, to exploit "the subliterary story of adventure, deliberately contrived for a mass audience."[20] Erastus Beadle produced the first of his famous "dime novels" in 1860. As production expanded, Beadle's editors, like their rivals and predecessors, found that nothing sold like the Wild West. And this discovery neatly coincided with the border troubles of the Southwest, the expansion of silver mining, and the opening of the cattle plains, which produced as models the likes of Jesse James, Wyatt Earp, and "Doc" Holliday.

The special appeal of the James boys rests in part upon unique circumstances. Jesse and Frank, during the Civil War, had ridden with Quantrill's Raiders, confederate guerilla-banditti on the Missouri border. And what set them apart from similar desperadoes, before and after, was the local popularity which made it hard to pursue or convict them in home territory. Jesse, at the height of his career in 1876, was not only the most famous criminal in our history, but the best

16. Frank Richard Prassell, *The Western Peace Officer: A Legacy of Law and Order* (Norman: University of Oklahoma Press, 1972), p. 12.

17. W. Eugene Holton, *Frontier Violence: Another Look* (New York: Oxford University Press, 1974), especially chs. 2, 4, 5, 7.

18. Robert W. Dykstra, *The Cattle Towns: A Social History of the Kansas Trading Centers* (New York: Knopf, 1968), pp. 144–46.

19. Prassel, *The Western Peace Officer*, p. 69.

20. Henry Nash Smith, *Virgin Land: The American West as Symbol and Myth* (Cambridge, Mass.: Harvard University Press, 1950), pp. 86–87. For western dime novels, see especially ch. 9.

American example of the "social bandit."[21]

The conditions which give rise to "social banditry" were roughly duplicated in postwar Missouri. These include hard times, a sense of economic exploitation, and an alien machinery of justice. Under these circumstances a local outlaw, careful to prey only upon outsiders and above all exploiters, may become a hero. The James boys, nemeses of banks and railroads, appear to qualify. And what is most remarkable is the way in which the biographical facts and especially the legends about Jesse conform to patterns found all over the world. Common elements include not only the original act of persecution which drives the local youth into outlawry and the act of betrayal which kills him, but even specific anecdotal material originally attributed to Robin Hood, the most notable original.

The phenomenon of social banditry, however, is at best only a partial explanation of the popularity of western badmen.[22] The wide open spaces of plains and mountain country, almost deliberately lacking in social context, serve as background for most of the hard cases of the era. Very little is known about the actual lives and exploits of such characters.[23] And more important than the embittering confederate experiences of a John Wesley Hardin or the New York slum background of a William Bonney, for example, are the free-floating myths, the projected fantasies, which attached themselves to these types. And life inevitably followed art: by the time of Wild Bill Hickok's 1876 assassination at a poker table in Deadwood, he had already played in Buffalo Bill's Wild West Show and been the subject of so many newspaper and magazine pieces that he and his interviewers must have memorized the formulas.[24]

The real significance of the gunfighters, then, lay not in the predictable role they played in the history of settlement but in the much larger role they continued to play in the national imagination. The fascination with outlawry and the glorification of violence are universal. But other elements are distinctively American, part of older and continuing traditions. These include the sacrosanct right to bear arms and the concomitant notion that, although villains too can shoot, ultimately "the gun is its own antidote."[25] Also, the blurred line between legitimate and illegitimate violence, often illustrated in the career lines of western toughs who operated alternately inside and outside the law, had older origins in vigilantism and duelling. All of these, added to a national self-image which stressed physical courage and self-reliance, found expression in the gunfighter. If Wyatt Earp had not existed, it would have been neces-

21. On "Social Banditry," see Eric Hobsbawm, *Bandits!* (New York: Delacorte Press, 1969).

22. Attempts to fit Billy the Kid into this Robin Hood mold, as champion of small ranchers and Mexicans in Lincoln County, New Mexico, seem clearly posthumous and strained. See Kent Ladd Steckmesser, *The Western Hero in History and Legend* (Norman: University of Oklahoma Press, 1965), ch. 9.

23. See Joseph G. Rosa, *The Gunfighter: Man or Myth?* (Norman: The University of Oklahoma Press, 1969).

24. Henry M. Stanley reports that Hickok, in an interview, claimed with a straight face to have killed over 100 white men, all with good cause. Steckmesser, *The Western Hero,* p. 124.

25. Kennett and Anderson, *The Gun in America,* pp. 251–252.

sary to invent him. Indeed, in large part, we did and continue to do so.

URBAN CRIME AND RIOT: ORDER AS PROGRESS

The historical study of ordinary urban violence is relatively new. And as a result, the field has, from the first, reflected current awareness of social theory on the one hand and hard quantitative methods on the other. The emphasis is less on distinctively "American" behavior than on wider patterns of development, in an effort to understand the process of social change itself. Drawing upon the experience of other societies as well as other disciplines, historians have sought especially to understand the two outstanding transformations of this period—the urban and the industrial.

Recent studies of collective violence reflect these concerns. The period from the 1830s through the 1850s was the most riotous in our history; one conservative estimate is that 1,000 lives were lost as a result.[26] Some of the reasons for this have already been outlined, but there are a number of other levels of explanation which, without denying these, seek to fit the phenomenon into other contexts.

One approach has involved a new look at the composition and activities of mobs in general. The traditional nineteenth-century view stressed the dangerously irrational behavior of human beings in groups.[27] Mobs, largely comprised of the "lowest" elements in the population, offered the protection of anonymity to their members as well as a giddy sense of excitement; the result was fickle, irresponsible behavior, as the crowd proved less moral or intelligent than the sum of its individual parts. In 1957, however, George Rude began a reexamination of these assumptions in his seminal study of *The Crowd in History*.[28] In eighteenth- and nineteenth-century France and England, it appears, collective violence was a traditional, sometimes tolerated, form of political expression for groups otherwise lacking in political leverage. Most mobs were composed of ordinary working-class people. Their purposes varied, but their targets, more often property than persons, were usually selected with these purposes in mind. The mob might be wrongheaded, but it was not blind and rarely out of control.

Rude's analysis may be applied to many of the popular disturbances of the Jacksonian Era.[29] Philadelphia's "anti-railroad riots," for example, occurred when the distant state legislature chartered a railroad to run in the streets of Kensington, despite unanimous opposition from the city's own representatives.[30]

---

26. David Grimsted, "Rioting in Its Jacksonian Setting," *American Historical Review*, vol. 77, no. 2 (April 1972), pp. 361–397.

27. The older views are among those surveyed in Stanley Milgram and Hans Toch, "Collective Behavior: Crowds and Social Movements," in *Handbook of Social Psychology*, ed. Gardner Lindzey and Elliot Aronson, 2nd. ed. (Reading, Pa.: Addison-Wesley, 1968), vol. 4, pp. 542–84.

28. George Rude, *The Crowd in History: A Study of Popular Disturbances in France and England, 1730–1848* (New York: John Wiley and Sons, 1964).

29. It is noteworthy that many of the detailed conclusions of Rude's analysis have been independently replicated by some of the authors below, as well as by the Kerner Commission report on the black riots of the 1960s, without any prior knowledge of Rude's work.

30. Michael Feldberg, "Urbanization as a Cause of Violence: Philadelphia as a Test Case," in *The Peoples of Philadelphia: A*

With the normal political avenues blocked, residents turned to direct action, battling work crews and sheriff's men, firing the property of the railroad and its supporters. Rioters justified their actions in terms of a popular traditional right of direct resistance to unpopular authority. And their well-run campaign helped to win enough support to block construction.

But while much crowd violence in this period may be regarded as an extension of the legitimate political process, governed by traditional restraints, any analysis which relies upon coolly rational calculation is, at best, incomplete. Psychologists may distinguish between "instrumental" and "expressive" violence—one rational and goal-directed, the other an irrational venting of emotion. But the distinction is difficult in practice. Then as now, rioting and street fighting were, above all, dominated by young males. And whatever the issues, there is a clear sense that much was done out of frustrations only partly understood and imperfectly expressed. And some of it was done for the sheer hell of it.

Drink, sport, and violence were all strong ingredients in Jacksonian working-class culture. And in Philadelphia, in this respect a representative city, all three ingredients found institutional expression in the city's numerous volunteer fire companies.[31] In the second quarter of the nineteenth century, the means and ends of what had once

been competition merely to be first at fires escalated ominously. The volunteers, once "gentlemen," were increasingly being recruited from the working classes. Rival companies allied with street gangs of young neighborhood toughs. With religious and political differences often superimposed on earlier frictions, and with perhaps something like community control at issue, firemen engaged not only in pitched battles but also in arson and murder in attempts to best each other. And whenever there was trouble in Philadelphia—attacks on blacks, election riots, church burnings—it appears that the volunteers were in the thick of it.

One important aspect of these riots, routs, and tumults is that they mark a stage in the development of the city. Through the eighteenth century and into the nineteenth, the mechanisms of social order—save in the rare emergencies when the militia might be called—were largely informal.[32] While its residents were divided by class and occupation, the old "walking city" was small enough to permit easy communication. Its population was normally governed by a small and easily recognized elite, leading a stable electorate of middle-class householders and artisans. While many feared the city's lower classes —blacks, laborers, and sailors ashore—social authority was never truly threatened.[33]

But, like other urban centers in the same era, Philadelphia was no

---

History of Ethnic Groups and Lower Class Life, 1790–1940, ed. Allen F. Davis and Mark Haller (Philadelphia: Temple University Press, 1973), pp. 58–61.

31. Bruce Laurie, "Fire Companies and Gangs in Southwark: The 1840's," in *Peoples of Philadelphia*, pp. 71–88.

32. Sam Bass Warner, Jr., *The Private City: Philadelphia in Three Periods of Its Growth* (Philadelphia: University of Pennsylvania Press), ch. 1.

33. John K. Alexander, "Poverty, Fear, and Continuity: An Analysis of the Poor in Late Eighteenth Century Philadelphia," in *Peoples of Philadelphia*, pp. 13–36.

longer a town but becoming a city. And its spreading area and mounting population were outgrowing the old system of governance.[34] De Tocqueville had noted, in his visit of 1831, that America was a nation of joiners; in the cities, part of this eagerness to belong was a reaction to the loss of older forms of association. "The mid-nineteenth century was par excellence the era of the urban parish church, the lodge, the benefit association, the social and athletic club, the political club, the fire company, and the gang."[35] What marked the last two, however, was the fact that they not only compensated for a wider sense of membership but also worked to subvert it. At best, the companies and their supporters tended to divide the city into hostile neighborhoods. At worst, they raised the threat of anarchy as they expressed all existing tensions in fire and blood. Private citizens, organized as sheriff's posses or militia companies, were subject to the same pressures and emotions as the firemen and found it hard to control them. And it was eventually recognized that to pit one group of residents against another was a poor way of keeping the peace.

All of Philadelphia's leadership was united, by the 1850s, in a determined effort to maintain public order.[36] One obvious response, inspired here as elsewhere by the riot problem, was to create a professional police force. At the same time a variety of other institutions served, less directly, to contain social violence. The rise of an organized party system, notably, has been credited with "the institutionalization . . . of conflicts which formerly could seek only fragmentary, irregular, and violent expression."[37] By the time of the Civil War, the era of massive street battles was over.[38] Professionalization of police and politics both proved effective steps in providing the discipline necessary to hold together the disparate population of the modern city.

While useful as far as it goes, however, an explanation of popular violence solely in terms of population growth, group differences, and conscious political decisions must still be supplemented with another approach. Not only Rude but also a number of observers from Karl Marx to Charles Tilly have suggested that collective violence not only is a natural feature of political life, but that its forms and objects may indicate something about the social and economic structure as well.[39] Tilly has labeled as "primitive violence" those ancient conflicts, without clear instrumental goals, between rival churches, clans, or perhaps soccer fans. "Reactionary violence," common in eighteenth- and nineteenth-century Europe, is the defensive response of such groups as handicraft workers threatened by industry, who resist the process of modernization in the state or economy and justify their cause with appeals to tradition. "Modern collective violence," finally, is the product of such organized groups as labor unions, which accept the centralized state and industry and seek to increase their power within them.

With this analysis in mind, it ap-

34. Warner, *The Private City*, pp. 49ff.
35. Ibid., p. 61.
36. Russell K. Weigley, "A Peaceful City: Public Order in Philadelphia from Consolidation through the Civil War," in *Peoples of Philadelphia*, pp. 155–173.

37. Warner, *The Private City*, p. 152.
38. Weigley, in *Peoples of Philadelphia*, p. 158.
39. See Charles Tilly, "Collective Violence in European Perspective," in *Violence in America*, ed. Graham and Gurr.

pears that much of Philadelphia's Jacksonian violence may be characterized as either "primitive," "reactionary," or some combination of the two. Attacks on black neighborhoods and battles between immigrants and nativists belong in the first category. Groups such as the handloom weavers, whose sputtering rearguard action against encroaching machinery erupted in such incidents as "the Battle of Nanny Goat Market," provided the second.[40]

Historians have noted more generally that the long depression which began in 1837 was essential to subsequent violence, whatever its apparent purpose. The collapse of the earlier trades' union movement, changing job patterns, and a heritage of insecurity help account for the increased hostility displaced upon black or Irish scapegoats.[41] And it is especially significant that the fire companies were largely made up of artisans from traditional crafts rather than workers in the city's new factories. These men, hard drinking and independent, used to setting their own pace and hours, were truly "relics of a pre-industrial age."[42] While their local power centers were challenged by such political developments as municipal consolidation and professional policing, their whole way of life was threatened by a new economic order as intolerant of untidy violence as it was of casual work habits.

Support for this sort of analysis is provided, finally, by studies of purely individual criminal violence, such as robbery, murder, and as-

sault.[43] Jacksonian cities were as troubled by street crime as by riot.[44] And it appears that the same elements were involved in both: boisterous, often boozy young men, as quick to take advantage as offense. Were the streets in fact more dangerous than those of a later period? There is little direct statistical evidence, but there are some strong clues.

Then as now, violence often came in bottles. And the historian can almost smell the fumes arising from the record. The consumption of alcohol during these years was, by later standards, very high; in Boston, during the 1820s, about one in every 65 inhabitants was engaged in selling liquor.[45] The rate of serious crime appears equally steep; while no reliable index stretches back before mid-century, the figures begin to descend as soon as they appear. Contrary to both sociological theory and popular impression, population growth by itself does not generate criminal violence. In the cities especially, the late nineteenth century appears far more sober and peaceful than the earlier half.

The most inclusive explanation for this development is that it resulted from new economic pressures. Drinking and fighting, except in off hours and designated

40. On weavers, see Feldberg, in *Peoples of Philadelphia*, pp. 62–65.

41. Laurie, in *Peoples of Philadelphia*, pp. 72–75.

42. Ibid., p. 83.

43. The thesis about individual violence and the new economic order sketched below, and relevant bibliography, are more fully outlined in Roger Lane, "Urbanization and Criminal Violence in the Nineteenth Century: Massachusetts as a Test Case," in *Violence in America*, ed. Graham and Gurr, pp. 445–459; and Roger Lane, "Crime and the Industrial Revolution: British and American Views," *Journal of Social History*, vol. 7, no. 3 (Spring 1974), pp. 287–303.

44. David R. Johnson, "Crime Patterns in Philadelphia, 1840–1870," in *Peoples of Philadelphia*, pp. 89–101.

45. Lane, *Policing the City*, p. 111.

places, are incompatible with modern economic rationality. What is tolerable in farmers, artisans, and the self-employed generally is intolerable in those who must work closely together, in large organizations, under tight supervision. One may easily imagine Philadelphia's firemen and similar free spirits hooting at workmen from the new Baldwin Locomotive Works, or the mills of Manayunk, sullenly aware that their own rough habits belonged to the past and that sobriety and regularity were the hallmarks of the industrial future.

The pressures were certainly mounting. The decades just before the Civil War encompassed not only our sharpest urban growth but the decisive movement toward large-scale manufacturing. At the same time, several new institutions and organizations served, consciously and unconsciously, to promote the required behavior. Excessive drinking was the target of the temperance movement as well as of professional police. The prison, the asylum, and the poorhouse all date from this era also; each sought to "reform" their inmates through an orderly, routinized regimen, in a setting remarkable for its resemblance to the factory.[46] And the public schools, made universal and compulsory for the first time, taught obedience in unison to rod, rule, and bell, to children who would find these disciplines all too "relevant" in later life.

The results were already apparent in the Centennial City. Philadelphia by that time was full of "in-migrants" not yet broken into its routines, as well as rebels who defied them. Revolt of another sort was smoldering also: the great Railroad Strike of the next year would usher in "modern collective violence" with a vengeance, as the United States would come to lead the world in labor violence.[47] But the visitors who flocked to the industrial exhibits of 1876 strolled through streets far quieter than those of any earlier generation.

CONCLUSION

Deeper problems remained unsolved, here and across the nation. The Revolutionary generation, in its optimism, had hoped that the mild, free, and rational institutions of the new Republic would, in themselves, reduce the impulse to criminal disorder. Their successors, early in the nineteenth century, hoped that prosperity and a wholesome environment would eliminate crime and poverty alike (the connection has long been understood).[48] By the time of the Civil War, bitter experience had eroded this confidence. Some forms of violence, in the year in which Colonel Custer was ambushed at the Little Big Horn, were being outgrown. But troublesome habits and attitudes persisted from the past, and continued growth generated new problems as it buried the old. The nation was still the largest, the most polyglot, the most open and disorderly in the Western world. It would have troubles enough to last a century more.

46. David J. Rothman, *The Discovery of the Asylum: Social Order and Disorder in the New Republic* (Boston: Little, Brown & Co., 1971).

47. Philip Taft and Philip Ross, "American Labor Violence: Its Causes, Character, and Outcome," in *Violence in America*, ed. Graham and Gurr.

48. Rothman, *Discovery of the Asylum*, pp. 59–71.

ANNALS, AAPSS, **423,** Jan. 1976

The Great American Search: Causes of Crime 1876–1976

By Travis Hirschi and David Rudisill

ABSTRACT: Biology, psychology, and sociology have successively dominated American criminology over the last 100 years. Given that the biological and psychological approaches were both oriented toward the characteristics of the offender, they were easy to test in principle, and their eventual decline is now interpreted as a consequence of their failure to survive empirical tests. With the rise of the sociological view, there was a corresponding decline in testability, especially with reference to the characteristics of the offender, and there followed a lengthy period of theoretical development virtually independent of research. The sociological theories prominent during this period stressed the multiplicity of cultures in American life, on the one hand, and the differential distribution of opportunity to achieve common goals, on the other. With the rise of large-scale research conducted by sociologists, these theories were themselves subject to test, and theories more closely grounded on the results of research became possible. At the moment, sociological theorizing focuses on the effects of the processing of offenders by agencies of social control.

Travis Hirschi is Professor of Sociology at the University of California, Davis. He is the author of Causes of Delinquency.

David Rudisill is a doctoral student in sociology at the University of California, Davis, specializing in deviance and research methods.

ONE hundred years ago American criminology located the causes of crime in the biology of the offender. Since then criminology has successively placed these causes in the offender's psychology and in the social, then cultural, aspects of his environment. Today, attention has moved from the attributes of the offender to the attributes of those in a position to judge or define him. Since criminology has drawn from the full range of biological and social sciences over this 100-year period, it is not surprising that, collectively, it has produced a long and varied list of causes of crime.

In this paper we briefly summarize a succession of organizing views or paradigms that have dominated academic criminology since 1876. Such a summary inevitably suggests the evolution of theory, and such evolution, most of us have been trained to believe, reflects the influence of research. In the history of criminology, there is occasional merit to this view. Some of these explanatory systems simply ran into trouble with the facts, and their decline may be traced to such trouble. In most cases, however, shifts in theoretical emphasis have been partly independent of the results of research. Like the theory it replaced, the new theory was derived from a well-established academic discipline. Using ordinary strategies of the discipline, its independence from research could be enhanced by interpreting previous data in a new light and by guiding attention to research areas not previously explored.

Organizing the history of the field as a "succession of paradigms," therefore, distorts history by suggesting (1) the existence of clear schools of thought; (2) the complete demise of older paradigms; and (3) the rigid adherence of members of a school to their own view to the exclusion of others. In fact, clear schools of thought exist in criminology only insofar as the academic discipline feeding them itself presents a unified point of view. And, as is well known, no academic discipline in America, especially sociology—the major parent discipline of criminology for perhaps fifty years—can be characterized as monolithic. The older paradigms are, it turns out, simply quite healthy academic disciplines that have turned their attention elsewhere. As a consequence, none of them may be said to be without influence today. (The biological view, it is true, survives mainly outside academia, where it is periodically fed by the popular press.) Finally, the ideology of criminology is pridefully eclectic. Nevertheless, in the paper that follows, we locate major views on the causes of crime within reasonably distinct time periods and may seem to suggest that during these periods their influence was absolute. Such has never been the case.

CONSTITUTIONAL DEFECT

Between the publication of Robert Dugdale's *The Jukes* in 1877 and Charles Goring's *The English Convict* in 1913, American views of the causes of crime reflected the dominance of biology as an explanatory scheme and the predominance of physicians in the study of the criminal.

Dugdale traced the genealogy of a New York "family" whose name "had come to be used generically as a term of reproach." Although Dugdale was basically an environmentalist and his assertions on the nature-nurture issue were properly cautious, the name of the family he studied was soon used generically as an illustration of hereditary crime. This is not surprising. The biological orientation of American criminology antedated even the work of Lombroso, the Italian positivist whose view that the criminal is a distinct species or subspecies of man quickly found an American following upon its introduction in the 1880s.[1]

It is fair to say, however, that American views were typically less extreme than Lombroso's. Most American scholars did not see the criminal as a biologically distinct animal. Instead, they believed merely that crime was inherited. The mechanism of inheritance varied from one scholar to another. Some, indeed, adopted the Lombrosian idea of atavism. Others believed either in the direct inheritance of criminality or in the inheritance of biological defects that led or were conducive to criminality, such as "pauperism" and "criminal neurosis."

Whatever the mechanism of heredity, the fact that heredity is important was rarely questioned. In 1910, even the prominent sociologist Franklin Giddings could accept the possibility that "crime is correlated with the crossing of vicious blood with a more vigorous outside strain."[2]

The death knell of this school of thought is generally taken to have been sounded by Charles Goring, whose methodologically sophisticated comparisons of Oxford students and English convicts led him to the conclusion that there is no such thing as a physical criminal type.[3] Although not all parts of the theory of biological defect were so directly or easily tested, the failure of the "physical type" aspect of the theory made it easy to believe that the theory as a whole was defective. An occasional scholar has resurrected the view that criminals are organically distinct or inferior; however, this view has not been a force in American criminology for about 60 years.[4]

FEEBLEMINDEDNESS

An important reason for the easy acceptance of the finding that biological defect theories were erroneous was the ready availability of a cognate explanatory variable. Such constructs as moral imbecility and idiocy had been in the literature for many years. By the time organic defect theories were falling from academic favor, these constructs had become feeblemindedness, evidence for which was appearing in

1. An excellent review of American thought on the biology of crime is Arthur E. Fink, Causes of Crime: Biological Theories in the United States, 1800–1915 (Philadelphia: University of Pennsylvania Press, 1938).
2. Robert L. Dugdale, The Jukes: A Study in Crime, Pauperism, Disease, and Heredity (New York: G. P. Putnam's Sons, 1910), p. v.

3. Charles Goring, The English Convict (Montclair, N.J.: Patterson Smith, 1972, first published in 1913).
4. The strongest modern statement of the view of criminals as organically inferior is Ernest A. Hooton, Crime and the Man (Cambridge, Mass.: Harvard University Press, 1939). Incidentally, Hooton does not agree with our assessment of Goring's methodology, and he emphatically disagrees with the conclusion that Goring's work somehow provided a definitive test of Lombroso's theory. For a balanced summary of current thinking, see Saleem A. Shah and Loren H. Roth, "Biological and Psychophysiological Factors in Criminality," Handbook of Criminology, ed. Daniel Glaser, (New York: Rand McNally & Company, 1974), pp. 101–173.

tests of mental ability. In the same study in which he concluded that Lombroso was wrong, Goring reported that feeblemindedness was the single most important correlate of crime. Goring did not doubt that feeblemindedness was inherited. At the same time, in America, Henry H. Goddard was taking an identical position:

The hereditary criminal passes out with the advent of feeble-mindedness into the problem. . . . It is hereditary feeble-mindedness, not hereditary criminality that accounts for [the criminal type].[5]

Like the physical type theories, feeblemindedness was a directly testable hypothesis, and such tests appeared in great volume in the literature, all showing a marked preponderance of feeblemindedness among criminals and delinquents. At the time, distributions of mental ability in the general population had not been established, and researchers were forced to guess about the proportion of feebleminded. None of them dared guess that this proportion could be anything like that found in samples of criminals and delinquents, where estimates ran as high as 90 percent. Testing of the World War I draft army, however, revealed that nearly a third of the general population was feebleminded when measured by the same standard applied to criminals. And, even worse, the overall distribution of mental ability in the draft army turned out to resemble very much that of adult prisoners.[6]

The idea that the less intelligent will also be less likely to foresee and appreciate the consequences of their acts remains so plausible that most contemporary textbooks in criminology still address the question of the intelligence of criminals. Their conclusion is that intelligence makes no difference. The literature cited in support of this conclusion typically dates to the 1920s and 30s, suggesting that intelligence, like physical defect, has recently been ignored. Actually, the rise of the multiple factor approach, which did not require that a cause of crime be both necessary and sufficient, at the same time made room for intelligence, and it, along with many other factors, is often included in research studies even today.

THE MULTIPLE FACTOR APPROACH

In *The Jukes*, Dugdale reports "the method employed has been to avoid theory lest I should unconsciously fall into the error of being dominated by foregone conclusions."[7] The American distrust of grand theoretical schemes came to full flower in 1915 in the work of William Healy, who concluded that the case study of the offender "should be ever a barrier to the acceptance of general social or biological theories of crime."[8] Freed from many of the a priori categories of the past, Healy and those who followed him were able to examine

5. Henry H. Goddard, *Feeble-mindedness: Its Causes and Consequences* (New York: Macmillan Co., 1914), p. 8.
6. Carl Murchison, *Criminal Intelligence* (Worcester, Mass.: Clark University, 1926). The distinction between adults and juveniles is a continual source of confusion in American

criminology. In many cases, it is not known how far the results of research on juveniles can be extrapolated to adults, and vice versa. The no-difference conclusion with respect to intelligence among adults, if true, does not seem to hold among juveniles.
7. Dugdale, *The Jukes*, pp. 1–2.
8. William Healy, *The Individual Delinquent* (Boston: Little, Brown & Co., 1915), p. 32.

a large number of possible causes of crime. In a famous example, a British scholar announced the discovery of "more than 170 distinct conditions conducive to childish misconduct."[9]

Between 1915 and the 1950s, the multiple factor approach dominated American research on the causes of crime and delinquency, and it characterizes much of this research today.[10] The case study emphasis has given way to emphasis on the empirical correlates of criminal behavior, but the emphasis on the facts, whatever their relevance to any particular theory, is retained. This approach allows research to incorporate variables from theories both dead and alive: family relations, school performance, social class, and even body type and intelligence. (Incidentally, measures of school attitudes or performance appear to be the best predictors of delinquency.)

Though the multiple factor approach dominated research in American criminology, it soon encountered the charge that its virtues were, after all, vices. The multiple factor approach—and indeed all positivistic approaches—centers its search for the causes of crime on the peculiarities of the offender. With the ascension of sociology to dominance in criminology about 50 years ago, it was confidently believed that such peculiarities were unnecessary to an explanation, that

the causes of crime could be shown to be normal social processes operating on normal human material.

The gap between positivistic explanation, with its emphasis on individual differences, and sociological explanation, with its emphasis on the normal response of normal people to normal (or abnormal) situations, is nowhere better seen than in the subsequent history of criminology. For several decades following the rise of sociology, criminological research and theorizing were largely independent enterprises. It was only after the growth of large-scale survey research following World War II that sociologists came to dominate systematic research on crime. Like researchers of earlier periods, they were interested in the theories of their own discipline, theories that had by then dominated the field for some time.

DIFFERENTIAL ASSOCIATION

One of the most prestigious of these theories, and perhaps the clearest example of the sociological effort to normalize crime, is Sutherland's straightforward assertion in 1939 that crime is learned. This learning takes place "in interaction with other persons . . . principally within intimate personal groups." In the end, the "person becomes delinquent because of an excess of definitions favorable to violation of law over definitions unfavorable to violation of law." This is the famous principle of differential association.[11]

According to this theory, crime is positively valued by criminals. Such positive valuation is supplied by

9. Cyril Burt, *The Young Delinquent* (London: University of London Press, 1944), p. 600.

10. See Sheldon and Eleanor Glueck, *Unraveling Juvenile Delinquency* (Cambridge, Mass.: Harvard University Press, 1950); and Marvin Wolfgang, Robert Figlio, and Thorsten Sellin, *Delinquency in a Birth Cohort* (Chicago: University of Chicago Press, 1972).

11. See Edwin H. Sutherland and Donald R. Cressey, *Principles of Criminology*, 9th ed. (Philadelphia: J. B. Lippincott Co., 1974).

their learning environment or culture. If crime is positively valued in the criminal's own culture, it is "crime" only insofar as some other culture is able to impose such a definition on it. The model implicit in the theory, then, is that of a colonial power imposing its values on innocent natives. Since there is no reason to expect that cultures differ with respect to the individual characteristics of their members, the relevance of such differences is implicitly denied.

If such individual differences are discovered, they cannot embarrass the theory. Such "causes" must operate through a culture conducive to criminality. In the absence of such a culture, none of these causes, singularly or in combination, would produce criminal behavior. The theory is thus compatible with all known facts about crime. By declaring individual properties irrelevant, or at least inessential, it has the effect of dampening interest in their exploration. Once individual characteristics become problematic —that is, researchable questions— the theory quickly runs into competition with the positivistic theories it tried so hard to define away. For example, the major empirical fact taken as support for the theory is the tendency of delinquents to associate with other delinquents, a fact that may also be taken as support for the view that criminality *precedes* differential association.

OPPORTUNITY OR STRAIN THEORY

At about the same time Sutherland first published his theory of differential association, Robert K. Merton was publishing a similarly sociological theory of deviant behavior which, nonetheless, differs markedly in emphasis. Where Sutherland saw various cultures in America, some of which are conducive to criminality, Merton saw only a single culture, a culture emphasizing the traditional Protestant virtues: success, hard work, ambition, and the like. Into this common culture with its emphasis on striving, Merton introduced the fact of differential opportunity. While all are led to believe there is "room at the top," in fact there is not room for all, and legitimate means of getting there are not equally distributed through the class system. In such a situation, the "culturally induced success-goal" exerts pressure on the disadvantaged to engage in criminal behavior as the only available means of attaining it.[12]

The most prestigious and influential theories of delinquency in American sociology since Merton have followed his lead, emphasizing differences in opportunity among social groups, especially socioeconomic classes. All of them suggest that these differences stem from the social structure rather than individual characteristics. Equality of opportunity, then, is the surest cure for crime.

To the extent that opportunity is itself a function of individual ability and desire, these theories compete with traditional explanations based on individual differences. For example, the major source of support for opportunity theories has been the greater rates of criminality in the lower socioeconomic classes. This fact also provides a point of entry for the positivist, who may

12. Robert K. Merton, "Social Structure and Anomie," *American Sociological Review* 3 (October 1938), pp. 672–682. See also Richard A. Cloward and Lloyd E. Ohlin, *Delinquency and Opportunity* (New York: The Free Press, 1960).

ask how much of these class differences are *due to the operation of equal opportunity* on persons differentially equipped to take advantage of it.

LABELING-CONFLICT THEORIES

Differential association and opportunity theory disagree on the value structure of American society. Most American criminologists have sided with differential association, believing in a plurality of value systems, and in the corollary idea that crime is a socially imposed category. In a currently popular elaboration, behavior that could be characterized as "illegal" is held to be widespread throughout society. Further, such behavior is uncorrelated with any personal or even social characteristic of those so behaving. Responding to their own stereotypes and political needs, agents of the criminal justice system—which itself represents the powerful social classes—differentially select from this immense pool of "offenders" the poor, the powerless, and the unlucky. Such selection is said to create the correlations upon which positivistic theories of crime depend. According to this view, the sources of the behavior eventually characterized as criminal—that is, questions of etiology—are theoretically uninteresting.

Unfortunately, consumers of the criminological literature typically come for answers to the question of causation, that is, "Why do they do it?" They therefore infer that this description of "how the system works" also explains criminal behavior. The consumer infers that "criminals are created through a process of discriminatory selection, ostracizing stigmatization, and de-

humanizing punishment."[13] If criminals are created in this manner, and criminals commit illegal acts, then we have an explanation of differential criminal activity—a differential, not incidentally, previously denied. If such differentials in behavior are possible, then selection need not be totally arbitrary or discriminatory, and indeed analogous social processes may themselves "create crime." Once again, then, a radical attempt to save the offender from those who would explain his behavior falls victim to "what the layman wants to know" about crime.

CONTROL THEORY

The one sociological account of criminality not designed as an explicit alternative to positivistic explanations is control theory. This theory emphasizes the potentiality for failure in the process of socialization. It asks "not so much why we behave badly as how we can be induced to behave well."[14] Crime, in this view, is not the result of positive training or of unsatisfied desire,

13. Eugene Doleschal and Nora Klapmuts, "Toward a New Criminology," *Crime and Delinquency Literature* (December 1973), p. 612. We distinguish between the authors of labeling or conflict theories and consumers of these theories because there appears to be a clear failure of communication at some point. Despite the repeated assertions of the labeling theorists that they have nothing to say about the etiology of crime, their theory is perhaps the most popular theory of crime causation currently available. See Edwin Lemert, *Social Pathology* (New York: McGraw-Hill, 1951); and Edwin Schur, *Radical Non-Intervention* (Englewood Cliffs, N.J.: Prentice-Hall, 1973).

14. Gwynn Nettler, *Explaining Crime* (New York: McGraw-Hill, 1974), p. 216. Nettler is an excellent source for critical summaries of all the sociological theories mentioned in this paper.

but rather the expression of "natural" tendencies. This view thus draws from a wide variety of sociological and psychological work on the development of "moral" behavior. Crime is automatically explained by explaining the behavior of the law-abiding. The delinquent is then seen, for example, as "a person relatively free of the intimate attachments, the aspirations, and the moral beliefs that bind most people to a life within the law."[15] Since the theory grants the possibility that some may be easier to teach than others, and that some cultures may be more effective teachers than others, it can draw from many perspectives, including those summarized earlier. Unlike more purely sociological theories, this theory is likely to emphasize the role of the family. Unlike more purely psychological theories, it emphasizes the significance of variation in group membership across the life cycle. With this latter emphasis, the theory can attempt to account for one of the major facts of crime ignored by other theories: the considerable variation in criminal behavior over the life of the "offender."

Given its connections with major concepts of several social scientific disciplines, it is not surprising that such a theory has been around for some time.[16] At present, control theory can be more properly described as a general stance toward the question of crime. Particular control theories differ markedly in the specific causes they emphasize. Even so, the theory has had the salutary effect of directing attention to, rather than away from, the results of research.

OVERVIEW

Interest in the causes of crime, as they are typically defined by the layman, has progressively declined among American academicians over the last 100 years. In the beginning, the academic mood was highly optimistic, reflecting the prevailing faith in the ability of science to explain human behavior. This optimistic mood was no doubt enhanced by the corollary belief that explanations automatically yield practical solutions: If crime is inherited, sterilization or isolation of offenders will eventually lead to its disappearance. Further, crime is sufficiently evil that such mild measures of social defense are easily justified.

The decline of the biological perspective was accompanied by increasing complexity of explanation, and a corresponding breakdown in the obviousness of the connection between cause and cure. At the same time, the cure was directed less and less toward the "social evil" and more and more toward treatment of the offender.

With the rise of sociology to dominance in criminology, explanatory attention moved away from the offender toward social processes creating him. Such explanatory schemes automatically shift the focus from cure to prevention. (In fact, some of them had no immediately apparent implications for either.)

15. Travis Hirschi, *Causes of Delinquency* (Berkeley: University of California Press, 1969), preface.

16. Explicit statements may be found in Albert J. Reiss, "Delinquency as the Failure of Personal and Social Control," *American Sociological Review* 16 (1951), pp. 196–207; Jackson Toby, "Hoodlum or Businessman: An American Dilemma," in *The Jews*, ed. Marshall Sklare (New York: The Free Press, 1958), pp. 542–550; Walter C. Reckless, *The Crime Problem* (New York: Appleton-Century-Crofts, 1973).

While research on the characteristics of individual offenders continued, it did so at a much reduced rate and was not tied to then dominant explanatory schemes. "Crass empiricism" and "sanctimonious theorizing" were, according to their respective antagonists, the order of the day.

When respectable research re-emerged in the fifties, it focused on the causes of crime suggested by leading sociological theories—such as group membership and social class—but it was not restricted to such "causes." In fact, in many ways it resembled the pre-sociological multiple factor approach, and therefore its "findings" resembled those of earlier periods. The traditional correlates of crime—age, sex, ethnicity, low social position, low intelligence, urban residence, family disruption, and poor school performance—were rediscovered.

Recent developments in sociological theorizing once again reflect dissatisfaction with this research emphasis on the characteristics of the offender. This time, however, the shift in emphasis has been more emphatic. For example, in one view, "crime" is a social construction more or less independent of the behavior it is alleged to denote. It follows that "criminal" is also a socially constructed category populated by persons whose behavior is identical to that of those not so labeled. Examination of the properties of offenders, therefore, shows only "how the system works." It says nothing about the causes of crime.

Such a view shifts attention to the processing of "offenders" and finds a cure for "crime" in modification of the social reaction to it. What evidence is there that differential processing is important in the production of criminal behavior? Ironically, even while the new theory was focusing attention on the *impact* of processing, many scholars were concluding that the various strategies of treatment or rehabilitation suggested by the old theories *have no impact* on the likelihood of subsequent criminal behavior. No theory, it would seem, can take comfort from such facts.

ANNALS, AAPSS, **423**, Jan. 1976

The Growth of Crime in the United States

By HAROLD E. PEPINSKY

ABSTRACT: The growth of crime in the United States has been viewed as a social problem since the founding of the Republic. From at least the middle of the nineteenth century, this growth can be explained as an outcome of the development of crime measurement technology. American crime measurement specialists have consistently operated under a pair of assumptions: that crime is underreported rather than overreported in crime statistics and that rates of crime generally increase. These assumptions have become the foundation of a self-fulfilling prophecy. Efforts have been devoted to detecting larger rates of crime by using each measure that has been developed, and new measures have continued to be created to supplement the old. Recently, for instance, police departments "refined" their procedures for compiling offense reports, so rates of offenses known to the police climbed dramatically. And the victim survey was developed to supplement police data, with the victim data interpreted as indicating that crime rates are increasing far faster than we had previously imagined.

It is proposed that those engaged in crime measurement be given incentives to report fewer offenses. Otherwise, regardless of change in the level of interpersonal conflict in American society, the prophecy of American crime measurement specialists can be expected to continue to fulfill itself, with an unabated growth of crime.

Harold E. Pepinsky is an Assistant Professor of Criminal Justice at the State University of New York at Albany. He has written articles and chapters on Chinese law, police, white-collar crime, and on general macroscopic issues of law and social control. He is the author of a forthcoming book entitled Crime and Conflict: A Study of Law and Society.

INTERACTION of two sets of beliefs accounts for much of the history of crime measurement in the United States:

There has always been too much crime. Virtually every generation since the founding of the Nation and before has felt itself threatened by the spectre of rising crime and violence.[1]

And:

There is general agreement as to the importance of official and trustworthy statistics of crime, criminals, criminal justice, and penal administration. The eagerness with which the unsystematic, often inaccurate, and more often incomplete statistics available for this country are taken up by text writers, writers in the periodicals, newspaper writers, and public speakers speaks for itself. Most of those who write and speak on American criminal justice assume certain things to be well known or incontrovertible. But as one looks for the facts underlying such assumptions he soon finds they are not at hand.[2]

Generally speaking, those engaged in measuring crime have taken the position that the gathering and interpretation of crime statistics can and should be free from a priori assumptions. But, of course, such assumptions must be introduced into interpretations of the significance of these or any social statistics. The assumptions that have been accepted in the field of crime measurement in our country appear to have had some untoward consequences.

THE GROWTH OF CRIME MEASUREMENT

European concern for and initial development of crime statistics apparently preceded those in America. The earliest call for crime statistics found by Sellin and Wolfgang[3] in their historical survey was that made in the seventeenth century by an Englishman, Sir William Petty.[4] Nationwide crime (conviction) statistics were first collected in France in 1827.

The most comprehensive survey of the early history of crime measurement in the United States is that done by Louis Newton Robinson.[5] According to his survey, the earliest American crime statistics collected on a statewide basis were judicial statistics in New York in 1829. By 1905, 25 states had legislation providing for compilation of statistics on numbers of people prosecuted and convicted in their courts. Statewide prison statistics followed on the heels of judicial statistics, beginning with Massachusetts in 1834.

Judicial statistics thus became the first indicator of how much crime there was and of trends in rates and numbers of crimes to be used in the United States. These data soon drew criticism for being incomplete, as early as 1836 by Henry Lyfton Bulwer for the French figures,[6] ac-

---

1. President's Commission on Law Enforcement and Administration of Justice, Task Force Report: Crime and Its Impact—An Assessment (Washington, D.C.: Government Printing Office, 1967), p. 19.

2. National Commission on Law Observance and Enforcement, No. 3: Report on Statistics (Washington, D.C.: Government Printing Office, 1931), p. 3.

3. Thorsten Sellin and Marvin E. Wolfgang, The Measurement of Delinquency (New York: John Wiley and Sons, Inc., 1964), p. 7.

4. William Petty, The Petty Papers: Some Unpublished Papers of Sir William Petty (Boston: Houghton-Mifflin Company, 1927).

5. Louis Newton Robinson, History and Organization of Criminal Statistics in the United States (Boston: Houghton-Mifflin Company, 1911).

6. Henry Lyfton Bulwer, France: Social, Literary, Political (London: Richard Bentley, 1836), vol. 1, pp. 169–210.

cording to Biderman and Reiss.[7] Robinson repeatedly echoed this criticism for American figures in 1911.[8]

The criticism of judicial statistics had two aspects. On the one hand, it pointed to the likelihood that not every case of the kind being measured got into the statistics. For instance, Robinson concluded that many court convictions did not get reported in the state figures.[9] On the other hand, the criticism pointed to the likelihood that the commission of a substantial number of crimes never led to conviction in the first place. Robinson asserted the belief that state crime statistics would always fail to include some crimes.[10]

The number of crimes that goes unreported by any measure has come to be known among crime measurement specialists as "hidden crime" or, more menacingly, as "the dark figure" or the "dark number." This purported bias in crime rate or crime incidence measurement has been a consistent source of concern in the United States, in this century at least. The possibility that the dark figure is not constant or does not vary consistently in relation to some population base, has also led to concern that crime statistics may not indicate whether crime is really increasing or decreasing over time.

With this aura of doubt, practically all American crime measurement specialists have persistently clung to two assumptions: (1) that crime is consistently underreported rather than overreported in crime statistics and (2) that rates of crime tend to increase over time, with but a few possible exceptions.

Scientists can never be certain about causes and effects, but, consistently with the history of American crime measurement, it can be postulated that the growth of crime in our society can be accounted for as an outcome of widespread acceptance of these two assumptions. A self-fulfilling prophecy appears to have been established, leading, first, to a growth in crime measurement and, in turn, to widespread popular consensus that crime itself continues to grow in our society.

By 1911, Robinson was already making the kind of argument that would be used to support the expansion of the data base for crime measurement.[11] The "main difference" between judicial and prison statistics, he argued, was that the former were "far more complete" than the latter. In itself, this was a fairly restrained conclusion about which kind of data was likely to approach a "true" picture of the number or rate of crime. But arguments of this kind have had a greater significance, for they have provided a logic for extending the crime data base indefinitely. If judicial statistics are more nearly complete than prison statistics (since not all those convicted of crimes were sentenced to prison), then are not arrest statistics more nearly complete than judicial statistics (since some of those arrested, though presumably guilty, were not convicted)? As one would expect, by 1931, police arrest statistics were compiled statewide in Massachusetts and "for nearly

7. Albert D. Biderman and Albert J. Reiss, Jr., "On Exploring the 'Dark Figure' of Crime," *Annals of the American Academy of Political and Social Science* 374 (November 1967), pp. 1–15.

8. Robinson, *Criminal Statistics*.

9. Ibid., pp. 38–68.

10. Ibid., p. 7.

11. Ibid., pp. 7–8.

half of the cities over 30,000 inhabitants."[12]

Before arrest statistics could become established as the successor to judicial statistics as the source of an authoritative crime measure, the police had developed another, still more inclusive, measure of crime: "offenses known to the police." These were drawn from police reports of offenses they had discovered themselves or of offenses reported to them by citizen complainants. With these statistics, crime could be measured independently of any knowledge of who was committing the offenses. As early as 1927, at the Convention of the International Association of Chiefs of Police, it was proposed that police offenses known data be made the primary basis for national crime statistics, and a legal mandate was given to the Federal Bureau of Investigation (FBI) to begin compiling such data in 1930.[13] By 1931, offenses known data were reported for 14 American cities.[14]

For a while, crime measurement seemed to go into remission. While the FBI tried to encourage more areas to report offenses, the country, caught in the throes of trying to recover from the Depression, seemed to lose interest in finding more hidden crime. The nationally reported rates of offenses known for serious crimes declined steadily into World War II.[15]

A presidential address to the American Sociological Association by Edwin H. Sutherland in 1939 signaled a return to concern for finding hidden crime.[16] Sutherland's thesis, as developed in a later article,[17] was that most of the hidden crime was committed by businessmen and professionals in the higher socioeconomic classes. He proposed that crime data include such figures as those for injections against antitrust violators. While initial resistance to Sutherland's proposed extension of crime measurement—as by Paul W. Tappan[18]—was strong, there are now signs that acceptance of finding a growth in white-collar crime is coming of age. Reluctance to find widespread criminality among the upper classes of a society is understandable. But now that Americans have shown enough tolerance of such a discovery to force the resignation of a president, the history of measurement of street crime is showing signs of recapitulating itself among the higher social strata. To illustrate, a recent article based a report of a sharp rise in white-collar crime on FBI data indicating that the number of white-collar crime convictions increased by 30 percent from the period of January 1972–June 1973 to July 1973–December 1974.[19] This new area for the growth of crime is finally beginning to open up to serious attention by specialists in crime measurement.[20]

16. Edwin H. Sutherland, "White-Collar Criminality," *American Sociological Review* 5 (February 1940), pp. 1–12.

17. Edwin H. Sutherland, "Is 'White-Collar Crime' Crime?," *American Sociological Review* 10 (April 1945), pp. 132–39.

18. Paul W. Tappan, "Who Is the Criminal?," *American Sociological Review* 12 (February 1947), pp. 96–102.

19. Colman McCarthy, "White Collar Crime," *Washington Post,* 11 April 1975.

20. At least one other channel has been opened for the growth of crime—that of juvenile delinquency statistics. Suffice it to

12. National Commission, *No. 3: Report on Statistics,* p. 87.

13. Ibid., p. 10.

14. Ibid., p. 87.

15. President's Commission, *Task Force Report,* pp. 19–20.

Meanwhile, during the decades of the forties and the fifties, the FBI, at that time the leader in the development of national crime statistics, concentrated on trying to get full and reliable offenses known data from law enforcement authorities across the country. Nationally reported rates of offenses known climbed steadily.[21] It is possible that people were really committing crimes at ever higher rates. It is also plausible to infer a connection between the assumptions of crime measurement and the upward trend. How, after all, is a law enforcement agency to demonstrate that its offenses known data are more nearly complete without showing increases in the figures recorded?

Though one can only guess at whether the growth of crime in the forties and fifties was at all a product of a self-fulfilling prophecy in the field of crime measurement, particular evidence in support of this inference is available for the decade of the sixties. In 1957, Thorsten Sellin wrote an article that strongly criticized inadequacies in the FBI's system of crime reporting.[22] In response to this criticism, a consultant committee made recommendations for revision of FBI procedures which the latter adopted.[23] But the Sellin criticism and the FBI response generated rather than abated attention to the shortcomings of official crime statistics. A wave of articles critical of FBI offenses known data began to appear at the beginning of the sixties.[24] Much of the criticism was directed at supposed variations in the ways different law enforcement agencies gathered and compiled their offenses known data, but the criticism that got the most substantial response was that of the incompleteness of offenses known data. Law enforcement agencies began making overt efforts to revise their reporting practices to give evidence that their figures were more nearly complete than ever before. The effects of revised reporting practices were particularly dramatic in New York City, where the rate of offenses known to the police was 72 percent higher in 1966 than in 1965.[25] The "true" increase in the New York rate was estimated to be 6.5 percent, based on the assumption that the previous trend there had actually remained unchanged. Thus, even where the size of an increase in an offenses known rate strained credulity, crime measurement's self-fulfilling prophecy operated to sup-

---

note that the growth of delinquency figures has been aided dramatically in recent years by the use of self-report measurement, which has made it possible to find delinquent acts committed by practically every adolescent. See, for example, Travis Hirschi, *Causes of Delinquency* (Berkeley: University of California Press, 1969).

21. President's Commission, *Task Force Report*, pp. 19–20.

22. Thorsten Sellin, "Crime in the United States," *Life Magazine* 48 (9 September 1957), p. 48.

23. Federal Bureau of Investigation, *Uniform Crime Reports: Special Issue* (Washington, D.C.: Government Printing Office, 1958).

24. For example, Ronald H. Beattie, "Criminal Statistics in the United States," *Journal of Criminal Law, Criminology, and Police Science* 51 (May–June 1960), pp. 49–65; David J. Pittman and William F. Handy, "Uniform Crime Reporting: Suggested Improvements," *Sociology and Social Research* 46 (January 1962), pp. 135–43; and Marvin E. Wolfgang, "Uniform Crime Reports: A Critical Appraisal," *Pennsylvania Law Review* 111 (April 1963), pp. 708–38.

25. Bernard Weinraub, "Crime Reports up 72% Here in 1966: Actual Rise Is 6.5%," *New York Times*, 21 February 1967.

port the conclusion that the crime rate was increasing, nevertheless.

A survey of recent national offenses known data reveals some interruptions in the operation of the prophecy that crime is growing, but the interruptions appear to be temporary.[26] During the administration of President Nixon, efforts were made to demonstrate that crime rates could be reduced through administration policy. The District of Columbia was a primary demonstration area for Nixon's "war on crime" policy, and for several years the official offenses known rates for some serious offenses showed declines. The District of Columbia police were criticized for manufacturing the declines through artifice, such as by reporting burglaries and grand thefts (felonies or serious crimes) as petit thefts (misdemeanors or minor crimes). Suffice it to note that the declines, like Nixon's second term in office, were short-lived. A number of other cities joined the competition, reporting drops in offense rates, which were more than compensated for by their suburban brethren. This anomaly, too, appears to have been temporary, for each year more of these cities have returned to reporting increases in their rates.

The criticism in the early sixties of the inadequacies of official crime data had another effect on crime measurement. A technological innovation, the victim survey, resulted. The first victim surveys were commissioned by the President's Commission on Law Enforcement and Administration of Justice and completed in 1967.[27] The victim survey approach has proven to be a major breakthrough in crime measurement. In one victimization study, it has already proven possible to find 10 times the rate of officially reported offenses.[28]

Typically, respondents in victim surveys are asked to report offenses that have been committed against them during the preceding one-year period. Albert J. Reiss, Jr., tried an experiment which indicates that a substantial potential for the growth of crime still exists within the victim survey approach.[29] He had a sample of people interviewed who were known to have reported offenses to the police within the preceding month. Twenty percent of the offenses that had been reported to the police went unreported in the victim survey.

Interpreting the growth of crime measurement in light of the postulated self-fulfilling prophecy, it is safe to project a continued growth of crime for the American future.

---

mission on Law Enforcement and Administration of Justice, Field Surveys I: Report on a Pilot Study in the District of Columbia on Victimization and Attitudes Toward Law Enforcement (Washington, D.C.: Government Printing Office, 1967), ch. 2, pp. 26–118; Philip H. Ennis, "Crime Victimization in the United States: Report on a National Survey," in President's Commission on Law Enforcement and Administration of Justice, Field Surveys II (Washington, D.C.: Government Printing Office, 1967); and Albert J. Reiss, Jr., "Measurement of the Nature and Amount of Crime," in President's Commission on Law Enforcement and Administration of Justice, Field Surveys III: Studies in Crime and Law Enforcement in Major Metropolitan Areas (Washington, D.C.: Government Printing Office, 1967), vol. 1, pp. 1–183.

28. Paul D. Reynolds, Victimization of the Residents and Their Perceptions of Community Services—1971 (Minneapolis, Minn.: Metropolitan Council of the Twin Cities, 1972), p. 49.

29. Reiss, "Measurement of Nature and Amount of Crime," p. 150.

---

26. These data are to be found in Federal Bureau of Investigation, Crime in the United States: Uniform Crime Reports (Washington, D.C.: Government Printing Office, annual).

27. Albert D. Biderman et al., "Incidence of Crime Victimization," in President's Com-

Indeed, given the ingenuity that American crime measurement specialists have displayed in conceptual innovation and technological refinement, the potential for the growth of crime in our society seems limitless.

A MODEST PROPOSAL

The assumption that it is desirable to lower rates of crime implicitly if not explicitly underlies practically all research and planning in the field of criminal justice. Measures of crime rates were intended at least in part to serve as criteria by which success or failure to meet this objective could be assessed. It has generally been presumed that the measures are independent of the objective. The preceding survey of the history of American crime measurement suggests otherwise: that a general failure to reduce rates of crime has been preordained by the assumptions upon which the development of crime measures has rested.

The problem stems from the belief that all hidden crime must be accounted for before one can know whether crime rates have really been reduced. It has commonly been assumed that the amount of crime that can be found at any time and place is finite—that the limits of defining behavior as crime are determined by the terms of formal legislation. This assumption is tenuous. The limits of change are yet to be seen in perceptions of whether one knows that an act has occurred which fits a statutory definition of a crime. What is perceived as a "suspicion" on one occasion can be perceived as an "established fact" on another. A memory that is perceived as being "distorted" on one occasion can be perceived as being "accurate" on another. An act that is perceived as being an "innocent altercation" on one occasion can be perceived as an "assault" on another. What is perceived as an "act of spite" on one occasion can be perceived as a "theft" on another. The author can testify to having seen such ambiguities arise routinely in the work of police patrolmen.[30] The pressure to find more and more hidden crime can be expected to create new ambiguities in the minds of those who might report offenses and to raise the probability that ambiguities will be resolved in favor of making reports. In this sense, the growth of crime measurement is likely to continue to lead to a growth in what is seen as the "real" rates of crime.

English practice indicates that the presumption used to resolve ambiguities underlying police offenses known data need not invariably favor reporting the highest available rate. American offenses known data on murder and involuntary manslaughter have long been regarded as the most nearly valid indicator of true crime rates. British Home Office reports on murder, including figures on lesser forms of criminal homicide, stress caution about accepting police figures at face value.[31] Police offenses known figures on murder are freely adjusted in these reports, including an

30. Harold E. Pepinsky, "Police Decisions to Report Offenses" (diss., University of Pennsylvania, 1972).
31. Evelyn Gibson and S. Klein, *Home Office Studies in the Causes of Delinquency and the Treatment of Offenders, No. 4: Murder—A Home Office Research Unit Report* (London: Her Majesty's Stationery Office, 1961); and Evelyn Gibson and S. Klein, *Home Office Research Studies, No. 3: Murder, 1957–1968—A Home Office Research Report on Murder in England and Wales* (London: Her Majesty's Stationery Office, 1969).

average reduction in initial police figures of about 14 percent per year for acquittals at trial—noting, "Deaths initially recorded by the police as murder may turn out not to be the result of crime. . . ."[32] American officials have no comparable practice of lowering offense rate figures.

In addition, the increases in American rates that result from a change in data bases, as in the shift from police data to victim survey data, stand to be interpreted as indicating that rates of crime are "really" increasing. It is difficult to isolate the changes due to changes in method of measurement, and the salience of the higher rates tends to be seriously questioned. The logic may be problematic, but in the confusion it appears that such rate increases reinforce the confidence of those measuring crime that the rates are, in fact, increasing.

Why not abandon attempts to determine real rates of crime? Little would be lost if the attempts are bound to fall short of success. There are rather straightforward ways to lower measured rates of crime if this can be accepted as a desirable objective in itself. The police department in Orange, California, substantially lowered the rates of serious offenses known by paying patrolmen to report fewer offenses, without any indication that life in the city was descending into chaos.[33] The experience of the promotion of the growth of crime by the growth of crime measurement could be put to use in reducing rates of crime; a new prophecy could be constructed to replace the old, in the hope that the new prophecy would be even remotely as effective in fulfilling itself as the old one has been.

Perhaps this proposed strategy of crime rate reduction is too threatening to pursue. Perhaps pursuit of the strategy presents an unacceptable risk of toleration of wrongful conduct. But if we are not prepared to accommodate ourselves to this kind of risk, the history of crime measurement in the United States suggests we had better be prepared to face the inevitability of a continued growth of crime. At present, it is hard to conceive of a way out of this dilemma.

32. Gibson and Klein, *Home Office Research Studies*, No. 3, pp. 1, 8.

33. John M. Greiner, *Tying City Pay to Performance: Early Reports on Orange, California, and Flint, Michigan* (Washington, D.C.: Labor-Management Relations Service of the National League of Cities, National Association of Counties, United States Conference of Mayors, 1974), pp. 5–16.

American Women and Crime

By Rita J. Simon

ABSTRACT: The topic of women and crime is currently enjoying a vogue, because women, in general, and research related to many aspects of women's lives are now popular topics for research. This article analyzes the relationship between the contemporary woman's movement, the role of women in crime, and the changing socioeconomic and political statuses of American women. Statistics on female arrest patterns for different types of offenses going back four decades are presented. The changes in women's propensities for committing different types of crimes are discussed and explanations about why these changes have occurred are offered. Statistics describing American women are compared with female crime data available for some 25 different countries. The extent to which women are victims of various types of offenses is also discussed. In its conclusion, the article offers some prognosis for the short-run future on how American women are likely to participate in criminal activities.

Rita J. Simon is Professor of Sociology, Law, and Communications Research at the University of Illinois. For the 1974–75 academic year, she was on leave, teaching in the Law School of Hebrew University, Jerusalem. Professor Simon is the author of a recently published monograph on Women and Crime. *She has also authored* The Jury and the Defense of Insanity, Public Opinion in America, *and* Payment for Pain and Suffering *(with Jeffrey O'Connell), as well as edited several books on law and society. Professor Simon is on the Board of Directors of the Law and Society Association.*

ON THE occasion of the Hamlyn Lectures at Sheffield University, in 1963, Lady Barbara Wooton observed:

It is perhaps rather curious that no serious attempt has yet been made to explain the remarkable facts of the sex ratio in detected criminality; for the scale of the sex differential far outranks all the other tracts (except that of age in the case of indictable offenses) which have been supposed to distinguish the delinquent from the nondelinquent population. It seems to be one of those facts which escape notice by virtue of its very conspicuousness. It is surely, to say the least, very odd that half the population should be apparently immune to the criminogenic factors which lead to the downfall of so significant a proportion of the other half. Equally odd is it, too, that although the criminological experience of different countries varies considerably, nevertheless the sex differential remains.[1]

Much has happened in the dozen or so years since Lady Wooton made these remarks. The main thrust of this article will be to describe those changes, to explain why they have occurred, and to make some prognosis about their implications for the future.

The topic, women and crime, is currently enjoying a wave of interest unknown at any previous time. Interest in the female offender is, I believe, a specific manifestation of the increased general interest and attention that women have been receiving since the latter part of the 1960s. Women themselves have been largely responsible for their increased notoriety. Having organized into a visible and vocal social movement, whose objectives are the attainment of greater freedom and more responsibility, they have also succeeded in drawing attention to themselves. One of the consequences of this attention has been to question and to research many aspects of women's roles that have hitherto been of little interest or concern to social scientists, clinicians, and law enforcement officials.

The movement for woman's liberation has changed a lot of things about women's reality; and it has been at least partially responsible for changes in women's behavior vis-à-vis criminal activities, as well as scholars' perceptions of the types of women who are likely to engage in crime. In 1966, Rose Giallombardo characterized the image of the woman offender as follows:

Women who commit criminal offenses tend to be regarded as erring and misguided creatures who need protection and help rather than as dangerous criminals from whom members of society should be protected.[2]

How similar that sounds to the observations of the Gluecks, who wrote, in 1934:

The women are themselves on the whole a sorry lot. The major problem involved in the delinquency and criminality of our girls is their lack of control of their sexual impulses.[3]

How strange these observations sound when one notes that, in 1970, four of the FBI's ten most wanted fugitives were women. Daniel Green, writing a few months ago in the *National Observer*, commented:

1. Lady Barbara Wooton, "A Magistrate in Search of the Causes of Crimes," *Crime and the Criminal Law*, 1963, pp. 6–8.

2. Rose Giallombardo, *Society of Women: A Study of a Women's Prison* (New York: John Wiley & Son, Inc., 1966), p. 7.

3. Sheldon Glueck and Eleanor Glueck, *Five Hundred Delinquent Women* (New York: Alfred A. Knopf, Inc., 1934), p. 96.

Before the advent of militant feminism, female radicals were little more than groupies in the amorphous conglomeration of revolutionary and antiwar groups that came to be known collectively in the '60s as The Movement. Like camp followers of old, they functioned principally as cooks, flunkies, and sex objects.

Sexual equality came to the Movement in the gas-polluted streets of Chicago during the '68 Democratic Convention. Enraged by the tactics of Mayor Daley's police, Middle American daughters raised for gentler things shrieked obscenities and hurled rocks as ferociously as veteran street fighters. From then on, guerrilla women were dominant figures in the splintered Movement, particularly the defiantly militant Weatherman faction, which they purged of "*macho sexism*" and renamed the Weather Underground.[4]

What role has the woman's liberation movement played in changing both the image of the female offender and the types of criminal activities that she is likely to commit? The rhetoric of the woman's movement has emphasized similarity between the sexes. Kate Millet, for example, argues that all of the significant behavioral differences between the sexes are those that have been developed by culture, environment, and sexist training.[5] Others in the movement have emphasized that women are no more moral, conforming, or law-abiding than men. They have urged their sisters to neither bask in feelings of superiority nor entrap themselves into wearing masks of morality and goodness.

In their contacts with law enforcement officials, women in the movement are prepared to trade preferential and paternalistic treatment for due process in civil and criminal procedures. Movement lawyers have claimed that women defendants pay for judges' beliefs that it is more in man's nature to commit crimes than it is in woman's. Thus, they argue that when a judge is convinced that the woman before him has committed a crime, he is more likely to overreact and punish her, not only for the specific offense, but also for transgressing against his expectations of womanly behavior.

The existence of such statutes as the "indeterminate sentence" for women, or the sanctioning of a procedure whereby only convicted male defendants have their minimum sentences determined by a judge at an open hearing and in the presence of counsel, while the woman's minimum sentence is decided by a parole board in a closed session in which she is not represented by counsel, are cited as evidence of the unfair, punitive treatment that is accorded to women in the court.[6]

The position that some supporters of the Equal Rights Amendment (ERA) have taken vis-à-vis prisons also illustrates the willingness of the woman's movement to accept the responsibilities of equality. The movement recognizes that the stereotypes that are held of women in the larger society provide some advantages to female inmates. For example, physically, penal institutions for women are usually more attractive and more pleasant than the security-oriented institutions for men. The institutions tend to be

4. Daniel A. Green, "The Dark Side of Women's Liberation: Crime Takes a Female Turn," *National Observer*, September 1974, p. 2.

5. Ibid., p. 2.

6. For a more detailed discussion of how the indeterminate sentence is applied to women, see: Linda Temen, "Discriminatory Sentencing of Women Offenders," *Criminal Law Review* 11 (winter 1973), p. 355.

located in more pastoral settings and they are not as likely to have the gun towers, the concrete walls, and the barbed wire that so often characterize institutions for men. Women inmates usually have more privacy than men. They tend to have single rooms; they may wear street clothes rather than prison uniforms; they may decorate their rooms with such things as bedspreads and curtains, that are provided by the prison. Toilet and shower facilities also reflect a greater concern for women's privacy. Advocates of ERA have written that they would eliminate these differentials by subjecting both men and women to the same physical surroundings in sexually integrated institutions. "Ideally, the equalization would be up to the level presently enjoyed by the women. But, if a State faces an economic roadblock to equalizing up, the ERA would tolerate equalization down to a lower, more economically feasible level."[7]

One of the major goals of the contemporary woman's movement is equal opportunities with men for positions and jobs that carry prestige and authority. While the objectives of the woman's movement of the 1920s were to get women out of their homes and into factories and offices, today success is more likely to be measured by the proportion of women in managerial and professional positions, by the proportion of women who have completed college and university, and by the absence of lower salary scales for women who hold the same types of jobs as men.

A review of census data indicates that the gap between men and

women who occupy management and professional positions is as great today as it was 25 years ago. In 1948, for example, 29 percent of the women employed in white-collar positions occupied professional and managerial slots; in 1971 the percentage was 33. Among men, in 1948, the proportion of white-collar positions represented in the managerial and professional subcategories was 61 percent; in 1971 it was 70 percent. Between 1950 and 1970, the proportion of women who graduated from college increased by 70 percent; but as of 1971 there were still almost six men for every four women who completed four years of college. On the matter of income, the annual earnings of women between 1956 and 1970 decreased in comparison to those of men (1956: women—$3,619, men—$5,716; 1970: women—$4,794, men—$8,845).

Notable changes have occurred, however, in the proportion of married women employed on a full-time basis between 1950 and 1970— a shift from 24.8 percent to 41.1 percent—and especially among married women with children of school age (6–17 years), where there has been an increase from 28.3 percent to 49.2 percent.

There is still much to be done before the woman's movement can claim success in achieving equality between men and women in jobs involving occupational prestige and high incomes. But the increase in the proportion of women who hold full-time jobs, the consciousness that the movement's rhetoric has succeeded in raising, along with the changes that have occurred in women's legal rights in such areas as personal property, abortion, and divorce laws, have all contributed to altering women's overall status as

7. R. R. Arditi et al., "The Sexual Segregation of American Prisoners," *Yale Law Journal* 82 (November–May 1973), p. 1266.

well as increasing opportunities and propensities that women have for committing crimes. What changes have already occurred in the area of crime will be described in some detail in the following pages.

WOMEN AS CRIMINALS

Table 1 describes the proportion of women who have been arrested for all crimes, for all serious crimes, and for serious violent and property crimes from 1932 to 1972.[8] The average rates of change in the proportion of women arrested between 1953 and 1972, between 1958 and 1972, and between 1967 and 1972 are also shown here. The last period is particularly crucial, because we would expect that during this period the rate of change would be marked by the greatest increase.

The average increase in the proportion of women arrested for serious crimes is greater than the average increase in the proportion of women arrested for all crimes. The data also show that the average rate of increase was greatest in the period from 1967 to 1972—.52 for all crimes and .84 for serious offenses. Note

8. It may appear that this discussion uses arrest statistics as proxies for describing crime rates among men and women without regard for the hazards of doing so. While the hazards are recognized, unfortunately there are no other data prior to these statistics that provide information about the characteristics of the suspect as well as the offense he or she is believed to have committed. Criminologists usually prefer to use statistics for determining crime rates that are computed on the basis of crimes known to the police, but those statistics do not identify the suspect in any way. It is also recognized that the proportions of arrests vary considerably from one type of offense to another. Arrest rates are more accurate proxies for behavior in violent types of crimes than they are for crimes against property.

also that from 1961 onward the percentage of women arrested for serious crimes was greater than the percentage of women arrested for all offenses.

The popular impression that in recent years women have been committing crimes of violence at a much higher rate than they have in the past is disputed by the statistics in Table 1. In fact, the increase in the proportion of arrests of women for serious crimes is due almost wholly to the increase in property offenses. Indeed, the percentage of women arrested for crimes of violence shows neither an upward nor a downward trend. The news item that, in 1970, four out of the FBI's most wanted fugitives were women must be juxtaposed against those statistics, which tell quite a different story.

The percentages for property offenses, however, show that big changes have occurred. In 1932, about one in every 19 persons arrested was a woman. In 1972, one in 4.7 persons arrested was a woman. Not only has there been a consistent increase in the percentage of women who have been arrested for property offenses, but also the biggest increases have occurred in the period beginning in 1967. This last finding is most congruent with our major hypothesis—that women's participation in selective crimes will increase as their employment opportunities expand and as their interests, desires, and definitions of self shift from a more traditional to a more liberated view. The crimes that are considered most salient for this hypothesis are various types of property, financial, and white-collar offenses.

Table 2 describes the percentage of female and male arrests, for serious crimes and for serious property and violent offenses within the total

TABLE 1

Percentage of Females Arrested for All Crimes, for All Serious Crimes, and for Serious Violent and Property Crimes: 1932–1972

Year*	All Crimes	Serious Crimes†	Violent Crimes	Property Crimes
1932	7.4	5.8	6.5	5.3
1933	7.2	5.9	7.1	5.2
—	—	—	—	—
1935	6.9	6.0	7.3	5.3
1936	7.3	6.4	8.0	5.7
—	—	—	—	—
1938	6.8	5.4	7.0	4.6
—	—	—	—	—
1942	12.0	8.9	9.8	8.3
1943	16.1	10.1	10.5	9.9
—	—	—	—	—
1946	10.7	7.7	7.7	7.7
1947	10.3	8.0	8.3	7.8
—	—	—	—	—
1949	9.9	8.0	9.9	7.3
1950	9.6	8.1	9.4	7.2
—	—	—	—	—
1953	10.8	9.4	11.9	8.5
1954	10.9	8.9	11.6	8.2
1955	11.0	9.1	12.0	8.4
1956	10.9	9.0	13.5	8.0
1957	10.6	9.3	13.1	8.5
1958	10.6	9.7	11.9	9.3
1959	10.7	10.5	12.7	10.0
1960	11.0	10.9	11.8	10.8
1961	11.3	11.5	11.6	11.4
1962	11.5	12.4	11.5	12.6
1963	11.7	12.7	11.6	12.9
1964	11.9	13.5	11.6	13.9
1965	12.1	14.4	11.4	14.9
1966	12.3	14.8	11.3	15.6
1967	12.7	15.0	10.8	16.0
1968	13.1	15.0	10.3	16.1
1969	13.8	16.6	10.6	17.9
1970	14.6	18.0	10.5	19.7
1971	15.0	18.3	10.9	20.1
1972	15.3	19.3	11.0	21.4
Average rate of change (per year) 1953–72	+0.23	+0.52	−0.05	+0.68
Average rate of change 1958–72	+0.35	+0.68	−0.07	+0.86
Average rate of change 1967–72	+0.52	+0.84	+0.04	+1.07

Source: For the data in tables 1–4, *Uniform Crime Reports* (Washington, D.C.: U.S. Department of Justice, Federal Bureau of Investigation).

* Not all of the years between 1933 and 1953 are included; but the periods of the depression, the Second World War, and the immediate postwar years are included in the sample. Between 1933 and 1953, the data reported in tables 1–5 are based on fingerprint records received from local law-enforcement officials throughout the United States. They are limited to arrests for violations of state laws and local ordinances. But not all persons arrested are fingerprinted. Beginning in 1953, the system was changed, and the figures from 1953 through 1972 describe all arrests in cities with a population of more than 2,500. While recognizing that the sources for the pre-1953 data are different than those collected later, I think that for purposes of comparison—for example, male versus female arrests—they are worth presenting.

† Serious crimes, according to the *Uniform Crime Reports* published by the FBI, are criminal homicide (murder, nonnegligent manslaughter, and manslaughter by negligence), forcible rape, robbery, aggravated assault, burglary, larceny, and auto theft. We have omitted forcible rape from our calculations because women are never charged with such an offense.

TABLE 2

FEMALES AND MALES ARRESTED FOR CRIMES OF VIOLENCE AND PROPERTY AND FOR SERIOUS
CRIMES COMBINED, AS PERCENTAGES OF ALL ARRESTS IN THEIR
RESPECTIVE SEX COHORTS: 1953–1972

| | VIOLENT CRIMES | | PROPERTY CRIMES | | SERIOUS CRIMES | |
YEAR	FEMALES	MALES	FEMALES	MALES	FEMALES	MALES
1953	2.2	2.0	5.6	7.2	7.8	9.2
1954	2.2	2.1	6.0	8.2	8.2	10.3
1955	2.3	2.1	6.2	8.3	8.5	10.4
1956	2.3	1.9	5.9	8.4	8.2	10.3
1957	2.2	1.8	7.1	9.0	9.3	10.8
1958	2.1	1.9	7.8	9.0	9.9	10.9
1959	2.3	1.9	8.3	8.9	10.6	10.8
1960	2.5	2.4	9.9	10.2	12.4	12.6
1961	2.5	2.4	10.9	10.8	13.4	13.2
1962	2.4	2.4	12.2	10.9	14.6	13.3
1963	2.5	2.4	13.4	12.0	15.9	14.4
1964	2.6	2.6	15.4	13.0	18.0	15.6
1965	2.6	2.7	16.3	12.8	18.9	15.5
1966	2.8	3.0	17.3	13.1	20.1	16.1
1967	2.8	3.2	18.0	13.7	20.8	16.9
1968	2.5	3.5	18.2	14.3	20.7	17.8
1969	2.6	3.6	19.6	14.3	22.2	17.9
1970	2.5	3.6	21.3	14.8	23.8	18.4
1971	2.7	3.2	21.5	15.3	24.2	19.2
1972	2.9	4.4	22.3	14.8	25.2	19.2
Average rate of change, 1953–72	+0.04	+0.13	+0.88	+0.40	+0.92	+0.53
Average rate of change, 1958–72	+0.06	+0.18	+1.04	+0.41	+1.11	+0.59
Average rate of change, 1967–72	+0.02	+0.24	+0.82	+0.22	+0.90	+0.46

NOTE: When the data are examined in this way, only the years in which all arrests have been recorded are included.

male and female arrests for all crimes.

In 1953, one out of 12.8 female arrests was for serious crimes as opposed to one out of slightly less than 10.9 male arrests. But two decades later, more women were arrested for serious offenses (about one out of four) than were males (about one out of five). The average rate of change among the women was greater during each of the three time periods than it was for the men. But the time span from 1967 to 1972 does not show a greater increase when compared with time periods that extend farther back. The percentage increase of men who have been arrested for violent offenses over the two decades is almost four times the percentage increase for women. For property offenses, it is the percentage increase for women who have been arrested that is three times the percentage increase for men.

Table 3 describes women's participation in the specific offense categories that are included in the index of serious offenses from 1932 to 1972 (type I offenses). Note that among all six offenses, only one shows a

TABLE 3

FEMALES ARRESTED AS PERCENTAGE OF ALL ARRESTS FOR TYPE 1 OFFENSES, 1932–1972

YEAR	CRIMINAL HOMICIDE	ROBBERY	AGGRAVATED ASSAULT	BURGLARY	LARCENY/ THEFT	AUTO THEFT
1932	8.7	3.3	8.6	1.7	9.3	1.6
1933	9.7	4.4	8.3	1.9	8.4	1.4
1935	9.9	4.6	8.0	1.7	8.3	1.7
1936	10.0	4.8	8.7	1.9	8.5	1.8
1938	9.6	3.9	7.9	1.5	7.1	1.5
1942	13.2	5.0	10.8	2.2	12.6	2.3
1943	13.2	5.3	11.7	3.1	15.5	2.2
1946	10.8	4.6	8.5	2.5	12.9	2.1
1947	11.3	4.5	9.4	2.7	12.4	2.2
1949	12.8	4.5	10.6	2.5	11.9	2.4
1950	13.5	4.3	10.6	2.5	11.5	2.7
1953	14.1	4.3	15.9	2.0	13.9	2.6
1954	14.2	4.2	15.9	2.2	13.0	2.5
1955	14.2	4.2	16.0	2.3	13.3	2.6
1956	14.8	4.3	17.6	2.3	12.6	2.5
1957	14.7	3.9	17.5	2.0	13.2	2.7
1958	16.4	4.5	15.7	2.4	14.3	3.2
1959	16.8	4.6	16.4	2.7	15.4	3.2
1960	16.1	4.6	15.3	2.8	16.8	3.6
1961	15.9	4.9	15.2	3.2	18.0	3.7
1962	17.2	5.1	14.7	3.6	19.6	3.9
1963	15.9	4.9	14.9	3.3	20.1	3.7
1964	16.6	5.3	14.4	3.7	21.4	4.3
1965	16.3	5.3	14.4	3.8	23.2	4.2
1966	15.9	5.1	14.0	3.8	24.0	4.1
1967	15.4	5.2	13.6	4.1	24.8	4.3
1968	15.4	5.5	13.1	4.1	25.2	4.9
1969	14.8	6.3	13.2	4.3	27.2	5.1
1970	14.8	6.2	13.3	4.6	29.0	5.0
1971	16.0	6.4	13.9	4.8	29.1	6.0
1972	15.6	6.6	13.9	5.1	30.8	5.7
Average rate of change, 1953–72	+0.08	+0.12	−0.10	+0.16	+0.89	+0.16
Average rate of change, 1958–72	−0.06	+0.14	−0.13	+0.19	+1.18	+0.18
Average rate of change, 1967–72	+0.04	+0.28	+0.06	+0.20	+1.20	+0.28

marked increase over time. After 1960, the proportion of women who have been charged with larceny or theft in any given year is much greater than is the proportion in any of the other offense categories, property as well as violent. It is interesting to note that until about 1960 the proportions of women who were arrested for homicide and aggra-vated assault were similar to those arrested for larceny, but in 1972 the percentage in the larceny category had almost doubled the 1960 percentage; whereas from 1960 on, the proportions have remained roughly the same for the homicide and aggra-vated assault offenses.

Table 4 describes trends in the proportion of women arrested for

TABLE 4

OTHER CRIMES, FEMALES ARRESTED AS PERCENTAGE OF ALL PEOPLE ARRESTED
FOR VARIOUS CRIMES: 1953–1972

YEAR	EMBEZZLEMENT AND FRAUD	FORGERY AND COUNTER- FEITING	OFFENSES AGAINST FAMILY AND CHILDREN	NARCOTIC DRUG LAWS	PROSTITUTION AND COMMERCIALIZED VICE
1953	18.3	14.0	9.3	15.7	73.1
1954	14.4	13.4	9.6	17.5	70.1
1955	15.6	15.2	9.8	17.1	68.8
1956	15.5	16.6	9.1	16.3	62.9
1957	14.4	14.8	9.0	15.6	69.2
1958	14.3	15.1	8.6	16.4	69.0
1959	14.9	16.2	8.9	16.2	65.2
1960	15.7	16.8	9.7	14.6	73.5
1961	15.7	17.5	11.2	15.4	71.8
1962	17.6	18.1	11.0	15.1	76.1
1963	18.3	18.7	11.5	14.2	77.0
1964	19.5	19.3	11.3	14.1	81.2
1965	20.7	19.2	11.0	13.4	77.6
1966	21.8	20.9	12.1	13.8	79.3
1967	23.4	21.4	11.4	13.7	77.2
1968	24.4	22.3	10.9	15.0	78.0
1969	26.3	23.2	11.4	15.5	79.5
1970	27.8	24.4	11.3	15.7	79.1
1971	27.4	24.8	11.6	16.3	77.4
1972	29.7	25.4	12.3	15.7	73.5
Average rate of change, 1953–72	+0.60	+0.60	+0.16	0	+0.02
Average rate of change, 1958–72	+1.10	+0.74	+0.26	−0.05	+0.32
Average rate of change, 1967–72	+1.26	+0.80	+0.18	+0.40	−0.74

selected offenses in the type II category.[9] The figures show that in 1972 approximately one in four persons arrested for forgery was a woman and one in 3.5 arrests for embezzlement and fraud involved a woman. If present trends in these crimes persist, approximately equal numbers of men and women will be arrested for fraud and embezzlement by the 1990s, and for forgery and counterfeiting the proportions

9. The Type II offenses shown in table 4 have been included because there has been a change in the arrest pattern for women or because they are offenses for which arrest rates for women are consistently high.

should be equal by the 2010s. The prediction made for embezzlement and fraud can be extended to larceny as well. On the other hand, if trends from 1958 to 1972 continue, fewer women will be arrested for criminal homicide and aggravated assault.

In summary, the data on arrests indicate the following about women's participation in crime: (1) The proportion of women arrested in 1972 was greater than the proportion arrested one, two, or three decades earlier. (2) The increase was greater for serious offenses than it was for all type I and type II offenses combined. (3) The increase in female arrest rates among the serious offenses was caused almost entirely by women's greater participation in property offenses, especially in larceny.

The data show that, contrary to impressions that might have been gleaned from the mass media, the proportion of females arrested for violent crimes has changed hardly at all over the past three decades. Female arrest rates for homicide, for example, have been the most stable of all violent offenses. Further probing of female arrest rates in the type II offenses revealed that the offenses that showed the greatest increases were embezzlement and fraud and forgery and counterfeiting. The increases were especially marked for the period from 1967 to 1972. None of the other offenses included in either type I or type II, save larceny, showed as big a shift as did these two white-collar offenses. Should the average rate of change that occurred between 1967 and 1972 continue, female arrest rates for larceny/theft, embezzlement, and fraud will be commensurate to women's representation in the society, or, in other words, roughly equal to male arrest rates. There are no other offenses among those contained in the uniform crime reports, save prostitution, in which females are so highly represented.

Two final observations: (1) it is plausible to assume that the police are becoming less "chivalrous" to women suspects and that the police are beginning to treat women more like equals; (2) police behavior alone cannot account for both the large increases in larceny, fraud, embezzlement, and forgery arrests over the past six years and for the lack of increase in arrests for homicide, aggravated assault, and other violent crimes.

The more parsimonious explanation is that as women increase their participation in the labor force their opportunity to commit certain types of crime also increases. As women feel more liberated physically, emotionally, and legally, and less subjected to male power, their frustrations and anger decrease. This explanation assumes that women have no greater store of morality or decency than do men. Their propensities to commit crimes do not differ, but, in the past, their opportunities have been much more limited. As women's opportunities increase, so will the likelihood that they will commit crimes. But women will be most likely to commit property, economic, and financial types of offenses. Their greater freedom and independence will result in a decline in their desire to kill the usual objects of their anger or frustration: their husbands, lovers, and other men upon whom they are dependent, but insecure about.

CROSS NATIONAL ARREST STATISTICS

A brief comparison of female arrest statistics in the United States with those collected by the International Criminal Police Organization for 25 countries all over the world in 1963, 1968, and 1970 shows that the United States moved from eighth place in 1963 to fourth place in 1968 to third place in 1970.

But the heterogeneity of the countries that rank directly above and directly below the United States makes it difficult to draw any conclusions about the types of societies that are conducive to high female arrest rates. Among those countries closest to the United States, there is, on the one hand, the West Indies, Thailand, and Burma; and, on the other hand, Portugal, West Germany,

Luxembourg, France, Austria, and Great Britain.

Perhaps more sense can be made of the rankings when they are broken by types of offenses. The offense categories that are included in the International Criminal Statistics and their definitions are listed in footnote 10. Table 5 compares the United States' female arrest statistics with other countries' for offense categories I, III (A and B), IV, and VI.[10]

For property and financial crimes —such as larceny, as defined by the FBI statistics, and fraud—the United States ranks second and first, respectively. Countries that rank directly above and below are those of Western Europe such as West Germany, Austria, and the Netherlands. For crimes of violence and

10. I. Murder: Any act performed with the purpose of taking human life, no matter under what circumstances. This definition excludes manslaughter and abortion, but not infanticide.
II. Sex offenses: Each country uses the definitions of its own laws for determining whether or not an act is a sex crime; rape and trafficking in women are also included.
III. Larceny: Any act of intentionally and unlawfully removing property belonging to another person. This category includes such a wide variety of offenses, that it was subdivided into:
A. major larceny: robbery with dangerous aggravating circumstances (for example, armed robbery, burglary, housebreaking)
B. minor larceny: all other kinds of larceny (for example, theft, receiving stolen goods)
IV. Fraud: Any act of gaining unlawful possession of another person's property other than by larceny. This category includes embezzlement, misappropriation, forgery, false pretenses, trickery, deliberate misrepresentation, swindle in general.
V. Counterfeit currency offenses: This includes any violation in connection with manufacture, issuing, altering, smuggling, or traffic in counterfeit currency.
VI. Drug offenses: This category covers any violation involving illicit manufacture of, traffic in, transportation of, and use of narcotic drugs.

drugs, American women rank sixth and seventh and are surrounded by a heterogeneous collection of countries that include the West Indies, New Zealand, West Germany, Scotland, and Canada. The positions of the United States and the countries of Western Europe in the larceny and fraud rankings are consistent with the hypothesis that, in those societies in which women are more likely to be employed in commercial and white-collar positions and to enjoy legal and social rights, they are also more likely to engage in property and economic types of crimes.

CONVICTIONS AND SENTENCES

Examination of convictions and sentencing patterns between men and women over time is difficult because of the absence of judicial statistics at the level of state courts. The federal statistics that are available from 1963 to 1971 are consistent with the arrest data in that they show that over the eight-year time span, the highest proportion of women have been convicted for fraud, embezzlement, and forgery. These same offenses also show the greatest increase in the proportion of females who have been convicted between 1963 and 1971.

California statistics from 1960 through 1972 do not show that the increase in convictions has followed the increase in arrests for the same types of offenses.[11] Although there has been an increase of 31 percent in the proportion of women convicted for all types of crimes from 1962 to 1972, that increase has been due solely to the higher conviction rates for violent offenses.

New York State statistics on the

11. The state of California maintains the most comprehensive crime and judicial statistics in the 50 states.

TABLE 5

RANKING OF COUNTRIES BY PERCENTAGE OF WOMEN ARRESTED FOR VARIOUS CRIMES: 1963, 1968, 1970

COUNTRY	ALL CRIMES		MURDER		MAJOR LARCENY		MINOR LARCENY		FRAUD		DRUGS	
	RANK	PERCENT	RANK	PERCENT	RANK	PERCENT	RANK	PERCENT	RANK	PERCENT	RANK	PERCENT
West Indies	1	28.9	11	13.3	13	3.4	11	16.3	5.5	15.4	—	—
New Zealand	2	25.3	4	16.9	8	4.2	6	19.6	5.5	15.4	5	14.2
Thailand	3	17.3	19	4.2	15	3.0	14	14.4	13	10.1	11	4.6
West Germany	4	16.4	8	15.0	10	3.8	1	25.5	2	21.8	3	14.6
Luxembourg	5	16.2	—	—	2.5	8.7	13	15.4	14	9.5	—	—
United States	6	15.2	6.5	15.4	7	5.3	2	24.8	1	23.5	7	11.1
Austria	7.5	13.8	3	22.0	2.5	8.7	4	22.6	3	20.8	4	14.3
France	7.5	13.8	12	12.8	1	8.8	8.5	16.6	4	18.7	—	—
England and Wales	9	13.5	6.5	15.4	16	2.6	7	18.5	8	14.4	—	—
Tunisia	10	12.8	1	27.0	4	8.5	18	7.3	20	4.6	12	3.5
Israel	11	12.1	22	2.8	17	2.5	19	6.8	17	6.6	8	7.7
Korea	12	11.5	2	22.4	9	4.0	16	10.0	15	8.2	2	23.1
Scotland	13	10.9	10	13.4	11	3.7	8.5	16.6	7	14.5	—	—
Netherlands	14	10.4	15	8.1	13	3.4	3	23.5	9	13.1	—	—
Ireland	15	10.1	13	12.5	5	6.5	10	16.5	11	10.6	—	—
Monaco	16	7.5	—	—	—	—	—	—	—	—	—	—
Tanzania	17	6.9	9	14.1	19	2.2	21	4.2	21	2.1	—	—
Cyprus	18	6.7	17	6.5	18	2.4	17	7.7	19	4.7	9	6.8
Finland	19	6.6	16	6.9	13	3.4	12	15.9	12	10.3	—	—
Japan	20	4.6	5	16.5	20	1.2	5	20.5	16	7.0	1	24.1
Malawi	21	4.2	20.5	4.0	22	.9	23	2.6	22	1.7	14	1.0
Hong Kong	22	3.0	20.5	4.0	21	1.0	22	4.1	18	5.5	13	2.2
Fiji	23.5	1.9	18	4.5	23	.3	20	5.1	23	.8	—	—
Brunei	23.5	1.9	—	—	—	—	—	—	—	—	10	4.8
Canada	—	—	17	10.0	6	5.5	15	13.4	10	11.8	6	13.9

proportion of female commitments to correctional institutions by type of offenses from 1963 to 1971 reveal an overall decline and no significant changes within any of the offense categories.

The proportion of female commitments to all state penal institutions declined between 1950 and 1970 from 5.1 percent to 4.7 percent.

On the whole, using the rather meager statistics that are available, it appears that the courts have not been adapting their behavior to meet the changing roles that women, and perhaps the police in their interactions with women, are performing. In interviews that were conducted with about 30 criminal trial court judges in the Midwest in the winter of 1974, we found that most of the judges had not observed, and did not anticipate, any changes either in the numbers or types of women or in the types of offenses that women were likely to be charged with in the immediate future. Most of the respondents said that they expected to continue to be easier on women than on men, when it came to passing sentence.

WOMEN AS VICTIMS OF CRIMES

This section shifts the focus of this article and turns the issue on its head by examining the role of women as victims of criminal acts. One of the issues to which the woman's movement has directed much of its efforts has been the treatment of women who are victims of rape. The movement has been critical of the legal system and has demanded changes in the standards of proof and identification that are required. It has pointed to the police and demanded that they behave more humanely. It has insisted that medical and psychological facilities be made available and has called for changes in the manner and circumstances under which women who claimed they had been raped are examined. It has also demanded that the services of a therapist be made available to the victim as soon as possible after she has reported the attack. The movement itself has been instrumental in setting up "rape hot lines" in many communities.

For all the attention that has been devoted to the female as "rape victim," it is interesting to note the proportions of men and women who have been victims of all types of criminal acts. For example, Wolfgang reported the characteristics of victims of criminal homicide from 1948 to 1952 and found that 76.4 percent were men and 23.6 percent were women. In 1972, the FBI reported that 22.2 percent of all murder victims were women.

In 1971, under the auspices of the Law Enforcement Assistance Administration, the Bureau of the Census conducted victimization surveys in Montgomery County, Ohio (Dayton), and in Santa Clara County, California (San Jose). In Dayton, 16,000 persons over the age of 16 and in San Jose, 28,000 persons over the age of 16 were victims of assault, robbery, or personal larceny at least once during 1970. The proportion of female victims in each city is shown below:

	Dayton	San Jose
Women as a percent of:		
Assault victims*	31	34
Robbery victims	36	34
Personal larceny victims	49	30

* Includes persons who reported they were raped.

It is obvious that the percentage of women victims is less than their representation in each of the communities. Even when rape victims are included in the assault categories, the proportion of assault victims is less than the 50 percent that one might expect simply on the basis of female representation in the community.

The following statistics allow for comparison between women and other categories in the two communities by showing rates of victimization per 100 population.

	Victimization Rates	
	Dayton	San Jose
Persons victimized by:		
Assault*	3.2	3.3
Robbery	0.8	0.8
Personal larceny	0.4	0.2
Women victimized by:		
Assault*	1.9	2.1
Robbery	0.6	0.5
Personal larceny	0.4	0.2

* Includes persons who reported they were raped.

	Victimization Rates	
	Dayton	San Jose
Young men between 16 and 24 victimized by:		
Assault	11.7	9.2
Robbery	1.7	2.4
Personal larceny	0.8	1.0

Minority group members:*		
Assault	3.1	3.9
Robbery	1.6	1.0
Personal larceny	0.8	0.3

* Dayton figures are for black persons; San Jose figures are for persons of Spanish origin or descent.

These figures, along with the national data on homicide, indicate that women are *less* likely to be victims of crimes than are men, and especially young men. Of course, one might argue that the relevant comparison is not the proportion of female victims by their representation in the society, but the proportion of female victims by the proportion of female offenders. If it is men — and especially men between the ages of 16 and 24 — who commit the highest proportion of criminal acts, then perhaps one should expect persons in that category to also account for the highest proportion of victims.

In their report to the *National Commission on the Causes and Prevention of Violence*, Mulvhill and Tumin described the results of a survey of victim and offender patterns for four major violent crimes in 17 large American cities. The crimes were: criminal homicide, aggravated assault, forcible rape, and robbery (armed and unarmed).[12] Table 6 describes the sex of the offender and the sex of victim for one of those types of offenses.

12. They obtained a 10 percent random sample of 1967 offense and arrest reports from the following cities: Atlanta, Boston, Chicago, Cleveland, Dallas, Denver, Detroit, Los Angeles, Miami, Minneapolis, New Orleans, New York, Philadelphia, St. Louis, San Francisco, Seattle, and Washington.

TABLE 6

SEX OF VICTIM AND OFFENDER FOR AGGRA-
VATED ASSAULT ARRESTS, 17 CITIES, 1967

SEX OF OFFENDER	SEX OF VICTIM		
	MALE	FEMALE	TOTAL
Male	56.6	27.0	83.6 (727)
Female	9.3	7.1	16.4 (142)
Total	65.9 (573)	34.1 (296)	100 (869)

NOTE: The figures represent percentages; those in parentheses are numbers of offenses.

The Mulvhill–Tumin data also show the following characteristics:

1. For all four offense categories, at least two-thirds of both the victims and the offenders are men. Armed robbery is almost exclusively a male situation: 90 percent of the victims and 95 percent of the offenders are men.

2. In the case of criminal homicide, 34 percent of the interactions are intersexual, and the roles performed by the men and women are divided almost equally—16.4 percent female offender/male victim, 17.5 percent male offender/female victim. There is a greater likelihood that the victim of a homicide perpetrated by a woman will be a family member (most likely her spouse) than when the homicide is committed by a man. Women are also more likely to kill members of their family than are men. White and black women share that propensity almost equally.

3. In the other offense categories, when the situation is intersexual, there is a much greater likelihood that the male will be the offender and the female the victim. For aggravated assault cases, the ratio of male-female victims is 3:1, in armed robbery, 2.5:1; and in unarmed robbery, 13:1.

These 1967 data are consistent with those obtained in the 1971 victimization surveys of Dayton and San Jose in that they also portray the male as being the victim much more frequently than the female. These data serve the additional function of dramatizing the extent to which violent crime is still very largely a male enterprise (males are both the perpetrators and the victims). Only 3.8 percent of all the criminal homicides, 7.1 percent of all the aggravated assaults, and .9 and 2.9 percents of all the armed and unarmed robberies were acts perpetrated by females against females. Finally, the 1967 data also show that, when violent offenses are intersexual, the woman's role is much more likely to be that of the victim and the male's that of the offender. Homicide is the exception.

CONCLUDING REMARKS

In the last three or four years, all of the mass media—films, newspapers, television, magazines, and radio—have agreed upon a common theme vis-à-vis women and crime. They have claimed that more women are engaging in more acts of violence than have been engaged in by American women at any time in the past. And they have attributed much of the females' greater propensities for violence to the woman's movement. The fact that, in 1970, four women made the FBI list for the ten most wanted criminals served as prima facie evidence of the accuracy of their perceptions. The Patty Hearst scenario also did much to convince the mass media that the image they were projecting about the increased propensities for violence by American women was indeed an accurate one.

But examination of national statistics over several decades reveals quite a different picture and, admittedly, one that lacks the drama of the media-created image. Women's participation in crime, especially serious crime, has increased. And the increase has been especially marked from 1967 on. But the types of serious crime that women are engaging in, in growing numbers, are crimes of property. They are economic and financial types of offenses. It is larceny, embezzlement, fraud, and forgery that are proving so attractive to women, and not homicide, assault, and armed robbery.

The increase in the first group of offenses and the decline in the second are, I believe, related in the following manner. With the woman's movement, a much greater proportion of women are working outside the home which provides more women with greater opportunities to embezzle, to commit fraud, and to steal than are available to housewives. The fact that these women are working also enhances their feelings of independence. The woman's movement supports these feelings by offering women a new image of themselves; and laws have changed so as to provide women with more legal and social independence. All of these factors, I believe, reduce the likelihood that women will attack or kill their most traditional targets: namely, their husbands or their lovers, other women with whom their men have become involved, or their unborn babies.

The factors cited above have provided women with the economic independence to take care of themselves and with a legal and social status that allows them to live without the protection of a man and to determine the fate of their own bodies. At least in the short run, then, I think we will continue to see an increase in women participating in property, fiscal, and economic offenses. Violent offenses will remain relatively stable or decline. The expectation, or the fear, that large numbers of young women will turn to radical politics and become revolutionaries has little evidence to support it. The Patty Hearsts and the Emily Harrises are probably as rare a phenomenon as was Ma Barker.

ANNALS, AAPSS, 423, Jan. 1976

The Heritage of Cain: Crime in American Fiction

By M. E. GRENANDER

ABSTRACT: For almost two centuries American fiction has featured crime, but its treatment in popular literature, which strokes the norms of a mass audience, has been quite different from that in high art, which examines critically the assumptions and values of our society. A study of serious fiction can, therefore, probe fundamental issues for us: How does literature define crime? Why does this definition differ occasionally from the statutory one? What crimes has fiction taken most seriously? How does fiction assess the criminal's circumstances and motivation? What is the literary attitude to criminal responsibility? What is the victim's role in crime? How is the criminal apprehended? How does the trial contribute to equity? How are legal professionals, the jury, and the insanity defense portrayed? How does literature rank criminal punishments? We can postulate tentative answers to these rather open-ended questions, but in a larger sense their value is heuristic, forcing us to reconsider some hypotheses we may have taken for granted.

M. E. Grenander is Professor of English at the State University of New York at Albany. Educated at the University of Chicago, she has been Visiting Professor of American Literature (Fulbright) at Lille and Toulouse, France. She is author of the Twayne Ambrose Bierce and of numerous articles on English and American authors, including essays on Thomas Szasz in the Nation and The Civil Liberties Review. Among her specialties is the interdisciplinary analysis of ideas. A recent president of the New York State American Studies Association, she held a senior scholar's stipend from the National Endowment for the Humanities last summer.

CRIME, a recurrent literary theme in many countries since the fraternal murder in Genesis, has been a pervasive constant in American fiction from the early days of the Republic. To deal with it in an article, I have slighted popular literature, which reflects the prevailing ethos, in order to concentrate on enduring works, which subject their culture to searching criticism.[1] I shall, however, briefly indicate the norms promulgated in three genres of popular fiction which lean heavily on crime before turning to more fundamental critiques.[2]

1. In this connection, see a thoughtful article by R. Gordon Kelley, "Literature and the Historian," *American Quarterly* 26 (May 1974), pp. 140–59.
2. I list in chronological order here the novels and stories on which I have drawn for this essay. Since all of them are standard works available in a number of different editions, I do not give complete bibliographical details: Charles Brockden Brown, *Wieland* (1798) and *Arthur Mervyn* (1799); Edgar Allan Poe, "The Murders in the Rue Morgue" (1841), "The Mystery of Marie Rogêt" (1842–43), "The Gold-Bug" (1843), and "The Purloined Letter" (1845); Nathaniel Hawthorne, *The Scarlet Letter* (1850); Harriet Beecher Stowe, *Uncle Tom's Cabin* (1852); Herman Melville, *Benito Cereno* (1855) and *The Confidence-Man: His Masquerade* (1857); Hawthorne, *The Marble Faun* (1860); Edward Everett Hale, "The Man without a Country" (1865); Bret Harte, "The Luck of Roaring Camp" (1868), "Tennessee's Partner" (1869), "The Outcasts of Poker Flat" (1869), and "The Idyl of Red Gulch" (1869); William Dean Howells, *A Modern Instance* (1882); Mark Twain, *Adventures of Huckleberry Finn* (1884); Howells, *The Rise of Silas Lapham* (1885); Henry James, *The Princess Casamassima* (1885–86); Ambrose Bierce, "An Occurrence at Owl Creek Bridge" (1890); Melville, *Billy Budd, Foretopman* (ca. 1890); Stephen Crane, *Maggie: A Girl of the Streets* (1893); Mark Twain, *Pudd'nhead Wilson* (1894); Crane, "The Blue Hotel" (1898); Frank Norris, *McTeague: A Story of San Francisco* (1899); Theodore Dreiser, *Sister Carrie* (1900); James, *The Golden*

WESTERNS, SPY THRILLERS, AND DETECTIVE STORIES

The western story reflects a frontier society's desire for an uncomplicated system of law and order, easily understood and administered, coupled with distrust of nuances of right and wrong which are difficult to decipher and interpret. The common man of the western plains always wins.[3] The spy story also operates in a matrix of accepted values. The spy in popular thrillers is always either good or bad, depending on whether he is "ours" or "theirs." The sympathetic portrayal of a foreign agent working to subvert American values would be unconscionable to readers of mass fiction. The detective story has a more complicated history. Edgar Allan

Bowl (1904); Willa Cather, "Paul's Case" (1905); F. Scott Fitzgerald, *The Great Gatsby* (1925); Dreiser, *An American Tragedy* (1925); Ernest Hemingway, "The Killers" (1927) and *A Farewell to Arms* (1929); William Faulkner, *The Sound and the Fury* (1929), "A Rose for Emily" (1930), and *Sanctuary* (1931); Margaret Mitchell, *Gone with the Wind* (1936); Walter Van Tilburg Clark, *The Ox-Bow Incident* (1940); Richard Wright, *Native Son* (1940); James Gould Cozzens, *The Just and the Unjust* (1942); Robert Penn Warren, *All the King's Men* (1946); Willard Motley, *Knock on Any Door* (1947); Herman Wouk, *The Caine Mutiny* (1951); Faulkner, *Requiem for a Nun* (1951); Ralph Ellison, *Invisible Man* (1952); Flannery O'Connor, "A Good Man Is Hard to Find" (1953); Faulkner, *A Fable* (1954); Vladimir Nabokov, *Lolita* (1955); Robert Traver, *Anatomy of a Murder* (1958); Harper Lee, *To Kill a Mockingbird* (1960); Ken Kesey, *One Flew Over the Cuckoo's Nest* (1962); Saul Bellow, *Herzog* (1964); Rex Stout, *The Doorbell Rang* (1965); Bernard Malamud, *The Fixer* (1966); Mario Puzo, *The Godfather* (1969); Nicholas Meyer, *The Seven-Per-Cent Solution* (1974); Richard Condon, *Winter Kills* (1974).
3. See Philip Durham and Everett L. Jones, eds., *The Western Story: Fact, Fiction, and Myth* (New York: Harcourt Brace Jovanovich, Inc., 1975).

Poe invented it in his "tales of ratiocination": "The Murders in the Rue Morgue" (1841), "The Mystery of Marie Rogêt" (1842–43), "The Gold-Bug" (1843), and "The Purloined Letter" (1845). Their appeal lay in working out answers to a puzzle which was only incidentally a crime. However, since the person who solved it was usually a detective, tales and novels in this form came to be called "detective stories," a term Poe himself did not use.

Since Poe's time, the detective story has split into two categories, the classic and the hard-boiled, each with distinguishing characteristics. The classic detective story's appeal is almost totally intellectual. But the tough-guy detective novels of Dashiell Hammett, Raymond Chandler, and their followers elicit, like the western, a gut reaction favoring macho simplicities. The plot of both species proceeds along a clearly marked path, with the actual crime committed in the early pages and the detective methodically reasoning from effect to cause, in order to discover who committed the crime and why—revelations that are not conveyed to the reader, except through clues on which he can exercise his own wits, until the end of the story. The criminal then meets justice, which may be highly idiosyncratic rather than conventional. Its manner is immaterial; the reader wants the puzzle solved, and when his suspense is ended, he is satisfied.

The classic detective solves a puzzling crime set in the framework of a society's fundamental values. The tough-guy detective plays his role against a corrupt backdrop, but he, too, corrects a perceived injustice. Like the western hero, he triumphs single-handedly, often using extralegal methods to satisfy the average man's yearning for a

justice he can comprehend, and reflecting an urbanized version of the frontier code.[4] Neither species of detective story leaves the moral loose ends lying about with which high art teases our minds; and, almost by definition, neither can probe society's values for us. The detective story must share, not challenge, its readers' assumptions; otherwise they will not care about the solution of its puzzle. Although Nero Wolfe, in Rex Stout's *The Doorbell Rang* (1965), does take on the FBI as his adversary, such a confrontation could occur in popular fiction only when doubt about the FBI was already widespread in society.

WHAT IS A CRIME?

In serious fiction, defining crime is crucial. In the real world, whatever the state calls a crime *is* a crime, and popular fiction tends to agree. "Right feeling," however, may not agree; and serious fiction is on the side of right feeling. The legality of chattel slavery is a cautionary example of the bad guidance our laws have sometimes offered. Hence, literature can be of tremendous importance in challenging current definitions of criminality. The victimless crimes frequently taken for granted in popular fiction are almost never examined from a legal point of view in high art: adultery, drug addiction, prostitution, gambling, and drunkenness. On the other hand, certain actions seem always to have been regarded as criminal in the fiction of American literary masters. These

4. See William Ruehlmann, *Saint with a Gun: The Unlawful American Private Eye* (New York: New York University Press, 1975). John M. Reilly presents a Marxist perspective in "The Politics of Tough Guy Mysteries," *University of Dayton Review* 10 (Summer 1973), pp. 25–31.

actions have involved threats to life, to the person, to liberty, to property, and to the society itself. The consensus on these as "crimes," whatever their legal status may be, accords with the view that, fundamentally, all "customs and institutions" are built on a bedrock of "universal, deep mental structures."[5]

Victimless crimes

Nicholas Meyer's recent best seller about Sigmund Freud and Sherlock Holmes, *The Seven-Per-Cent Solution* (1974), reflects contemporary mental health ideology in its attitude to Holmes's drug addiction. But even though drug addiction, prostitution, gambling, drunkenness, and adultery are sometimes crimes in popular literature, they have not been in serious American fiction. Indeed, victimless crimes are often not reprehensible even in pop literature.

Although the high-minded hero of Charles Brockden Brown's early *Arthur Mervyn* (1799) is zealously bent on reforming prostitutes, Stephen Crane analyzed their plight more searchingly in *Maggie: A Girl of the Streets* (1893), relating it to harsh family treatment, poverty, and male chauvinism. However, a sentimental stereotype of the prostitute with a heart of gold, along with the gentlemanly gambler and the amusing drunkard, had already begun to emerge in semi-popular fiction. Bret Harte made a career of presenting these stereotypes, which turned conventional cultural values upside down, in such local color short stories as "The Luck of Roaring Camp" (1868), "The Idyl of Red

Gulch" (1869), "The Outcasts of Poker Flat" (1869), and "Tennessee's Partner" (1869). In "The Blue Hotel" (1898) Crane portrays a professional gambler as mannerly, just, and moral; and Margaret Mitchell continued the tradition of the wise and kindly prostitute in *Gone with the Wind* (1936).

Drunkenness and adultery are special cases. Although the former is not a crime per se in fiction, actions harming others which are exacerbated by drunkenness are. Adultery has seldom been represented as criminal, even though statutes against it are still on the books in many states (including New York). But since it may have very serious consequences, popular sentimental literature of the nineteenth century imbued it with pathos and melodrama; and three great American novels subjected it to searching analyses: Nathaniel Hawthorne's *The Scarlet Letter* (1850), Henry James's *The Golden Bowl* (1904), and Robert Penn Warren's *All the King's Men* (1946). By and large, however, since World War I, adultery has seldom been taken seriously in popular literature, where it tends to be treated as a lighthearted jest. It is not portrayed as criminal even in the fiction of John O'Hara, John Cheever, and John Updike, where it is a staple element.

Threats to life, to the person, and to liberty

Although American fiction writers have always taken murder seriously,[6] they may explore refinements in its definition. Thus, James

---

5. Gunther S. Stent, "Limits to the Scientific Understanding of Man," *Science* 187 (21 March 1975), p. 1053.

6. See David Brion Davis, *Homicide in American Fiction, 1798–1860: A Study in Social Values* (Ithaca, N.Y.: Cornell University Press, 1957).

Gould Cozzens's *The Just and the Unjust* (1942) deals with the trial of defendants who are legally guilty of first-degree murder, although they did not actually kill their victim. Harper Lee's *To Kill a Mockingbird* (1960) treats rape conventionally from the orthodox male point of view, but it is examined much more searchingly in Richard Wright's *Native Son* (1940) and Robert Traver's *Anatomy of a Murder* (1958). The psychological destruction of the victim as an aftermath of her experience is underlined in William Faulkner's *Sanctuary* (1931) and its sequel, *Requiem for a Nun* (1951), and is given a particularly poignant twist in Vladimir Nabokov's *Lolita* (1955), where the victim is a child.

Kidnapping is important in *The Just and the Unjust*, but it is slavery as a crime against humanity that has fired American writers — in Mark Twain's *Adventures of Huckleberry Finn* (1884), Herman Melville's *Benito Cereno* (1855), and Warren's *All the King's Men*. Much of the pathos of *Huckleberry Finn* lies in Huck's unquestioning belief that he is committing a crime by not surrendering Jim to the authorities. He does not doubt the morality of the law; he simply decides to break it. But the very conventional Tom Sawyer goes along only because he knows that Jim is free, manumitted in his dead mistress' will. Both Tom and his creator were playing it safe. Mark Twain wrote his novel about an antebellum society years after the abolition of slavery. Moreover, helping the kindly and paternalistic Jim flee to freedom is hardly an offense to right feeling.

Melville, however, said "NO! in thunder" to slavery while it was still legal by showing its victims reacting with murderous violence in *Benito Cereno*, which turns the institution upside down. A band of African Negroes who are cargo on a South American slaver have mutinied, killing the whites or holding them hostage. The experience of the Castilian Chilean captain, Don Benito Cereno, as a helpless slave forces him to recognize the horror of human bondage. Although he is rescued from the insurrectionists, he cannot cope with the ethical inferno he has glimpsed and succumbs to his monstrous vision.

This novella, written while slavery was under statutory protection in the United States, was created with great subtlety so that the horror of what the blacks do is fully apparent. Nevertheless, Melville was mounting an extraordinarily effective attack against the perverted laws which allowed so intelligent and resourceful a person as Babo, leader of the mutineers, no role except that of a slave. *Benito Cereno* poses mutiny and murder against the evils of a legalized crime against humanity. Something similar is done in our time by Ken Kesey, whose *One Flew Over the Cuckoo's Nest* (1962) uses murder to criticize the psychiatric torture and enslavement institutionalized in contemporary society.

Threats to property

Theft in American fiction sometimes finances flight from intolerable circumstances, as in Theodore Dreiser's *Sister Carrie* (1900), Willa Cather's "Paul's Case" (1905), and Faulkner's *The Sound and the Fury* (1925). More sophisticated thefts occur as early as *Arthur Mervyn*, where Thomas Welbeck's forgery and fraud are portrayed as outright villainy. In some cases, however, "white-collar" crimes have been left shadowy—as in F. Scott Fitzgerald's *The Great Gatsby* (1925)—or they raise refined ethical questions, underlining the gray area they occupy. Melville's novella *The Confidence-Man: His Masquerade* (1857) was based on the activities of an actual New York criminal, who prefaced his touch by asking his intended victim, "Are you really disposed to put any confidence in me?"[7] His query created the generic name for the class of criminal he typified. At the time, some observers pointed out that his crimes were made possible not by stupidity but by generosity, a moral dilemma Melville's fable explores.

William Dean Howells's interest in the relationship of social problems to economic questions underlies his exploration of white-collar crimes in *A Modern Instance* (1882) and *The Rise of Silas Lapham* (1885). The corporate bribery of Judge Montague Irwin when he was the state's attorney general plays a key role in *All the King's Men*.

Threats to society

Fiction may present the betrayal of a subculture which threatens the parent society. Long before Mario Puzo's popular *The Godfather* (1969), Ernest Hemingway's classic "The Killers" (1927) presented this inversion of values.[8] But crimes threatening the social order itself (riots, mutiny, treason, and revolution) are the most fundamental a

society can face, since they deal with its very existence. The resourcefulness and courage of one man or a small handful of men control incipient riots in *Huckleberry Finn*, *To Kill a Mockingbird*, and *Native Son*. Walter Van Tilburg Clark's *The Ox-Bow Incident* (1940) portrays a mob lynching, and Ralph Ellison's *Invisible Man* (1952) an explosive riot. In all these novels, a mob forms when it perceives that justice has not been, and is not going to be, done. Its perception may or may not be accurate; however, if its complaints are handled with dispatch and firmness, the danger of its eruption into violence is greatly lessened.

Analyses of both treason and revolution require such an epic approach that most fiction has not attempted them. Exceptions are Edward Everett Hale's harrowing short story, "The Man without a Country" (1865), and James's *The Princess Casamassima* (1885–86), which includes magnificent portrayals of the cold-hearted dedicated revolutionary, the inept bumblers who tend to surround such a figure, and the women of high rank drawn into the revolutionary cause through boredom. More fundamentally, James's novel presents the revolutionary's classic dilemma: a given society's values and graces are inextricably intertwined with its misery and injustice.

Mutiny, a microcosmic threat to the social order, has been more manageable. Melville's *Benito Cereno* and *Billy Budd* (ca. 1890) examine it with extraordinary penetration and subtlety. World War I was the background for Hemingway's *A Farewell to Arms* (1929) and Faulkner's *A Fable* (1954); World War II, for Herman Wouk's *The Caine Mutiny* (1951). *Billy Budd* and

---

7. Johannes Dietrich Bergmann, "The Original Confidence Man," *American Quarterly* 21 (Fall 1969), pp. 560–77.

8. An analysis of this short story, making clear the locus of its plot, is R. S. Crane, "Ernest Hemingway: 'The Killers,'" in *The Idea of the Humanities*, vol. 2 (Chicago: University of Chicago Press, 1967), pp. 303–14.

The Caine Mutiny are of special interest in portraying mutineers sympathetically, but nevertheless unequivocally holding them accountable for their crime.

THE CRIMINAL

Habitual, occasional, manipulated, and inadvertent

American fiction has dealt with both the habitual criminal, whose offenses are a way of life with him, and the individual who, for whatever reason, commits an isolated crime. Examples of the former are found in Mark Twain's *Pudd'nhead Wilson* (1894), Willard Motley's *Knock on Any Door* (1947), *Anatomy of a Murder*, "The Killers," and, of course, the rash of current popular fiction dealing with Mafia figures. There is a depressing sameness about all these petty criminals, described in *The Just and the Unjust*: their principal problem was "how to make a living; and criminals who made good ones were as rare as millionaires. The rank and file could count on little but drudgery and economic insecurity." Nerveracked and in perpetual danger, they would "kill a man in a paroxysm of malignity and terror as soon as look at him."

Fiction also portrays characters who commit an occasional isolated crime, exemplified by Lieutenant Frederic Manion, in *Anatomy of a Murder*, who kills his wife's rapist; Hurstwood in *Sister Carrie*, a responsible businessman who commits an atypical theft; Clyde in Dreiser's *An American Tragedy* (1925), who drowns his pregnant lower-class girl friend in order to free himself for a socially advantageous marriage; and the badly trained dentist in Frank Norris's *McTeague* (1899), who murders his wife. The aristocratic Judge Irwin in *All the King's Men* once accepted a lucrative bribe; self-righteous Adam Stanton in the same novel murders the unscrupulous governor he discovers is his sister's lover. The adolescent in "Paul's Case" commits a single embezzlement in order to have one gaudy fling before he commits suicide. The protagonist in Faulkner's "A Rose for Emily" (1930) murders her lover, but continues to hold her head high. All these are characters who are not professional criminals, but are impelled to their isolated crimes in order to safeguard what they perceive as respectability in a lawabiding society whose code they subscribe to.

A third type of criminal may become the cat's-paw for a more intelligent one who escapes the consequences of action he has initiated. The fanatic's killings in Charles Brockden Brown's *Wieland* (1798) were triggered by a ventriloquist, and Steven Maryk is maneuvered by Tom Keefer in *The Caine Mutiny* into a breach of discipline leading to his court-martial. Mr. Wilson was told by Tom Buchanan that Jay Gatsby owned the hit-and-run car that had killed Mrs. Wilson. The murders of Willie Stark and Adam Stanton in *All the King's Men* are also committed through manipulation.

Finally, there is the inadvertent misdeed which is a criminal accident, like Billy Budd's blow at Claggart and automobile manslaughters such as those in *The Great Gatsby* and *The Just and the Unjust*.

Criminal psychology

Miriam and Donatello in Hawthorne's *The Marble Faun* (1860) offer an example of the "deepening tangle of dark impulses and mixed motives" described by the narrator in *Anatomy of a Murder*. The relation between the criminal's ethical principles and his passions gives us three different kinds of motivation. If both impel him, he will be completely stable; he *wants* to commit a crime, and he has embraced principles which justify it. Although the latter may deviate from the principles of his society, giving rise to the legalistic concept of "insanity" discussed later in this article, the criminal holding them will suffer no pangs of conscience; he can act with cold efficiency and complete ruthlessness.

Criminals whose passions and principles coalesce are Tom in *Pudd'nhead Wilson*; Hemingway's gangsters in "The Killers"; and Nick Romano, the young Chicago hoodlum in *Knock on Any Door*. Paul Muniment, the revolutionary chemist in *The Princess Casamassima*, is quite prepared for murder to further his goals. *McTeague* presents two paired psychopathologies in the Zerkows and the McTeagues, both of which result in the wives' brutal murder by their husbands. The adolescent in "Paul's Case" feels no remorse after embezzling his employer's funds, nor does the necrophiliac Emily Grierson after poisoning her faithless lover in "A Rose for Emily." The murderous Misfit in Flannery O'Connor's "A Good Man Is Hard to Find" (1953) says, "I ain't the worst [man] in the world . . . . I never was a bad boy that I remember of." In *Billy Budd*, a tantalizing attempt is made to present the evil Claggart's "natural depravity" as a phenomenon that has puzzled the courts, giving rise to "the prolonged contentions of lawyers with their fees" and the "yet more perplexing strife of the medical experts with theirs." The passions and principles of Bigger Thomas powerfully coincide in *Native Son*. He smothers the drunkenly comatose Mary Dalton in terror at being discovered in her bedroom, then stuffs both her hacked-off head and decapitated corpse into the roaring furnace. Although her murder was accidental, he draws psychic strength from it, justifying his crime as an existential choice affirming his personality. He also rationalizes it as an expression of race hatred, but shortly rapes and then murders his Negro mistress, Bessie, battering her head in with a brick and throwing her body down an air shaft. In the concluding pages of the novel, faced with impending death, he says, "What I killed for I *am*!"

Two types of more ambivalent motivation are found in criminals whose principles war with their passions. Such characters are in conflict and extremely unstable. Hyacinth Robinson, the young bookbinder in *The Princess Casamassima* who becomes embroiled in a revolutionary cadre, exemplifies those who justify their crime intellectually but recoil from it. Hyacinth's revolutionary ethics support the duke's assassination; when the crunch comes, however, his humane instincts prevent him from killing his intended victim. The obverse character has right principles, but overwhelming passion drives him to an act he knows is evil. Great artists have been fascinated by the psychological complexities of such a character, who will inevitably be gnawed by conscience. Shakespeare and Moussorgsky have given us the archetypes in Macbeth and Boris Godunov, but

American fiction offers less grand examples: the murderer swayed by religious mania in *Wieland* and *The Scarlet Letter*'s Arthur Dimmesdale, consumed by remorse.

Criminal responsibility

Few writers have presented criminals not responsible for their own destinies, since the term *character*, as literary critics use it, derives from the moral choices an individual makes throughout his life. Depriving him of responsibility, for good or ill, dehumanizes him into a driven puppet to whom the reader can have only a vaguely humanitarian response. The rare instances of such a fictional agent seem to be embodiments of contemporary intellectual movements. A possible reason for Wieland's manipulation by ventriloquism into killing his family may be that Brown wrote the novel during the heyday of the great Austrian hypnotist, Franz Anton Mesmer (1734–1815). In the late nineteenth century, writers following Zola were fascinated by the doctrines of naturalism, whose tenets of determinism and overpowering instincts were used by Stephen Crane and Frank Norris to account for the murders in "The Blue Hotel" and *McTeague*.

Although current biomedical research demonstrates that neural circuits are "anything but diffuse and non-selective," scientists in the 1930s believed that the nervous system was functionally almost infinitely malleable.[9] Their views supported an organismic psychology which put almost total stress on

9. For a nontechnical account of the evolution of neuroscientific thinking on this matter, see Roger W. Sperry, "Left-Brain, Right-Brain," *Saturday Review* 2 (9 August 1975), pp. 30–33.

family and social factors as conditioning determinants for behavior, theories with important consequences for sociology and penology. If delinquency were directly attributable to adverse cultural influences, then crime would simply be the result of the criminal's upbringing. This reductionist doctrine, beguiling in its simplicity, found its way into fiction. Two novels, in particular, dramatized it explicitly: *Native Son* and *Knock on Any Door*. A more sophisticated exploration of blame-shifting occurs in *The Caine Mutiny*, which makes the point that no matter how good a seaman an officer is, he must also understand and deal effectively with his fellows. Thus, although it was "really" Keefer who was responsible for the *Caine* mutiny, Maryk nevertheless pays an appropriate penalty by having his dreams of a naval career dissipated because he had unwisely trusted a shallow coward.

Indeed, Maryk's fate underlines a paradox about nearly all the protagonists discussed in this section whose creators have attempted to divert criminal responsibility from their shoulders. With the single exception of Crane's gambler in "The Blue Hotel," all the murderers meet death as the appropriate punishment for their brutal crimes: Wieland commits suicide, McTeague dies horribly under the desert sun, Romano and Thomas are both electrocuted. In every case, despite the authors' lip service to doctrines which attempt to absolve criminals from the consequences of their actions, the reader feels that justice has been done.

THE VICTIM

Fiction rarely portrays crime as the victim sees it. One reason, since the crime is frequently murder, is that he simply disappears from the scene, although he may not disappear from the plot: Barney Quill, dead before *Anatomy of a Murder* begins, permeates the novel. The victim may be someone who deserved to die, like the macho rapist Quill, or over whose loss the reader can feel few pangs, such as the brutal policeman in *Knock on Any Door* or Bob Ewell in *To Kill a Mockingbird*, stabbed barely in time to prevent his killing the Finch children. On the other hand, fictional portrayals of murder victims, when they do occur, seize the imagination powerfully. Trina McTeague's grisly death is painted with harrowing intensity, as is the family murder in "A Good Man Is Hard to Find."

Such examples offer clues for a relatively arcane area of investigation: to what extent do the victim's own attitudes and behavior contribute to his demise? After the witnesses in "The Blue Hotel" tumble into the street, "the corpse of the Swede, alone in the saloon, had its eyes fixed upon a dreadful legend that dwelt atop of the cash-machine: 'This registers the amount of your purchase.' " The white Mary Dalton in *Native Son*, whose condescending pseudoliberalism toward her father's new black chauffeur takes the form of getting drunk with him so that he has to carry her to her bedroom and put her to bed, invites her death. Claggart in *Billy Budd* solicits his own destruction by falsely accusing the Handsome Sailor of fomenting mutiny. Barney Quill courts murder by raping the wife of the man who subsequently killed him.

More subtly, fiction suggests that the victim may fail to exercise ordinary prudence in an intimate situation, treating someone dangerous with unwary compassion. A pathetic example of this tendency is revealed by the horrified Bessie Mears in *Native Son*, whose premeditated murder by Bigger Thomas occurs after he has coerced her into joining him in an extortion scheme based on Mary Dalton's death. She agrees to go off with him to a deserted building, where he rapes and beats her, throwing her body down an air shaft. The point is made explicit by his own lawyer, Boris Max. He consistently describes Bigger not as a responsible individual, but as the symbol for a collective entity so bestialized that "at the sight of a kind face it does not lie down upon its back and kick up its heels playfully to be tickled and stroked. No; it leaps to kill."

THE WITNESS

Graphic examples of human slaughter in fiction, as witnesses actually perceive it, emphasize the concrete incident or dramatize specific clues. In "A Rose for Emily," the "witnesses" are the Jefferson townspeople; what they see is not the crime itself, but signs from which a particularly bizarre necrophilic murder is inferred. It is never made explicit, however; the reader himself is forced to be a witness, drawing his own conclusions. Other crimes or their immediate aftermath are vividly described. Thus Trina McTeague discovers Maria Zerkow's body with the throat cut; her coming upon Maria's corpse ominously foreshadows the discovery that someone will later make of her own. In "The Blue Hotel," a small group in a western saloon witness the braggart Swede's murder. When the gambler's knife shot forward, "a human body, this citadel of virtue, wisdom, power, was pierced as easily as if it had been a melon. . . . The bartender found himself hanging limply to the arm of a chair and gazing into the eyes of a murderer." Another direct account is presented in *All the King's Men*. Dr. Adam Stanton, discovering that his sister is the governor's mistress, shoots Willie Stark and is immediately gunned down by his bodyguard. The description by Jack Burden, the narrator, is peculiarly poignant because he is inextricably tangled with all these characters.

APPREHENDING THE CRIMINAL

The detective

Poe's "The Murders in the Rue Morgue" and "The Purloined Letter" created the detective's special attributes, emphasizing his analytical or deductive powers. Sometimes he is a member of the official force; sometimes a professional private detective, like Nero Wolfe; sometimes merely a dilettante with a loose, informal police connection who dabbles in crime for the sheer joy of solving its puzzles, like Poe's C. Auguste Dupin himself. His idiosyncrasies set him apart from the ruck of mortals. Dupin is a bookworm, fond of nocturnal rambles through the Paris streets, who shutters his house during the day and lives by candlelight. Nero Wolfe, so immensely obese that he rarely stirs from his New York City brownstone, is an orchid fancier and a dedicated gourmand. David Wilson is an educated eastern lawyer, whose whimsical deadpan humor alienates him from the literal-minded yokels of Dawson's Landing. Ostracized and lonely, he takes up fingerprinting as a hobby and, through this means and his native wit, solves the murder in *Pudd'n-*

head Wilson. Although the classical detective is, above all, an intellect, like Dupin or Nero Wolfe, the hard-boiled detective employs violence as his primary weapon. He is a very tough guy, cynical in his attitude toward his fellow mortals, and often displaying superhuman prowess at the bottle and in bed. Although he tends to be an expert marksman and a good fighter, he has no Marquis of Queensberry scruples. His physical skills are brutal and ruthless, more those of the barroom brawler than the adroit boxer.

The police

Fictional police, whether city, county, or state, are usually remarkably efficient. Their procedures frequently involve large numbers of professional personnel, sophisticated and expensive technology, and even effective extra-legal measures. However, unless one of their number is himself the detective, they lack imagination and tend to be intellectually pedestrian. The relationship between key officials in a police force and the analytical detective or lawyer (such as Perry Mason in the Erle Stanley Gardner series) is, therefore, apt to be one of grudging mutual respect. Again, Poe's tales furnish an outline, with Dupin describing the Parisian police and their prefect as attaining their surprising results with an ordinary criminal through "simple diligence and activity." But a felon whose cunning is "diverse in character from their own" foils them.

Dupin's condescending attitude appears also in *Anatomy of a Murder*, which describes "alert good-looking young state police troopers" with their acurate charts and measurements as being like eager math professors. The Chicago police in

Native Son, however, are impassive functionaries. They methodically protect Bigger Thomas, who has murdered two women in particularly brutal fashion, from an angry mob. In both *Native Son* and *Knock on Any Door*, the Chicago police are white. By the time of Saul Bellow's *Herzog* (1964), however, they are blacks, still functioning with the stolid efficiency described in Wright's novel.

Although ruthless police brutality is seldom emphasized in the classic detective story, it is apt to be shared with the hero himself in the hard-boiled species. In serious fiction, procedures outside the law may achieve a rough justice. The Chicago force in *Knock on Any Door* use violent methods to identify and apprehend the murderer, clearly guilty but against whom only circumstantial evidence exists. In *To Kill a Mockingbird*, the county sheriff exculpates the reclusive Arthur Radley by making up a complicated accidental-death story to account for the stabbing of Bob Ewell.

The FBI

Although city police, county sheriffs, and—especially—state troopers are often treated with respect and some admiration, the Federal Bureau of Investigation has come in for a severe drubbing. *The Doorbell Rang* pits Nero Wolfe against J. Edgar Hoover and his minions. With its widespread cadre of highly trained agents, costly electronic surveillance gadgetry, and nationwide tentacles, the FBI is one of the most formidable adversaries the portly detective has ever come up against. His abhorrence of and contempt for the powerful agency and its unscrupulous tactics are given extensive coverage in this popular novel, which concludes with an unnamed figure (clearly Hoover) ringing Wolfe's doorbell to admit defeat.

The FBI also appears in an unfavorable light in a serious novel, *The Just and the Unjust*. Its agents, with extensive legal education and experience, know just how much they can get away with in torturing a suspected criminal, Stanley Howell, into admitting his guilt. Hard-faced and efficient, they are careful to leave no marks on his body as a record of what they have done, but reduce him to such a physical wreck that his attorney has to ask for repeated recesses. Judges, attorneys, and local police all suspect what has happened and regard the FBI agents with distaste.

THE TRIAL

Although detective stories conclude with the apprehension of the culprit, on the assumption that due punishment will be meted out once he is caught, serious fiction often examines the trial, a "fascinating pageant" where his legal guilt or innocence is established. Both *The Just and the Unjust* and *Anatomy of a Murder* center on trials; and trials are significant in *Billy Budd*, "The Blue Hotel," *Knock on Any Door*, *To Kill a Mockingbird*, and *The Caine Mutiny*. *Anatomy of a Murder*, *Knock on Any Door*, and *The Just and the Unjust* describe the trial as an intensely partisan contest in which lawyers seek not truth but victory. In revealing imagery, it is a "snarling jungle"; a savage, "primitive, knock-down, every-man-for-himself" combat; a "damned hard battle" for "survival itself." Other metaphors are of a show, play, or "raw drama" whose "main actors lose all if they fail." In the trial as duel, the opposing lawyers, whose weapons are their "wits and brains," are "masters of overstatement, flamboyantly fighting for victory, for reputation, for more clients, for political advancement, for God knows what."

The reader of American fiction can pick up a certain expertise about courtroom tactics and strategy. Both *To Kill a Mockingbird* and *The Just and the Unjust* emphasize that aimless fishing on cross-examination is usually foolish and dangerous. Although the jury is an incalculable element, another bit of lore is that it telegraphs its findings as soon as it comes into the courtroom, never looking at a defendant it has convicted. Its verdict is supposed to be based on factual evidence brought out by the opposing lawyers combined with law relayed by the judge. However, following this procedure does not always give the result readers feel is just. Hence, the jury (to the exasperation of lawyers, judges, and reviewing bodies) may render a verdict which, although not in accord with the evidence and the law, nevertheless satisfies the reader's gut desire for equity.

The prosecuting attorney

According to Paul Biegler, the narrator of *Anatomy of a Murder*, "being a public prosecutor was perhaps the best trial training a young lawer could get . . . , but as a career it was strictly for the birds." Mitchell Lodwick, prosecuting attorney in this novel, is a clean-cut but inexperienced young man elected for his glamor as a football star and war veteran. Abner Coates of *The Just and the Unjust* and his superior, Martin Bunting, the district attorney, are honest, logical, and straightforward, doing a workmanlike and completely persuasive

job. Kerman and Buckley, the prosecutors in *Knock on Any Door* and *Native Son*, are very different types—unsympathetic, driving careerists bent on swelling their records with convictions. Both see their duty as one of protecting society by upholding its laws. When necessary, Kerman clothes his disreputable witnesses in presentable clothes; and he coaches them with cajolery and threats, acquiescing in their being beaten up by the police to get their testimony. Nick Romano's counsel describes prosecutors as not caring "if a man is innocent or guilty. They're out to make a record for themselves." However, *The Just and the Unjust* gives a different slant: "A miscarriage of justice, with some good, brave man in the interesting and dramatic plight of standing trial for what he never did" is an implausible thousand-to-one chance, given the detailed process by which a prisoner is indicted and brought to trial.

The defense attorney

Defense lawyers, whatever their ethics or abilities, are portrayed as infatuated with the law. Although money is their primary professional motivation, they all want desperately to win their cases. Biegler says that "a lawyer caught in the toils of a murder case is like a man newly fallen in love: his involvement is total." Boris Max, Bigger Thomas' Communist lawyer in *Native Son*, is more the personification of a dialectical thesis than a fully characterized individual, but in his single-minded adherence to collectivist ideology he is sincere. In this respect he resembles the wise, scholarly Atticus Finch, in the sentimental and rather dated *To Kill a Mockingbird*, who is otherwise unique. Max and Finch, however, are unlike most criminal defense lawyers in American fiction, who tend to be at best indifferently honest. More typical than either is the defense attorney in *Anatomy of a Murder*, who considers truth only as a last resort. According to *The Just and the Unjust*, which presents lawyers more favorably than most American fiction, an attorney is a "professional liar."

Defense lawyers, if successful, are incomparably better paid than prosecutors. Good examples are Servadei and his partners, prominent shysters in *The Just and the Unjust*; and the amusing old windbag in *Anatomy of a Murder*, Amos Crocker, who weeps and roars his way through filibusters instead of making jury arguments. However, the fullest characterization of the type is Andrew Morton, who takes up Nick Romano's case in *Knock on Any Door*. A skillful mouthpiece for organized crime, he has luxurious, well-staffed offices and a magnificent home on Chicago's Gold Coast. Although he knows quite well that Nick murdered the policeman Dennis Riley in a particularly brutal fashion, he does not hesitate to spin an elaborate web of false testimony in an effort to secure an acquittal, going even farther than Kerman in suborning perjury. His tactics are so shrewd that the reader expects their success until Nick breaks down on the witness stand and confesses.

The defense attorneys in *Anatomy of a Murder* and *The Caine Mutiny*, Paul Biegler and Barney Greenwald, are somewhat more ethical, being careful to stay within the letter of the law. However, they do not hesitate to violate its spirit. Biegler artfully coaches his client, Frederic Manion; and Greenwald, Steve Maryk's lawyer in *The Caine Mu-*

tiny, establishes that Lieutenant Commander Philip Queeg, against whom Steve had mutinied, was a "neurotic" and "paranoid." Greenwald's ploy gets Maryk acquitted at the general court-martial, but he is deeply ashamed of what he has done. At the subsequent victory dinner, he shows up drunk and says that if he were writing a novel its hero would be Captain Queeg. "You're guilty," he announces to Maryk. "I got you off by phony legal tricks."

The most admirable defense lawyers in the fiction I have studied are Parnell McCarthy in *Anatomy of a Murder* and Harry Wurts in *The Just and the Unjust*. McCarthy, most of whose own clients have fallen away because of his drinking, is Biegler's learned and industrious assistant. Wurts is a buffoon in his personal life, and his sterling qualities as a trial lawyer tend to be further obscured because the novel is told from the prosecution's point of view. But he is resourceful, bold, and acute. He has a real feel for the law, a passionate faith in the adversary process through which legal justice operates, and an acute insight into the psychology and foibles of the ordinary men and women who become jurors.

The judge

Judges come off far better in American fiction than do lawyers, being wise and humane scholars who attempt to administer even-handed justice. Since our legal system charges them with instructing the jury in matters of law, they are often impartial founts of legal knowledge and may state the thesis in didactic novels and stories. Even Montague Irwin in *All the King's Men* had been, except for his single lapse, a "just judge" who had "done good." Others, like Judge Weaver in *Anatomy of a Murder* and the homespun Judge Taylor in *To Kill a Mockingbird*, are able, learned, and seldom reversed. *The Just and the Unjust*, with its three judges, gives us the fullest description of judicial attitudes and proprieties. The curt, severe Judge Vredenburgh is irascible, but he is also astute, competent, and fair. Judge Irwin, the "reserved and aloof" president judge, is strict, but has an air of "austere sweetness." Hating facts as symptoms of the "folly and unreason pandemic in the world," he balances them precisely against the statutes; but opposes any legislation which would enhance "the principle, false among free men, of preventing a choice instead of punishing an abuse." His rambling charge to the jury impresses on them what they need to know, his circumlocutions giving them time to mull over each point. It is, however, Abner's invalid father, Judge Coates, who presents the novel's thesis, pointing out the importance of the jury in granting an equity that impersonal law may not provide.

Probably the most famous judge in American literary history is Captain the Honorable Edward Farfax Vere, commanding officer of H.M.S. *Indomitable* in 1797, when mutiny was a constant threat. A handsome young impressed seaman, Billy Budd, was falsely accused of mutiny in front of Vere by the mysteriously depraved master-at-arms, Claggart. Unable to speak because of a stammer which afflicts him during moments of great stress, Billy knocks Claggart down, inadvertently killing him. "Fated boy!" breathes the appalled Captain Vere. Although he feels an almost paternal fondness for the luckless sailor, he appoints a drum-head summary court-martial to try him for murder during an act of mutiny. After the trial—whose facts are not in doubt—he reminds the members of the court what naval law prescribes, and they bring in the inevitable verdict. Starry Vere then reports it to the prisoner in a long and presumably emotional last interview. That his course was the right one is borne out by subsequent events. Billy Budd dies blessing Captain Vere, mutiny is averted, and an authorized naval publication approves the salutary promptness of the punishment. The point of Melville's story is that in the affairs of men time, place, and circumstance render necessary a judgment which may run contrary to the scruples of that higher justice only the absolute rectitude of eternity can afford.

The jury

American fiction makes its most telling point about our legal system in defense of the jury's key role in the vast, lumbering machinery of the law. Even *To Kill a Mockingbird*, which presents the jury in a negative light, concedes its educational value. Although juries preserve a rough equity, they are neither particularly wise nor able. The unpredictability of their verdicts is stressed repeatedly, but is paradoxically the very quality that makes a jury trial democratic, since its weathervane results are never preordained. Yet, as Biegler tells Manion,

"Even jurors have to save face. . . . If the judge—who's got a nice big legal face to save, too—must under the law virtually tell the jurors to convict you, . . . then the only way they can possibly let you go is by flying in the face of the judge's instructions—that is, by losing, not saving, face."

This is precisely what happens in *The Just and the Unjust*, where these theories are given their fullest expression. Two issues confront the jury: (1) Was Frederick Zollicoffer murdered? (2) Was he murdered in the course of a kidnapping? As Judge Vredenburgh carefully instructs the jurors, if they believe the evidence points to a "yes" vote on both these questions (and it clearly does), they are legally bound to bring in a verdict of first degree murder against Zollicoffer's kidnappers. Such a verdict, at the time and place in which the novel occurs, would have resulted in the execution of the two defendants. However, they did not actually fire the shots that killed the victim. That action was performed by their leader, subsequently captured and shot in an attempted escape. The dry, matter-of-fact district attorney, Marty Bunting, methodically explains the obvious to the bored jury. If they believe what the evidence establishes, they should bring a verdict of first-degree murder against Howell and Basso and assign the death penalty. But to the judge's exasperation and the dismay of the district attorney and his assistant, they bring in a verdict of second-degree murder, whose maximum sentence is twenty years' imprisonment. Even the defendants' city shyster, Servadei, recognizes their decision as "the caprice of a lot of stubborn yokels who could not be counted on to play the game according to the rules."

The scholarly President Judge Irwin then delivers a long, stern lecture to the confused and sulky jurors, stating that it would be inappropriate to thank them, since they had failed to understand their position and their responsibilities and had not discharged their duty properly. He then makes a nod in an outrageously implausible direction: "You had a right to find, if that was what the evidence meant to you, that neither of these men took part in any kidnapping." Since the evidence could not possibly support this conclusion, he ends by giving them a wintry smile and an indication of what their consciences must support: "You were sworn to give a true verdict according to the evidence."

The Just and the Unjust traces the way in which the jury arrives at its preposterous decision, what the immediate consequences of such a verdict are, and how its larger implications support our system of criminal justice and our society as a whole. Why did this willful jury astoundingly find against reason, law, and fact for second-degree murder, when its verdict obviously should have been first-degree murder? The novel suggests a number of answers. To begin with, though killing Zollicoffer, a drug peddler and low criminal, was,

of course, a crime, his death was no loss—even a gain—to society at large. Thinking along this line, a jury might do something silly, like deciding the defendants were not so bad after all. . . . To counter with law or logic was hard, for in adopting such a line of thought, a jury already had declared the intention to abandon both. Collective entities—a jury, a team, an army, a mob—often showed a collective apprehension and a collective way of reasoning that transcended the individual's reasoning and disregarded the individual's logic. The jury, not embarrassed by that need of one person arguing alone to explain and justify what he thought, could override any irrelevancy with its intuitive conviction that, irrelevant or not, the point was cogent.

Another reason is advanced by an FBI witness, "a liar but . . . certainly no fool," who "thought the jury was jibbing at executing two men for something they argued a third man had really done." Harry Wurts, the dedicated and skillful defense attorney, had underlined this point in addressing the jurors. He described as barbarous, futile, and disgraceful eighteenth-century laws making scores of crimes punishable by death. They were eventually abolished, he says, because juries refused to "bring in verdicts of guilty. Jurors might not be able to make the law; but they had something to say about justice."

Wise Judge Coates, however, puts the jury's decision in its broadest context. "A jury has its uses. . . . There isn't any known way to legislate with an allowance for right feeling. . . . Justice is an inexact science" mediating the ancient conflict between liberty and authority. Although the Finch family in *To Kill a Mockingbird*, bitterly disappointed at the jury's verdict, discuss the possibility of changing the law so that "only judges have the power of fixing the penalty in capital cases" or even of doing away with juries entirely, Judge Coates undermines these naïve notions.

"The jury protects the Court. It's a question how long any system of courts could last in a free country if judges found the verdicts. It doesn't matter how wise and experienced the judges may be. Resentment would build up every time the findings didn't go with current notions or prejudices. . . . A jury can say when a judge couldn't, 'I don't care what the law is, that isn't right and I won't do it.' It's the greatest prerogative of free men. . . . They may be wrong, they may refuse to do the things they ought to do; but freedom just to be wise and good isn't any freedom. We pay a

price for lay participation in the law; but it's a necessary expense."

These theories are implemented in "The Blue Hotel." In that story, the gambler who killed the Swede got a light sentence because "there was a good deal of sympathy for him in Romper." However, the negative side of the equation hinted at by Judge Coates is provided by the rather peculiar jury in *To Kill a Mockingbird*, which includes no townspeople, only farmers, no blacks, and no women. Perhaps in part because of its unrepresentative composition, its verdict is only too predictable, but nevertheless flouts both evidence and law. Still Atticus Finch regards it as the "shadow of a beginning. That jury took a few hours. An inevitable verdict, maybe, but usually it takes 'em just a few minutes."

INSANITY AND CRIME

Ambiguity vexes the whole question of insanity and crime. On the one hand, fiction probes rather deeply into the aberrations I have described under "Criminal Psychology" without suggesting that they excuse their possessors from responsibility for their actions. On the other hand, insanity as a legal concept nearly always results in a perversion of justice for two quite contradictory reasons. Although an insanity defense may allow the perpetrator of a crime to be freed (as in *Anatomy of a Murder*), it may also, quite to the contrary, result in abrogation of his constitutional rights and a far more severe punishment than he would have received had he been declared sane and guilty. This is what happens in *One Flew Over the Cuckoo's Nest*.

Insanity and *sanity* as legal ploys in fictional works are terms with so little relevance to questions of criminal responsibility that shrewd lawyers can manipulate them in almost any direction they choose, capitalizing on the absence of consensus among psychiatrists. Thus, although Barney Greenwald believes that Steve Maryk has foolishly allowed himself to be misled by the venal Tom Keefer, he nevertheless agrees to defend him and cynically maneuvers "expert" witnesses into indicating that Captain Queeg, who had been pronounced medically sane by three navy psychiatrists, was a paranoid neurotic. The labels Greenwald pins on Queeg can then be distorted to justify Maryk's actions.

"Insanity" can also be applied to the defendant. Paul Biegler in *Anatomy of a Murder* constructs the entire case for Frederic Manion, being tried for killing his wife's rapist, on a plea of temporary insanity, a "decently plausible legal peg" for the jurors to hang an acquittal on. Manion learns his lesson so fast and so thoroughly that he successfully cons not only the judge and jury but even his own attorney, and the gambit works. The jurors find Manion "not guilty by reason of insanity"; he is released from custody on a writ of habeas corpus and, in a matter of minutes, walks out of the courtroom a free man.

Nevertheless, the comments on this book by the psychiatric scholar, Professor Thomas S. Szasz, are instructive. Dr. Szasz writes that although the jury's refusal to convict Manion "makes sense," his crime had "nothing to do with insanity." Szasz goes on to point out that "if the defense of insanity is sustained, . . . there are two basic possibilities" for the defendant, with an outcome like Manion's rare and becoming rarer. Much more likely is the alternative that acquitting him by reason of insanity will warrant his transport to an insane asylum after his trial, to be confined there until " 'cured' or until 'no longer dangerous to himself and others.' " Accordingly, Szasz recommends abolition of the insanity plea on two grounds: (1) it should not be used to excuse crime; (2) its consequences for the defendant are customarily dire.[10]

American fiction supports his reasoning. Pretty Boy Romano, the murderer in *Knock on Any Door*, is adamant against being pronounced insane. His celebrated lawyer, Andrew Morton, announces: "We can build a case on insanity or temporary insanity." Romano, however, refuses: "No. I ain't going to cop no plea on insanity! Leave that angle out, see!" Bigger Thomas reacts the same way when the state's attorney tries to elicit his cooperation by suggesting a hospital examination to determine that he's "not responsible." Bigger's angry reaction is immediate: "He was not crazy and he did not want to be called crazy. 'I don't want to go to no hospital.' " Although both Romano and Thomas are electrocuted for their murders, *One Flew Over the Cuckoo's Nest* suggests that acquittal by reason of insanity would have been more horrible. McMurphy, who has naïvely chosen a mental hospital in preference to the prison farm after committing a minor offense, gradually realizes the unlikelihood that he will ever be released. Subjected to a series of technologically refined

10. Thomas S. Szasz, *Law, Liberty, and Psychiatry* (New York: Macmillan & Co., 1963), pp. 138–39; *Ideology and Insanity* (Garden City, N.Y.: Doubleday Anchor, 1970), pp. 107, 109.

tortures, he is finally murdered by a fellow-inmate to rescue him from the empty existence awaiting him after part of his brain has been surgically destroyed.

PUNISHMENT

Punishment in American fiction covers a wide spectrum. It may not be assigned at all, as in the case of a shy recluse in *To Kill a Mockingbird* who stabbed the murderous drunk assaulting his neighbor's children. It may take the form of blocking the defendant's career plans after his acquittal (Steve Maryk in *The Caine Mutiny*). It may entail imprisonment, either short-term (as in Manion's case) or long-term (Tom Robinson in *To Kill a Mockingbird* or Yakov Bok in Bernard Malamud's *The Fixer* [1966]). It may involve indefinite incarceration in a mental hospital, with such ancillary tortures as electroshock and lobotomy (*One Flew Over the Cuckoo's Nest*). Or it may involve execution: hanging in *Billy Budd* and Ambrose Bierce's "An Occurrence at Owl Creek Bridge" (1890); electrocution in *Knock on Any Door* and *Native Son*.

Death is by no means the worst of these punishments. After the protagonist of *Knock on Any Door* began his relentless criminal descent, he was neither attractive nor sympathetic; yet, once sentenced, he achieved a brief integrity, recognizing what he had become and what he had done to his family. He is brave and composed at his actual electrocution. In death Nick Romano becomes, if not a hero, at least someone whose stoicism compels a measure of admiration. Peyton Farquhar, the captured Confederate spy, faces hanging with manly resolution. As his neck breaks, he

has a vivid fantasy of escaping to be reunited with his wife and family. Consequently, his last moments are happy ones. Billy Budd goes even beyond Farquhar's experience, achieving a brief glory when he hangs. Just before he dies, he says clearly, "God bless Captain Vere!"—words enhanced by his spiritualized appearance as his body swings in the mystically rosy dawn.

Extended imprisonment is a much worse prospect for the condemned criminal than death. Manion tells Biegler that he'd "sooner die" than spend his days in prison. Tom Robinson, falsely accused of rape and convicted, cannot stand confinement. He makes a futile, desperate dash for freedom from the prison farm, where he is being held pending his appeal, and is promptly gunned down by the guards. A wrenching account of a long, tortured imprisonment makes up the bulk of *The Fixer*. Since the novel's setting is anti-Semitic Czarist Russia, this punishment has no direct relevance to American society, but it does reveal a distinguished modern American writer's attitude toward the crippling psychological effect of prolonged detention and the extraordinary resources a prisoner must call upon to withstand it.

Probably the worst punishment a criminal can undergo, as portrayed in American fiction, is incarceration in a hospital for the insane. Even mass fiction is beginning to hint at this. Richard Condon's mystery thriller, *Winter Kills* (1974), for example, portrays a ruthless industrial magnate delivering the ultimate threat: being "locked away for a long time" in a mental institution, "and I'm going to . . . see that you get a prefrontal lobotomy to help you wait for the years to go past." A gruesome account of the harrowing effects such a commitment can have is presented in *One Flew Over the Cuckoo's Nest*. The protagonist in this novel, who has unwittingly exchanged the limited hardships of a prison farm for the Kafkaesque horrors of a mental hospital, gradually comes to understand the capricious and arbitrary nature of the length of his confinement and the punishments that can be visited upon him. After being subjected to repeated electric shock convulsions which impair his memory, he undergoes a lobotomy which destroys his personality. Rather than allow this hollow shell to endure as an object lesson to those who confront the institution's staff, his best friend, another patient, murders him and escapes.

CONCLUSIONS

Certain tentative generalizations emerge from this rapid survey. Literature for a mass audience tends to confirm accepted values. Critical examination of these values in such fiction serves as a warning signal that sizable numbers of people are already beginning to doubt them. The negative treatment of the FBI in a popular detective novel is a cautionary example to the literary historian who remembers how widely read Harriet Beecher Stowe's *Uncle Tom's Cabin* (1852) was before the Civil War.

At a more fundamental level, high art diagnoses cancers in the body politic still unnoticed by most people. The horrors brought on by slavery in *Benito Cereno* are analogous to the institutionalized repression of *One Flew Over the Cuckoo's Nest*. If we follow this line of thinking, serious fiction suggests questions to which social scientists, including criminologists and penologists, should direct special attention. The dubieties that trouble the mind after one reads widely in the American fiction portraying crime indicate issues of basic importance to society. The exploration of values our literary masters have undertaken forces us to reexamine cultural assumptions that, in our everyday lives, we often take for granted.

ANNALS, AAPSS, **423**, Jan. 1976

Psychoanalysis and Crime: A Critical Survey of Salient Trends in the Literature

By JOHN J. FITZPATRICK

ABSTRACT: Psychoanalytic studies of criminal motivation generally have followed the salient trends within the historical development of psychoanalytic theory. The first trend, initiated by Sigmund Freud in an essay entitled "Criminals from a Sense of Guilt" (1916), highlighted the motivational priority of unconscious psychosexual conflict. Social and economic factors were minimized. Psychoanalytic ego psychologists subsequently have questioned the explanatory adequacy of the libido theory and have modified the theoretical orientation of psychoanalysis. This theoretical reorientation has been reflected in recent psychoanalytic studies of crime, which not only seek to account for the contextual diversity of antisocial behavior but also emphasize the etiological significance of character development, the adaptational functions of the ego, and the important role played by the environment in the criminal's life.

John J. Fitzpatrick received his doctorate in American History from the University of California, Berkeley, where he also taught in the American Studies program and the History Department. He is co-editor of the Group for the Use of Psychology in History Newsletter and an expanded version of a bibliography that appeared in the History of Childhood Quarterly, which has been published as A Bibliography of Psychohistory (Garland Publishing, 1975). He is a psychohistorian and fellow in the Interdisciplinary Studies Program of the Menninger Foundation, a faculty member of the Menninger School of Psychiatry, and a special student of the Topeka Institute of Psychoanalysis.

CRIME is an exceedingly diverse and complex phenomenon that has been rooted in the social and economic nexus of contemporary America as much as in the psychodynamics of the individual criminal. It shares many of the characteristics that Richard Hofstadter has attributed to violence in America. It has exhibited an "extraordinary frequency . . . [and] sheer commonplaceness in our history . . . , [a] persistence into very recent and contemporary times, and . . . [a] rather abrupt contrast with our pretensions of singular national virtue."[1] Crime in America also lacks both a geographical center and an ideological tradition. Criminals are among not only the poor and the uneducated, but also the privileged and the powerful. The dimensions of crime range from impulsive assaults and murders, usually committed by acquaintances, to calculated embezzlements and perjuries of corporate officials and political leaders.

These many varieties of crime have spawned an almost equal number of analytic explanations to account for their occurrence. For example, sociologists have studied the demographic factors influencing a normative group of criminals, historians have examined changes in the patterns of crime during different chronological periods, and psychoanalysts have endeavored to uncover the essential psychodynamics that account for the etiology of antisocial behavior. Each of these perspectives has made a significant contribution to our understanding of crime which is limited only by the theoretical and methodological boundaries of the respective disciplines. However, in this paper, I will focus only on the psychoanalytic explanations of crime, which are rooted in a theory of human behavior initially adumbrated by Sigmund Freud during the early twentieth century.[2]

All psychoanalytic studies of crime are characterized by two trends which reflect the historical development of psychoanalytic theory. The first, initiated by Freud in an essay written in 1916 entitled "Criminals from a Sense of Guilt," emphasizes the motivational priority of instinctual expression and unconscious psychosexual conflict. The second trend, following the later discoveries of the psychoanalytic ego psychologists, minimizes the role of instincts and highlights selected adaptational and environmental factors which impel one toward criminal behavior.

INSTINCT THEORY OF CRIMINAL BEHAVIOR

Freud's theory of psychosexual development is the cornerstone of psychoanalytic theory and psycho-

1. Richard Hofstadter, "Reflections on Violence in the United States," in *American Violence: A Documentary History*, ed. Hofstadter and Michael Wallace (New York: Alfred A. Knopf, 1970), p. 7.

2. See Staff Reports, "Violence in America: Historical and Comparative Perspectives" and "Crimes of Violence," *Staff Report to the National Commission on the Causes and Prevention of Violence*, 13 vols. (Washington, D.C.: Government Printing Office, 1969), vols. 1, 2, 11–13; Daniel Bell, "Crime as an American Way of Life: A Queer Ladder of Social Mobility," *The End of Ideology* (Glencoe: The Free Press, 1960), pp. 115–36; Sheldon and Eleanor Glueck, *Toward a Typology of Juvenile Offenders: Implications for Therapy and Prevention* (New York: Grune & Stratton, 1970); Richard A. Falk, Gabriel Kolko, and Robert Jay Lifton, eds., *Crimes of War: A Legal, Political-Documentary, and Psychological Inquiry into the Responsibility of Leaders, Citizens, and Soldiers for Criminal Acts of War* (New York: Random House, 1971).

analytic studies of criminal behavior. It posits that a child progresses through three distinct, yet overlapping, stages of sexual development which culminate in an oedipal conflict between the child and his parents. During the developmentally crucial crisis, the child unconsciously desires to eliminate the parent of the same sex and to have intimate erotic relations with the parent of the opposite sex. In most children, fantasy is accompanied by a great deal of anxiety and guilt feeling but is sufficiently repressed and controlled as not to eventuate either murder or incest. However, Freud and his early followers found that criminals are not able to master their oedipal conflict, and consequently they suffer from an acute, albeit unconscious, sense of guilt that seeks alleviation through punishment. Freud wrote in 1916 that some adults steal and murder principally because of a sense of guilt which has lingered in their unconscious since childhood. Economic gain, revenge, and passions of the moment might be the superficial reasons given for a person's criminal behavior, but Freud held that guilt feeling over an imagined oedipal sin accounts for the antisocial behavior. The guilt feeling, he wrote, "derived from the Oedipus complex and was a reaction to the two great criminal intentions of killing the father and having sex with the mother."[3]

Two representative psychoanalysts who worked within the tradition begun by Freud were August Aichhorn, director of the Austrian Institute for Delinquents, and Edward Glover, founder of the London Institute of Criminology. They were trained in psychoanalysis by Freud and Karl Abraham, respectively. Following an analysis of a number of youth who had committed a variety of antisocial acts, Aichhorn concluded in his classic study of juvenile delinquency, *Wayward Youth* (first published in 1925), that their delinquencies were "the result of an interplay of psychic forces."[4] While a small fraction of the criminal behavior was due to the adolescents' inadequate upbringing or economic hardships, Aichhorn's investigations led him to reiterate Freud's conviction that "dissocial behavior essentially arose out of unconscious guilt feelings or the need for punishment."[5]

Edward Glover's essays span a period from 1922 to the late 1950s and reflect the instinctual vantage point of psychoanalysis initially outlined by Freud. Like Aichhorn and Freud, Glover emphasizes the etiological priority of intrapsychic conflicts and minimizes the existential context of behavior. He felt that crime resulted from "a conflict between the primitive instincts with

3. Sigmund Freud, "Criminals from a Sense of Guilt," in *The Standard Edition of the Complete Psychological Works of Sigmund Freud*, 24 vols. (London: The Hogarth Press, 1953–74), vol. 14, pp. 332–33. See also "The Ego and the Id," *Standard Edition*, vol. 19, p. 52; "Dostoevsky and Parricide," *Standard Edition*, vol. 21, pp. 186–87. The *Standard Edition* is very skillfully edited and contains many explanatory annotations by the editors. The standard textbook of psychoanalysis is Otto

Fenichel, *The Psychoanalytic Theory of Neurosis* (New York: W. W. Norton, 1945). The basic assumptions of psychoanalytic theory are explained in David Rapaport, *The Structure of Psychoanalytic Theory: A Systematizing Attempt* (New York: International Universities Press, 1960).

4. August Aichhorn, *Wayward Youth* (New York: The Viking Press, 1963), pp. 3, 38, 70.

5. Ibid., p. 231. Several useful elaborations of Aichhorn's work are contained in *Searchlights on Delinquency: New Psychoanalytic Studies*, ed. Kurt R. Eissler (New York: International Universities Press, 1949).

which man is endowed and the altruistic codes inculcated by adult society."[6] The model of socialization implied in Glover's theory is the family, which not only embodies the social prohibitions against aggression and incest handed down from one generation to the next, but also provides the child with a set of acceptable values to emulate. A person's character, as well as his overtly criminal proclivities, is determined by the vicissitudes of his resolution of the oedipal conflict. Faulty resolution leads to a life of crime or neurosis.[7]

According to this view (which still prevails in some psychoanalytic circles) people do not commit crimes because of an overly permissive conscience but because of a rigid and severe one which had inculcated a strong sense of unconscious guilt over imagined/fantasized oedipal crimes. They commit crime in order to be punished for an offense that seems less offensive than their fantasized oedipal transgression. Thus, in the early psychoanalytic literature, crime was conceptualized as an atonement ritual.

The most extreme proponent of this viewpoint was the American psychoanalyst, Edmund Bergler. He wrote in the mid-1940s that "only the unconscious anticipation and acceptance of punishment makes crime possible for the criminal, since

it appeases his inner conscience." Furthermore, "the social factors in crime play a relatively subordinate motivational role" to the vicissitudes of the criminal's intrapsychic conflicts.[8]

These early psychoanalytic studies of crime highlight the irrational, infantile, and unconscious dynamics of crime. Yet the explanatory emphasis attributed to these factors is not confined to the early literature; it represents an enduring and unique, though problematic, trend within psychoanalysis, and, as such, it can be found in many of the contemporary studies of criminal behavior.[9] Adelaide M. Johnson and Stanislaus Szurek, who studied the

6. Edward Glover, *Roots of Crime* (New York: International Universities Press, 1960), p. 7.

7. Ibid., pp. 102, 133, 285–86, 297–303. See, also, Melanie Klein, "Criminal Tendencies in Normal Children," and "On Criminality," in *Contributions to Psychoanalysis* (London: The Hogarth Press, 1948), pp. 185–201, 278–81; Anna Freud, "Certain Types and Stages of Social Maladjustment" in *Searchlights on Delinquency*, ed. Eissler, pp. 193–204.

8. Edmund Bergler, "Psychopathology of Imposters," in *Selected Papers of Edmund Bergler, M.D.: 1933–1961* (New York: Grune & Stratton, 1969), pp. 731–32; Bergler, " 'Crime and Punishment,' " *Selected Papers*, pp. 755–56, 768. See, also, Bergler, "Malignant Masochism," *Selected Papers*, p. 822; Theodor Reik, *The Compulsion to Confess: On the Psychoanalysis of Crime and Punishment* (New York: Farrar, Straus and Cudahy, 1945, 1957, 1959).

9. See Kate Friedlander, "Formation of the Antisocial Character," *The Psychoanalytic Study of the Child* 1 (1945), pp. 189–203; Friedlander, *The Psychoanalytic Approach to Juvenile Delinquency* (London: Routledge and Kegan Paul, 1947); Walter Bromberg, "Psychopathic Personality Concept Evaluated and Reevaluated," *Archives of General Psychiatry* 17 (December 1967), pp. 641–45. See, also, issues of the *Archives of Criminal Psychodynamics* (1955–1962); Robert M. Lindner, *Rebel without a Cause: The Psychoanalysis of a Criminal Psychopath* (New York: Grune & Stratton, 1944). A psychiatric profile of Jack Ruby, which is marred by excessive use of jargon, is contained in Walter Bromberg, *Crime and the Mind: A Psychiatric Analysis of Crime and Punishment* (New York: Macmillan Co., 1965), pp. 136–54. Bromberg and Manfred S. Guttmacher conducted the psychiatric examinations of Ruby while Roy Schafer administered the psychological tests. Schafer's court testimony can be found in *Trauma* 6 (December 1964), pp. 17–58.

parents of a number of delinquents as well as the delinquents themselves, found that there was a striking similarity between the parents' regressive and unintegrated impulses and the behavior of their children. Family interactions demonstrated "the subtle manner in which one child in the family of several children might unconsciously be singled out as the scapegoat to act out the parent's poorly integrated and forbidden impulses." The neurotic needs of the parent were vicariously gratified by the child. A mother's unconscious promiscuity might find expression and gratification in her daughter's illicit sexual adventures, while the father's lack of conscience about theft often results in his son's antisocial acts. Johnson and Szurek attributed the etiology of such behavior to the parent's "unconscious permissiveness or inconsistency toward the child in those spheres of behavior."[10] This intriguing insight into a generational pattern of motivation deserves further research and elaboration by psychoanalysts.

In spite of the impressive efforts by psychoanalysts to uncover the heretofore neglected unconscious infantile dynamics underlying some types of criminal behavior, psychoanalytic studies of crime depending upon the instinct theory as an explanatory base have proved to be inadequate for a number of reasons. First, the assumption that behavior, criminal or otherwise, is primarily an overt manifestation of an infantile unconscious conflict is questionable. While unconscious conflicts exert an obvious impact on behavior, behavior is subject to multiple determinants, and it remains an unproven assumption that what is unconscious exerts a more basic motivational influence than conscious or social determinants. Second, the instinct theory's reliance on the etiological primacy of the oedipal conflict has been modified by the recent studies of ego psychologists and the British school of object-relations theory.[11] Third, viewing crime as the symbolic expression of an unconscious conflict minimizes the motivational role of precipitating factors within the environment and reflects a general lack of appreciation of the contextual diversity of motivating influences. And fourth, the focus on the family as the primary agent of socialization for the child has opened instinct theorists to the criticism that they have ignored the rest of the world in their conceptual schemes.[12]

10. See the essays by Adelaide M. Johnson and Stanislaus Szurek in *Searchlights on Delinquency*, pp. 115–27, and 225–45; Johnson and Szurek, "The Genesis of Antisocial Acting Out in Children and Adults," *Psychoanalytic Quarterly* 21 (July 1952), pp. 323–43; Szurek, "Notes on the Genesis of Psychopathic Personality Trends," *Psychiatry* 5 (1942), pp. 1–6.

11. See D. W. Winnicott, "The Antisocial Tendency," *Collected Papers: Through Pediatrics to Psycho-Analysis* (New York: Basic Books, 1958), pp. 306–15; Sydney Smith, "The Adolescent Murderer: A Psychodynamic Interpretation," *Archives of General Psychiatry* 13 (October 1965), pp. 310–19; Joseph Satten et al., "Murder without Apparent Motive: A Study in Personality Disorganization," *American Journal of Psychiatry* 117 (July 1960), pp. 48–53.

12. The methodological problems enumerated above are not unique to the early psychoanalytic studies of crime. They are inherent in the instinct theory and characterize all facets of applied psychoanalysis prior to the introduction of ego psychology. See, for example, Fred Weinstein and Gerald Platt, *Psychoanalytic Sociology: An Essay on the Interpretation of Historical Data and the Phenomena of Collective Behavior* (Baltimore: The Johns Hopkins University Press, 1973); Weinstein and Platt, "The Coming

SOCIOLOGICAL AND HISTORICAL INTERPRETATIONS

Franz Alexander, a psychoanalyst and author of numerous monographs on crime, accepted the Freudian proposition that most criminal behavior was rooted in unconscious oedipal conflicts.[13] He and his co-authors, however, moved beyond the instinct theory and tried to account for the variety of motivational factors observed in their analyses of psychopaths by introducing an explicitly sociological and historical context to the study of criminal behavior. While Alexander and his co-workers described specific character deficiencies among some criminals that accounted for their antisocial behavior, they also observed that a number of criminals appeared to be neither neurotic or psychopathic but merely victims of an existential dilemma which forced them to identify with other criminals in a criminal subculture.[14]

After migrating to the United States in 1930, Alexander found, through many of his clinical observations, that the frontier ideology of individualism—the ethos of success and private gain—which contrasted with the prevailing social condition of a "highly organized and standardized industrial civilization," placed a peculiar stress on the psychological development of American criminals. Many of them, he felt, responded to this stress by rejecting the social ethic of conformity and embracing, instead, a life of pathological "individualism and adventure" in crime.[15]

The theory and substance of Alexander's numerous studies of criminal behavior represent a move away from the instinctual bias of earlier psychoanalytic literature. He discarded two of the instinct theory's assumptions about culture that limited its explanatory usefulness. Alexander held that culture can not be conceptualized merely as either a magnified individual or a force that exerts a constant and common impact on all the people exposed to it. Instead, culture reflects a multiplicity of phenomena that need to be studied in their own right to determine how they influence the exceedingly complex etiology of crime.[16] Two factors that, in retrospect, seem to have pushed Alexander's work in the direction of an integrated analysis of the unconscious and symbolic with the social existential were: (1) developments within the history of psychoanalytic theory, which increasingly emphasized the importance of external reality and the ego as determinants

Crisis in Psychohistory," *Journal of Modern History* 47 (June 1975), pp. 202–28; John J. Fitzpatrick, "Erik Erikson and Psychohistory: A Critical Assessment," forthcoming.

13. Franz Alexander and Hugo Staub, *The Criminal, the Judge, and the Public: A Psychological Analysis* (Glencoe: The Free Press, 1956), pp. 30, 93–108, 139–49.

14. Ibid., p. 45 passim. See, also, Franz Alexander and William Healy, *Roots of Crime: Psychoanalytic Studies* (New York: Alfred A. Knopf, 1935); and Alexander, *The Scope of Psychoanalysis, 1921–1961: Selected Papers of Franz Alexander* (New York: Basic Books, 1961).

15. Franz Alexander, *Our Age of Unreason: A Study of the Irrational Forces in Our Social Life* (Philadelphia: J. B. Lippincott Co., 1942), pp. 301–07.

16. Franz Alexander, "Psychoanalysis and Social Disorganization," "Psychoanalysis Revised," "Educative Influence of Personality Factors in the Environment," in *Scope of Psychoanalysis*, pp. 384–411, 137–64, 424–39. See, also, Martin Grotjahn, "Franz Alexander, 1891–1964; The Western Mind in Transition," in *Psychoanalytic Pioneers*, ed. Alexander et al. (New York: Basic Books, 1966), pp. 384–98.

of behavior, and (2) his own psycho-social point of view.[17]

Alexander's insight that a culture's ideology, in addition to accidental social factors and intrapsychic conflicts, needs to be accounted for to arrive at the etiology of criminal behavior has been extended by Erik Erikson. Moreover, the studies of delinquency conducted by Erikson share Alexander's working assumption that the unique circumstances of American history and social structure have encouraged some people to pursue a criminal career. American society has invited a succession of interactions between the developing child and his culture which not only provide for his individual development but also adapt him to the culture, or segment of culture, that he will work, love, and play in for the remainder of his life. The developmentally crucial stage of the individual's life cycle is adolescence, and it is here that Erikson has located the tension that often results in criminal behavior.

Adolescence is the crucial period when youth in America are confronted with vocational choices, ideological commitments, and various other identity issues. It also is the period when society allows youth to experiment with a limited series of identities so they may eventually commit themselves to one that will provide an organizing core for the remainder of their lives. The existential choices involved in this process, however, overwhelm the potential criminal. Delinquency for him, thus, becomes one means of resolving this tension. His delinquent choice, in turn, is reinforced, confirmed, and consolidated by the attitude of society toward his anti-social behavior.[18]

CONCLUSIONS

Although the work of Freud, Aichhorn, Glover, Alexander, and Erikson does not exhaust the copious, albeit fragmentary and unsystematic, psychoanalytic research analyzing the motives for criminal behavior, their work does summarize the salient themes and points of view which have evolved in the literature since Freud's initial essay in 1916.[19] Their explanations of motivation have followed the pre-

17. See, for example, Anna Freud, *The Ego and the Mechanisms of Defense* (New York: International Universities Press, 1966); Heinz Hartmann, *Ego Psychology and the Problem of Adaptation* (New York: International Universities Press, 1958); Heinz Hartmann, Ernst Kris, and Rudolph M. Loewenstein, "Some Psychoanalytic Comments on 'Culture and Personality,'" in *Psychoanalysis and Culture: Essays in Honor of Geza Roheim*, ed. George B. Wilbur et al. (New York: International Universities Press, 1951), pp. 3–31; and Roy Schafer, "An Overview of Heinz Hartmann's Contributions to Psycho-Analysis," *International Journal of Psycho-Analysis* 51 (1970), pp. 425–46.

18. Erik Erikson, "Ego Identity and the Psychosocial Moratorium," in *New Perspectives for Research on Juvenile Delinquency*, ed. Helen Witmer and Ruth Kotinsky (Washington: Government Printing Office, 1955), and Erik H. Erikson and Kai T. Erikson, "The Confirmation of the Delinquent," *Chicago Review* 10 (Winter 1957), pp. 15–23. See, also, Ruth Eissler, "Scapegoats of Society," in *Searchlights on Delinquency*, pp. 288–305; Lauretta Bender, "The Genesis of Hostility in Children," *American Journal of Psychiatry* 105 (October 1948), pp. 241–45.

19. The connection some psychoanalysts have hypothesized between the death instinct and criminal behavior has not been discussed in this paper because it plays an insignificant role in the literature. For an elaboration of this point of view, however, see Bruno Bettelheim, "Violence: A Neglected Mode of Behavior," *The Annals* 364 (March 1966), pp. 50–59; Karl A. Menninger, *Man against Himself* (New York: Harcourt Brace Jovanovitz, Inc., 1938); and Menninger, *The Crime of Punishment* (New York: The Viking Press, 1968).

vailing theoretical orientation of psychoanalysis, first by highlighting the intrapsychic substrate of behavior and then by emphasizing the etiologically significant issues raised by ego psychologists: the adaptive functions of the ego, character development, and the role of the environment.

While the seemingly endless variety of criminal activity cannot be understood solely from any methodological perspective, psychoanalytic studies of motivation continue to provide us with a unique opportunity for coming to grips with the dynamics of individual behavior, which have been neglected by social scientists preoccupied with patterns, trends, and statistical norms of criminality. In order to fully utilize this potential, however, future psychoanalytic studies of criminal behavior must augment the existing scholarship by developing a research model that conceptually integrates individual dynamics and character development with the social and phenomenological context of human activity.

Annals, AAPSS, **423**, Jan. 1976

Mafia: The Prototypical Alien Conspiracy

By Dwight C. Smith, Jr.

ABSTRACT: The attractiveness of alien conspiracy theories in American public opinion stretches back to the early days of the Republic. "Mafia" has been the name of one such theory. When placed in context with other conspiracy theories, such as the Bavarian Illuminati scare of 1798–1799 and the Red Scare of 1919–1920, the reasons for emergence of a "Mafia" theory in 1890–91, and again in 1946–1963, become clear. Contemporary public opinion regarding crime is heavily influenced by the post-World War II resurgence of "Mafia" claims, though the evidence behind them is questionable. The role of "Mafia" as a force in public policy is clear, however, and events of the last decade suggest that the consequent shifts in legal strategies, and an increasing sense of injustice generally, have been greater threats to American society than the presumed alien conspiracy behind the anti-Mafia policies.

Dwight C. Smith, Jr., is Director of Institutional Research at the State University of New York at Albany. Educated at Yale and Syracuse Universities, he is the author of The Mafia Mystique. Before joining the Albany staff in 1967, he was Assistant Deputy Director for Systems Planning and Research of the New York State Identification and Intelligence System.

AMERICANS have always been sensitive to threats from rival national interests. The historic roots of this cultural trait have been evident since the early days of the Republic, as a newly-won independence had to be maintained against political pressures from the mother country and from her European rivals. In a world arena dominated by the politics of nationalism, few of us seriously question the authenticity or the propriety of that concern.

Lurking behind this concern, however, is a parallel cultural thread with potentially greater significance to American public policy: a recurring apprehension that somewhere "out there" is an organized, secret, alien group that is poised to infiltrate our society and to undermine our fundamental democratic beliefs. "It" is more foreboding than the known national rival, because conspiracies can set to work in our midst without a public declaration of intent or an overtly hostile act; even before we know it, "they" can be overrunning our internal defenses and overwhelming any instinct to resist. The precise nature and composition of the conspiracy varies with the times; its structure is generally vague and indistinct; but to those convinced by its signs, there is no room for argument as to its existence and no escape from the ominous future that it portends. It may be a reflection of a human fear of the foreign devil, some enduring examples of which (notably the Elders of Zion) have gained international appeal; but for the United States, the concept of conspiracy has occupied an important and sometimes respected position in our value structure.

HOW DOES AN ALIEN CONSPIRACY THEORY DEVELOP?

There is a broad, though shallow, thread of willingness to believe in the alien conspiracy in public opinion. At the fringes are anxious persons of varying political persuasions, whose apprehensions approach paranoia as they detect their favorite conspiracies behind every public event. But even in the middle, "sensible" ground, it remains painfully obvious that Americans are susceptible to the lures of conspiracy advocates when their accusations touch the right cultural anxieties. In four instances since 1798, charges of a secret alien conspiracy[1] have captured sufficient attention to affect public opinion and public policy well beyond the scope of events triggering the original cry. In sequence, the villains have been the Bavarian Illuminati, whose threat became evident during the presidency of John Adams; the original "Mafia," which burst on the American scene in 1890; the Bolsheviks of the Red Scare that followed World War I; and the revived and partially domesticated "Mafia" of the mid-1960s.

In each case, three conditions have been present. First, there was a feeling of unease over the prospect that forces beyond our borders do, or might, exercise undue influence over the scope and direction of domestic social change—an unease sufficiently widespread to support a new look at persons and events at the edge of what Kai Erikson has called "the community's traditional boundary network."[2] Second,

1. I distinguish the bona fide alien conspiracy from the domestic variety, which tends to be more common but less foreboding in the long run.
2. Kai T. Erikson, *Wayward Puritans* (New York: John Wiley & Sons, 1966), p. 69.

a moral entrepreneur, in Howard Becker's words,[3] has to take the stage to focus public attention on the conditions, or values, of American life that are at stake. Third, it must be possible to construct a set of facts, or assumptions of fact, that can be used by the entrepreneur as evidence supporting a conspiratorial explanation of potential changes for the worse.

The Illuminati were a threat to religious values. They are long since forgotten, perhaps because we no longer consider religion to be as important as did the New England clergy of the late eighteenth century. The Bolsheviks were a threat to political values; and they still haunt us, though faith in a Communist conspiracy has become almost respectable since the days of the Red Scare, a recognized arm of Soviet foreign policy rather than just a shadowy plot. "Mafia," in contrast, was a criminal threat, which perseveres in contemporary public opinion as a prototypical alien conspiracy, still up to its evil ways. A complex set of conditions led to its original discovery, to its reappearance 50 years later, and to its continuing influence today in American public opinion. By reviewing first the Illuminati and the Red Scare episodes, we may gain a perspective from which the reasons for the perseverence of "Mafia" in public opinion will be clearer.

A THEOLOGICAL CONSPIRACY: THE
BAVARIAN ILLUMINATI,
1798–1799

The spectre of the Bavarian Illuminati was first raised in this

3. Howard S. Becker, *Outsiders* (New York: The Free Press, 1963), p. 147ff.

country in 1798 by the Reverend Jedediah Morse of Charlestown, Massachusetts, who, with many of his fellow New England clergy, found rapidly shifting social and political conditions threatening to an established sense of order. Political cleavages that had emerged on a national scale following adoption of the constitution stimulated their apprehension. Concern for resiliency of a new nation was heightened by the swiftness with which new crises followed upon each other; in the brief span of six years, for example, the Republic had to absorb such disparate and critical events as the arrival of Citizen Genet, the brief appearance of the secret Democratic Societies, John Jay's unpopular treaty with England, the XYZ Affair, and the passage of the Alien and Sedition Acts. Lurking behind it all was the anti-establishment, anticlerical French Revolution.

Conservative churchmen were particularly vulnerable to rumors that atheistic forces were arrayed against them. A growing demand for religious tolerance was inexplicable simply as a popular cause; there had to be a driving force behind it, using the issue of religious freedom as a smokescreen for an attack on religion itself. The absence of an identifiable force was simply proof that it was secret; and the necessity of exposing it required a search for its true identity. The French Revolution was the obvious place to look. Not only was it antireligious in its own right, but the supporters of tolerance in this country were also known to be sympathetic to it. Morse's prominence in the Illuminati controversy came about because he was the first to "expose" to Americans a conspiracy that both explained the

French Revolution and could be linked to the cause of tolerance here.

The Order of the Illuminati is so distant from contemporary religious or philosophical thought that a brief account of its history may be helpful here.[4] The order had enjoyed a brief life in Bavaria, from 1776 to 1787. Its original mission was to advance the cause of truth and reason. Their opponents, said the order's founder Adam Weishaupt, were the Jesuits who controlled education through the enforcement of dogmatic instruction that suppressed all liberal ideas. Weishaupt's argument was not antireligious; he wanted to rescue Christianity from "the advocates of supernaturalism and the enemies of reason,"[5] and that led him and the order to frequent early utterances hostile to current Christian dogma. When read apart from Weishaupt's basic intent, and in association with other records of the order, those statements were interpreted as evidence that the order was "devoted to the overthrow of religion and the State, a band of poisoners and forgers, an association of men of disgusting morals and depraved tastes."[6] On the basis of that interpretation, coupled with the reminder that such a cause also challenged political authority, the Elector of Bavaria suppressed the order.

But he could not suppress the memory of the order when the French Revolution erupted a few years later. The order was resurrected then, to explain the Revolution as simply an attack on religion— that is, as if no other economic, social, intellectual, or historic factors had any bearing on it. Somehow, a secret conspiracy had so thoroughly infiltrated French life that on command it could rise up and overthrow an otherwise stable monarchy. That conspiracy was the Illuminati, which had—so the argument went —subjugated the Freemasonry of France to its diabolical conspiracy against both thrones and altars. The explanation suffered at every turn from the lack of evidence, but the legend survived. Jedediah Morse's attention was drawn to it through the writings of an Englishman, John Robison, who charged that

AN ASSOCIATION HAS BEEN FORMED for the express purpose of ROOTING OUT ALL THE RELIGIOUS ESTABLISHMENTS, AND OVERTURNING ALL THE EXISTING GOVERNMENTS OF EUROPE . . . the most active leaders in the French Revolution were members of this Association . . . [it] still exists, still works in secret, and . . . its emissaries are endeavoring to propagate their detestable doctrines . . . [I]t still subsists without being detected, and has spread into all the countries of Europe.[7]

When he came to Robison's unsupported assertion that several lodges of the Illuminati had been established in America prior to 1786, Morse instantly grasped the "truth." He lost little time in passing the word to his congregation. "The astonishing increase in irreligion," Morse preached, gave reason "to

4. A detailed analysis of the Illuminati and its effect on New England is contained in Vernon Stauffer, *New England and the Bavarian Illuminati* (New York: Columbia University Press, 1918).

5. Ibid., p. 160. Weishaupt considered Jesus of Nazareth to be the grand master of the Illuminati (see p. 159).

6. Ibid., p. 182.

7. John Robison, *Proofs of a Conspiracy against All the Religions and Governments of Europe, Carried on in the Secret Meetings of the Free Masons, Illuminati, and Reading Societies* (Edinburgh, Scotland: n.p., 1797), pp. 10, 11, 15. Quoted in Stauffer, *Bavarian Illuminati*, p. 203.

suspect that there is some secret plan in operation, hostile to true liberty and religion. . . ."[8] The Illuminati were at the bottom of it; they were the principal cause of virtually every event that had shaken established governments during the previous two decades. Morse concluded: "In this situation of things, our duty is plain. . . ."[9]

There were no Illuminati in the United States, but once Morse's sermon was printed and widely distributed, the dispute over their presumed existence continued for more than a year. After Morse's charges were espoused by Timothy Dwight in a public address on July 4, 1798, the reality of the Illuminati became an accepted article of faith for the Federalist cause. It was an attractive argument for them because it forced their opponents[10] into the impossible position, given the absence of facts in the case, of having to prove a negative condition. Once it became known, however, that Robison's European "proofs" had been discredited, and that Morse knew that to be the case even while continuing to press the existence of the Illuminati in this country, calmer heads prevailed and the controversy faded from view. But the damage had been done. Morse had demonstrated that American public opinion could be swayed by theories framed by the necessities of a desired conclusion—that working backward from a particularized anxiety, one could create the evidence to justify public fear by embroidering the past with a conspiratorial cause. The specific presumptions about the Illuminati dropped from sight, as the New England clergy turned to other matters of faith and morals; but Morse's methodology survived for the benefit of future supporters of conspiracy theories.

A POLITICAL CONSPIRACY: THE RED SCARE, 1919–1920

The Red Scare of 1919–1920 emerged at another anxious time for Americans. The struggle to organize labor was stretching social structures: the wartime legacies of inflation and unemployment added to domestic uncertainty. The debate over immigration, buttressed by wartime appeals for national solidarity, had reappeared in the context of a xenophobic, near-fanatical 100 percent Americanism. Just over the horizon lay bolshevism, whose influence could be detected, by observers prone to conspiracy theories, wherever the accustomed order was under attack.

The unexpected event that triggered the Red Scare was the news that 36 bombs had been mailed from New York City, timed to arrive on May Day at the homes of prominent American business and political leaders.[11] Only one reached its

8. Jedediah Morse, *A Sermon, Delivered at the New North Church in Boston, in the morning, and in the afternoon at Charlestown, May 9th, 1798, being the day recommended by John Adams, President of the United States of America, for solemn humiliation, fasting and prayer* (Charlestown: n.p., 1798), p. 19. Quoted in Stauffer, *Bavarian Illuminati*, p. 232.

9. Ibid., p. 25. Quoted in Stauffer, *Bavarian Illuminati*, p. 237.

10. Jefferson, "the arch apostle of the cause of irreligion and free-thought," and his supporters were the principal targets of the Federalist clergy. See Stauffer, *Bavarian Illuminati*, p. 121.

11. This event, and subsequent federal action under Attorney General Palmer, is described in Stanley Coben, *A. Mitchell Palmer: Politician* (New York: Columbia University Press, 1963), chs. 11, 12, pp. 196–245.

destination, causing minor injury and property damage, but the implications flowing from simply the intent of the act were explosive enough. Police and Justice Department officials immediately described the attempt as an IWW-Bolshevik plot, intended to signal a May Day reign of terror. Public reaction to their charges was swift. Mobs formed in various cities, sometimes assisted by local police, to attack radical meetings and parades. The resulting riots became further proof to the public at large of the strength of the radicals and of their willingness to resort to force, and the public clamor for action by the Justice Department reached a fever pitch.

Attorney General A. Mitchell Palmer became the moral entrepreneur of the day, using the bombing incident as his justification for mobilizing public opinion against a radical, Bolshevik-inspired conspiracy. His cause had more substance than Morse's Illuminati: there were at least five known organizations that might threaten the country;[12] the May Day bomb threats, though not solved, were obvious conspiratorial signs; the Bolshevik cause was an indisputable force on the international scene, widely believed to be fomenting conspiratorial activity; and Palmer was in a position to do more than preach. After coopting the Department of Labor, which had the power to deport alien Anarchists, Palmer acted. In nationally coordinated raids on November 7, 1919, and January 2, 1920, federal agents and local police descended on the meeting places of Anarchists and Communists.

To the public at large, the raids were an immediate success. Thousands of supposedly dangerous alien radicals had been rounded up for deportation. Their roundup gave proof that the conspiracy threat was real, while simultaneously throttling it. But success was short-lived; by midsummer the Red Scare had become wholly discredited.

Two factors contributed to its demise. First, once it became evident that Palmer's agents had been overzealous in their pursuit of radicals, an inevitable backlash set in. There had been an almost casual disregard of arrest and search warrants, a widespread use of violence and harassment, denial of counsel, and protracted detention of innocent persons in abominable facilities.[13] Even the Labor Department, in the person of Acting Secretary Louis F. Post, drew back from Palmer's leadership when the facts emerged. By applying constitutional standards, Post dismissed the great majority of deportation cases brought to him for action. Palmer and his staff were enraged, but in the ensuing controversy (conducted largely in the context of impeachment hearings against Post) prominent members of the legal profession issued a strong condemnation of the Palmer Raids[14] that cut sharply into the attorney general's support.

12. There were three groups with anarchist leanings: the Union of Russian Workers, El Ariete, and L'era Nuovo; and there were the American Communist Party and its factional offshoot, the Communist Labor Party.

13. An example: 39 men arrested in Lynn, Massachusetts, for being in a meeting hall often used by radicals had come together solely for the purpose of forming a cooperative bakery. Coben, *A. Mitchell Palmer*, p. 229.

14. "For more than six months we . . . . have seen with growing apprehension the continued violation of [the] Constitution and breaking of [the law] by the Department of

Second, the Justice Department had confused the quasi-romantic rhetoric of radical pamphleteering with a determination to act, and its cause faltered when widely trumpeted prophecies of future radical violence failed to materialize. Following the original bomb plot of May 1919, the Bureau of Investigation forecast a Day of Terror for July 4; but nothing happened. The following spring, the department tried again, warning of a gigantic conspiracy involving general strikes, assassinations, and bombings on May Day; when nothing happened once again, public opinion turned, and Palmer became the butt of derisive editorial cartoons.

Palmer had been able to mobilize public opinion to a much greater extent than Jedediah Morse. But when his conspiracy turned out to be ephemeral, the Red Scare collapsed. Its demise was so thorough that Congress adjourned for the summer in 1920 without passing a peacetime sedition law that had been widely supported less than six months earlier. Yet Palmer had revalidated a point: alien conspiracies can be sold to an expectant public, even to the extent of temporarily condoning illegal government action.

A CRIMINAL CONSPIRACY: THE ORIGINAL "MAFIA," 1890–1891

"Mafia" became a popular American alien conspiracy theory in 1890, as proof of the apparent criminal bent of the southern European and as a consequent justification for restricting immigration. One event gave rise to the theory: the murder, on October 15, 1890, of the New Orleans Superintendent of Police David Hennessey.[15] "Mafia" entered the case for three reasons. First, Hennessey allegedly told friends who came to his aid after he had been ambushed that "the Sicilians have done for me"; that centered attention on the Sicilian colony of the city. Second, he was known to have taken the side of the Provenzanos against their rivals, the Matrangas, in a dispute over stevedoring rights; the Matrangas thus became the obvious Sicilian suspects in the murder and the eventual defendants in court. Third, the Provenzanos found it convenient, being under suspicion themselves for an earlier ambush of the Matrangas, to allege to reporters that the Matrangas were leaders of a local Mafia group with some 300 adherents.

The charges of "Mafia" had no place in the murder trial that followed; they were strictly a matter of public opinion. They prevailed in the highly charged atmosphere of New Orleans because the allegations came from friends of Hennessey. No one questioned the Provenzanos or sought proof of their charges: allegations sufficed.

From a more objective vantage point, one might question the gullibility of the New Orleans citizenry, but a closer examination would suggest that the city's leaders were not really concerned about either the reality of a Mafia or the necessity of requiring the niceties of legal

---

Justice." National Popular Government League, *To the American People: Report upon the Illegal Practices of the Department of Justice* (Washington, D.C.: Government Printing Office, 1920), p. 3.

15. A detailed description of the event and its aftermath is contained in Dwight C. Smith, Jr., *The Mafia Mystique* (New York: Basic Books, 1975), pp. 27–40.

proof. Rather, they were intent upon exacting revenge for a fallen hero, and for that purpose charges of "Mafia," true or not, were a convenient justification for what would follow. Sicilians had to be punished, one way or another. After all, as a dispatch from New Orleans pointed out two days after Hennessey died, "it is the first time in the criminal history of the city that the Sicilians have attacked any one save those of their nationality."[16] The community was patient at first: "We owe it to our duty as American citizens to try the law first, and to try it thoroughly,"[17] was the counsel of the mayor's Committee of Fifty that investigated the case. But when the Matranga group that stood trial the next spring was acquitted, the true sentiments of the community prevailed. Led by members of the Committee of Fifty, a mob descended on the parish prison the following day and shot or lynched 11 of the Matrangas then in custody, including five who had not been on trial at all.

As far as New Orleans was concerned, the event could have ended there. Vengeance had been obtained. But a lynching of such proportions could not pass unnoticed; besides, three of the mob's victims had been Italian citizens. The affair thus became an international incident. The charges of "Mafia" were even more convenient then, because they served to rationalize, in a crude way, the blatantly illegal lynch mob.[18] Consequently, the New Or-

leans incident survived for the next quarter century as proof that there was a Mafia and as a standard argument ("look what happened in New Orleans") in the fight for greater restrictions on immigration.

An international debate over the reality of Mafia required more than the assertions of the Provenzanos, however well they might have satisfied the citizenry of New Orleans. There was external support for their tale, in the form of evidence that bands of men did exist in southern Italy in defiance of the law, and that "Mafia" was associated with certain aspects of illegal behavior in Sicily. There might be some logic, then, in assuming that illegal activity and "Mafia" had reached the United States with the immigrant flood. But what was that illegal behavior, and what was "Mafia"? The New Orleans case established an image of the Mafia as a gang of cutthroats, held together by fearsome blood oaths and dedicated to crime; was that accurate?

Contemporary scholarship[19] suggests that it was not. Events in Sicily that we have subsequently called Mafia were essentially localized patron-client relationships, held together by an attitude (or "state of mind") rather than formal oaths of allegiance, to which the word "Mafia" was generally applied. It existed in the absence of a strong governmental presence. The mafioso person served to mediate, in a heavily stratified economy, between absent landlords and landless peasants; inevitably, men of a mafioso character obtained influ-

16. *New York Times*, 19 October 1890, p. 1.

17. Ibid., 28 October 1890, p. 1.

18. Ironically so, since the mob was much more assuredly a band of "death-bound assassins," as the New Orleans City Council initially described Hennessey's assailants.

19. See, especially, Anton Blok, *The Mafia of a Sicilian Village, 1860–1960* (New York: Harper & Row, 1975; and Henner Hess, *Mafia and Mafiosi: The Structure of Power* (Farnborough, Eng.: D. C. Heath Ltd., 1973).

ence that extended also into political affairs. The system was dependent upon patronage and upon the ability of a "man of respect" to utilize violence when necessary, to maintain his authority as middleman. To call it "organized" required attributing to its practitioners a self-conscious sense of structure well beyond either the necessities of their circumstances or their sense of being.

The phenomenon of Mafia had emerged in response to cultural conditions, not as an organization independent of its surroundings that could decide to export itself. If traces of similar behavior were to be found in this country, it would be because the American environment provided comparable measures of nonexistent governmental machinery, a stratified society, and the consequent need to establish patron-client linkages. As Francis Ianni has suggested,[20] those cultural imperatives formed the basis of the immigrant colony; thus the village culture that had supported mafioso behavior in Sicily survived with the immigrant tide to support it here. The citizens of New Orleans, and their counterparts in other cities, might well have observed patron-client relationships at work. The critical question for the day was how to interpret what was seen. Instead of recognizing what it really represented—that the American system, by denying adequate legal protection for the immigrant and by allowing exploitation of his labor for the benefit of an established native class, had stimulated the growth of extralegal social mechanisms— American observers took the easy

way out by blaming it all on an alien conspiracy.

The original New Orleans Mafia scare died down after President Benjamin Harrison indemnified Italy on behalf of the three Italian citizens murdered by the lynch mob. But Mafia legends built around the Hennessey case survived. Every new instance of Italian-associated criminal behavior became an occasion for resurrecting the Mafia story and provided even more evidence to support pressures for immigration control. But, unfortunately for the honest-intentioned immigrant, public fear of a Mafia did little to rescue him from conditions in which mafioso behavior was a necessity of life.

"MAFIA" REVIVED, 1946–1963

As the previous accounts have illustrated, there was fertile ground in America for conspiracy scares in 1798, 1890, and 1919. Each occasion had its own reasons for unease over the prospect that an alien force might secretly be undermining our social and political institutions: a sense of irreligion spreading from the French Revolution; the prospect of lawlessness as a characteristic of certain immigrants; and the threat of an impending Bolshevik uprising. Each had its own moral entrepreneurs: Jedediah Morse; the Committee of Fifty; and Attorney General Palmer. Each had its own set of facts with which an entrepreneur could exploit a latent sense of unease against his preferred villains: Robison's *Proofs*; Hennessey's murder; and radical pamphleteering.

The results varied. Religious tolerance was stronger nationally than the orthodoxy of New England in 1798: Morse was discredited, and

20. Francis A. J. Ianni, *A Family Business* (New York: Russell Sage Foundation, 1972), pp. 43–54.

the Illuminati were forgotten. Justice was more important than empty warnings in 1919: Palmer was also discredited, though both public opinion and formal government policy eventually concluded that his Red Scare was in reality a strategic weapon of our principal foreign rival, the Soviet Union—at which point it ceased to be an alien conspiracy in its own right. The original Mafia scare, on the other hand, had considerably more staying power as a conspiracy theory. Immigrants continued to pour into the country, and charges of excessive criminal tendencies among some of them continued as well. Mafia remained the latent explanation, to be resurrected as in the Petrosino murder case of 1909,[21] whenever an unsolved crime could be linked to Italians.

The second "Mafia" scare was different. It had its own moral entrepreneurs, the Federal Bureau of Narcotics. But national unease, in the years following World War II, was directed at the political implications of international communism rather than at criminals; and there was no clear set of facts yet to substantiate an appeal to widespread anxieties over a criminal conspiracy. The "Mafia" of the immigration years had been virtually dormant[22] when narcotics agents at-

tempted to revive it in 1946. There was a certain residual sense of foreboding attached to it still, but public opinion simply was not responsive. For seventeen years the bureau labored to produce a receptive mood toward a criminal threat and a convincing set of facts that would reestablish "Mafia" in the public eye. Each time their charges appeared, there was a brief flurry of public interest, as the press dusted off and reprinted old stories for a new generation; but though interest may have seemed intense each time, it rapidly waned and "Mafia" would fade again from view. This was true of the charges by the bureau in 1946 that Frank Costello was the kingpin of Harlem's Mafia;[23] of the Kefauver Committee's narcotics-inspired claim in 1951 of "a sinister criminal organization known as the Mafia";[24] of the efforts by narcotics agents to link Vincent Squillante with the Mafia during the McClellan committee's 1957 investigation of labor racketeering in Long Island's garbage-collection industry;[25] and even of stories associated with the so-called Apalachin Conclave of November 1957 and the subsequent state and federal investigations that it inspired.[26] It was not until the testimony of Joseph Valachi in the fall of 1963 that the concept of a real alien conspiracy called Mafia took hold permanently.[27] Other law enforcement agencies then took over the Narcotics Bureau's cause. Their efforts culminated in 1967, when the President's

21. See Smith, *The Mafia Mystique*, pp. 45–54.

22. Between 1918 and 1943 there were only four domestic incidents (aside from a few dispatches from Sicily describing Mussolini's anti-Mafia campaign) in which the *New York Times* saw fit to identify "Mafia" with the facts of the case. They occurred in 1921, 1925, 1926, and 1928, and each reference was incidental to the story. None of them had anything to do with the "proof" of Mafia, or Cosa Nostra, that Joseph Valachi produced in 1963. See ibid., pp. 62–65. In 1944 Vito Genovese was identified upon his arrest in Rome as a person associated with

the Mafia, but his notoriety in that case rapidly faded from view. Ibid., pp. 121–123.

23. Ibid., pp. 123–127.

24. Ibid., pp. 131–151.

25. Ibid., pp. 156–162.

26. Ibid., pp. 162–216.

27. Ibid., pp. 217–242.

Crime Commission officially blessed the concept of a Mafia conspiracy.[28]

The motives of the Narcotics Bureau have been variously ascribed to the need for a cause to compete with the FBI's Communist menace or to the inevitable circumstance of being directed toward the one area of crime that required a high degree of cooperation and international connections. But a closer examination of the bureau's history suggests that its main challenge in the period under question was to explain failure. The notion of total suppression of illegal narcotics use through importation control was a self-proclaimed mission, and it had not been attained. How better to explain failure (and, incidentally, to prepare the ground for increased future budgets) than to argue that, dedicated though it might be, the bureau was hard pressed to overcome an alien, organized, conspiratorial force which, with evil intent and conspiratorial methods, had forced its ways on an innocent public?[29]

Obviously, the bureau's strategy was neither that cynical nor that clear; this description is simply a retrospective summary of a position that emerged through a series of tactical skirmishes with the entrepreneurs who found the profits in narcotics to be worth the risk. The bureau's efforts ultimately succeeded, and we can point to two conditions that made it possible. First, the bureau's early charges laid the groundwork for a set of expectations regarding what organized crime "ought" to look like that would be receptive, finally, to the proper evocations of proof. Second, the bureau found in Joseph Valachi a sufficiently plausible witness to lend substance to its conspiracy charges. Viewed in a more neutral light, Valachi appears to be substantially less knowledgeable and informative than his captors alleged; his principal strength, however, lay not in what he said but in his role as an insider, repenting, in effect, through his "confession." For the supporters of the Narcotics Bureau, that gesture was more important than the presumed facts that he put forth, since by his admission he justified the bureau's moral entrepreneurship. As Kai Erikson put it in describing the early Puritan approach to criminality and the criminal, "To repent is to agree that the moral standards of the community [the bureau] are right. . . ."[30]

COMMERCIALIZATION OF "MAFIA": 1969

The President's Crime Commission's endorsement of a "Mafia" theory was rapidly and widely adopted elsewhere. The period during which proof might have been required seemed to have passed. Popular commentators and scholars alike now talked and wrote of an American Mafia as an established fact. Two years later, however, the moral entrepreneurs of law enforcement were outflanked by a new

28. "Today the core of organized crime in the United States consists of 24 groups operating as criminal cartels in large cities across the nation. Their membership is exclusively men of Italian descent. . . ." President's Commission on Law Enforcement and Administration of Justice, *Task Force Report: Organized Crime* (Washington, D.C.: Government Printing Office, 1967), p. 6. See also Smith, *The Mafia Mystique*, pp. 248–251.

29. Smith, *The Mafia Mystique*, pp. 184–188.

30. Erikson, *Wayward Puritans*, p. 195.

breed of "Mafia" pushers, the commercial entrepreneurs. Inspired by the success of Mario Puzo's *The Godfather*,[31] virtually everyone out to make money—especially those in the publishing and entertainment industries—jumped on the bandwagon. "Mafia" became a household word; its images remain public property, no longer under the control of the law-enforcement community.[32]

In these circumstances, it is no longer possible to say with certainty that there is or is not an organization called Mafia. Accepted conclusions of labeling theory argue strongly that after a quarter century of having been labeled as mafiosi, a sense of group identification and acceptance of the label would have occurred to a number of Italian-Americans even if there had been no basis for it previously.[33] The characteristics of illicit marketplaces argue strongly that an entrepreneur labeled as a mafioso would have little incentive to deny it (except in certain law-enforcement circumstances), given the increased status and power that expectations associated with the label would carry.[34] One could argue, then, that if there was a Mafia today, it would owe its existence to the efforts of

the Federal Narcotics Bureau and their legal and commercial disciples. If that was the case, however, the resulting organization would have no direct historic links either to social organisms of nineteenth-century Sicily or to its immigrant colony counterparts in this country; the assertions of a foreign creation or alien ideology would be without foundation.

On the other hand, it is always possible, though improbable, that an organization called Mafia predates the Narcotics Bureau's postwar crusade. Whether its roots ran back to Sicilian soil or were simply based in the social circumstances of the United States might be the subject for an interesting debate for the social historian to pursue, but the more important questions lie elsewhere: do the imagery and concepts associated with "Mafia" direct us toward the critical characteristics of a specified group of persons, or do they really serve to divert us from analyses that may have much greater significance for the American scene?

IS A CONSPIRACY CHARGE MORE THREATENING THAN THE CONSPIRACY? THE "MAFIA" EXPERIENCE

The charges of "Mafia" in the fifties and sixties had not been exclusively figments of the imagination. There were individuals and events continuously coming to the attention of law-enforcement personnel during that time who were collected into a category called "organized crime." However they might be interpreted, the persons and events were real. Led by the Narcotics Bureau, most law-enforcement personnel called them evidence of a Mafia. The result, for contemporary theories of crime con-

---

31. Mario Puzo, *The Godfather* (New York: G. P. Putnam's Sons, 1969).
32. See Smith, *The Mafia Mystique*, pp. 292–305.
33. "Mafia" acts, then, as the master trait, in the sense intended by Becker, *Outsiders*, pp. 32–39.
34. Crime reporters from localities in which "Mafia" expectations are particularly strong have provided their share of anecdotal evidence for this argument. An example of the effects of rumored Mafia or Cosa Nostra connections is contained in Norman Miller's account of the enterprising Tony DeAngelis. See Norman C. Miller, *The Great Salad Oil Swindle* (New York: Coward-McCann, Inc., 1965), pp. 26–30.

trol, was to isolate a small group of men of Italian descent and to accuse them, as members of a particular organization, of having perfected organized crime in America. They were the embodiment of the alien conspiracy: a group of men motivated by criminality and a sense of loyalty foreign to an open, democratic society, united by an organization designed for crime that was based on violence and focused on crime and corruption. They were charged with corrupting and intimidating both business and government, as if no other group in America had ever tried to influence a Congressman or bribe a policeman or bypass antitrust laws or reach a greedy hand into the White House.

This interpretation came about by misreading three parts of the evidence. First, law-enforcement observers noted that their group of suspects held a shared sense of identification and were often engaged in cooperative action, and interpreted that behavior as proof of a secret organization. From another perspective, however, one might ask whether they had any choice. The suspects were, after all, engaged in enterprises in adjoining portions of the marketplace and would have had reasons for collaboration and group identification similar to those in the conditions governing activities of lawyers or insurance salesmen in other parts of the market spectrum. Besides, being branded by the moral entrepreneurs as "outsiders," they had few social openings except among themselves. Second, observers were prone to see evidence of violence, which clearly marked the suspects as alien to the social order, but were slow to acknowledge evidence of corruption that might just as easily have marked them as being within the mainstream of

lightly regulated business affairs. Third, observers forgot that they had begun by assembling evidence of Italian wrongdoing; when the evidence was later analyzed, its exclusively Italian coloration became proof that only Italians engaged in organized crime.

The result was a misinterpretation of a much wider range of activities that are inherently American, not alien, and fundamentally linked to a free-market economy. These activities might be better known as *illicit enterprises*.[35] Rather than being the outgrowth of some alien, violent, criminal organization, they are businesses supported informally by networks of mutual obligations—some of which can be reinforced by bonds of kinship—that are based as much on corruption as on violence and are focused on providing patron-client type favors and enforcement (or security) services.

A misreading of the evidence by the law-enforcement community led to a group of strategies that do not effectively address the problems of illicit enterprise. They focus on legal action that might put some entrepreneurs, Italians or otherwise, behind bars but would do little to change the structures of their marketplaces. More importantly, however, though ostensibly aimed at destroying organized crime, those strategies have themselves been more threatening to this country than the illicit behavior they were supposed to control. They have been threatening on two counts. First, they have affected law enforcement beyond the confines of organized crime control; second, they have had a significant impact

35. For a more complete description of "illicit enterprise," see Smith, *The Mafia Mystique*, pp. 335–345.

on the corruption of justice in the United States.

The strategies in question are those of the 1968 Omnibus Crime Control and Safe Streets Act and the 1970 Organized Crime Control Act. They were justified as weapons in a courtroom campaign against a conspiratorial foe; they included wiretapping and eavesdropping, investigative grand juries, wider witness-immunity provisions, stronger perjury laws, and extended sentences in organized crime cases. They were supported by a finding that organized crime was such a threat to this country that to control it we would be justified in modifying the existing balance between privacy and order. In the context of existing "Mafia"-oriented assumptions of the nature of organized crime, the argument seemed plausible. But no sooner were new laws on the books than government agencies began finding new conspiracies to fight. The antiwar movement of the late sixties soon became the target, as the men who exercised government control became the ogres stifling political dissent—victims indeed of the paranoia that thrives on, and reinforces, allegiance to a conspiracy theory.[36]

36. For evidence that the Justice Depart-

"Mafia"-induced strategies of crime control also served as a smokescreen for the continued erosion of justice and equity in America. By focusing on violence as a principal characteristic of Mafia organizations, law enforcement agencies have evaded the continuing problem of corruption in the criminal justice system. The "head-hunting" strategy only placed greater premium on the power-brokering skills of the entrepreneur. His success has obvious repercussions. When the shady dealer can stay on the street—Wall Street or Broadway—by co-opting political leaders and law-enforcement personnel, he spreads a message that "equal justice" is not a cherished value but a hollow phrase. It is this fact of life, not the illegal nature of certain services, that still represents the greater threat of illicit enterprise; it is a fact of life that an alien conspiracy theory dominated by traditional "Mafia" images is unable to comprehend.

ment still endorses generalized anti-conspiracy strategies, see Jerrold K. Footlick, Jon Lowell, and Anthony Marro, "How to Get Your Man," Newsweek, 1 December 1975, pp. 113–114.

Blacks, Crime, and American Culture

By JOHN A. DAVIS

ABSTRACT: Attempts to understand crime patterns among blacks in the United States have systematically failed to consider the impact of slavery and resultant racist policies on black self-esteem. This paper explores the thesis that cultural domination was fundamentally more damaging than economic domination to black self-esteem. The ruthless attacks on blacks and black culture, usually justified by legal interpretations by whites, destroyed their faith that justice could be secured in this society. Data is presented which indicates that social inequalities have been perpetuated under the law and blacks were aware of this. Indeed, the law appears as a major instrument of racial oppression and, historically, many blacks have resisted oppression through illegal acts. Economic oppression of blacks *under the law* and their resistance created the condition in which the connection between crime and punishment lost the power to constrain antisocial acts. Blacks often secretly admired resistance, particularly those who felt oppressed, while whites developed extreme paranoia that blacks were out to take their lives and property. The euphemism "crime in the streets" is the perpetuation of this paranoia. The records show that blacks mainly victimize blacks. Chances are far greater for a white to be victimized by another white than by a black. The predominant crime pattern among blacks is against property, and the rate is not significantly higher than for whites. In crime against persons, black rates are higher than white rates.

John A. Davis is an Assistant Professor of Sociology at UCLA. He specializes in criminology and deviant behavior. His primary interest is the development of sociological understanding of the role of the black perspective on the actions and attitudes of black people.

THIRTY-ONE years ago, Gunnar Myrdal stated that the Negro problem was not only America's greatest failure but also America's incomparable opportunity for greatness.[1] He entitled his work *An American Dilemma*, and arguments raged as to whether or not a real dilemma existed in the minds and souls of white America. Since the mid-sixties, American blacks have argued that no dilemma exists, because white America has never accepted the black man as an equal human being.

The brutal suppression inflicted upon blacks by whites is the result of a paranoid state directly related to attitudes toward crime and blacks. The feeling is that crime is the embodiment of evil[2] and blacks are therefore more "crime prone" because they are more distant from "good," which is white. This dichotomous thinking is reflected in public attitudes as well as the formulations of criminologists about "causes" of crime.

BLACK CULTURE AND THE AMERICAN EXPERIENCE

The black man is seen as "made in America," his background and tradition buried in the watery graves of the millions who died on the passage over. He has no past worth mentioning, and his presence is seen as the expression of the tolerance of his benefactors. His future depends on his ability to internalize the dominant culture. However, there is a growing school of thought among black scholars that Afro-American

1. Gunnar Myrdal, *An American Dilemma* (New York: Harper & Row, 1944), p. 1021.
2. Karl Menninger, *The Crime of Punishment* (New York: Viking Press, 1968).

culture has important differences from the dominant American culture. The foundation of this argument rests on the assumption that cultural habits are extremely resilient, so many of the African traditional modes remain, especially within the southern black population. Although the formal cultural structure (for example, family, communal living, social stability, and so forth) was destroyed by the institution of slavery, the habits remained, only severed from their roots. Blacks were left with habits and preferences which could not be understood and which were ridiculed by the dominant society. This cultural attack may have had consequences more detrimental to blacks than the personal attacks. The attempt to validate the inherent inferiority of blacks "scientifically" has been constant from the time of U. B. Phillips to the present arguments of Shockley and Jensen.

The systematic attack on blacks affected both blacks' and whites' attitudes, and the primary basis of the attack was cultural. Whites justified their racist practices through cultural attitudes and blacks suffered as a result. The suffering is expressed in various ways by social scientists, but the most direct expression is through the concept of self-hatred. This development was well understood by Fanon when he stated:

Every colonized people—in other words, every people in whose soul an inferiority complex has been created by the death and burial of its local culture originality—finds itself face to face with the language of the civilizing nation; that is, with the *culture* of the mother country. The colonized is elevated above his jungle status in proportion to his adoption of the mother country's cultural standards.[3] (emphasis added)

The point to this is that, although the black man's culture may not have been destroyed, his understanding and appreciation of his culture was severely damaged. Afro-Americans were left in a cultural wasteland with no sense of belonging. Rejected and depreciated by the dominant American society, separated from and resentful of their African background, blacks were surrounded by a sea of cultural and personal confusion. They came to hate themselves. It is amazing that black people even survived the early American experience and a small wonder that blacks have tended to commit crimes against themselves.

LAW AND INEQUALITY

One cannot understand crime without understanding the nature of the social order in which it occurs. Crime in America takes place within a capitalistic system where greater emphasis is placed on property rights than on human rights.[4] The paramount value within the society is profit, and individual value is measured by the ability to amass profits. Those individuals having great wealth form a sort of Interest Group[5] and influence the formation of laws to protect their interests. Only acts that violate laws are criminal, no matter how reprehensible

the act.[6] The great debate which followed Edwin Sutherland's work on white-collar crime is an example of this definitional problem.

Statute law exists to protect the interests of powerful groups in the United States. These materialistic interests derived from profit are secured through exchange. Some men benefit and others are burdened by this exchange, and laws protect the system through which this unequal exchange is perpetuated. Therefore, in the area of property, the order which derives from the enforcement of laws perpetuates material inequality. Human value is attached to materialism, and those who own little or nothing have less value and, to the degree that they adopt the values of the system, lower self-esteem. This fact may be reflected in aggressive impulses resulting from despair, hopelessness, and frustration.

On the other hand, the laws regulating crimes against persons may be more equal in the sense that they cover the interests of practically all groups in society and therefore reflect a lower level of inequality. However, the *dynamic* aspect of law (that is, enforcement) has been shown to reflect differences depending on the interest group of the victim and victimizer. There is also evidence to show that a definite relationship exists between economic exploitation and the potential to aggress against others. Edwin Schur[7] reflects this position when he

3. Franz Fanon, *Black Skin, White Masks* (New York: Grove Press, 1967).
4. Herman and Julia Schwendinger, "Defenders of Order or Guardians of Human Rights?," *Issues in Criminology* 5 (summer 1970).
5. Richard Quinney, *The Social Reality of Crime* (Boston: Little, Brown and Co., 1970), p. 12.

6. Edwin H. Sutherland and Donald Cressey, *Criminology* (Philadelphia: J. B. Lippincott, 1970), p. 12.
7. See Edwin M. Schur, *Law and Society: A Sociological View* (New York: Random House, 1968); and Schur, *Our Criminal Society* (New Jersey: Prentice-Hall, 1969).

suggests that America is a criminal society because it is an unequal society. The oppression necessary to maintain an unequal system, and the inability to affect the imposing value system based on materialism, negatively affects the self-esteem of those burdened by the system.

SELF-ESTEEM AS PROTEST

Self-esteem, including self-respect and feelings of success, is based on a physical and social environment in which the person can find order and security.[8] Much of the literature dealing with self-esteem assumes the importance of compatibility between the person and his environment. But what if a person is oppressed and is aware of the source and nature of his oppression? What if his or her burning desire is to remove the source of that oppression? Self-esteem then becomes functionally related to oppression. A particular form of opposition takes place: self-esteem is expressed in the form of protest, and protest takes on many forms.

Although there are many sources of oppression, the dominant sources in America are economic and racial oppression. The action aspect of law is the mechanism used by the dominant society to keep opposition under control. Racial oppression has economic features. Indeed, the initial impetus to enslave blacks may have been primarily economic. However, the system developed to justify the perpetuation of slavery took on racial qualities independent of economic considerations. These developments had an impact on both blacks' and whites' beliefs and attitudes.

Although there is little hard data on early opposition to racial oppression among black slaves, we can gain some insight through the analysis of early folktales and folk heroes. "High John the Conqueror" is a folktale describing a folk hero who successfully resisted oppression through the use of his wits:

That's the kind of plantation John lives on. But it didn't bother John none. He was a *be* man. Wasn't no disputing that. High John loved living, and, although he was a slave, he made up in his mind that he was gon' do as much living and as little slaving as he could. He used to break the hoes—accidentally, of course. Set ol' mass'a barn of fire. Accidentally, of course. He always had a hard time getting to the field on time, and when he did get there, somehow the mule would accidentally tramp down a whole row of cotton before the boss man knew what was happening. Ol' massa was never sure, though, whether or not John was doing all this on purpose, because John would work real hard some years and make a good crop. The next year, though, it seemed like everything he touched got destroyed.[9]

The theme of opposition to oppression is repeated over and over again in terms of either covert attacks on property owned by slaveholders or flight from the oppressive situation.

Opposition to oppression can also be seen in a number of accounts of slave resistances. The Denmark Vesey conspiracy of 1822[10] took place in Charleston, South Carolina. Slaves were enlisted from a distance of 80 miles, and thousands were in-

8. Abraham H. Maslow, *Motivation and Personality* (New York: Harper & Row, 1970).

9. Julius Lester, *Black Folktales* (New York: Grove Press, 1969), p. 93.

10. Herbert Aptheker, *A Documentary History of the Negro People in the United States* (New York: The Citadel Press, 1951), p. 74.

volved. The 1831 publicized case of Nat Turner[11] also involved thousands of rebellious slaves, and it was an uprising in which approximately 60 whites lost their lives as did approximately 100 blacks. The response of whites was to hang all participating and suspected blacks. Furthermore, night riders were organized to put down any secret meetings among slaves. The night riders had the authority of "policemen," and their expressed purpose was to intimidate and harass slaves.

Other blacks outside the South openly encouraged slaves to rebel. Most notable of these calls was issued by Henry Highland Garnet and David Walker. Garnet was a twenty-seven-year-old Presbyterian minister who, in 1843, stated:

Nearly three million of your fellow-citizens are prohibited by law and public opinion (which in this country is stronger than law) from reading the Book of Life. Your intellect has been destroyed as much as possible and every ray of light they have attempted to shut out of your minds. The oppressors themselves have become involved in the ruin. They have become weak, sensual and rapacious—they have cursed you—they have cursed themselves—they have cursed the earth which they have trod. . . . They endeavor to make you as much like brutes as possible. When they have blinded the eyes of your mind —when they have embittered the sweet waters of life—then and not till then, has American slavery done its perfect work. TO SUCH DEGRADATION IT IS SINFUL IN THE EXTREME FOR YOU TO MAKE VOLUNTARY SUBMISSION.[12]

David Walker was less eloquent and more direct. He was an agent for a black newspaper in Boston, and he issued an appeal to slaves which urged a bloody rebellion if the oppressors did not grant liberty. According to William Katz, the copies of his appeal were found throughout the South and the slaveholders panicked, offering a reward for Walker dead or alive.[13] The occurrence of opposition to the *symbol* of oppression (property) was much more frequent than to persons, yet the few violent attacks on whites kindled a deep fear in their hearts, and they reacted with intense brutality. This set the stage for the public attitude that the "criminal" acts against oppression were basically against persons.

The legal decisions of the Supreme Court and the legislature generally reflected the public opinion, which was anti-slave. However, the fact that the North may have been anti-slavery does not mean it was pro-slave. Opposition to slavery was basically an economic phenomenon supported by powerful manufacturing interests. These interests were pitted against the equally powerful agrarian interest of the South, and the political compromise was a sort of balance-of-power decision reflected in a number of legislative decisions, such as the Missouri Compromise. The judiciary also reflected the guiding sentiment of that time. This culminated in the Dred Scott Decision of 1857, in which Judge Roger Taney declared that the Missouri Compromise was unconstitutional, stating, that "the Negro has no rights which a white man is bound to respect."[14] In the case of *Plessey* v. *Ferguson* (1898), the Supreme Court held that laws which segregate people be-

11. Ibid., p. 119.
12. Ibid., p. 226.

13. William Loren Katz, ed., *The American Negro: His History and Literature* (New York: Arno Press, 1969), p. 165.
14. Ibid., p. 415.

cause of their race did not violate the United States Constitution. This decision solidified the Separate but Equal Doctrine, which held until the Brown Decision in 1954. Even though the ruling had clear implications for desegregation of schools, we find that schools are as segregated today as they were then.

Clearly, blacks in this country could not redress their grievances through law. The law and its enforcement was against the interests and well-being of the black man. Under such oppressive conditions, resistance to law is resistance to oppression. W. E. B. Dubois explored this problem in an early work.[15] He described the Convict Lease System which developed in southern states after the Civil War. This system was a form of cheap labor for plantation owners who could "lease" blacks convicted of crimes. Since there were few jobs for blacks, a large number could easily be arrested as vagabonds. The system produced a large pool of laborers for agrarian interests.

The effect of the system on the black perspective was to link crime and slavery to white suppression. Dubois states that, under the system, punishment lost its deterrent effect and criminals gained pity in the eyes of black men. He feels that this system was the crowning blow to the faith held by blacks in the integrity of the courts and the fairness of juries. Here, again, one can find expressions of this phenomenon in folktales, as seen by the following Paul Lawrence Dunbar tale, "Ole Sis Goose":

Ole Sis Goose was er-sailin' on de lake, and Ole Br'er Fox was hid in de weeds.

By an by Ole Sis Goose swum up close to der bank and Ole Br'er Fox lept out an cotched her.

"O yes, Ole Sis Goose, I'se got yer now, you'se been er' sailin' on der lake er long time, en I'se got yer now. I'se gwine to break yer neck en pick yer bones."

"Hole on der', Br'er Fox, hold on, I'se got jes' as much right to swim in der lake as you has ter lie in der weeds. Hit's des' as much my lake es hit is yours, and we is gwine to take dis matter to der cotehouse and see if you has any right to break my neck and pick my bones."

And so dey went to cote, and when dey got dere, de sheriff, he wus der fox, en de judge, he wus er fox, and der tourneys, dey wus fox, en all de jurymen, dey was foxxes, too.

En dey tried Ole Sis Goose, en dey 'victed her and dey 'scuted her, and dey picked her bones.

Now, my chilluns, listen to me, when all de folks in de cotehouse is foxes, and you is des' er common goose, der ain't gwine to be much jestice for you pore cullud folks.

Historically, the first crime was the crime of the dominant society *against* the black man. He was dehumanized by a totally oppressive system; ruled out of the human family by social theorists, by custom, and by law; excluded from meaningful participation in decisions affecting his life; and socially atomized through assaults on his native culture. The damage inflicted upon blacks by these beastial assaults had, from one point of view, a detrimental effect on their self-esteem, resulting in the citation of various character and behavioral traits among blacks as justification for excluding or criminalizing—the height of racist thinking. But out of this damage also grew a richer self-esteem in direct response to op-

15. W. E. B. Dubois, *Notes on Negro Crime* (Atlanta, Ga.: Atlanta University Press, 1904).

pression: an irrepressible conviction to rise up and recreate the black culture that was.

HISTORICAL PATTERNS OF CRIME AMONG BLACKS

The attempt to determine the rates and changes in patterns of crime bears all of the limitations of statistical analysis presented in the literature.[16] Nevertheless, it is the only national data presently available, and attempts to interpret this data still have utility.

The most startling fact about patterns of crime among blacks is that, basically, the predominant pattern is the persistence of crimes against property over the years. This pattern is very consistent with the class-based pattern among all ethnic groups in the United States. Furthermore, the disproportionate rate of crimes against property is found primarily among males. This is reflected in the statistics presented in table 1 for the year 1880. The data indicate that of those offenses charged, 57 percent were for crimes

16. John I. Kitsuse and Aaron V. Cicourel, "A Note on the Uses of Official Statistics," *Social Problems* 11 (1963), p. 131; Roger Hood and Richard Sparks, *Key Issues in Criminology* (New York: McGraw-Hill, 1970), pp. 25–32.

against property and 24 percent for crimes against persons. Ninety-three percent of the offenses were charged against males.

The same patterns are repeated in subsequent years, as can be seen in tables 2 and 3. From table 2, we can see that in 1965, assuming the nonwhite category is composed basically of blacks, the percentage of victimization among blacks in crimes against property (burglary, larceny, and motor vehicle theft) is 75 percent and in crimes against persons (rape, robbery, aggravated assault), 25 percent.

A similar pattern may be seen in table 3, which presents victimization data for 1973. However, the striking feature of both these tables is the lack of any substantial differences in rates of property crime between blacks and whites. Indeed, if anything, the white rate is somewhat higher than the black rate. Although this may be explained to some extent by the fact that a higher proportion of whites are victimized by blacks for larceny then vice versa (table 4), the difference is not so great as to explain the high white victimization rates. It is more easily explained by the fact that whites possess more property which can be stolen. This observation serves to highlight the "reality" upon

TABLE 1

NUMBER OF OFFENSES CHARGED FOR THE YEAR 1800

	ALL COLORED	COLORED MALE	COLORED FEMALE
All offenses	16,562	15,381	1,181
offenses against government	117	116	1
offenses against society	1,072	809	263
offenses against persons	3,918	3,691	227
offenses against property	9,510	9,027	483
miscellaneous	317	259	56
not stated	1,610	1,476	140

SOURCE: *Ninth Atlanta Conference*, 1904, p. 13.

TABLE 2

VICTIMIZATIONS BY RACE AND TYPE OF CRIME (1965) RATES PER 100,000

OFFENSES	WHITE	NON-WHITE
Total	1,860	2,592
forcible rape	22	82
robbery	58	204
aggravated assault	186	347
burglary	822	1,306
larceny ($50 and over)	608	367
motor vehicle theft	164	286
Number of respondents	27,484	4,902

SOURCE: NORC SURVEY reported in *The Report of the President's Commission on Law Enforcement and the Administration of Justice* (Washington, D.C.: Government Printing Office, 1967), p. 39.

which the social fact of black=criminal has been based. The black rate of violent crime is, however, substantially greater than that for whites; yet it must be emphasized

that it still accounts for a minor portion of black crime. The data is also evidence of the historical preoccupation of whites with property—thus they commit more property crimes. The black has suffered not only substantial property deprivation, but personal and cultural destruction; thus his higher rate of crime against persons. The highly intraracial nature of violent personal crime as evidenced in table 4 is further support for this view.

Another factor which may affect the race differences in rates of crime against persons may be the selective nature of law enforcement. Numerous studies have demonstrated that blacks get differential treatment from police and from the courts.[17] There is some indication

17. William J. Chambliss, "Sociological Analysis of the Law of Vagrancy," *Social*

TABLE 3

NUMBER AND RATE OF PERSONAL VICTIMIZATIONS BY TYPE OF CRIME (1973)

RACE OF VICTIM AND TYPE OF CRIME	VICTIMIZATIONS		
	NUMBER (THOUSANDS)	PERCENT	RATE[1]
Black			
total	2,255	100	132
crimes of violence	801	36	47
rape and attempted rape	29	1	2
robbery and attempted robbery	245	11	14
assault and attempted assault	527	23	31
crimes of theft	1,454	64	85
personal larceny with contact	118	5	7
personal larceny without contact	1,336	59	78
White			
total	18,211	100	127
crimes of violence	4,642	25	32
rape and attempted rape	129	1	1
robbery and attempted robbery	856	5	6
assault and attempted assault	3,657	20	26
crimes of theft	13,569	75	95
personal larceny with contact	31	2	3
personal larceny without contact	13,118	72	92

SOURCE: *Current Population Reports* issued by the U.S., Department of Commerce (Washington, D.C.: U.S., Bureau of Census, 1974), p. 164.

1. The victimization rate, a measure of the occurrence among population groups at risk, was computed on the basis of the number of victimizations per 1,000 population age 12 and over.

TABLE 4

PERCEIVED RACE OF OFFENDER AND THE RELATIONSHIP OF OFFENDER TO VICTIM
BY TYPE OF CRIME

SUBJECT	ALL CRIMES AGAINST PERSONS	CRIMES OF VIOLENCE	RAPE	ROBBERY	ASSAULT	PERSONAL LARCENY WITH CONTACT
Black victims						
perceived race of						
offender by victim						
all offenders						
(thousands)	519	468	26	83	359	51
percent	100	100	100	100	100	100
black	87	88	89	93	87	71
white	8	8	11	0	10	13
relation of						
offender to victim						
all offenders						
(thousands)	519	468	26	83	359	51
percent	100	100	100	100	100	100
stranger	51	47	74	74	39	84
not stranger	49	53	26	26	61	16
White victims						
perceived race of						
offenders by victim						
all offenders						
(thousands)	3,060	2,916	96	358	2,463	144
percent	100	100	100	100	100	100
black	21	20	31	41	16	43
white	74	75	62	52	79	41
relation of						
offender to victim						
all offenders						
(thousands)	3,060	2,916	96	358	2,463	144
percent	100	100	100	100	100	100
stranger	59	57	71	76	54	91
not stranger	41	43	29	24	46	9

SOURCE: U.S., Bureau of Census (Washington, D.C., 1974), p. 165.
NOTE: Includes only crimes committed by single offender.

that the police, because of racist views, see certain criminal acts as "normal" for black communities and are slower to respond to calls. Should this be the case, the crime rate in the black community would reflect police practices as well as other factors.

CONCLUSION

Crime among blacks is a complex *reaction* to oppression. It consists principally of predatory acts against property and it occurs primarily within the black community with blacks as the primary victims. The present-day cry of "crime in the streets" continues a long history of overreaction by members of the

Problems 12 (summer 1964); Irving Pillavin and Scott Briar, "Police Encounter with Juveniles," *American Journal of Sociology* 70 (September 1964); George W. Crockett, "Racism in the Law," *Science and Society* (spring 1969); Edward Green, "Race, Social Status and Criminal Arrest," *American Sociological Review* 35 (June 1970), p. 18.

dominant society to an unreal threat. The social scientists and, in this instance, criminologists, have played a major role in perpetuating this fear through theories and research which define the black community as prototypical of the criminal environment. The criminal justice system, and particularly law enforcement, reify these positions through actions based on discretionary powers. The black community itself reflects the exclusion and oppression it has to live under through the bitterness expressed both internally and externally. The violence within the community is an expression of the bitterness turned inward. Racism is the value system on which the entire problem rests. It certainly has economic roots, but it has taken on a reality of its own.

ANNALS, AAPSS, **423**, Jan. 1976

Progress and Prosecution

By JACK M. KRESS

ABSTRACT: Possessing awesome and almost unlimited discretionary powers, the district attorney is the most important figure in America's modern system of criminal justice administration. These powers stem primarily from the unique fact that the public prosecutor exists in a system which was initially premised on a common law concept of private prosecution. The discretion involved in charging and plea-bargaining decisions exemplifies the power granted a civil law official to administer a common law jurisprudence. The value of a return to private prosecution as a control upon unfettered prosecutorial discretion is explored, as well as the suggestion of increased internal guidelines for the exercise of the prosecution function.

Jack M. Kress is an Assistant Professor at the School of Criminal Justice of the State University of New York at Albany. A graduate of Columbia Law School, Professor Kress has studied criminology at Cambridge University in England and served for four years as Assistant District Attorney to Frank S. Hogan, the late District Attorney of New York County. Professor Kress has written on the subjects of plea bargaining and the rules of evidence and is currently working on Criminal Law and Criminal Justice. *He has acted as a consultant for the United Nations and the Police Foundation and is presently co-directing a major Law Enforcement Assistance Administration-sponsored study aimed at reducing unjustified sentence variations in state courts.*

THE familiar office of public prosecutor or district attorney is a distinctive and uniquely American contribution to common law jurisprudence. Whereas Americans typically describe their legal system as based upon the English common law, in terms of both its procedural attributes and substantive state penal codes, the public prosecutor is a figure virtually unknown to the English system, which is primarily one of private prosecution to this day. "The very institution of public prosecution is largely an American invention."[1]

This might appear to be a point of only minor interest except for the central role of the district attorney in American's modern system of criminal justice administration. He is *the* pivotal figure in the justice process. "To a considerable extent he is police, prosecutor, magistrate, grand jury, petit jury, and judge in one."[2] "The prosecutor has more control over life, liberty, and reputation than any other person in America."[3]

Although we possess enormously detailed records of many trivial aspects of our justice system, the

derivation of the office of public prosecutor surprisingly remains an historical mystery. The major theories advanced suggest that the office evolved from trends already extant in the common law, that the idea was borrowed from the civil law, or that the concept grew de novo out of the colonial experience.

THE COMMON LAW TRADITION

It is worthwhile attending to the prosecution machinery in England. In common law, a crime was viewed not as an act against the state, but rather as a wrong inflicted upon the victim. The aggrieved victim, or an interested friend or relative, would personally arrest and prosecute the offender, after which the courts would adjudicate the matter much as they would a contract dispute or a tortious injury. Thus, there was no common law analogue to the American district attorney until 1879, when the office of director of public prosecutions was created. At least in theory, this common law system of private prosecution still exists in Great Britain today. For example, although 88 percent of cases brought to court are "police" prosecutions, the police officer, just as the director of public prosecutions, is legally "acting not by virtue of his office but as a private citizen interested in the maintenance of law and order."[4] His only

1. Frank W. Miller, *Prosecution: The Decision to Charge a Subject with a Crime* (Boston: Little, Brown and Co., 1969), p. 54, n. 22.

2. Raymond Moley, *Politics and Criminal Prosecution* (New York: Minton, Balch & Co., 1929), p. vii. See, also, National Advisory Commission on Criminal Justice Standards and Goals, *Report on Courts* (Washington, D.C.: Government Printing Office, 1973), p. 227; and Kenneth Culp Davis, *Discretionary Justice: A Preliminary Inquiry* (Baton Rouge: Louisiana State University Press, 1969), pp. 188–214.

3. Robert H. Jackson, *Journal of American Judicature Society* 24 (1940), p. 18. This statement by the late Justice Jackson was made while he was Attorney General of the United States.

4. Patrick Devlin, *The Criminal Prosecution in England* (London: Oxford University Press, 1960), p. 17. Even today, the director of public prosecutions only handles approximately 8 percent of the prosecutions brought in England, generally limited to those which were formerly capital in nature. Further, his powers and duties are far more limited than those of any local county prosecutor in the United States. See R. M. Jackson, *Enforcing the Law* (London: Macmillan & Co., 1967), pp. 44–54; and Edward Tindal

differentiation from a private citizen is a slightly broader power of arrest, after which arrest the officer hires a solicitor to prepare the case on his personal behalf against the defendant.

This system of private prosecution had its critics, few though they were. There were those who argued that, since the laws were publicly adopted and promulgated, their enforcement and execution should be public, in order to prevent private prosecution—and hence the courts —from becoming an instrument for private vengeance. Indeed, as early as 1534, Henry VIII proposed "that the sergeants of the common weal act as public prosecutors to enforce penal statutes throughout the country."[5] His proposal was rejected by Parliament, however, as were all others until 1879.[6] Some commentators have pointed to those rejected proposals as potential sources for colonial adaptation which already existed within the English tradition. Others have suggested that the Anglican churchwarden, the Crown's attorney general, or royal revenue agents provided the otherwise absent ancestral link.[7] But as these are so distant in form from a true public prosecutor, and as historical research has unearthed no specific nexus between these, they seem unlikely progenitors of the American district attorney.

The final argument in favor of a common law derivation of public prosecution is that the whole proclaimed notion of private prosecution is a legal fiction. Glanville Williams contends that calling the present practice of English prosecution "private" is engaging in semantic gymnastics: "In fact, . . . a prosecution by a policeman or other official is brought in pursuance of superior orders or under statutory authority and at public expense, so that it is unreal to describe it as a private prosecution."[8]

Similarly, Professor John H. Langbein researched sixteenth-century practice and concluded that the early English magistracy performed significant prosecutorial functions: "the justices of the peace became the ordinary public prosecutors in cases of serious crime."[9] Langbein

Atkinson, *The Department of the Director of Public Prosecutions* (Toronto: The Canadian Bar Association, 1944).

5. Brian A. Grosman, *The Prosecutor: An Inquiry into the Exercise of Discretion* (Toronto: University of Toronto Press, 1969), p. 11. See T. F. T. Plucknett, "Some Proposed Legislation of Henry VIII," *Royal Historical Society Transactions* (Fourth Series, 1936), p. 119; and National Commission on Law Observance and Enforcement, *Report on Prosecution* (popularly known as The Wickersham Commission, Report #4) (Washington, D.C.: Government Printing Office, 1931), pp. 6–7.

6. Leon Radzinowicz, *A History of English Criminal Law: The Reform of the Police* (1957), p. 3. See, also, Philip B. Kurland and Waters, "Public Prosecution in England, 1854–79; An Essay in English Legislative History," *Duke Law Review* 4 (1959), p. 493; and Glanville Williams, "The Power to Prosecute," *Criminal Law Review* (1955), pp. 596, 601.

7. See W. Scott Van Alstyne, Jr., "Comment: The District Attorney—A Historical Puzzle," *Wisconsin Law Review* (1952), pp. 125, 138; and Julius Goebel, Jr., and T. Raymond Naughton, *Law Enforcement in Colonial New York* (Montclair, N.J.: Patterson Smith, 1944), pp. 328–330.

8. Williams, "The Power to Prosecute," p. 603. Bear in mind, however, that this is clearly a minority view. See Devlin, *Criminal Prosecution*, and Jackson, *Enforcing the Law*, and Jay A. Sigler, "Public Prosecution in England and Wales," *Criminal Law Review* (1974), p. 642.

9. John H. Langbein, "The Origins of Public Prosecution at Common Law," *The American Journal of Legal History* 17 (October 1973), p. 313.

sees the English justice of the peace (JP)—whose primary role as preliminary examining magistrate should not be confused with that of a trial judge—as filling both the investigatory and forensic roles of the modern prosecutor, thus resembling the present-day French *Juge d'Instruction*,[10] and traces the origins of these powers to two statutes passed in 1554–1555, which required inquiry of the prisoner by the JP and "transformed the role of the private accuser from option to obligation."[11]

While Langbein restricts his vision to early English history, a logical extension of his argument would appear to suggest that "The Prosecuting JP," as Langbein refers to him, was firmly established by the time of the American colonization. Glanville Williams lends support to this view and suggests that the prosecuting JP lasted well into the nineteenth century, when newly created police forces finally assumed their functions.[12]

Therefore, the appearance of a separate public prosecutor in the colonies might be explained as a fairly logical next step, that is, a pragmatic division of the separate magisterial and prosecutorial functions, not unlike that which eventually occurred in Great Britain. Unfortunately, this is only an ex-

trapolation of a theory already grounded on scant evidence; Professor Langbein apparently intends to apply his thesis only to a narrow class of "serious" felonies falling short of state trials.[13] More research is certainly required before we may support such a so-far undocumented claim of influence upon the colonies.

THE FRENCH PROCUREUR

There are two major systems of Western law. We are naturally most familiar with the common law system which obtains in the English-speaking nations of the world; but the remainder of Western civilization operates under Roman or civil law, which utilized an inquisitorial system necessitating a public prosecutor for all relevant periods of American colonization and statehood.[14] Thus, it is natural to ask

10. See Robert Vouin, "The Role of the Prosecutor in French Criminal Trials," *American Journal of Comparative Law* 18 (1970), p. 483; Robert Ferrari, "French and American Criminal Law: Three Points of Resemblance," *Journal of American Institute of Criminal Law and Criminology* 8 (May 1917), p. 33; and Devlin, *Criminal Prosecution*, pp. 11–12.

11. Langbein, "Origins of Public Prosecution," p. 322.

12. Williams, "The Power to Prosecute," p. 601.

13. Professor Langbein's acknowledged acquaintance with European jurisprudence may also cause him to give an entirely different meaning than we do to the term "public prosecution." His description of American prosecutorial practice certainly displays a lack of familiarity with our federated system: "In the American system the state's chief lawyer in the jurisdiction, the attorney general, is nominally responsible for prosecuting crime, aided by however many district attornies and their hirelings," "Origins of Public Prosecution, p. 315. See text at note 26.

14. See Williams, "The Power to Prosecute," p. 596; and A. C. Wright, "French Criminal Procedure," *Law Quarterly Review* 44 (July 1928), pp. 324, 329; and *Law Quarterly Review* 45 (January 1929), p. 92. This use of the term "civil law" to refer to the European legal system as a whole should not be confused with the same term which divides common law litigation between civil and criminal matters. This is especially important to bear in mind as modern American forms of private prosecution (such as *qui tam* actions and multiple damage suits) straddle this latter civil/criminal distinction: see

whether the American colonies somehow chose to adopt a civil law official, perhaps from France or Holland, to administer a common law jurisprudence.

The most frequently claimed source of the public prosecutor is France, but it is well to note that the evidence for French influence is entirely circumstantial, based on the similarity of prosecutorial institutions rather than on any direct link; for example, the Louisiana Territory was not purchased from France until 1803, a century after the Connecticut legislature established a modern public prosecutor's office. The concept of public prosecution was, however, well established in France by the time of America's colonization. As Montesquieu put it in 1748, "we have to-day an admirable law: it consists in what the prince wants, laid down to see that the laws are carried out, and which places an officer in each court to prosecute all crimes in his name. . . ."[15] In modern France, the state-appointed *procureur public* receives complaints, supervises police behavior, and initiates investigations. He also prepares charges and controls the conduct of the trial and all other phases of a prosecution.

The Wickersham Commission argued in 1931 that France was obviously the primary source of the public prosecutor since revolutionary America reacted against all things British and displayed a concomitant adulation for the French.[16] Theoretically, this hypothesis could neatly answer the vexing question of why a continental-style prosecutor —and not substantive Roman law— was adopted, for, after all, it was not English law but English law *enforcement* against which the Americans rebelled. This particular argument fails, however, owing to the fact of the public prosecutor being deeply engrained in America in "good old colony times," well before any anti-English fervor developed. In May of 1704, the Connecticut Assembly passed the law which is generally recognized as creating the first permanent office of public prosecutor on a colony-wide basis:

Henceforth there shall be in every countie a sober, discreet and religious person appointed by the countie courts, to be attorney for the Queen [this was in the reign of Queen Anne] to prosecute and implead in the lawe all criminals and to doe all other things necessary or convenient as an attorney to suppresse vice and immoralitie. . . .[17]

Virginia commissioned county attornies in 1711 and public prosecution was firmly established as the American system by the time the Judiciary Act of 1789 created United States district attorneys to prosecute federal crimes.

THE DUTCH SCHOUT

But France is not the only claimed civil law ancestor of the public

"Comment: Private Prosecution: A Remedy for District Attornies' Unwarranted Inaction," *Yale Law Journal* 65 (December 1955), pp. 209, 222–223.

15. Charles Louis Montesquieu, *The Spirit of the Laws* (1748), book 16, ch. 8. See, also, Morris Ploscowe, "Development of Inquisitorial and Accusatorial Elements in French Procedure," *Journal of Criminal Law, Criminology and Police Science* 23 (September–October 1932), p. 372.

16. Wickersham Commission, Report #4, p. 7. See, also, Roscoe Pound, "The Influence of French Law in America," *Illinois Law Review* 3 (May 1908), p. 354.

17. Quoted in Wickersham Commission, Report #4, p. 7. See, also, Walter M. Pickett, "The Office of the Public Prosecutor in Connecticut," *Journal of Criminal Law and Criminology* 17 (November 1926), p. 348.

prosecutor. "This officer, common in civil law countries, is possibly a legacy from the Dutch administration in what is now New York."[18] It is argued that the American district attorney is a direct descendant of Holland's *schout*, a public official who prosecuted all criminal cases under Dutch law (records do clearly indicate that *schouts* practiced in the New World, at least in New Amsterdam—later New York City[19]). The theory is premised on the fact that the Netherlands was the only power besides England which actually governed portions of areas which became the original 13 states: the colony of New Netherland claimed control of parts of what are today Connecticut, New York, New Jersey, Pennsylvania, and Delaware. These, indeed, seem to be the states where the public prosecutor first made his appearance in the English colonies.[20] By 1686, Pennsylvania appears to have had at least one prosecuting attorney on its public payroll and, by that same year, there was a public prosecutor in a New Jersey Quaker community. Further, district attorneys existed all over New Jersey by 1747 at the latest.

Intriguing as the Dutch hypothesis is, the Netherlands' claims beyond New Amsterdam were exaggeratedly based on a small settler population, and their total popula-

tion base, even when concentrated in Manhattan, was quite small at all times. Further, their period of political control was, in any event, quite brief, lasting only from 1653 until 1664[21] and it is questionable if this was sufficient time for the institution of the *schout* to take root —especially as it then had to lay dormant under English rule for a number of years before its first reappearance in a state with a concededly minimal Dutch population![22]

This search for the source of public prosecution has also seen a claim advanced for the Scottish system "where prosecutions are conducted by procurators-fiscal working under the supervision of the Lord Advocate."[23] As the public prosecutor was such a basic feature of civil law systems, it is not difficult to imagine rival claims being advanced on behalf of any of the other major immigrant groups, such as the Germans or Poles, which formed significant minorities within the colonies. Indeed, it is probably this ethnic conglomerate facet of the colonies which has led otherwise cautious historians to opt for a "spontaneous combustion theory for the creation of the public prosecutor in America."[24]

---

18. Sanford H. Kadish and Monrad G. Paulsen, *Criminal Law and Its Processes: Cases and Materials*, 2nd ed., (Boston: Little, Brown and Co., 1969), p. 1034.

19. Van Alstyne, "Comment: The District Attorney."

20. Ibid., p. 134. But Van Alstyne's claim that Virginia did not possess a public prosecutor before the Revolution (pp. 137–138) is mistaken. See Wickersham Commission, Report #4, p. 7.

21. And again for one year in 1673–1674.

22. For further evidence contrary to Van Alstyne's otherwise fascinating thesis, see, for example, Goebel and Naughton, *Law Enforcement*, and the statement in note 20.

23. Brian A. Grosman, "The Role of the Prosecutor in Canada," *American Journal of Comparative Law* 18 (1970), pp. 498, 499. See, also, W. G. Normand, "The Public Prosecutor in Scotland," *Law Quarterly Review* 54 (July 1938), p. 345; and Jackson, *Enforcing the Law*, pp. 45–46.

24. Van Alstyne, "Comment: The District Attorney," p. 125. See, also, sources cited in note 7.

THE STRUCTURE OF PROSECUTION

Whatever the derivation of the office, it rooted quickly and firmly into American life with remarkably few changes in form or function over the following two centuries. We should now describe the present state of public prosecution in America.

The prosecuting attorney, or district attorney as he is most commonly known,[25] unlike his European counterparts, is not a career official or civil servant. He is usually a respected local attorney, elected on a county-wide basis, compensated by county funds, and generally autonomous from the control of both the governor and the attorney general of his state.[26] To aid him in his investigatory capacity, the prosecutor has both the informal assistance of local police and, in almost every state, contingent funds to be used for the hiring of special non-police investigators where needed. Very few states statutorily prohibit the private practice of law (although the private defense of *criminal* cases

is usually prohibited); indeed, only in the larger metropolitan areas do we find full-time prosecutors. Most of America's 2,700 prosecutors serve in small offices with one or two assistants.[27] These assistants, or deputies, to the district attorney are usually chosen by him with the approval of the county governing body —often on the recommendation of political party officials sharing the affiliation of the elected district attorney—and these assistants even more frequently engage in only part-time prosecution.

Three structural reforms are suggested by this analysis: an end to political involvement by the prosecutor; the centralization of inefficiently small, county-wide offices; and the end to potential conflicts of interest by insisting that all prosecutors hold office on a full-time basis. It is interesting to note that it is precisely in these areas that the American prosecutor differs so markedly from both his English and European counterparts, who are usually full-time career officials appointed by a central administration authority.

Roscoe Pound recognized the pivotal role of the prosecutor a half century ago and diagnosed the central ailment of that office: "Undoubtedly the bane of prosecution in the United States of today is the intimate connection of the prosecutor's office with politics."[28] By this statement, Pound meant to attack both the corrupting influence of

---

25. In our federated system, prosecutors have many other designations, including circuit solicitor, commonwealth attorney, county attorney, criminal district attorney, district attorney general, etc.

26. This section of the paper attempts to summarize the practice of 50 states and therefore is subject to qualification in virtually every respect. As an example of the difficulties of generalization, consider that up until 1959, county attorneys in Utah did not even have to be members of the bar! For a comparative analysis of state statutes, see Earl H. DeLong and Newman F. Baker, "The Prosecuting Attorney: Provisions of Law Organizing the Office," *Journal of the American Institute of Criminal Law and Criminology* 23 (April 1933), p. 926; and Duane R. Nedrud, "The Career Prosecutor," *Journal of Criminal Law, Criminology and Police Science* 51 (September–October 1960), p. 343.

27. National Advisory Commission, *Report on Courts*, p. 227.

28. Roscoe Pound, *Criminal Justice in America*, 1924, 1930 (New York: Da Capa Press, reprinted 1975), p. 183. See, also, Wickersham Commission, Report #4, pp. 14–15.

political bosses upon the operation of the office as well as the inclination of the district attorney himself to "make a record" so as to foster his own political ambitions. Pound urged permanent staffing and increased salaries under civil service conditions to supply continuous experience and end the rapid turnover of assistant district attorneys. Pound saw the district attorney as possessing too *little* discretion and urged the appointment process for prosecutors as a means to insure the prosecutor freedom from political checks on his behavior.[29] Supporters of the elective system, however, argue the necessity to control the enormous and virtually unreviewable power of the public prosecutor and contend that "the check of periodic elections—a direct accounting of stewardship—is a mechanism exemplifying the power of the people over their servant."[30]

The other two structural reforms suggested are interrelated, owing to fiscal realities. Traditionally, the jurisdiction over which a public prosecutor operates is territorially defined, usually as a county, but sometimes as a circuit or district. This means that in sparsely populated areas the cost of funding a full-time prosecutor might be prohibitive for the local taxpayers to bear and/or that the meager salary they could afford to pay a full-time district attorney would attract less able occupants to the office. Therefore, these less densely populated areas have generally preferred to allow their prosecutors a private legal practice to insure that more

qualified applicants would seek the office. The unfortunate trade-off, of course, has been the appearance, and sometimes the reality, of a conflict of interest.

The only practical way to achieve the ideal of a full-time district attorney would be to end strictly territorial jurisdiction and apply another standard, one which would take into account the fact that twentieth-century crime, "once a matter of strictly local concern, has become interstate and even international in character, employing the full range of modern means of transportation and communication."[31]

A logical new standard could be one of productivity or workload, but this might seem too close to the undesirable "fee" system which obtained in many offices up to a half century ago. "For this reason it is worth while at least to consider whether or not it is preferable for a state to have its prosecutors serve districts of nearly equal population."[32] After all, if legislators are chosen on this principle, it seems reasonable for the all-important administrators of the law to be similarly representative. Some would centralize our legal system to an even greater degree, but such proposals are opposed by a strong tradition of local control of law enforcement, as well as a more modern distaste of anything even remotely resembling a national police force.[33]

---

29. See, also, DeLong and Baker, "The Prosecuting Attorney," p. 962.

30. American Bar Association [ABA] Standards for Criminal Justice, *The Prosecution Function and the Defense Function* (approved draft, 1971), p. 19.

31. Ibid., p. 22. See, also, Standard 2.3(b), urging that "the offices of chief prosecutor and his staff should be full-time occupations" (p. 27); and Wickersham Commission, Report #4, pp. 10–16.

32. DeLong and Baker, "The Prosecuting Attorney," p. 962. See, also, ABA Standard 2.2 and commentary, *The Prosecution Function*, pp. 50–57.

33. See Richard A. Myren, "Should the United States Adopt a National Substantive Criminal Code for Serious Offenses?" *Journal*

THE FUNCTIONS OF THE PROSECUTOR

The multiple and often contradictory roles which the district attorney is expected to fill explain much of the power—as well as the problems—of the office. "On the one hand, the prosecutor is the leader of law enforcement in the community."[34] When there is public pressure for a "war against crime," it is he who is expected to lead it with public statements, strong direction, and vigorous prosecution. Further, we call ours an adversary system and expect the district attorney to try to convict a defendant in court just as we expect the defense attorney to do all in his power to acquit the same defendant. This public belief, however, is contradictory to standards enunciated by the organized bar: "The responsibility of a public prosecutor differs from that of the usual advocate; his duty is to seek justice, not merely to convict."[35] Thus it is that the store of anecdotes of every prosecutor invariably includes a number of cases where he has dismissed charges against a seemingly guilty defendant, often after a lengthy and expensive investigation.

A too often ignored point should be made here. In the American system of criminal justice, the crime victim does *not* have an attorney in court. Many European countries permit the victim a separate counsel,[36] and in a system of private prosecution, the complainant obviously makes all decisions regarding his case. The American district attorney, however, represents the state and not the victim. This is why he rarely consults a victim with regard to charging or plea negotiations and almost never informs him of the results of the case in which the victim may have been injured or robbed. When the crime victim speaks of the assistant district attorney as being *his* attorney, he is spouting the myth of an adversary process and not the realities of a situation where he may never be informed of his rights to receive compensation or to refuse to testify.

THE CRIMINAL JUSTICE PROCESS

In order to fully understand the present function of the prosecutor, a brief synopsis of the criminal justice process is in order. In most cases, a defendant is arrested by the police with minimal investigation and only after a citizen complaint of crime. The defendant is fingerprinted and taken to the prosecutor, who prefers initial charges. The defendant is then brought before a magistrate who explains the charges against him, sets bail, and assigns counsel. There follows a preliminary hearing before a judge (or a grand jury session presided over by the prosecutor), followed by an official presentment (or indictment) of charges upon which the defendant

---

of Criminal Justice 2 (summer 1974), p. 103. One recent example of the "distaste" referred to is the strongly felt opposition occasioned by the Federal Bureau of Investigation's announcement of plans to centralize computerized crime data banks.

34. ABA Standards, *The Prosecution Function*, p. 19. See, also, National Advisory Commission, *Report on Courts*, p. 249.

35. American Bar Association, *Code of Professional Responsibility*, EC 7–13 (final draft, 1969). The Supreme Court put it that the interest of the United States Attorney's office "is not that it shall win a case, but that justice shall be done." *Berger* v. *United States*, 295 U.S. 78, 88 (1939).

36. See Vouin, "The Role of the Prosecutor," and Hans-Heinrich Jescheck, "The Discretionary Powers of the Prosecuting Attorney in West Germany," *American Journal of Comparative Law* 18 (1970), p. 508.

is arraigned and pleads either guilty or not guilty. A not guilty plea is followed by a series of preliminary motions and a jury trial resulting in either acquittal or conviction. Upon a conviction, whether by plea or by trial, a defendant is sentenced to either probation or imprisonment and may appeal his conviction and/or his sentence—prosecutors are permitted to appeal neither an acquittal nor a sentence which they regard as excessively lenient.

In a few instances, the district attorney assumes a less reactive stance than this summary indicates, serving as informal counsel to the police and actually initiating and supervising the investigatory process. This is particularly true with regard to serious crimes, such as homicide, or complicated ones involving fraud or organized criminal activity. The Watergate Special Prosecution is one cogent and visible example of this "pro-active" role. Even in the usual situation, however, prosecutors are reconsidering their passive stance and are screening more and more cases brought to them by the police and other agencies of investigation.[37]

In most jurisdictions, the process of formal charging is accomplished by the district attorney's filing of presentment papers against the defendant. In a shrinking number, the time-consuming and often *pro forma* presentation of evidence before a body of grand jurors is required. Today, most American jurisdictions

"have come to the logical result of the system of public prosecutions and done away with grand juries, a proper check on private prosecutions as a regular and necessary stage in a criminal proceeding."[38] In either method, however, the district attorney's role is often described as being a "quasi-judicial" one, and he is put to a high standard of self-discipline in charging.[39]

The forensic, trial role of the district attorney is probably the one most familiar to a lay public, although it is doubtful whether the restrictions upon his presentation are fully appreciated. The prosecutor must turn all exculpatory materials discovered by him over to the defendant (even if he disbelieves them), although there is no reciprocal obligation on the defense attorney. The prosecutor is not allowed to assert his personal belief in the guilt of the defendant, nor may he characterize the defendant by any unfavorable epithet, such as hoodlum or criminal. Similarly, the prosecutor is prohibited from offering the jury any evidence of the defendant's prior criminal record unless the defendant takes the witness stand, nor may he comment adversely on the defendant's failure to take the witness stand, should the defendant choose not to do so.

DISCRETION

Whatever the historical genesis, it is the overlay of the public prosecutor upon a system premised on private prosecution that provides the

37. See, for example, National Center for Prosecution Management, *A System for Manual Evaluation of Case Processing in the Prosecutor's Office* (Washington, D.C.: LEAA Grant #71-DF-1093). See, also, Donald M. McIntyre, Jr., ed., *Law Enforcement in the Metropolis* 97–116 (Chicago: American Bar Foundation, 1967); and, generally, Miller, *Prosecution.*

38. Pound, *Criminal Justice in America*, p. 109.

39. See, for example, ABA Standards, *The Prosecution Function*, p. 44; and, generally, Miller, *Prosecution.*

American office with its unique complexion. Most pertinently, the one feature inevitably noted by observers of American justice is the vast amount of independence and discretion lodged with this locally elected official—far more than that possessed by any of his European counterparts: "One of the most striking features of the American system of criminal justice is the broad range of largely uncontrolled discretion exercised by the prosecutor."[40] This is only logical, given the historical background: "Obviously, if prosecution is essentially a private matter, the person prosecuting ought to be able to call it off" or make settlements or commence proceedings as he wishes.[41] But America has gone a significant step farther. In England, there was a check upon unfettered private prosecution in that the English Attorney General had the power to *end* the private prosecution by informing the court that the Crown was unwilling for the prosecution to continue. America's county prosecutors inherited not only the power of the private initiator but also that of the attorney general and thus the additional power to monitor and mitigate their own decisions, thereby making their discretion almost total—well nigh unreviewable in theory and even less reviewed in practice.[42]

As we have seen, the unique status of the public prosecutor in American jurisprudence was fairly fixed by the time of the Revolution, and the ensuing two centuries have served only to solidify his position. Today, however, a number of his attributes have been called into question, and serious changes in the shape of future prosecution have been suggested. More and more we may see how prescient the great Roscoe Pound was a half-century ago:

More than one bad feature of American criminal justice of today comes from want of accord between the law in the books and the administration of law in action when an organized police and organized bureau of public prosecution function under a system of legal rules presupposing private arrest and private prosecution.[43]

In one form or another, the central issue today is prosecutorial discretion: Is there enough of it? Is there too much? Can it be channeled? Can we control it so as to avoid the excesses of imperial behavior and/or corruption?

"Discretion," it should be noted, is a word that requires precise definition. I do not mean it to be synonymous with "corruption," which can take place no matter how structured a system is; for corrupt activity, a prosecutor may, of course, be prosecuted himself. Nor do I

40. Wayne R. LaFave, "The Prosecutor's Discretion in the United States," *American Journal of Comparative Law* 18 (1970), p. 532. See, also, *United States* v. *Cox*, 342 F.2d 167 (5th Cir. 1965); and the interesting statement contained in President Gerald Ford's Proclamation of 8 September 1974, "Granting Pardon to Richard Nixon," which noted the former president's criminal liability and then added: "Whether or not he shall be so prosecuted depends on findings of the appropriate grand jury and on the discretion of the authorized prosecutor." None of this is meant to imply, however, that prosecutorial discretion is a purely American phenomenon. See Shigemitsu Dando, "System of Discretionary Prosecution in Japan," *American Journal of Comparative Law* 18 (1970), p. 518.

41. Kadish and Paulsen, *Criminal Law and Its Processes*, p. 1034. See, also, Glanville Williams, "Discretion in Prosecuting," *Criminal Law Review* (1956), pp. 222, 223.

42. See Wickersham Commission, Report #4, pp. 18–19.

43. See Pound, *Criminal Justice in America*, p. 108.

mean it to apply to errors of judgment that may be involved in the assessment of the sufficiency of evidence; such errors will occur in any system run by human beings. Frank W. Miller uses the term to refer to charging or plea-bargaining decisions which reflect an honest "judgment that full enforcement would not be in the overall community interest."[44] Though I generally prefer this more cautious use of the term, for present purposes even Kenneth Culp Davis's broad definition would suffice: "A public officer has discretion whenever the effective limits on his power leave him free to make a choice among possible courses of action or inaction."[45]

CHARGING AND PLEA BARGAINING

From the earliest stages of the criminal justice process, the prosecutor may engage in that most contentious practice: plea bargaining. In order to understand plea bargaining, we must remember the vast amount of discretion with which an historically private prosecution system has invested the modern district attorney. The first major exercise of that discretion is in the decision to charge, not to charge, or not to charge as fully as the evidence might warrant.[46] A number of often conflicting considerations go into this charging decision.

First, there is what might be termed a "legal" decision as to whether or not there is sufficient evidence to suggest—not merely a presentment which only requires evidence of a probability of guilt, but, looking ahead to a trial—the likelihood of securing a jury conviction by the higher evidentiary standard of proof beyond a reasonable doubt. This requires an early assessment of both the quality and quantity of available evidence. For example, in even very serious assaults between family members, most complainants eventually refuse to press charges, and a district attorney would be remiss not to consider this likelihood.

Second, there are "systemic" considerations, including an assessment that full prosecution might not be in the public interest. Scarce prosecutorial resources must be efficiently allocated, and therefore there will usually not be full enforcement of laws against private gambling, for example, the enforcement of which laws would likely lose the district attorney a good deal of public respect and support.[47] Full prosecution might be perceived as too costly or dangerous for the nation as a whole, as former United States Attorney General Eliot Richardson argued it would be in his statement accepting Spiro Agnew's plea.[48] The cooperation of the suspect may also be an important consideration, as in the tactic of letting the small fish go in order to catch the big fish.[49]

44. Miller, *Prosecution*, p. 293. See, also, Charles Breitel, "Controls in Law Enforcement," *University of Chicago Law Review* 27 (1960), p. 427.

45. Davis, *Discretionary Justice*, p. 4.

46. For a full treatment of the charging decision see, generally, Miller, *Prosecution*.

47. See Orvill C. Snyder, "The District Attorney's Hardest Task," *Journal of Criminal Law, Criminology and Police Science* 30 (1939), p. 167; and Frank G. Remington et al., *Criminal Justice Administration: Materials and Cases* (New York: Bobbs-Merrill, 1969), pp. 276–326.

48. See Jack M. Kress, "The Agnew Case: Policy, Prosecution and Plea Bargaining," *Criminal Law Bulletin* 10 (January–February 1974), p. 80.

49. See John Kaplan's interesting confessional, "The Prosecutorial Discretion—A

Third, the availability of realistic alternatives to criminal prosecution —such as psychiatric or drug rehabilitation programs—will be considered.[50]

While this analysis relates primarily to the decision *not* to charge, contrary factors might lead a prosecutor to press fully all charges. Full prosecution might be a reflection of media or public pressure, as in the case of a highly publicized local child rapist, or might actually be perceived as a social service for the defendant, as where the local drunk is felt to require an extended "drying out" period in the town jail.

The issues of charging and plea bargaining are closely related, and lesser degrees of the factors suggested above will be involved in the district attorney's willingness to participate in the plea negotiation process. Owing to the enormous caseloads confronting urban prosecutors, it would be both physically impossible and morally undesirable for there to be full prosecution in every case.[51] Guilty pleas account for well over 90 percent of the convictions secured by prosecutors, and, in larger offices, "going rates" for particular crimes become established and well known to the defense bar.[52]

The American bar was, at one time, unanimous in its condemnation of plea bargaining[53] but has recently performed an about-face and is nearly unanimous in support of it: "Properly conducted, plea discussion may well produce a result approximating closely, but informally and more swiftly, the results which ought to ensue from a trial, while avoiding most of the undesirable aspects of that ordeal."[54] The 1973 Presidential Crime Commission did, however, urge the abolition of plea bargaining,[55] and there appears to be no abatement of the widespread public impression that there is just "something dirty" about the whole notion of bartered justice.

Comment," *Northwestern University Law Review* 60 (1965), p. 174 and especially p. 187.

50. Increasing the number and effectiveness of these alternatives is generally recognized today as a desirable reform and is usually referred to as "diversion" from the official criminal justice system. See National Advisory Commission, *Report on Courts*, pp. 27–41.

51. "If every policeman, every prosecutor, every court, and every postsentence agency performed his or its responsibility in strict accordance with rules of law, precisely and narrowly laid down, the criminal law would be ordered but intolerable. Living would be a sterile compliance with soul-killing rules and taboos. By comparison, a primitive tribal society would seem free, indeed," Breitel, "Controls in Law Enforcement," p. 427. See, also, Arthur Rosett, "The Negotiated Guilty Plea," *The Annals* 374 (November 1967), p. 70.

52. See, generally, Donald J. Newman, *Conviction: The Determination of Guilt or Innocence without Trial* (Boston: Little, Brown and Co., 1966); President's Commission on Law Enforcement and Administration of Justice, *Task Force Report: The Courts* (Washington, D.C.: Government Printing Office, 1967), pp. 9–13; and Arnold Enker, "Perspectives on Plea Bargaining," President's Commission, p. 108.

53. Note the frequent references to plea bargaining as an "abuse" in Wickersham Commission, Report #4, especially pp. 95–97.

54. ABA Standards, *The Prosecution Function*, p. 21. See, also, Chief Justice Warren Burger's praise of this process in *Santobello v. New York*, 404 U.S. 257, 260 (1971); and the concurring opinion of the prestigious American Law Institute in their *Model Code of Pre-Arraignment Procedure* (tentative draft, No. 5A, 1973).

55. National Advisory Commission, *Report on Courts*, p. 46. See, also, Albert W. Alschuler's reasoned attack, "The Prosecutor's Role in Plea Bargaining," *University of Chicago Law Review* 36 (1968), p. 50.

CONTROLS ON DISCRETION: A REBIRTH OF PRIVATE PROSECUTION?

Unlike Roscoe Pound, most observers of criminal justice administration have regarded the district attorney as possessing far too much unreviewable power stemming from the historic discretion we have accorded our private litigant/public prosecutor. Thus, they have begun to suggest various structuring devices to both guide and limit the exercise of discretion: "Half the problem is to cut back unnecessary discretionary power. The other half is to find effective ways to control necessary discretionary power."[56]

When we consider the subject of controls upon discretion, we must naturally look to the roots of that discretion which this paper finds in the unique conjunction of a public prosecutor and a system whose premises are based on private prosecution. Logically, we should either reinstitute private prosecution or more realistically adapt our system to the central role of the public prosecutor. The case for the former is stronger than one might imagine. One commentary is eloquent in its plea for the restoration of private prosecution as a control device to "balance the excesses of the district attorney's discretion with individual and community vigilance."[57] The same article documents the pragmatic value of this reform measure and pointedly reminds us that many civil law countries, including "France and Austria have also used private prosecution to restrain the discretion of the public prosecutor."[58] Defenders of Britain's continued system of private prosecution similarly urge its benefits as a control upon potential official abuse: "The power of private prosecution is undoubtedly right and necessary in that it enables the citizen to bring even the police or government official before the criminal courts, where the government itself is unwilling to make the first move."[59]

Whatever the value of a renaissance of private prosecution, the organized bar has strongly opposed this change.[60] Further, numerous judicial opinions have fought back attempts to allow a measure of private prosecution into our system: crime victims or private complainants are not "allowed to substitute their judgment, by invoking mandamus or similarly-purposed remedies, for those of the official who is responsible for the entire public."[61] This is in contradistinction to West German practice, for example, where there is sharp judicial scrutiny of charging practice, and the crime victim may not only insist upon judicial review, but may even appeal adverse findings.[62]

---

56. Davis, *Discretionary Justice*, p. 51. Davis's book is the seminal work in the recognition and control of discretion. See, especially, pp. 188–214.

57. See "Comment: Private Prosecution," p. 234.

58. Ibid., p. 224. See, also, Miller, *Prosecution*, pp. 327–334.

59. Williams, "The Power to Prosecute," p. 599. (Williams is a bit inconsistent here, however. See his contradictory statement at p. 603, referred to note 8.)

60. ABA Standards, *The Prosecution Function*, especially Standard 2.1 and commentary.

61. Miller, *Prosecution*, p. 295. See, also, for example, *United States* v. *Brokaw*, 60 F. Supp. 100 (S.D. Ill. 1945).

62. See Jescheck, "The Discretionary Powers of the Prosecuting Attorney in West Germany," p. 512. See, also, Davis, *Discretionary Justice*, pp. 191–195.

SUGGESTED SYSTEMIC CONTROLS ON DISCRETION

We would, therefore, do well at this point to address ourselves more to systemic adaptations. We must recognize, however, that our more than two centuries of primary reliance on public prosecution have provided theorists with additional arguments in favor of vast discretion: "(1) Because of legislative 'overcriminalization.' . . . (2) Because of limitations in available enforcement resources. . . . (3) Because of a need to individualize justice."[63]

The obvious answers to these arguments have often been made: (1) decriminalization, particularly of so-called "victimless" crimes;[64] (2) increased enforcement resources, both materially and through improved cooperation and communication[65] and even centralization of otherwise local and independent agencies;[66] and (3) a preference for equality of treatment over individualization to ensure the absence of bias or favoritism in prosecutorial decision-making.[67]

Normally, however, when we think of checking discretion, we consider less drastic overhauls as standing a greater chance of adoption. I have already alluded to the external pressures on a prosecutor that might be applied through the political process and the public criticisms of press and politician alike. In addition, there are obviously gross statutory and constitutional constraints already in existence, such as the very limits of state penal law formulations and the jurisdictional boundaries outside of which no prosecutor may operate. On rare occasions, there have been judicial inquiries into the motive for ordering prosecution,[68] and, in even fewer instances, courts have ordered prosecutions themselves.[69] When grand juries were more independent bodies than they are today, there was the occasional "runaway" grand jury, such as the one that called Thomas Dewey into national prominence in 1935.[70] Other suggested reform or control devices have included tighter professional entry and discipline procedures, with a more detailed code of ethics and stricter enforcement measures,[71] and the important one of closer administrative scrutiny.[72]

63. LaFave, "The Prosecutor's Discretion," pp. 533–534.

64. See, generally, Herbert L. Packer, *The Limits of the Criminal Sanction* (Stanford, Calif.: Stanford University Press, 1968); Troy Duster, *The Legislation of Morality* (New York: The Free Press, 1970); and Sanford H. Kadish, "The Crisis of Overcriminalization," *The Annals* 374 (1967), p. 157.

65. See, generally, National Advisory Commission on Criminal Justice Standards and Goals, *Criminal Justice System* (Washington, D.C.: Government Printing Office, 1973).

66. See Wickersham Commission, Report #4, pp. 13–16; DeLong and Baker, "The Prosecuting Attorney," p. 957; and Myren, "Should the United States Adopt a National Substantive Criminal Code?"

67. See American Friends Service Committee, *Struggle for Justice* (New York: Hill and Wang, 1971); and Andrew von Hirsch,

Doing Justice: The Voice of Punishments (New York: Hill and Wang, in press for 1976).

68. There are a few cases arguing that "selective enforcement" is improper. See, for example, *People* v. *Utica Daws Drug Co.*, 16 App. Div. 2d 12, 255 N.Y.S. 2d 128 (4th Dept. 1962), and Judge Bazelon's dissenting opinion in *Henderson* v. *United States*, 349 F. 2d 712 (D.C. Cir. 1965).

69. See Davis, *Discretionary Justice*, pp. 207–214.

70. See Martin Mayer, " 'Hogan's Office' Is a Kind of Ministry of Justice," *New York Times Magazine*, 23 July 1967.

71. ABA Standards, *The Prosecution Function*, p. 23.

72. Davis, *Discretionary Justice*, pp. 195–214.

One significant distinction may be drawn here between the discretion involved in the charging and in the plea bargaining decisions, which is that the courts have seriously attempted to curb and delineate the bounds of plea bargaining discretion, whereas charging discretion remains as unreviewed as ever.[73] The plea negotiation process has moved out into the open and has been placed under the visible scrutiny of the judge, who is now required to make certain that prosecution promises have been kept,[74] that no undue coercion has been placed upon the defendant to plead guilty,[75] that the defendant has understood his rights and the consequences of a plea, that the defendant has entered his plea voluntarily, and that there has been a factual basis for the plea.[76] Some have proposed that the prosecution offer detailed reasons for accepting a guilty plea,[77] and Donald J. Newman has suggested that, in cases of significant public interest, the prosecution publish a detailed summary of the evidence against the pleading defendant.[78]

Owing to the fact that our system allows defendants and not prosecutors the right of appeal, appellate courts have usually reviewed plea bargaining only where they perceived a defendant getting shortchanged in the bargain he received, usually because of either ignorance or fraud. Two other polar aspects of the prosecutor's plea bargaining discretion, however, have rarely been discussed. One is where the defendant is even more greatly shortchanged by never being offered a bargain at all! In such a situation, "no court has any jurisdiction to inquire into or review [the prosecutor's] decision."[79]

The second aspect may have even greater adverse consequences, and this is the result of the obvious fact that a defendant is most unlikely to appeal a bargain that is excessively lenient toward him. In this manner, society may be even more grossly shortchanged, as the entire thrust of our present plea bargaining system is toward undue leniency rather than undue harshness.[80]

THE PERMANENT TEMPORARY PROSECUTOR

In the limited space here available, I have only briefly alluded to some of the many suggested con-

73. "The federal courts are powerless to interfere with [the United States Attorney's] discretionary power. The Court cannot compel him to prosecute a complaint, or even an indictment, whatever his reasons for not acting." *Pugach* v. *Klein*, 193 F. Supp. 630, 635 (S.D.N.Y. 1961). See Roger P. Joseph, "Note, Reviewability of Prosecutorial Discretion: Failure to Prosecute," *Columbia Law Review* 75 (January 1975), p. 130.

74. *Santobello* v. *New York*.

75. See *Cortez* v. *United States*, 337 F. 2d 699, 701 (9th Cir. 1964).

76. See *People* v. *Selikoff*, 35 N.Y. 2d 227 (1974), and Federal Rules of Criminal Procedure, Rule 11.

77. See, generally, American Bar Association Standards for Criminal Justice, *Pleas of Guilty* (approved draft, 1968).

78. See Donald J. Newman, "The Agnew Plea Bargain," *Criminal Law Bulletin* 10 (January–February 1974), p. 85.

79. *Newman* v. *United States*, 382 F. 2d 479, 482 (D.C. Cir. 1967). See, also, *United States* v. *Berrigan*, 482 F. 2d 171, 174 (3rd Cir. 1973). This situation does not, however, appear to occur with the frequency of the second aspect to be discussed. Alschuler, "The Prosecutor's Role in Plea Bargaining," p. 105, challenges the propriety of the *Newman* decision. See, also, *United States* v. *Falk*, 479 F. 2d 616, 618 (7th Cir. 1973).

80. Richard Kuh, "Plea Copping," *New York County Bar Bulletin* 24 (1966–1967), p. 160; and Samuel Dash, "Cracks in the Foundation of Criminal Justice," *Illinois Law Review* 46 (1951), pp. 385, 392–393.

trols upon prosecutorial discretion. I should like, however, especially to highlight two major constraints which have been little commented upon yet which quite recently have become very visible, proven their practical value, and shown promise of becoming increasingly significant in the future. The first structural mechanism is that exemplified by the well-known Special Watergate Prosecution Task Force. In an ever growing list of instances, the superseding, special or "temporary" prosecutor has paradoxically begun to appear as a permanent fixture and hence a major influence upon the shape of future prosecutorial activity in America.[81]

In one sense, the very concept of the special prosecutor is an attempt to answer those difficult questions of "Who shall police the police?" and "Who shall prosecute the prosecutor?" These prosecutors have, so far, arisen on an ad hoc basis to deal with what have been seen as temporary situations, and their mandates have therefore been strictly limited in terms of financing, jurisdiction, and duration. For example, New York State recently authorized separate special prosecutions of corruption in New York City[82] and the crimes committed during the Attica prison riots.[83] These special prosecutions are a discretionary control device in that they have typically been employed in situations where the permanent prosecutor has been perceived as being unable or unwilling to positively exercise his discretion to prosecute. Thus, this is the control on the decision not to prosecute, particularly where it is feared that bias and/or corruption may have been an element in that negative decision.

FUTURE GUIDELINES FOR THE PROPER EXERCISE OF THE PROSECUTION FUNCTION

The second major constraint goes more to method and is more positive, in that it assumes a decent concern for equity on the part of the prosecutor. This is the check of the self-imposed internal guideline, sometimes solely self-administered, and occasionally publicly promulgated. While the district attorney is sometimes said to be the chief law enforcement administrator in the community, he has no direct authority over police, yet he can tell the police chief that his office simply will not bother to prosecute a "streaker" or some other low priority offender. Customary plea reduction offers for given offenses have the force of law if the defense bar is made aware of them. The United States Board of Parole recently adopted and published internal decision-making guidelines which

81. See ABA Standards, *The Prosecution Function*, especially Standard 2.10 and commentary, which recommends expansion of the concept. It should be noted, however, that the power to appoint special prosecutors has existed for a very long time. See De-Long and Baker, "The Prosecuting Attorney," pp. 957–961.

82. The Office of the Special Prosecutor commenced operations on 19 September 1972 by authority of an Executive Order issued by Governor Nelson A. Rockefeller. The Office grew out of a recommendation of the Commission to Investigate Allegations of Police Corruption in the City of New York, better known as the Knapp Commission.

83. The Attica special prosecutor was partly a response to recommendations by the McKay Commission. See New York State Special Commission on Attica, *Attica: The Official Report of the New York State Special Commission on Attica* (New York: Praeger, 1972).

have been well received.[84] Current research is testing the feasibility of implementing similar guides for judicial sentencing decisions.[85] One prosecutor has already taken the logical next step and literally published internal staff policy guidelines on plea bargaining.[86] These developments can only be encouraged as means of promoting equity and fairness in the future exercise of prosecutorial discretion.

84. Don M. Gottfredson et al., "Making Paroling Policy Explicit," *Crime and Delinquency* 21 (January 1975), p. 34.

85. The Law Enforcement Assistance Administration is presently sponsoring such a project, entitled "Sentencing in State Courts," which is being co-directed by Don M. Gottfredson, Jack M. Kress, and Leslie T. Wilkins.

86. Richard H. Kuh, "Plea Bargaining: Guidelines for the Manhattan District Attorney's Office," *Criminal Law Bulletin* 11 (January–February 1975), p. 48.

Criminal Sentencing in the United States: An Historical and Conceptual Overview

By Alan M. Dershowitz

ABSTRACT: The criminal sentence seeks to reduce the frequency and severity of crimes by employing the following mechanisms: (*a*) isolating the convicted criminal from the rest of the population, so that he is unable to commit crimes during the period of his enforced isolation; (*b*) punishing the convicted prisoner, so that he—and others contemplating crime —will be deterred by the prospect of a painful response if convicted; (*c*) rehabilitating the convicted criminal, so that his desire or need to commit future crimes will be diminished. During different periods of our history, the power to determine the duration of a convicted criminal's sentence has been allocated to different agencies: first to the legislature; then to the judiciary; and now—under indeterminate sentencing—to the parole board. The locus of sentencing authority has a considerable effect on such factors as the length of sentences, the degree of discretion, and the disparity among sentences. The century-long trend in the direction of indeterminancy seems to be ending. It is likely that the coming decades will witness a return to more legislatively-fixed sentences.

Alan M. Dershowitz is Professor of Law at Harvard Law School and an active civil liberties and criminal lawyer. He received his B.A. degree in 1959, from Brooklyn College, where he majored in Political Science, and his L.L.B. degree from Yale Law School in 1962, where he was Editor-in-Chief of the Yale Law Journal. He then served as law clerk to Chief Judge David Bazelon of the Court of Appeals in Washington, and then to Mr. Justice Arthur Goldberg of the United States Supreme Court. He has published two books and more than 60 articles in scholarly and popular magazines.

THE history of criminal sentencing in the United States has been a history of shifts in institutional responsibility for determining the sentence to be served by the convicted criminal. At different stages, this decision has been allocated in varying ways among the legislature, courts, parole agencies, and prosecutors. Although the primary object of the criminal sentence—to reduce the frequency and severity of crimes—has remained fairly consistent over time, different mechanisms of crime reduction have been emphasized at different periods in our history.

THE MECHANISMS OF THE CRIMINAL SENTENCE

The mechanisms of the criminal sentence include the following: (1) *isolating* the convicted criminal from the rest of the population so that he is unable to commit crimes during the period of his enforced isolation; (2) *punishing* the convicted prisoner so that he—and others contemplating crime—will be deterred by the prospect of a painful response if convicted; (3) *rehabilitating* the convicted criminal so that his desire or need to commit future crimes will be diminished.

Isolation

The mechanism of isolation operates directly to remove the criminal from the general population. It has been used throughout history, against all manner of "dangerous" beings. During the period of removal, the isolated criminal cannot generally commit crimes against the rest of the population. Imprisonment is not the only instrument of enforced isolation; banishment, exile, deportation, hospitalization, house arrest, and enforced enlistment in the military are other instruments of isolation that have been employed throughout history. In order to operate effectively, the removal of the convicted offender need not be accompanied by any pain other than that inherent in the isolation itself. Theoretically, isolation could be accomplished at any escape-proof area isolated from the law-abiding population.

Although the mechanism of isolation operates simply and directly, it does rest on a superstructure of complex assumptions, some of which are more easily demonstrable than others. It assumes that the population to be isolated includes a significant number of persons who, if permitted to remain in the general population, would commit crimes against that population. The actual number and seriousness of the crimes that would be committed by the population of those currently isolated is, of course, unknowable. Moreover, even if it could be determined how many crimes were ultimately prevented by isolating the prison population, that would still not tell us what percentage of the total serious crime is being prevented by isolating that population. For example, even if a large percentage of the prison population of a given jurisdiction would have committed several serious crimes had they been released rather than imprisoned, it may still turn out that these "prevented" crimes would have accounted for only a small percentage of the total serious crimes committed in that jurisdiction during the relevant period.

It is difficult to judge how "successful" isolation is as a mechanism of crime prevention without some controlled experiments which —for understandable reasons— society is reluctant to authorize.[1] Obviously, some crimes are being prevented; but that would be true if we were randomly to isolate any significant percentage of the population. For example, if all persons whose family name began with the letter A were isolated for a year, there would be some reduction in the frequency and seriousness of crime, since that population—like any randomly selected population —obviously includes some who would commit serious crimes. Moreover, the larger the group and the longer the period of isolation, the greater would be the number of serious crimes prevented.

It is obvious that the population of convicted criminals currently sentenced to prison includes a significantly larger percentage of future crime-committers than any randomly selected population. What is not obvious is that the population of those currently sentenced to prison included the largest feasible percentage of future crime-committers. Putting aside the question of "preventively" confining "dangerous" persons who have not "yet" been convicted of serious crimes,[2] there is still the critical question of whether the population of those currently selected for imprisonment *from among those convicted of serious crimes* includes the largest feasible percentage of future crime-committers.

There are a variety of considera-

tions that limit our ability and willingness to zero in on the population with the highest percentage of future serious crime-committers for confinement. Consider, for example, two defendants, one of whom has been convicted of pre-meditated murder but is unlikely to commit future crimes, the other of whom has been convicted of burglary but is extremely likely to commit future crimes. Surely the seriousness of the conviction would have to be given some weight in determining whether and for how long these defendants should be imprisoned. To the extent one focuses exclusively on the isolation aspect of imprisonment, the past conviction is not relevant except insofar as it confers "jurisdiction" on the system to imprison[3] and is predictive of future crime. Indeed, several forms of isolation that have been, and are currently, employed by our society ignore past culpability and purport to focus exclusively on prevention of future harms: mental hospitalization, quarantine, and confinement of material witnesses are illustrative of this genre of state intervention.

One of the reasons that so little attention has been paid to measuring the success of isolation as a means of reducing crime is that most isolated prisoners are thought to "deserve" their isolation, without regard to whether they would commit crimes during their period of isolation. Whatever crime reduction is achieved, the argument goes, is relatively costless, since the primary reason for the isolation is "punishment," and the crime reduction effect, if any, is merely incidental to the punishment.

1. See Alan M. Dershowitz, "Preventing Preventive Detention," *New York Review of Books*, 13 March 1969, p. 27.

2. See Alan M. Dershowitz, "Preventive Confinement: A Suggested Framework for Constitutional Analysis," *Texas Law Review* 51 (1973), pp. 1277, 1283–88.

3. See, Salielles, *The Individualization of Punishment*, p. 186.

Deliberate imposition of punishment

Pain, inconvenience, and loss of freedom, money, and status generally accompany isolation. But, at least in theory, that is not its purpose. When punishment is deliberately imposed on a convicted defendant, its purpose is precisely to produce a "hurt" that will serve to discourage future crimes by making it clear that conviction will be followed by the imposition of such a hurt. This mechanism of crime control is older than recorded history; and, like isolation, it can be used with some degree of effectiveness on animals, as well as humans.

It is completely clear and demonstrable—despite frequent protestations to the contrary—that some punishments deter some crimes by some people. Were it not for parking tickets, there would be more double-parking; and as the cost of using a parking lot approaches the cost of a parking ticket, there will generally be more instances of illegal parking. That is not to say, however, that ten-year sentences will deter more manslaughters than five-year sentences. It is almost impossible to demonstrate the precise effectiveness of a given punishment on a given crime.

It is certainly clear that the severity of the penalty alone does not serve as an adequate measure of its deterrent impact. Other probable operative factors include: the certainty and promptness of its infliction on all who commit the crime; the degree to which potential crime-committers are aware of the penalty, its certainty, and its promptness; and the relationship between the "benefits" of the crime and the "costs" of the punishment to potential crime-committers.

Of the three mechanisms of the criminal sentence discussed herein, only punishment—*qua* punishment—is designed to achieve purposes in addition to reducing the frequency and/or severity of criminal harms. Criminal punishment has always had important symbolic and other nonutilitarian goals. Immanuel Kant put it most extremely when he argued that even if no possible advantage can be found in punishing a given criminal, he must nonetheless be punished. To illustrate the categorical nature of this imperative, he constructed his famous example:

. . . Even if a Civil Society resolved to dissolve itself with the consent of all its members—as might be supposed in the case of a People inhabiting an island resolving to separate and scatter themselves through the whole world—the last Murderer lying in the prison ought to be executed before the resolution was carried out. This ought to be done in order that every one may realize the desert of his deeds, and that blood-guiltiness may not remain upon the people; for otherwise they might all be regarded as participators in the murder as a public violation of Justice.[4]

Most contemporary Western thinkers reject the Kantian notion of punishment as an end in itself. Most also reject the extreme opposite view—espoused by the Italian positivists during the last quarter of the seventeenth century[5]—that "punishment" and "justice" should have nothing whatever to do with

4. The Penal Law is a Categorical Imperative; and woe unto him who creeps through the serpent-windings of Utilitarianism to discover some advantage that may discharge him from the Justice of Punishment. . . ." Immanuel Kant, *Philosophy of Law*, trans. W. Hastie (Clifton, N.J.: Augustus M. Kelley, Pubs., 1887), pp. 195–196.

5. See, for example, Cesare Lombroso, *Criminal Man* (n.p., 1971).

criminal sentences; that considerations of "public safety" and "social defense" should be the sole determinants of whether and for how long a convicted criminal should be confined. The difficult question facing a concerned people in contemporary America is not whether considerations of justice and punishment should play any role in sentencing decisions, but rather what kind and how much of a role should these age-old factors be accorded in a rational sentencing system.

If considerations of justice and punishment were ignored, then sentencing determinations would rationally be made on the basis of a cost-benefit analysis of the desirability of a given sentence for each convicted defendant. Sentencing officials would consider such factors as: available space in prisons; likelihood that a given defendant, if permitted to remain free, would commit serious crimes; projected impact of the sentence on the future criminality of this defendant and others; and the balance of advantages and disadvantages to society of imprisoning the particular defendant.

To be sure, sentencing officials do consider such factors, especially in our current age of relatively indeterminate sentencing.[6] But they do not, for the most part, consider them in isolation from the gravity and culpability of the underlying crime. It is simply unjust to sentence a convicted burglar to a longer term of imprisonment than a convicted murderer, irrespective of the prag-

matic considerations that might incline a utilitarian sentencing official toward such a result. Some weight must be given to proportionality between the underlying crime and the punishment imposed. Where to strike the appropriate balance between "past-looking" considerations of proportionality and "future-looking" considerations of crime reductions is a question that has troubled, and will continue to trouble, concerned people for centuries.

Rehabilitation

Of the three mechanisms of criminal sentencing described herein, rehabilitation is the most complex and ambitious. While isolation works directly to build walls between the allegedly dangerous and endangered populations, and punishment works relatively directly to create disincentives to crime, rehabilitation seeks to alter the dynamics of the convicted criminal. It seeks to decrease his need to commit acquisitive crimes by increasing his ability to secure employment; it seeks to reduce his desire to commit certain crimes by redirecting his value system; it seeks to increase his control over antisocial needs and desires by restructuring his personality. To what extent these ambitious goals can be achieved in the context of a prison sentence is much disputed.

The nature of the issues raised by "rehabilitation" as a mechanism of crime reduction depends to some degree on the role ascribed to rehabilitation in sentencing theory and practice. If assumptions about a defendant's "need" for, and society's ability to effectuate, rehabilitation are used to justify a sentence of imprisonment or a decision not to release, then one kind of issue is presented: since the defendant pre-

6. See Alan M. Dershowitz, "Indeterminate Sentencing as a Mechanism of Preventive Confinement," in *Law in the United States of America in Sociological and Technological Revolution*, ed. John Hazard and Wenceslas Wagner (Brussels, Bel.: n.p., 1974).

sumably would have remained free, or would have served less time, but for rehabilitative assumptions, then the confiners have a significant burden of establishing the validity of these questionable assumptions. If, on the other hand, the confinement decisions—whether and for how long—are based exclusively on other factors, such as proportionality and dangerousness, and if rehabilitation is merely employed as an adjunct to the process of confinement, then different kinds of issues are raised. To the extent that rehabilitation is imposed on a prisoner without his consent or by employing threats concerning duration and/or conditions of confinement, serious questions are again raised—questions akin to those presented by using rehabilitation to justify confinement. To the extent, however, that rehabilitative facilities are simply made available to prisoners serving sentences justified on other "legitimate" grounds, the issues raised are somewhat less compelling.[7]

It cannot be said, in the United States today, that rehabilitative assumptions play no role in determining whether and for how long defendants have to be confined. The precise weight given to such assumptions varies enormously among judges.

Combining the mechanisms of the criminal sentence: the sentence of imprisonment

Although imprisonment has been used throughout the ages, it is only

during the last two centuries that it has emerged as the dominant form of criminal sentence. Despite recent shrill calls for its abolition, prison will remain the dominant form of criminal sentence for many generations to come. The reason for this is that the prison sentence conveniently combines, in one simple operation, the three primary mechanisms of crime reduction. All at once, it isolates, it punishes, and it provides—in theory at least—an appropriate setting for rehabilitation.

To illustrate the analytic confusion generated by this coalescence of functions, it may be useful to employ a heuristic device: postulate a system in which imprisonment may be used only to isolate. It may never be used to punish or to rehabilitate. Punishment must take the form of either a monetary deprivation, such as a fine or disqualification, or the immediate imposition of physical pain or dismemberment; rehabilitation may be compelled only on an "out-patient" basis and never in prison. Under this system, only those convicted defendants[8] who are demonstrably dangerous—who would commit serious crimes if not confined—could be imprisoned, and only so long as they remained dangerous.[9]

The number of convicted persons imprisoned under such a system

7. There still is room for questioning the goals sought to be achieved by rehabilitation, even voluntary rehabilitation. See "South Africa Plans Rehabilitation Centers for Blacks Violating Racial Laws," New York Times, 20 July 1975, p. 4, col. 1.

8. This formulation deliberately leaves out the entire issue of whether dangerous persons who have not been convicted may be "preventively" confined.

9. That such a system is not unthinkable is evidenced by the fact that it was proposed by early advocates of indeterminate sentencing: "No man be imprisoned unless it is clear that his freedom is dangerous to others, and that when once imprisoned, no man be free until the danger has ceased." C. Lewis, "The Indeterminate Sentence," Yale Law Journal 9 (1899), p. 17.

would almost certainly be lower than the number imprisoned today, though the amount of the reduction could not be calculated without defining the type and degree of dangerousness required for confinement. If, for example, only convicts with a very high likelihood (say 80 percent or more) of inflicting physical harm could be confined, then prison populations would be significantly reduced. If, on the other hand, all convicts with any significant likelihood (say 20 percent or more) of inflicting physical, psychological, or property harm could be confined, then the reduction would be far more modest.

The advantages of such a system are obvious. It would force sentencing decision-makers to think harder about the intended purpose or purposes of a criminal sentence: if the purpose were merely to punish —whether for deterrence or retaliation—then imprisonment could not be ordered; nor could it be ordered if the purpose were merely rehabilitative. Only if the judge concluded—on the basis of satisfactory evidence—that the convicted defendant met the standard of dangerousness could confinement be ordered.

In practice, of course, difficulties and confusion would persist. What if a sentencing judge concluded that a given defendant met the standard of dangerousness and also deserved serious punishment; could he then order physical and/or financial punishment over and above that inherent in the confinement; or could he conclude that the confinement satisfied both purposes? What if the judge concluded that a defendant met the standard of dangerousness and also needed rehabilitation; could he then com-pel rehabilitative efforts during the period of confinement; or would such efforts have to await the convict's release? Once sentencing functions are permitted to be combined—as they surely would be in real life—analytic confusions would be generated.

Another advantage of such a system would be that the expensive resource of imprisonment—expensive both in liberty and in material costs—would be reserved for those convicted defendants whose imprisonment produced the most immediate and demonstrable results.

The disadvantages of a system under which imprisonment would be used only against dangerous convicts are also obvious. It would deny society a major deterrent weapon against crimes committed by "nondangerous" and "nonrecidivating" offenders—white-collar, governmental, and political criminals— who are uniquely deterred by the threat of being imprisoned along with "common" criminals. It would also deprive us of the important education and symbolic message that certain crimes committed by the wealthy and powerful are as serious and as destructive of important values as are crimes of violence.

Another problem with the "model" system is that, by denying society the use of imprisonment as a punishment, it requires the creation and employment of other forms of punishment which may be deemed less "civilized." Whether whipping should indeed be considered less civilized than imprisonment is a debatable question, but the "cruel and unusual punishment" of our state and federal constitutions—such as currently interpreted—may impose serious constraints upon the employment of physical punishments other than imprisonment. In order to replace imprisonment, alternate punishments would have to be severe. Otherwise, nondangerous criminals convicted of serious crimes would be treated with undue leniency in comparison with dangerous criminals convicted of less serious crimes; and the seriousness of nonviolent, nonrecidivating crimes would be unduly diminished.

Consider, for example, the Watergate cases. It can be safely assumed that Messrs. Haldeman, Ehrlichman, and Mitchell are no longer dangerous (if for no other reason than that they are unlikely ever to be in positions where they could recidivate); nor are they in need of the kind of rehabilitation currently available in prison. But it would be immoral in the extreme for them to be spared imprisonment, since under current sentencing practices imprisonment is the most significant measure of how seriously society regards a crime. For these serious criminals to escape with only a fine would be to minimize their culpability. Were equivalently serious punishments, other than imprisonment, available, it might be fair—and effective—to impose such punishments on the likes of Haldeman et al. But in the absence of such alternative punishments, it would simply be unfair to fine them, since fines—especially at their current levels—are widely regarded as slaps on the wrist or criminal license fees. Yet, at one level, the absurdity of imprisoning these convicted criminals is patent: they simply do not need walls around them. It is only the symbolism of the imprisonment—and the accompanying stigma and deprivation—that justifies imposing this punishment.

The heuristic device employed above is simply intended to demonstrate both the confusion inherent in current sentencing practices—especially as it relates to the sentence of imprisonment—and the impossibility of simple solutions. Despite its criticisms, imprisonment is likely to continue as the dominant formal response to conviction for serious crime, not only for dangerous criminals, but also for nondangerous criminals convicted of serious crimes.

AN INSTITUTIONAL HISTORY OF CRIMINAL SENTENCING

The literature on the allocation of sentencing responsibility over the last two centuries is surprisingly spotty; authoritative historical accounts are lacking. Nevertheless, it is possible to describe, in general outline, several historical periods characterized by somewhat different sentencing systems.

The colonial period

During the colonial period, the primary mechanisms of sentencing were isolation and punishment. Colonial Americans used a variety of nonincarcerative techniques to protect their communities from the threat of crime. One effective method for both preventing and punishing offenses within a particular town was the enforcement of settlement laws: unwanted individuals were simply "warned out" (excluded) by the constable. Specific crimes were punished, according to the colonial criminal codes, with relatively specific penalties. Economic crimes were usually punished by a system of fines, in addition to orders of restitution. Offenders who simply could not pay were sentenced to forced labor, whipped, placed in the stocks, or perhaps branded with a symbol of their offense.

These same corporal penalties were also deemed appropriate for a wide variety of petty offenses. Colonial criminal codes sometimes gave a magistrate a measure of discretion concerning, for example, the duration of an offender's stay in the stocks or the pillory; but, in general, punishments were legislatively prescribed with some precision. Often, that prescription was death.

Incarceration as a punishment or as a "rehabilitative" technique was practically nonexistent. Although some communities had local jails, these institutions did not house convicted offenders serving criminal sentences, but were used to "hold" defendants who were awaiting trial or who had been unable to raise sufficient funds to pay court-imposed fines.

Thus, with few exceptions, criminal sentencing in the colonial period was primarily the responsibility of the legislatures. Statutes dictated relatively fixed sentences: the whip, the stocks, fines, death.

The pre-Civil War period

During the period following the Revolution (1790–1820), most states undertook rather complete revisions of their criminal codes, drastically limiting the operation of the death penalty. Similarly, flogging, whipping, branding, and other corporal punishments were abolished in many jurisdictions. Instead of violent physical penalties, the states developed a new—and, in many ways, quite innovative—form of criminal sentence: imprisonment, often with the most idealistic goals for the offender's benefit. When first proposed as a sentencing mechanism, imprisonment was seen as a "reformative" policy merely because it served as a substitute for capital punishment. However, incarceration rather quickly developed its own justifications as an intrinsically "reformative" institution; the penitentiary could, through carefully calibrated systems of discipline, labor, and religious exhortation, "cure" the offender of his criminogenic pathology.[10]

The underpinnings of this optimistic view of the potential for incarcerative reform of the individual offender were first set forth in 1787 at a meeting in the Philadelphia home of Benjamin Franklin. An influential group gathered there to hear Dr. Benjamin Rush deliver a paper concerning the establishment of a modern prison system. Rush urged a prison program which would (1) establish various inmates "classification" programs, for purposes of both inmate housing assignments and various "treatment" plans; (2) devise a self-supporting institutional system based on inmate piecework and agriculture; and (3) impose indeterminate periods of confinement on inmates who would then be released on the basis of evidence of their progress toward "rehabilitation." The Philadelphia Society for Alleviating the Miseries of Public Prisons organized to implement Dr. Rush's idealistic program. In 1790 the society succeeded in prevailing upon the state legislature to authorize the remodeling of Philadelphia's Walnut Street Jail in order to fashion a prison—a "cellhouse"—which could serve as a proving ground for the new theory of individualized reformative incarceration.

Over the next few decades—in

10. See David J. Rothman, *The Discovery of the Asylum* (Boston: Little, Brown & Co., 1971).

fact, until the 1870 Declaration of Principles—the practice and theory of criminal sentencing underwent very little substantive revision. The state codes were reworked and capital and corporal punishments gave way to sentences of imprisonment. Legislatures gave courts discretion—within ranges which were rather narrow compared to today's legislatively authorized punishments—to impose sentences which could then be altered only by the executive's pardoning power. Some nineteenth-century statutes set out punishments based on different gradations of offenses which had formerly had only one broad definition.

This period, encompassing almost the entire nineteenth century, can be fairly characterized as one in which the judiciary began to share responsibility with the legislature for criminal sentencing decisions. The legislature set the outside limits within which sentencing discretion could be exercised, but the statutes did not set out specific, detailed criteria to guide judicial sentencing. Once the sentence was imposed by the court upon the individual offender, it was "fixed": it did not include a minimum term and/or a maximum term subject to later decisions by other institutions or persons such as wardens. A sentence of two years meant 730 days (unless, of course, a pardon or some sort of commutation was forthcoming from the executive branch).[11]

In several senses, the sentencing process then in operation was in serious conflict with the developing rhetoric of reformative incarceration. First, despite hortatory calls to vocational and spiritual betterment, an inmate's response in the prison environment mattered very little in determining the duration of his sentence: whether he was a model prisoner or not, he was likely to serve the sentence pronounced by the court.

Second, the length of the sentence was almost invariably a function of how the court—and, in the first instance, the legislature—viewed the seriousness of the crime committed. Courts, as sentencing institutions, rarely concerned themselves with "correctional" goals other than simple punishment for a particular criminal act. If the conviction was for the felony of assault, a New York court, "on a consideration of all the circumstances of the case," could sentence an offender to imprisonment (in solitary confinement at hard labor, or to "simple" incarceration) for any term up to 14 years.[12] The relevant "circumstances," for a court in the nineteenth century, would include such considerations as the ferocity of the attack and the defendant's motive.

The post-Civil War period

An "enlightened" view of a sentencing system which would strongly reinforce rehabilitative rather than punitive purposes was given dramatic highlighting at the 1870 National Prison Congress. The delegates to that convention voted for a Declaration of Principles—a call for a variety of penal reforms, among them a radical alteration of the existing sentencing structure. The principles did pay lip service to the punitive rationale for sen-

11. Some states, such as New York, did, however, have "good time" laws which allowed an inmate to earn a set amount of sentence reduction through good behavior in prison.

12. See *Laws of New York* (1801), ch. 58.

tencing: "Crime is an intentional violation of duties imposed by law" and "[p]unishment is suffering . . . in expiation of the wrong done." Nevertheless, and more importantly, crime is:

a moral disease, of which punishment is the remedy. The efficiency of the remedy is a question of social therapeutics, a question of the fitness and the measure of the dose. . . . [P]unishment is directed not to the crime but the criminal. . . . The supreme aim of prison discipline is the reformation of criminals, not the infliction of vindictive suffering.[13]

With "reformation" as the uncompromised goal of the prison, it followed that release should be effected only upon its achievement. Thus, the Congress declared:

Peremptory sentences ought to be replaced by those of indeterminate duration—sentences limited only by satisfactory proof of reformation should be substituted for those measured by mere lapse of time.[14]

This principle had been most strongly urged by Zebulon Brockway, then the superintendent of the Elmira Reformatory in New York, who had addressed the delegates on "The Ideal of a True Prison System." His ideal was premised on the indeterminate sentence. According to Brockway, the "indeterminate sentence" and the "indeterminate reformatory" were the methods by which the reformation of the criminal and the protection of society could be most effectively achieved. Brockway rejected vengeance (pure punishment) as unjust and deter-

rence as a failure. He proposed, instead, a system of confinement under which:

all persons in a state, who are convicted of crimes or offenses before a competent court, shall be deemed wards of the state and shall be committed to the custody of the board of guardians, until, in their judgment, they may be returned to society with ordinary safety and in accord with their own highest welfare.[15]

The first explicit indeterminate sentence law for crimes in the United States was enacted at the behest of Zebulon Brockway in the state of Michigan in 1869. It was of extremely limited application, reserved solely for "common prostitutes" and providing for a three-year sentence which could be terminated at any time at the discretion of the inspectors of the Detroit House of Correction.[16] (The maximum punishment for prostitution had been far less than three years.) Eight years later, Brockway secured the enactment of the first indeterminate sentence law of more widespread penal application. His original proposal was for an indeterminate sentence law "without limitation," but "neither public sentiment in general nor the views of the legislators would accept this."[17]

Instead, New York enacted a modified provision which was typical of the statutes enacted in most states in the year following. The New York law limited the term of the sentence to "the maximum term pro-

13. *Transactions of the National Congress on Prisons and Reformatory Discipline,* (Albany, 1871), reprinted by the American Correctional Association, ed. Weed and Parsons (1970).

14. Ibid.

15. Zebulon R. Brockway, *Fifty Years of Prison Service* (London: Oxford University Press, 1912), p. 401.

16. Edward Lindsey, "Historical Sketch of the Indeterminate Sentence and Parole System," *Journal of Criminal Law and Police Science* 16 (1925), p. 9.

17. Ibid., p. 21.

vided by law for the crime for which the prisoner was convicted and sentenced," but left the determination of the exact amount of time to be served to the managers of the reformatory. By 1922, 37 states had similar forms of indeterminate sentencing and seven others had parole systems which were functionally similar to the indeterminate sentence.

As rehabilitation came to be recognized as the prison's primary function, a major reordering of sentencing power was implemented in order to allow the period of incarceration to fit the time required for the particular offender's reformation: hence, the proliferation of parole systems and the indeterminate sentence. Ironically, by the time indeterminate sentencing structures had been established, the belief in man's ability to better his moral faculties was giving way to various schools of physiological and ethnic determinism: the new criminologists suggested that some, if not most, criminal "types" could not overcome their propensities for deviant behavior. So, in a strange inversion, the indeterminate sentence could be used to prolong the incarceration of those offenders felt to be "incurable."

Medical terminology and methodology began to infuse the functioning of the prison system. Ideally, an inmate was carefully "classified" (diagnosed), and treatment plans were prescribed for his individual condition; prisoner's responses to his rehabilitative program was constantly monitored and evaluated; upon recovery from his criminal disease, he was paroled. Of course, some criminal syndromes had no known cures—and those inmates unable to demonstrate that the symptoms and cause of their disorders had somehow disappeared had to remain in prison to serve out their full sentences. The indeterminate sentence was essential to the working of this system. The large amount of discretionary power vested in correctional and parole personnel was necessary in order to give the clinicians (psychiatrists and psychologists, educators, social workers, employment counselors, and others) the needed leeway to tailor their efforts to each individual prisoner.

Current practices

The indeterminate sentence, which was once viewed as a special form of sentencing, has now emerged as the dominant sentencing structure in the United States. Nor is the indeterminate sentence a unitary concept of precise definition; it is very much a matter of degree. A sentence is more or less indeterminate to the extent that the amount of time actually to be served is decided not by the judge at the time sentence is imposed, but rather by an administrative board while the sentence is being served. Thus, a judicially imposed sentence of one day to life, the actual duration to be determined by the parole board after service of sentence has commenced, is entirely indeterminate; a judicially imposed sentence of life imprisonment with no possibility of parole (or other discretionary reduction) is entirely determinate. Between these terminal points of the continuum lies a wide range of more or less indeterminate sentences. A judicially imposed sentence of not less than five nor more than 10 years is partially indeterminate: although its maximum and minimum are fixed at the time of sentencing, the actual time to be served within those limits will be decided subsequently by some administrative authority. Another form of indeterminate sentence is the judicially imposed term of imprisonment for what appears to be a fixed period, say 10 years, but subject to the normal rules of parole, under which an administrative board has discretion to authorize release after a percentage of the "sentence" prescribed by statute has been served. Thus, all sentences subject to parole —the vast majority of prison sentences imposed in the United States today—are indeterminate to some degree.[18]

MODELS OF CRIMINAL SENTENCING

It is possible to extract from this history several possible models of prison sentencing. Among the "pure" models are the following:

1. *The legislatively fixed model*— The legislature determines that conviction for a given crime warrants a given term of imprisonment (for example, a first offender convicted of armed robbery must be sentenced to five years imprisonment). There is no judicial or administrative discretion under this model; the legislature has authorized but one sentence. In practice, of course, there

would still be discretion at various points in the process: the police and/or prosecutor generally have wide discretion to determine the charge (whether the taking was a robbery or some lesser form of larceny; whether the weapon constituted an "arm"); the executive generally has discretion to commute or pardon. In theory, however, the legislatively fixed sentence model is the least discretionary, in the sense that the sentence is determined in advance of the crime and without knowing who the criminal is.[19]

2. *The judicially fixed sentence model*—The legislature determines the general range of imprisonment for a given crime (for example, a first offender convicted of armed robbery shall be sentenced to no less than one and no more than 10 years imprisonment). The sentencing judge must fix a determinate sentence within that range ("I sentence the defendant to five years imprisonment"). Once this sentence is fixed, it cannot be increased or reduced by any parole board or adult authority; the defendant must serve five years.[20] Under this model, discretion is vested in the sentencing judge (how much depends on the range of imprisonment authorized by the legislature). On the day he is sentenced, however, the defendant knows precisely how long he will

---

18. The concept of indeterminacy is not applicable exclusively to punitive criminal sentences. Orders of involuntary confinement that do not bear punitive labels—such as commitment of the insane, addicts, juvenile delinquents, defective delinquents, and sexual psychopaths—are typically indeterminate; indeed, they tend to be even more indeterminate than criminal sentences. Commitments of the mentally ill, sexual psychopaths, and defective delinquents are wholly indeterminate as a general rule. "Nonpunitive" confinements of juveniles and addicts usually have upper time limits, but give administrative boards discretion to determine the actual duration of the confinement within these limits.

19. Under this model, the legislature does, of course, have enormous discretion to determine which crimes deserve what punishments. And since it is widely known what kinds of persons commit what kinds of crimes, various kinds of prejudice —economic, social, racial, and others—can operate.

20. This model does not consider good time provisions or other relatively automatic reductions, nor does it consider commutation or pardon.

serve; there is no discretion vested in the parole board or prison authorities.

3. *The administratively fixed sentence model*—The legislature nominally sets an extremely wide permissible range of imprisonment for a given crime (for example, a first offender armed robber shall be sentenced to a term of one day to life). The sentencing judge must— or may—impose the legislatively determined sentence ("You are sentenced to one day to life"). The actual duration of the sentence is decided by an administrative agency (for example, after five years of imprisonment, the adult authority decides that the prisoner is "ready" for release). Under this model, vast discretion is vested in the administrative agency and, in practice, in the prison authorities. And the defendant, on the day he is sentenced, does not know—though he probably can make an educated guess based on past practices—how long he will have to serve.

In addition to the "pure" models described above, there are obviously a number of mixed systems. For example, the most common American sentencing system operates as follows: the legislature determines the general range of sentences for a particular crime (a first offender armed robber may be imprisoned from three to 10 years). The judge may select any sentence within that range ("I sentence you to five years"). The parole board may then release him after a specific percentage of his sentence (say one-third) has been served.

An important deviation from these pure models is introduced by the phenomenon of prosecutorial plea bargaining, under which the sentence is determined—or at least critically affected—by negotiations between the prosecutor and the defense attorney. Such negotiations are possible under any of the pure systems, though they may take a different form depending on the model. For example, where the sentence is legislatively fixed, the object of the negotiations will probably be to reduce the charge from a more to a less serious one (thus directly reducing the legislatively determined sentence). Where the sentence is judicially determined, the object will probably be to reduce the sentence imposed by the judge. Where the sentence is administratively determined, the object will probably be to have the prosecutor put a good word in with the parole board. There can be no practical understanding of any sentencing system without an appreciation of the role that plea bargaining plays in it.

CURRENT TRENDS AND FUTURE PROSPECTS

The era of the indeterminate sentence—of the administrative model of sentencing—is quickly drawing to a close. Reaction is beginning to set in. In the past several years, several influential books were published criticizing the indeterminate sentence. The first, a report prepared for the American Friends Service Committee under the guidance of Professor Caleb Foote of Berkeley, recommended the abolition of indeterminate sentencing and the adoption of a system which proportions the punishment to the act committed (though it advocated the retention of "good time" reductions of sentence with proper safeguards).[21]

Jessica Mitford's more popular work, *Kind and Usual Punishment*,

21. A Committee Report prepared for the American Friends' Service Committee, *Struggle for Justice* (New York: Hill & Wang, 1971).

focuses particularly on indeterminate sentencing as it is practiced in California. After describing its humane-sounding qualities, she poses and attempts to answer the following questions:

Why, then, is [the indeterminate sentence] denounced by the supposed beneficiaries — prisoners and parolees — from coast to coast, its abolition one of the focal demands of the current prison rebellion? And why is it coming under increasing attacks from those criminologists, sociologists, lawyers, legislators who have taken the trouble to look closely at the prison scene and have informed themselves at first hand about the day-to-day realities of prison life?[22]

Mitford finds many reasons for this strident opposition, including "much longer sentences for most prisoners than would normally be imposed by judges,"[23] and total arbitrariness of the bureaucracy that rules every aspect of their existence"[24]—notably the actual duration of their confinement.

The most scholarly and thoughtful of these recent works is Judge Marvin Frankel's *Criminal Sentences: Law without Order*, which is a general critique of sentencing, especially in the federal courts. Finding that the "movement toward indeterminacy in sentencing is broad and powerful,"[25] Frankel articulates a "minority position" that "indeterminate sentencing, as thus far employed and justified, has produced more cruelty and injustice than the benefits its supporters envisage."[26] Doubting that rehabilitation, an important justification of indeterminancy, is possible in most cases, Judge Frankel opts for a "presumption . . . in favor of a definite sentence, known and justified on the day of sentencing (and probably much shorter than our sentences tend to run)." There should be:

a burden of justifying an indeterminate sentence in any particular case—a burden to be satisfied by concrete reasons and a concrete program for the defendant involved. The justification . . . would consist of identified needs and resources for effective rehabilitation. . . .[27]

In the United States, judicial doubts about the substantive wisdom of particular law enforcement techniques often are reflected initially by the imposition of procedural barriers. Courts feel more comfortable placing procedural, rather than substantive, limitations on legislatively authorized programs. As Justice Harlan once said: While courts "must give the widest deference to legislative judgments" concerning the substantive criteria for confinement, the judiciary has "been understood to possess particular competence" in assessing the "necessity and wisdom of procedural guarantees." It is not surprising, therefore, that the initial judicial limitations on indeterminate sentencing have taken the form of procedural safeguards. Several important decisions, dealing with a

22. Jessica Mitford, *Kind and Usual Punishment* (New York: Alfred A. Knopf, 1973), p. 81.

23. Ibid., p. 83.

24. Ibid., p. 87.

25. "A prestigious and influential scholarly product, the Model Penal Code, provides for broadly indeterminate sentences. A number of state legislatures, including several influenced by the Model Penal Code, have opted for indeterminancy in recent revisions of their laws." Marvin E. Frankel, *Criminal Sentences: Law without Order* (New York: Hill & Wang, 1973), p. 88.

26. Ibid. Judge Frankel acknowledges the impact of prisoners' complaints on resisting the trend toward indeterminancy: "Until the last couple of years, the trend toward indeterminant sentencing has seemed irresistible. Just recently, from the prisons and elsewhere, some voices of dissent have been heard."

27. Ibid., p. 98.

different point in the indeterminate sentence process, have imposed procedural barriers to the easy imposition of indeterminate sentences.[28] Courts have also begun to impose some substantive limitations on the indeterminate sentence.[29]

It is likely that a process of retrenchment is upon us: courts and legislatures will continue to reflect the growing academic and inmate criticism of indeterminate sentencing. What we may well witness over the next several decades is a return to an earlier stage in the inevitable cycle. Legislatures will assume greater responsibility for sentencing decisions. The role of the parole board will probably be significantly curtailed. The sentencing judge and prosecutor may also have limits imposed on their discretion. Then, before long, a reaction may again set in: complaints will be voiced against too much conformity and rigidity; a need for flexibility and discretion will be noted. And the cycle will turn once again.

28. See, for example, *Specht* v. *Patterson*, 386 U.S. 605 (1967); *Monks* v. *New Jersey*, 58 N.J. 233, 277 A, 2d. 193 (1971); *Morrissey* v. *Brewer*, 408 U.S. 471 (1972).

29. See, for example, *In re Lynch*, 8 Cal. 3rd 410, 503 P. 2d 921 (1972); Compare, *People* v. *Wingo*, 43 U. S. L. W. 2493 (1975).

No Excuse for Crime

By ERNEST VAN DEN HAAG

ABSTRACT: Criminologists often regard offenders as victims of conditions beyond their control or as "political prisoners," punished for "the inevitable consequences" of their socioeconomic status (S. I. Shuman). However, offenders do not become "political prisoners" unless their offenses were addressed to the sociopolitical system. Nor do crimes "inevitably" arise from poverty anymore than corruption inevitably arises from power. Therefore, neither poverty nor power are legal excuses. Criminal law always is meant to perpetuate the existing order, although Richard Quinney objects because the burden of legal restraint falls most heavily on the disadvantaged who are most tempted to disrupt the legal order. Yet the criminal law is meant to restrain those tempted to violate it. Quinney's view that socialism will solve "the crime problem" appears bereft of evidence. The comparative crime rates of blacks and whites are analyzed and the punitive and social reform approaches compared. They are found to be not alternative but cumulative.

Professor van den Haag is Adjunct Professor of Social Philosophy at New York University and Lecturer in Psychology and Sociology at the New School for Social Research. This essay is based upon a chapter from his forthcoming book, Punishing Criminals *concerning a very old and painful position.*

"Environment is the root of all evil—and nothing else! A favourite phrase. And the direct consequence of it is that if society is organized on normal lines, all crimes will vanish at once, for there will be nothing to protest against, and all men will become, righteous in the twinkling of an eye."[1]

EXCEPT in narrowly specifiable conditions, the law does not see offenders as victims of conditions beyond their control. But criminologists often do.[2] Paul Bator describes views shared by many:

. . . that the criminal law's notion of just condemnation is a cruel hypocrisy visited by a smug society on the psychologically and economically crippled; that its premise of a morally autonomous will with at least some measure of choice whether to comply with the values expressed in a penal code is unscientific and outmoded; that its reliance on punishment as an educational and deterrent agent is misplaced, particularly in the case of the very members of society most likely to engage in criminal conduct; and that its failure to provide for individualized and humane reha-

1. Fedor Dostoevski, *Crime and Punishment* (1866). Dostoevski's novel is directed against this notion, which he puts in the mouth of one of Raskolnikov's friends. The notion itself is still around. Thus, Alex Thio in *The American Sociologist*, vol. 9, no. 1 (February 1974), p. 48: ". . . laws benefit the powerful, for it is much easier and less costly for them to punish the powerless criminals than to eradicate the cause of the crimes by changing the basic structure of society . . . laws, by virtue of enabling the powerful to perpetuate the social-structural causes of murder, rape, arson and burglary, ensure the perpetuation of those crimes."

2. To legally excuse an offense, it must be shown that external conditions were such that a reasonable person, acting with normal diligence could not have avoided his act—unless it is shown that the offender lacked the mental competence to know what he was doing or that what he was doing was wrong.

bilitation of offenders is inhuman and wasteful.[3]

GHETTOES AND "POLITICAL PRISONERS"

Most criminologists are not quite so explicit. But some are. Consider two. S. I. Shuman, Professor of Law and Psychiatry at Wayne State University goes farther than Bator. Shuman maintains that "if the ghetto victim does what for many such persons is inevitable and is then incarcerated . . . he is in a real sense a political prisoner," because he is punished for "the inevitable consequences of a certain socio-political status."[4] If these consequences were indeed "inevitable," the punishment would be unjust, as Professor Shuman argues. Why, however, would the (unjustly) punished offender become a "political prisoner," as Professor Shuman also claims?

All punishments are imposed, or sanctioned, by the political order which the law articulates. Are all convicts, then, political prisoners? or all those unjustly punished? or all convicts who come from disadvantaged groups? If such a definition were adopted, every convict, all disadvantaged convicts, or everyone unjustly punished would be a political prisoner. "Political prisoner" would become a synonym for "convicted," for "disadvantaged," or for "unjustly punished."

If we want to distinguish between political and other prisoners, a "political prisoner" must be defined as someone imprisoned because he

3. Paul Bator, "Finality in Criminal Law and Federal *Habeas Corpus* for State Prisoners," *Harvard Law Review* 76 (1963).

4. S. I. Shuman, *Wayne Law Review*, March 1973, pp. 853–4. Professor Shuman's argument is more intelligent than most, but otherwise prototypical.

tried to change the political system. The aim of his crime determines whether or not the criminal is political; the offender who intended personal enrichment cannot become a political criminal independently of his actual intent, simply because a penalty is imposed for "the inevitable consequences of a sociopolitical status," which led him to enrich himself illegally. If any unlawful attempt to improve one's personal situation within the existing order "because of the inevitable consequences of a certain socio-political status" is a political crime, then all crimes committed by severely deprived persons are political. But is the ghetto dweller who becomes a pimp, heroin dealer, or mugger a political criminal just as the one who becomes a violent revolutionary? Ordinarily, an offender who did not address the political order is not regarded as a political criminal, whether he is a victim of politics or not, whereas an offender whose crime did address the political order is a political criminal, even if he is not a victim of politics. This usage permits a meaningful distinction, which Professor Shuman obliterates by making "political" refer to presumptive causes rather than to overt intentions.

Inevitable Crimes?

Professor Shuman goes on to claim that

arguing that inevitability is too strong a connection between crime and poverty or ghetto existence because not all such persons commit crimes, is rather like arguing that epilepsy or heart attack ought not to excuse because not all epileptics or persons with weak hearts are involved in a chain of events which results in injury.

He adds that "those poverty or ghetto victims who do not commit crimes are extraordinary."

Surely "extraordinary" is wrong here as a statistical generalization: most poor people do not commit crimes;[5] those who do are extraordinary, not those who don't. Perhaps Professor Shuman means that it takes more resistance within than it does outside the "ghetto" not to commit crimes, which is quite likely. But "inevitability"? Here, the analogy with epilepsy or heart diseases is unpersuasive. Such conditions serve as legal excuses only because they produce seizures beyond the control of the person affected. These seizures are legal excuses only when they are the cause of the crime or injury or of the failure to control it. Otherwise a "weak heart" or an epileptic condition is not an excuse. Thus, poverty could not be an excuse, unless it can be shown to produce seizures beyond their control which cause the poor to commit crimes.

Poverty does not produce such seizures. Nor would poverty deprive the victim, if he were to experience a seizure (of criminality?), of control in the way an epileptic seizure does the epileptic. Poverty affects motivation and increases temptation, as does sexual frustration or, sometimes, marriage—hardly an uncontrollable seizure. To have little or no money makes it tempting to steal; the poverty-stricken person is more tempted than the rich. But a poor person is not shorn of his ability to control temptation. Indeed it is to

5. Perhaps they do—if questionnaires rather than conviction records are followed. (The reliability of questionnaire data is as questionable as that of police records.) It seems likely that about three times as many crimes are committed as are recorded. If so, the statement "most poor people do not commit crimes" remains correct.

him that the legal threat is addressed. He is able to respond to it unless he suffers from a specific individual defect or disease which makes him incompetent.

There is a generous and strong moral bias in Shuman's arguments, although he does not seem fully aware of it. The bias was already noted by Friedrich Nietzche when he wrote in *Beyond Good and Evil*: "[writers] are in the habit of taking the side of criminals." Stated in undisguised moral terms, the argument goes: the poor are entitled to rob or rape because of the injustice they suffer—poverty. The moral nature of the argument is concealed by an erroneous factual claim: poor offenders can't help committing crimes and, therefore, should not be held responsible.

The nonfactual, moral nature or bias of the argument is easily revealed if "power" is substituted for "poverty." Suppose one were to credit fully Lord Acton's famous saying: "Power tends to corrupt and absolute power corrupts absolutely." Those who hold power, then, could be held responsible for criminal acts only to some degree, since they live in conditions which tend to corrupt them. Those who hold "absolute power" can not be held responsible for criminal acts at all. They would be "power victims," as ghetto dwellers are "ghetto victims." Their rapes would be political acts, and they would be political prisoners when punished for them. Power would become a legal excuse. "Absolute power" would be an absolute excuse.

This does not appear to be what Shuman advocates. Yet he urges that poverty (or slums) should be an excuse since—like power—it leads to crime. Shuman wants to excuse the poor and not the wealthy and

powerful, not because, as he suggests, poverty is causally more related to crime than wealth; rather, he sees deprivation as morally unjust and painful, and power and wealth as morally undeserved and pleasant, wherefore he wants to excuse the poor and punish the wealthy.[6] He is morally prejudiced against those corrupted by undeserved wealth—whom he gives no sign of excusing—and in favor of those corrupted by unjust deprivation.

The generosity of his prejudice leads Shuman to overlook a logical error in his argument. In some sense, everybody is what he is, and does what he does, as a result of his genetic inheritance and the influence of his environment—poverty or wealth or power—that interacted with his genetic inheritance and produced him and his conduct. This is no more the case for the poor than for the rich, for criminals than for noncriminals. However, there is no reason to believe that, except in individual cases (which require specific demonstration), genetics, or the environment, so compel actions that the actor must be excused because he could not be expected to control them.

Unless none of us is responsible for what he does, it would have to be shown why criminals, or why poor criminals, are less able to control their conduct and therefore

6. What are the psychological reasons (the scientific or causal as distinguished from the moral ones they rationalize) for excusing the slum-dwelling robber (who wishes to support his habit, or girl friend) and not the embezzler (who wishes to take his girl friend to Acapulco)? Wherein is the embezzler's ambition, greed, wish for prestige, sexual desire less strong, less excusable, or less predetermined by his character and experience than the slum dweller's?

less responsible than others. This cannot be shown by saying that they are a product of the conditions they live in. We all are. Nor can non-responsibility be claimed by showing that their living conditions are more criminogenic than others. Greater temptation does not excuse from responsibility or make punishment unjust. The law, in attempting to mete out equal punishment, does not assume equal temptation.

When it is used to excuse crime in the way advocated by Shuman, moral indignation about squalor, however well justified, may have the paradoxical effect of contributing to high crime rates. Crime becomes less odious if moral disapproval of poverty, slums, or ghettoes becomes intense, pervasive, and exculpatory enough to suggest to the "underprivileged" that they are entitled to take revenge through crime and, when they do, to be spared punishment. Those inclined to offenses will perceive the reduced certainty and severity of punishment in such a moral climate as a failure of society to defend its social order. Offenders, not unreasonably, will attribute this failure to doubts about the justification of the social order and to guilt feelings about those deprived by it, who are believed to be "driven to crime" and, when caught, to be unjustly punished "political prisoners."

In my opinion, Shuman is wrong, but Richard Quinney[7] is embarassing. After explaining "critical philosophy" (the Frankfurt pseudonym of Marxism) at remarkable length by means of pronouncements such as, "a critical philosophy is radically critical," and "Marx held

that only under the appropriate conditions can human possibilities be realized," Quinney concludes that "criminal law is an instrument . . . to maintain and perpetuate the existing social and economic order," as though revealing something interesting, or linked to the capitalist order. Yet the criminal law always defends the existing order and those who hold power in it by penalizing those who violate it; and the legal order never can do less than articulate the "social and economic order," capitalist or socialist. How could it be otherwise? If, within a given social order, some people lawfully are richer or more powerful than others, the criminal law must *inter alia* defend their advantages.

Further, in any social order those who are not affluent and powerful are more tempted to rebel, or to take what is not theirs, than those who are—who need not take what they already have. Hence, the burden of the law falls most heavily on the least privileged: the threats and punishments of the criminal law are meant to discourage those who are tempted to violate it, not those who are not. Marxists are as right in saying that the criminal law is addressed disproportionately to the poor as Anatole France was in his witticism: "the law in its majestic equality forbids rich and poor alike . . . to steal bread." However, that discovery is about as interesting as the disclosure that the prohibition law was meant to restrain drinkers rather than the teetotalers who imposed it. The criminal law would be redundant if it did not address those tempted—by taste or social position—to break it.

Quinney also asserts that with socialism "law as we know it" will disappear, for "the crime problem"

7. Richard Quinney, *Critique of Legal Order: Crime Control in a Capitalist Society* (Boston: Little Brown & Co., 1974).

will be solved "once society has removed all possibility of hatred" (August Bebel). Trotsky held similar views: under socialism

man will be incomparably stronger, more intelligent, more subtle. His body will be more harmonious, his movements more rhythmical, his voice more musical; his style of life will acquire a dynamic beauty. The average type of man will rise to the level of an Aristotle, Goethe, Marx. From this mountain crest, the new peaks will rise.[8]

Bebel and Trotsky had no experience of socialism when they wrote. Richard Quinney must be congratulated for managing to preserve or regain his innocence, untainted by the available theoretical and practical experience. Bereft of Quinney's innocence, I do not foresee a society —socialist or otherwise—in which men will not quarrel and envy each other, wherefore the criminal law will have to restrain them and protect the social order against those who are, or feel, disadvantaged by it. At present the societies which claim to be socialist seem to use legal punishments more than others.[9] I see no reason for maintaining that future socialist societies—whatever form of socialism they adopt—will need criminal law any less.

BLACK CRIME RATES

Crime among blacks occurs at a rate about 10 times higher than among whites, when blacks and whites are compared as groups. Most crimes are intraracial. The victims of violent crimes are almost as often black as the criminals. (The victims of property crimes committed by blacks and of assaultive crimes concerned with property, such as robbery, are more often white.) Some figures may give an idea of the gross difference. In 1970 blacks in the United States accounted for about 60 percent of all arrests for murder and, according to the FBI's figures, for 65 percent of the arrests for robbery.[10] (Blacks constitute 12 percent of the population.) The difference between black and white crime rates may well be explained by different environments. What has been said in the preceeding section should prevent confusion of such an explanation with a justification for individual offenders.

However, simple comparisons of black and white crime rates are misleading. They ignore the fact that a greater proportion of blacks are young and poor, and the young and poor of any race display the highest crime rates. In other words, the age- and income-related variances must not be attributed to race. The age-specific crime rates of blacks are only slightly higher than those of whites on the same socioeconomic level.[11] The remaining difference cannot be attributed to racially discriminating law enforce-

10. F. B. Graham, "Black Crime: The Lawless Image," *Harper's Magazine*, September 1970, p. 64.

11. See M. A. Forslund, "A Comparison of Negro and White Crime Rates," *Journal of Criminal Law, Criminology and Police Science* 61 (June 1970); E. R. Moses, "Negro and White Crime Rates," in M. E. Wolfgang et al., eds., *The Sociology of Crime and Delinquency* (New York: John Wiley & Sons, 1970); R. M. Stephenson and F. R. Scarpitti, "Negro-White Differentials in Delinquency," *Journal of Research in Crime and Delinquency* 5 (July 1968).

8. Leon Trotsky, *Literature and Revolution*, (New York: Russell & Russell, 1957).

9. Solzhenitsyn's *Gulag Archipelago* is only the latest illustration of this well-known phenomenon.

ment.[12] What discrimination there is may lead in the opposite direction. Crime is less often reported in black communities, and police are less inclined to arrest blacks for crimes against blacks then they are to arrest whites for crimes against whites.

The difference in crime rates should not come as a surprise. Blacks have been oppressed for a long time. Many are recent migrants from rural to urban areas who have the usual difficulties of acculturation faced by most immigrants. Their access to the labor market was, and still is, limited because of lack of training due to past discrimination. All this has some effect on the legitimate opportunities available to them and, as importantly perhaps, on the ability of individuals to utilize what opportunities there are.

Thus, we should expect a somewhat higher crime rate for blacks, and no explanation in *current* economic terms is needed. Such an explanation would not be supported by the available data. Between 1960 and 1970, the medium income of white families went up 69 percent; that of black families doubled. Whereas only 3 percent of black families earned more than $10,000 a year in 1951, 13 percent did so in 1971.[13] Thus disparity between the income (and the social status) of blacks and whites, though it remains considerable, has been diminished even faster than the difference between white poor and nonpoor. The difference between black and white crime rates has not decreased. Clearly the crude economic explanation—poverty—won't do. Possibly resentment of the remaining disparities has not decreased as these disparities have become fewer and less considerable. Resentment, then, could have prevented the black crime rates from falling as blacks become less deprived and the black-white difference in economic and social status become smaller.[14]

Continuing cultural differences, created by historical circumstances, probably contribute to the difference in crime rates of blacks and whites as well; but we know too little as yet to usefully describe, let alone explain, these cultural differences. Phrases such as "the culture of violence" merely describe what is yet to be understood.[15] Surely crime is largely produced by

12. See D. J. Black and A. J. Reiss, Jr., "Police Control of Juveniles," *American Sociological Review* 35 (January 1970); E. Green, "Race, Social Status and Criminal Arrest," *American Sociological Review* 35 (June 1970).

13. The figures used are in dollars of constant purchasing power, that is, they exclude the effects of inflation; they are taken from Ben J. Wattenberg and Richard M. Scammon, "Black Progress and Liberal Rhetoric," *Commentary*, April 1973, p. 35.

14. For teenagers, the economic picture is darker. And teenagers account for much crime. One-third of black teenagers were unemployed in 1971, against 15 percent of white teenagers. The high unemployment rate probably contributed to high crime rates in both cases, and the difference in the unemployment rate of white and black teenagers contributed to the difference in crime rates. The high teenage unemployment rates may be caused at least in part by minimum wage legislation, which requires that teenagers be paid a minimum, which often exceeds what their production is worth to employers. (The minimum wage rate for most other workers rarely is above what they are worth to employers.)

15. Ghettoization does not explain much, for, except for black ghettoes, the incidence of crime in ghettoes (ethnically segregated slums) is low. In Chinese or Jewish ghettoes there was little crime. On the other hand, variances in crime rates everywhere are associated with ethnic differences.

the life styles generated by the subcultures characteristic of those who commit it. But does this tell us more than that crime is produced by a crime-producing subculture?

ENVIRONMENT AND PERSONALITY

What are we to conclude? Many people, black and white, living under the conditions ordinarily associated with high crime rates—such as poverty or inequality—do not commit crimes, while many people not living under these conditions do. It follows that these conditions are neither necessary nor sufficient to cause crime. Crime rates have risen as poverty and inequality have declined. It follows that high crime rates need not depend on more poverty or inequality and are not remedied by less. More resentment may increase crime rates even when there is less poverty—but resentment is hard to measure and may increase with improving conditions, as was pointed out by Alexis de Tocqueville.[16]

Since the incidence of crime among the poor is higher than among the nonpoor, it is quite likely that when combined with other ingredients—not always easily discerned—poverty and inequality do produce high crime rates, probably by affecting motivations and temptations. Thus, poverty may be an important element—though neither indispensable nor sufficient by itself—in

16. Democracy in America. For example:

"It is natural that the love of equality should constantly increase together with equality itself, and that it should grow by what it feeds on. . . ."

". . . The mere fact that certain abuses have been remedied draws attention to the others and they now appear more galling; people may suffer less, but their sensibility is exacerbated. . . ."

the combination that produces high crime rates and explains the variance among groups. But recognition of the importance of poverty as a criminogenic condition should not lead us to neglect individual differences. Enrico Ferri, unlike some of his latter-day followers, did not neglect them. He wrote:

If you regard the general condition of misery as the sole source of criminality, then you cannot get around the difficulty that out of the one thousand individuals living in misery from the day of their birth to that of their death, only one hundred or two hundred become criminals. . . . If poverty were the sole determining cause, one thousand out of one thousand poor ought to become criminals. If only two hundred become criminals, while one hundred commit suicide, one hundred end as maniacs, the other six hundred remain honest in their social condition, then poverty alone is not sufficient to explain criminality.[17]

THE LEGAL AND THE SOCIAL APPROACH

Surely it is futile to contrast environmental (social) with individual (psychological) causation, as though they were mutually exclusive alternatives. Instead, we might ask in quantitative terms:

1. How much of the variance in crime rates—among social groups, or between two time periods—is controlled by specific differences in social conditions?

2. Which of these (a) can be changed; (b) at what cost, monetary or otherwise?

3. At what cost can we then reduce the crime rate in general, or

17. Enrico Ferri, The Positive School of Criminology, ed. Stanley E. Grupp (Pittsburgh: University of Pittsburgh Press, 1968), p. 60.

the variance, by changing social conditions? What specific social change is likely to bring about what specific change in crime rates and in variances?

To illustrate: if we assume that X percent of the variance between black and white crime rates is explained by the lower employment rates of black males, then we might be able to predict that a rise of X percent in the employment rate of black males would lead to a decline of X percent in the crime rate or in the variance. There are all kinds of pitfalls in such a simplified model. Employment rates, for instance, are determined by a variety of factors. Richard Cloward came to grief by assuming that employment rates are determined exclusively by employment opportunities.[18]

Still, in the apt words of Enrico Ferri: "Certain discreet shelters arranged in convenient places contribute more to the cleanliness of cities than fines or arrests."[19] Ferri

18. See Daniel Patrick Moynihan's *Maximum Feasible Misunderstanding* (New York: The Free Press, 1969) for an analysis of these pitfalls.

19. Enrico Ferri, *Criminal Sociology* (New York: Agathon Press, Inc., 1917), p. 24.

meant public urinals. But the principle applies to any change in the social or physical environment, and the questions it poses are always: (1) What is the ratio of the cost of the change in social conditions to the benefit (the reduction in crime rates) compared to the ratio of a change in other variables (for example, expenditures on police; higher or more regular punishments) to the benefit (the reduction in crime rates)? (2) Given these ratios, which change is preferable in view of other merits or demerits?

Parking violations can be reduced by better policing, higher fines, and more public garages. Very high fines would help, but may not be tolerable. More public garages will help, but may be too costly. Without some punishment for violation, there would be no incentive to use public garages, and without some legitimate opportunity, it is likely that the law will be violated unless punishments are extremely severe and certain. The alternatives—"improve social conditions" and "increase punishment"—are not mutually exclusive. They are cumulative. The question is, which combination promises the greatest benefits at the least cost.

ANNALS, AAPSS, **423**, Jan. 1976

Controlling "Dangerous" People

By JOHN MONAHAN AND GILBERT GEIS

ABSTRACT: The label "dangerous" often has been applied in America to persons whose major threat lay in the fact that they offended the moral or esthetic sensibilities of those holding power. In the America of the Revolutionary period, there was comparatively little violent crime, but by today's standards, punishments tended to be harsh and/or humiliating. The mentally aberrant were seen as especially dangerous, since their condition was traced to a devilish infestation, and they were handled with great brutality. Blacks, too, often restive under slavery, were regarded as dangerous persons. Today, similar kinds of ascriptions as "dangerous" are applied to criminals, mental patients, and minorities—with similarly unconvincing evidence to justify the treatment such persons often receive. Danger ought to be determined on a social basis, not by theological or medical dictation, and the category ought to include all (but only) forms of human and group action which represent real threats.

John Monahan is a psychologist and Assistant Professor in the Program in Social Ecology at the University of California, Irvine. He is editor of two 1975 books, Community Mental Health and the Criminal Justice System *and (with Duncan Chappell)* Violence and Criminal Justice.

Gilbert Geis, a sociologist, is Professor in the same program. He is the author or editor of six books, including Man, Crime, and Society *with Herbert A. Bloch (2nd. ed., 1970),* White-Collar Criminal *(1968), and* Public Compensation to Victims of Crime *with Herbert Edelhertz (1974).*

IT IS uncommonly difficult to try to place oneself inside the minds of persons living 10 generations ago in what had just become the United States of America and to attempt to make sense of things which they regarded as "dangerous." It is clear, from archival records, what persons then alive said and did about things such as crime, sexual "irregularities," race relations, and mental illness. But whether they did so out of an intellectual conviction, either factually or fictively based, that the behaviors and persons engaging in them represented a threat or manufactured the threat to justify their repressive measures is another matter.

There have always been real dangers out there, persons and things which, if left unchecked, will likely cause considerable harm to innocent parties. At the same time, however, humans have a long and pathetic record of dissimulation in regard to their oppression of persons they come to define as "dangerous."

The reading we take of the historical record is that "dangerousness" in Revolutionary America, as now, often was a convenient concept to hold down and put aside selected segments of those who represented real or imaginary threats, often because they were not being dealt with in a satisfactorily humane and intelligent manner. The self-fulfilling prophecy also flourished in Revolutionary times, as it does now: declared to be dangerous and derogated as dangerous, individuals and groups read their cues correctly and behaved according to the manner in which they had been defined.

Dangers are of many sorts. Among other things, there are threats to life or physical well-being, to possessions, and to values. The threats may be direct, as in the case of assault, murder, or catastrophes such as tornadoes or atomic bombs. They may also be more speculative. A person putting forward a different political view may be alleged to be dangerous because, if his position prevails, he will enroll others who will not abide by the "proper" rules in regard to the well-being of persons and property. Advocates of communistic economics often have been seen as dangerous in capitalistic societies—and vice versa.

When matters of esthetic or moral preference are proscribed, such as homosexuality or the use of "dangerous" drugs, the issue rarely is posed in terms of competing values; instead, the behaviors are transformed into threats to the integrity of the social system, physical dangers to the practitioners, and perils to innocent others (for example, young persons who purportedly stand in jeopardy of being corrupted). Patrick Devlin has set forth the rationale behind declaring some "different" behaviors to be minacious acts:

Societies disintegrate from within more frequently than they are broken up by external pressures. There is disintegration when no common morality is observed and history shows that the loosening of moral bonds is the first stage of disintegration, so that society is justified in taking steps to preserve its moral code as it does to preserve its government and other essential institutions.[1]

A difficulty inheres in the fact that retrospection other than Devlin's might conclude that now-defunct societies seemingly failed to identify real dangers and instead

1. Patrick Devlin, *The Enforcement of Morals* (London: Oxford University Press, 1965), p. 13.

concentrated on matters which today appear to have been trivial divergencies from regularity. Indeed, the ferocity of response may have been the catalyst which transposed minor deviants into major social saboteurs. It is possible, of course, in a Durkheimian sense, that scapegoating is functional for a society, in that it cements more substantially the bonds of regularity among the ambivalent.[2] But, in our view, the right of the individual to pursue idiosyncratic behavior, the necessity for the society to determine fairly what the real dangers are, and the need to respond to such dangers in ecumenical fashion—without fear or favor—are fundamental requirements of a just social order. The considerable bias that historically has entered into the denomination of "dangerousness" has been pinpointed by Thomas Szasz:

Drunken drivers are dangerous both to themselves and to others. They injure and kill many more people than, for example, persons with paranoid delusions of persecution. Yet, people labelled paranoid are readily committable, while drunken drivers are not.

Some types of dangerous behavior are even rewarded. Race-car drivers, trapeze artists, and astronauts receive admiration and applause. In contrast, the poly-surgical addict and the would-be suicide receive nothing but contempt and aggression. Indeed, the latter type of dangerousness is considered a good cause for commitment. Thus, it is not dangerousness in general that is at issue here, but rather the manner in which one is dangerous.[3]

2. Emile Durkheim, *The Rules of Sociological Method*, trans. S. A. Solovay and John H. Mueller (New York: The Free Press, 1938), pp. 68–71.

3. Thomas S. Szasz, *Law, Liberty and Psychiatry* (New York: Macmillan Co., 1963), p. 85.

In what way, and for what reasons, then, do societies select those dangers that they will note and act against? Clearly, the responses are a function of social structure, history, and the demography and ethos of a group, among other things. Below, we will attempt to depict some characteristics of the early period of the United States, as well as those of contemporary times, and to relate these to the manner in which certain kinds of persons and acts were declared to be dangerous and how these behaviors were handled.

THE SETTING: CIRCA 1776

At the time of the American Revolution, there were many menacing dangers to human life that have been extirpated today. Early death from disease was common; and the lethal vicissitudes of existence often were attributed to or rationalized in terms of theological givens. The Reverend Philip Fithian, a Princeton graduate (class of 1772), whose letters and diaries provide a fine sense of the Revolutionary-epoch trained mind at work, notes on New Year's Day of 1774 that "perhaps by the next [year] I shall have made a longer and more important Remove, from this to the World of Spirits!"[4] Fithian's diary is replete with reports of "Agues," "Fluxes," and "Quinsey," and sudden deaths therefrom. Nor was his concern untoward, for Fithian himself was to die of dysentery during the Revolution, at the age of 29.

At the same time, though, life was slow-paced, insularity common, and communication, by present standards, extraordinarily slow.

4. Philip Vickers Fithian, *Journals and Letters, 1774–1777* (Freeport, N.Y.: Books for Libraries, 1969), p. 78.

Fithian, for instance, took seven days on horseback to travel between his home in New Jersey and the plantation in Virginia, on which he was to assume a tutoring position. The distance was but 260 miles.[5] The slow, erratic communications tended to keep dangers localized, unlike today, when the nationwide path of motion pictures, such as "Jaws" and "The Exorcist," scatters homogenized fears through the nation.

In other ways, too, life in the late eighteenth century was benign in comparison with life today. In Pennsylvania, for instance, according to Arthur M. Schlesinger, there were only 38 persons convicted of murder from the time of the colony's settlement through late 1775. This was a rate of one for each three years. The corresponding figure for burglaries was less than one a year. And these statistics were registered despite a considerable mixture of nationalities, continuing frontier disorders, the presence of felons transported from Britain, and the temptation of the considerable wealth centered in Philadelphia during this period.[6]

Nonetheless, the response to crime indicated intense feelings regarding its danger or, perhaps, merely venomous cruelty. In the state of New York in 1776, there were 16 crimes, including housebreaking and forgery, which demanded the death penalty for the first offense.[7] "Terrifying and irrevocable retribution" could be the price for major crimes,[8] though the severity of sentences was at times mitigated by leniency and even laxity.[9] It is interesting to speculate about the relationship between the chanciness of Everyman's existence and the barbarity of Revolutionary-times' punishments; whether, in this regard, the striking decline in recourse to the death penalty today represents growing regard for human life or is primarily a function of the better chance we all have to live longer and a reluctance to end arbitrarily what may otherwise go on for some time.

Particularly notable in Revolutionary times, given the relatively few serious crimes, is the concentration on behaviors, such as fornication and adultery, which now would be regarded as peccadilloes or matters of personal choice. For these, there were publicly-administered sanctions, combining the supposed function of deterrence with that of entertainment in a period when life tended to be marked by hard work and, for many, pervasive boredom. As Carl Bridenbaugh has observed:

Public humiliation was regarded not only as heightening the punishment but also as a means of identifying the culprits to the community at large. The townspeople, for their part, found the sight a welcome relief from the daily routine. The whipping post, the stocks, the pillory, the ducking stool . . . all served as agencies of gruesome entertainment, with a constantly changing plot and cast of characters.[10]

5. Ibid., pp. 47–49.
6. Arthur M. Schlesinger, *The Birth of the Nation* (New York: Knopf, 1968), p. 105.
7. Frank Monaghan, "The Results of the Revolution," in *History of the State of New York*, ed. Alexander C. Flick (New York: Columbia University Press, 1933), vol. 3, p. 327.
8. Carl Bridenbaugh, *Cities in Revolt: Urban Life in America, 1743–1776* (New York: Knopf, 1955), p. 109.
9. Monaghan, "The Results of the Revolution," p. 327.
10. Bridenbaugh, *Cities in Revolt*, p. 111.

It would be presumptuous to maintain that these punishments proved not only ineffective, but also counterproductive. They may have kept some of the undecided conforming. But they also may have propelled others into behavior which offered not only some fun, but now had the added attraction of a bit of time in the limelight. All in all, it seems likely that the dangers to morals presented by most of the offenses in Revolutionary times were beyond the suasion of the punishments. If so, a great deal of unnecessary suffering, humiliation, and degradation was visited upon people to no significant avail. And the same unpleasant conclusion seems in order in regard to much of what society today defines as dangerous as well.

THE "DANGEROUSLY" INSANE

The belief that the psychologically disordered pose a danger to the society has been remarkably constant through the past 200 years, though the forms of expression that this view has taken have undergone considerable change.

Demoniacal possession was the causal explanation for most forms of mental disorder during the colonial period. Insanity was regarded as "the outbreak of the animal, violent, filthy, blasphemous and murderous elements of the fallen human soul, elements which had culpably been permitted to get the upper hand of the highest attributes."[11] The scourge, the rack, the stake and the gallows were the common methods of "treatment."[12]

That most versatile of our Founding Fathers, Benjamin Franklin, established the first hospital in the colonies "for the Reception and Care of Lunaticks." Franklin relied heavily upon the belief that the mentally ill were dangerous when he sought backing for the facility. His petition to the Pennsylvania Assembly, for instance, set forth the following claim:

That with the Numbers of People, the number of Persons distempered in Mind and deprived of their rational Faculties, has greatly increased in this Province; That some of them going at large are a Terror to their Neighbours, who are daily apprehensive of the Violences they may commit; And others are continually wasting their Substance, to the great injury of themselves and Family, ill disposed Persons wickedly taking Advantage of their unhappy Condition. . . .[13]

Once built, the hospital consigned patients to a cellar, where their scalps "were shaved and blistered; they were bled to the point of syncope; [and] purged until the alimentary canal failed to yield anything but mucus."[14] As late as 1808, "lunatics" were "bound, chained, and even flogged at the particular phases of the moon, to prevent the occasion of violence."[15] Other cures for the "dangerous" mentally disordered included the "bath of surprise," consisting of a trapdoor which suddenly opened under an unsuspecting patient, who had been induced to walk over it, thereby plunging him into a pool of ice water from which he was "frequently extracted more dead than alive." In the "well-cure," the

11. Francis Tiffany, *Life of Dorothea Lynde Dix* (Boston: Houghton Mifflin Co., 1892), p. 57.
12. Albert Deutsch, *The Mentally Ill in America*, 2d. ed. (New York: Columbia University Press, 1949), p. 24.

13. Quoted in ibid., p. 59.
14. Thomas G. Morton, *The History of the Pennsylvania Hospital, 1751–1895* (Philadelphia: Times Printing House, 1895), p. 10.
15. Deutsch, *The Mentally Ill*, p. 82.

patient was chained to the bottom of an empty well, and water was added slowly, "to instill in him the terror of approaching death."[16]

The centuries have mollified some of the more horrible expressions of American fear and scorn of the psychiatrically aberrant. But the view that they are threats dies hard. Post-World War II surveys, for instance, have found that the American public believes that persons diagnosed as mentally disturbed are substantially more dangerous than the remainder of the population.[17] The view is reflected in policies permitting involuntary civil commitment of persons deemed dangerous *and* mentally disordered. Those who may be equally dangerous, but without alleged mental disorder, proceed unhindered. Of the 45 jurisdictions with provisions for emergency hospital commitment, 38 limit this procedure to "mentally ill individuals who appear dangerous to themselves or others."[18] Yet "dangerous" is rarely defined in these statutes, and only the vaguest definitions of mental illness are provided. In some states, for example, mental illness is defined as "any condition which substantially impairs an individual's mental health," while other commitment laws circuitously declare that a mentally ill person is one whose condition requires hospitalization.[19]

Similarly, the idea that the mentally disordered are dangerous is reflected in the influential Model Sentencing Act, which defines as dangerous "the offender who has committed a serious crime against the person and shows a behavior pattern of persistent assaultiveness based on serious mental disturbances."[20] The act advocates an additional sentence of up to 30 years for such persons. Quixotically, no special provisions attach to the offender who commits a dangerous act *without* being mentally disturbed.

Today, two principle rationales lie behind the involuntary detention of individuals believed to be dangerous and disturbed. These insist, first, that the mentally ill are, by reason of their condition, more dangerous than other persons and, second, that mental disorder—and its presumed component of dangerousness—is susceptible to psychiatric treatment. Both arguments appear untenable, however. Studies indicate that the mentally ill as a group are, at most, slightly more dangerous than their fellow citizens and, indeed, there are inquiries which report them even less dangerous.[21] Nor does treatment appear to produce the kinds of results theories claim for it.[22]

16. Ibid., p. 81.

17. Judith G. Rabkin, "Opinions about Mental Illness: A Review of the Literature," *Psychological Bulletin* 77 (March 1972), pp. 153–171; Theodore R. Sarbin and James C. Mancuso, "Failure of a Moral Enterprise: Attitudes of the Public Toward Mental Illness," *Journal of Consulting and Clinical Psychology* 35 (October 1970), pp. 159–173.

18. Note, "Civil Commitment of the Mentally Ill," *Harvard Law Review* 87 (April 1974), p. 1204.

19. Ibid., p. 1202.

20. National Council on Crime and Delinquency, *Model Sentencing Act* (Hackensack, N.J.: Council, 1971), p. 456.

21. For a review of the studies, see John Monahan, "The Prevention of Violence," in *Community Mental Health and the Criminal Justice System*, ed. John Monahan (New York: Pergamon Press, 1975), pp. 13–54.

22. For a review of the studies, see Gilbert Geis and John Monahan, "The Social Ecology of Violence," in *Moral Development and Behavior: Theory Research and Social*

The advent of psychotropic medications in the 1950s reduced the degree of physical restraint imposed upon "disordered" patients and prisoners. The "well-cure" and the "bath of surprise" no longer are included in the mental hospitals' repertoire. But cures unknown at the time of the American Revolution—practices such as electroshock and psychosurgery—are now being used. And the underlying justification for the involuntary confinement and treatment of these "dangerous" persons has changed little since Benjamin Franklin penned his petition to the Pennsylvania Assembly.

OTHER DANGERS: BLACKS AND DRUGS

"The numerous slaves of colonial New York were regarded as a potential menace," an historian of the state notes.[23] Alistair Cooke finds the explanation in "a fear of being outnumbered, a terror of insurrection."[24] Another writer points out that "racial conflict between Caucasians and Negroes is one of the most persistent factors in American violence."[25] He observes that the first slave uprising took place in New York City in 1712, and was put down with great ruthlessness.[26]

Issues, ed. Thomas B. Lickona (New York: Holt, Rinehart, and Winston, in press, to be published in 1976).

23. Monaghan, "The Results of the Revolution," p. 328.

24. Alistair Cooke, America (New York: Knopf, 1974), p. 72.

25. Richard M. Brown, "Historical Patterns of Violence in America," in Violence in America, ed. Hugh D. Graham and Ted R. Gurr (New York: New American Library, 1969), p. 48.

26. Ibid.

The dramaturgy of race relations in the United States, both then and now, is an Alice-in-Wonderland scenario, which would be ludicrous were its consequences not so awful. Human aspirations for equality and dignity are thwarted. Persons maltreated and miserable, then, do things which might permit them some surcease from their condition. What they do is then declared dangerous, and as a consequence they suffer further ill-handling.

Responses to blacks during Revolutionary times were often near-hysterical. The biographer of Thomas Jefferson tells of the burning at the stake of a slave named Eve on a plantation near Jefferson's. She was accused of poisoning her master. The killing was not a lynching; the sheriff was carrying out the order of the local court.[27]

Not all citizens, then as now, went along with the prevailing dogma about where racial danger lay and how to respond to it. The Reverend Fithian, for instance, was enraged at the manner in which some Virginians dealt with slaves. He describes a black coachman who was chained to the chariot-box because he was said to be "inclined to run away." "This is the method," Fithian noted, "which This Tyrant makes use of to keep him when abroad; & So soon as he goes home he is delivered into the pityless Hands of a bloody Overseer."[28] Later, in a fine bit of prescience, Fithian shows an understanding of the possible consequences of degradation upon its victims:

The ill Treatment which this unhappy part of mankind receives here, would

27. Fawn M. Brodie, Thomas Jefferson: An Intimate History (New York: Bantam, 1975), p. 42.

28. Fithian, Journals and Letters, p. 136.

almost justify them in any desperate attempt for gaining that *Civility*, & *Plenty* which tho' denied them, is here, commonly bestowed on Horses![29]

The processes described above are not unique to race relations. Chein and his associates have documented the same pattern in the response to heroin addiction. After intensive investigation, Chein concluded that addicts were

individuals who had already failed to find alternative solutions to their problems and who had not received any effective help in doing so. [By using drugs], they would be seeking what seemed to them the best available treatment of their distress.[30]

American society, Chein notes, takes extraordinary pains to keep heroin from addicts, thus escalating its price, and it then declares that the addicts are social menaces because they engage in so great a volume of crime—to secure the drugs which have been priced beyond their ability to afford them through noncriminal activity. Similarly, the drug is outlawed because its use is said to be dangerous to the individual's health and well-being. Thousands of addicts thus die through overdose or contract serious diseases because they are blocked from trustworthy sources of the drug, sterile needles, pure drugs, and distilled water.

OVERVIEW

Conceptions of what constitutes a danger have changed substantially in the last two centuries in American society. Yet the change has been neither consistent nor unidirec-tional. In some areas, Americans appear more tolerant now of what was considered dangerous in 1776. In other cases, thinking appears to have solidified. And on many issues, only the rationale for the ascription of dangerousness has changed, not the ascription itself.

The psychologically disordered come within this last grouping. There was at the time of the Revolution, and there now is, a strong public belief that psychiatric diagnoses carry with them accurate harbingers of violent behavior. This belief has, for two centuries, been largely responsible for the policy of isolating the mentally ill from the community of their fellow citizens.

Two major changes can be traced in regard to the designation of certain classes of persons as dangerous over the past two hundred years. The most clearly recognizable is the *decreased reliance upon religion*. Witnesses to the Salem witch trials were still alive at the time of the American Revolution. The dangerous then were those who were said to have committed acts contrary to the will of God, as that will was interpreted by whichever brand of religiosity was dominant in a given place.[31]

Nature, as Spinoza declared, seems to abhor a vacuum. Corresponding to the decreased influence of religion in designating the dangerous has been an *increased reliance upon medical practitioners* to discern those who allegedly pose a threat to the established order. Psychiatrists decide which of the mentally different are too dangerous to remain at liberty, just as they decide on the civil commitment

29. Ibid., p. 248.

30. Isidor Chein et al., *The Road to H: Narcotics, Delinquency, and Public Policy* (New York: Basic Books, 1964), pp. 380–381.

31. See Kai T. Erikson, *Wayward Puritans* (New York: Wiley, 1966).

of narcotic addicts and on the presence of "sexual psychopathy."

The processes by which these things occur are instructive. Theodore Sarbin has posited a distinction between violence, which he suggests denotes action, and danger, which he regards as being based on a relationship of power. Human beings, Sarbin observes, often are defined as dangerous when they rebel against degrading procedures which attempt to transform their social identity. Such procedures put them in a condition of strain. They either must accept the identity as a nonperson, or brute, or engage in instrumental behavior which "radically alters the social system and reverses . . . the power relationship, thus affording [them] a more acceptable social identity." If they take the second course, their behavior comes to be perceived as "dangerous" by the persons whose power is being repudiated.[32]

Sarbin's view may be examined briefly in terms of an historical source of the Revolutionary period. Note in the following quotation how the Reverend Fithian, seeing what would be regarded by most of us as a minor deviation, indulges in a fiery process of verbal degradation. The event had been precipitated, Fithian speculates, by a presumed insult, or "perhaps one had mislaid the other's hat, or knocked a peach out of his Hand, or offered him a dram without wiping the mouth of the Bottle. . . ." A brawl ensues:

This spectacle, (so loathsome & horrible!) generally is attended with a crowd of People! In my opinion, (others may think for themselves) animals which seek after & relish such odious and filthy amusements are not of the human species, they are destitute of the remotest pretension to humanity; I know not how they came by their form, by the help of which they are permitted to associate with Men, unless it has been (unfortunate for the World!) by an intermixture of the meaner kinds of Devils with prostitute Monkeys! . . . I think all such should be deemed by the community infectious, & suspended at least any kind of intercourse. . . .[33]

Thus, on a much grander and more elaborate scale, are human beings transposed from the acceptable to the dangerous, and reclassified from their species to another.

In the future, hopefully, there will be a shift from the earlier religious and the present medical bases for determining the nature of danger to concern with social criteria. For the purpose of public policy in a democracy, danger should not be revealed by the will of God or found in medical pronouncements. Its ascription, as Jerome Skolnick has noted, is a social and political process,[34] and the future should openly treat it as such. Ethics and social morality, not theology and medicine, should guide its study.

The next century must shift emphasis from dangerous people to dangerous behavior. While individuals and their acts obviously are related, the assumption that a status of dangerousness can reliably be attached to a given person has been greatly overemphasized. The most meaningful definitions of danger to guide future policy and research appear to be those which link outcome to source. Things such as

---

32. Theodore R. Sarbin, "The Dangerous Individual: An Outcome of Social Identity Transformation," British Journal of Criminology 7 (July 1967), pp. 285–295.

33. Fithian, Journals and Letters, p. 243.
34. Jerome H. Skolnick, The Politics of Protest (New York: Simon & Schuster, 1969), p. 4.

building a defective car and smogging a city should be brought within the compass of the dangerous. Since the founding of the Republic, dangerousness largely has been confined to individual aberrations. Today, as never before, it is not the person, but the impersonal organizational behemoth which poses the greatest dangers to each of us.

Equity and Republican Justice

By LESLIE T. WILKINS

ABSTRACT: The incarceration of offenders (in prisons) with a view to their reformation was a social invention of the early Americans—the Quakers of Pennsylvania—some 200 years ago. The view that the goal of rehabilitation of offenders is either impossible or undesirable or both is now gaining ground rapidly. It has also become widely accepted, as the result of research and general experience, that the simplification of the problem of crime to the problem of the offender leads nowhere. The anchor points for moral values have been eroding, and reference to authority figures or symbols for guidance as to what is right and just is regarded as unsatisfactory. The concept of *equity* (which involves comparisons between items) has come to be preferred over the concept of *justice* (which refers to a fixed ideal). Parole determinations, for example, may be "arbitrary" but they must not be "capricious." Justification of punishment for socially damaging behavior relies on the idea of commensurateness ("deserts"). This raises to a new level of urgency the issue of doing justice in an unjust society—a difficulty which the prior philosophy of the treatment of offenders was able to avoid.

Professor Leslie T. Wilkins has been at the State University of New York's Graduate School of Criminal Justice, at Albany, since 1969. His first excursion into criminology was in 1952, when he collaborated with Dr. Hermann Mannheim in research published under the title of Prediction Methods in Relation to Borstal Training. In 1972 he was presented the Edwin H. Sutherland Award of the American Criminological Society. He has published widely, both in books and journal articles, and served as editor of learned journals and consultant to several national and international bodies.

IF WE who are in some position of authority today were required to report back to those who were in similar positions 100 or 200 years ago, we should shock and surprise them in many different ways. They would doubtless be surprised to learn of our advances in technology, and equally as surprised to hear of our lack of progress in the development and application of human sciences. They might even question whether the disparity in achievements was due to disparity in financial investment and inquire why "thing-research" had proved so much more attractive to funding agencies than "persons-research." They would be shocked to learn that crime was still regarded as a major problem, causing us great concern. As David Rothman points out:

. . . . the Enlightment view of man. . . shaped by his environment, replaced traditional Calvanistic notions of inate depravity. Thus would-be reformers had all the more reason to believe that if only the right influences could be brought to bear, the deviant would be cured.[1]

THE EARLY AMERICAN INVENTION

There seems to be little doubt but that the idea of the modern prison and the "correctional agencies" can be claimed as an early American social invention. A report on crime and punishment prepared for the American Service Committee and published in 1971 noted, "[T]he horror that is the American prison system grew out of an eighteenth-century reform by Pennsylvania Quakers and others against the cruelty and futility of capital and corporal punishment. *This two-hundred-year*-old experiment has failed"[2] (emphasis added).

There is little doubt of the good intentions and the strength of the beliefs of the Society of Friends of 200 years ago. They believed that offenders could be reformed. This belief has taken several turns since its expression in the "Penitentiary." Training, therapy, reeducation, or other means have been expected to lead to the rehabilitation or reintegration of the offender.

All these varieties of belief have at least one element in common: they claim that the probability that the individual will commit further crimes can be reduced by what is done to him; he will learn, by some means, not to do it again, his "problem" will be understood, or he will be "cured." This family of beliefs may be characterized as representing the "clinical medical model" for the treatment of offenders. What is to be done to the individual offender is oriented forward in time. It is not what he did which is the major criterion for action by the social agencies, but what he is likely to do in the future.

CONFLICTS OF GOALS

The major question with regard to decisions about offenders is, according to this theory, their efficiency. The test as to whether a "treatment works" is, of course, the test of the diminished probability of further criminal activity (recidivism). It is difficult to measure a change in an individual probability,

---

1. David J. Rothman, "Behaviour Modification in Total Institutions," *The Hastings Center Report* 5, no. 1 (February 1975), p. 17.

2. A Committee Report prepared for the American Friends Service Committee, *Struggle for Justice* (New York: Hill & Wang, 1971), p.v.

and hence philosophical arguments rather than hard data have been the support. For example, it is considered by some that goodness and truth are associated, and hence it follows that the medical-clinical model, being more humanitarian (that is, "good") must by that very token be more effective than less humanitarian means for dealing with offenders. We shall return to this claim later.

Contrasted with that class of tests which asks questions about the future and the probable behaviors of offenders as criteria for the disposition decisions are those philosophies which seek to justify the actions by reference only to the past. The test is based upon concepts of "just deserts"—not what he is likely to do, but what punishment is commensurate with the offense which he has committed.

A third class of concerns relates to questions of how the behaviors of others ("society") are likely to be influenced by what is done to the selected class of offenders. This is the idea of "general deterrence." If murderers are killed, will there be fewer murders? The issues of fact are somewhat easier in this area to establish than are assessments of any changed levels of personal probabilities, but there is some ground for disagreement as to the meaning of available data.

A fourth class of justifications for dealing with offenders in certain ways merely points out that if the individual is isolated from his potential victims, then he cannot victimize them! Such arguments discount totally the amount of crime which occurs within the prison community. Normal citizens may be spared some crime by the detention

of some criminals, but as Jones[3] has fully demonstrated, our prisons are dangerous places.

All the popular methods for dealing with crime, 200 years ago and today, focus upon the offender. The victim, the situation, the environment, and all other aspects of that complex incident we call crime tend to be ignored.[4] Perhaps that is why we have not been successful—we have attempted to simplify the problem of crime to the problem of the criminal. Excessive simplification is not an adequate specification of the problem, and no problem can be solved until it is properly specified. But we must leave this issue aside and hope that the next 200 years will see more progress. Let us examine a little more closely where we now are in relation to our action and thought about criminal justice.

THE "TREATMENT MODEL"

Until recently it was possible to classify attitudes toward offenders along much the same lines as political attitudes—there were the liberals and there were the conservatives. The liberals were characterized (by the conservatives!) as "soft on criminals," but saw themselves as identified with the "clinical-medical model"—the belief that the offender could be rehabilitated by educational or therapeutic means. The conservative

3. David Jones, "The Dangerousness of Imprisonment" (Ph D. diss., School of Criminal Justice, State University of New York at Albany, 1975).
4. See, for example, Oscar Newman, *Defensible Space: Crime Prevention through Urban Design* (New York: Collier Books, 1973); and Jeffrey C. Ray, *Prevention through Environmental Design* (Beverly Hills, Calif.: Sage, 1971).

viewpoint was characterized (by the liberals) as the lock-them-up-and-throw-away-the-key group.

The situation is now totally confused, but there is hope in that the confusion is recognized. There are some professionals in the correctional agencies who strongly believe in the "medical-clinical model"; they tend to differ as to what forms of treatment would be effective, and some are concerned as to whether those treatments which might be claimed to be effective are not also morally suspect. It is, notwithstanding, generally agreed that "treatment" must have some boundaries. Boundaries of time have been argued in the courts: specifically, whether a person may be held in incarceration longer than the maximum sentence in order to be "helped." Extension of time in prison, even when further training or treatment might be involved is, many claim, morally unjustified since it conceals additional punishment and further periods of isolation from society.

The arguments against additional time to facilitate "treatment" or training can be used in a more general way to throw doubt upon the claim that the "medical/treatment" model is, in fact, humanitarian. It may be possible to justify more demeaning practices if they can be classified as "treatment" than if the only justification were in terms of punishment. It can be accepted as morally viable to give electro-convulsive therapy, but to use the same procedures as punishment would be difficult to justify. Furthermore, if an offender is to be "treated," then it would seem logical to suggest that he be continued in "treatment" (in incarceration?) until he is cured. But it is his captors who determine when he is cured. If the decision to release is linked with the medical model and the idea of "cure," then any recidivism is due to "liberal" release procedures, since by definition, only those who will not offend again should be released.

This conveniently ignores the fact that the only way of knowing whether a person will commit further crimes is by placing him at some risk of doing so. The only feedback of information which the releasing agency will have is of those "inappropriately released" — successful releasees do not make news. If the risk of "inappropriate release" is reduced, the period of incarceration must increase. In short, the apparently progressive and humanitarian method of making the treatment fit the individual offender may be open to much more abuse than the tailoring of a punishment to fit the crime.

In practice, however, there is a strong tendency toward agreement on what is to be done in relation to the detention of offenders. Those who hold the "treatment" view are prepared to claim that those offenders who have committed the more serious crimes are the more difficult to reform and hence need to be detained longer than those whose crimes are the more trivial. There would, however, seem to be no essential correlation between the time to effect a "cure" and the event which triggered the decision to incarcerate. The claim can be made, of course, because there is no evidence that any form of "treatment" which has been put into effect to date has had any impact whatever upon the probability of offenders committing further crimes.

THE BAD, MAD, SICK CONFUSION

It is interesting to note that the confusion between the idea of "treatment" and the isolation of the offender or "sick" person and of punishment is extremely ancient. The identification of magical locations, shrines, healing springs, or whatever served to get the deviant or sick away from the society in which he normally lived. The essential idea of society seems to have been to insist that the deviant, the offender, the deranged, or the sick, "Get the hell out of here!"[5] For some, the galleys served well;[6] for others, the nomans' land outside the city walls (outlaws), and there was transportation. The latter took many forms, from merely the forcing of traveling merchants to take the deviants away and get them lost[7] to well-organized shipments to faraway places.

Michael Foucault[8] sees an association between the practical and symbolic action taken with regard to leprosy and (when this ailment disappeared from western Europe at the end of the Middle Ages) action taken with regard to "madmen" and "criminals." In his words,

[L]eprosy disappeared, the leper vanished, or almost, from memory; these [lazar houses] structures remained. Often, in these same places, the formulas of exclusion would be repeated, strangely similar two or three centuries later. Poor vagabonds, criminals, and "deranged minds" would take the part played by the leper. . . .[9]

In the case of leprosy, it is possible that the isolation of the victim did serve to reduce the incidence of the disease. In 1656, however, the founding of the Hôpital Général, Paris—with a staff doctor required to visit twice a week—made the association between sickness, laziness, crime, and madness much more clear. The directors had the powers of ". . . jurisdiction, of correction and punishment over the poor of Paris. . . ."[10] They (the directors) having "for these purposes stakes, irons, prisons, and dungeons in the said hospital . . . no appeal will be accepted from the regulations they establish within the said hospital. . . ."[11] Functional analysis could trace no medical model in the repressive operations of the Hôpital Général.

Similarly, today, functional analysis can trace no medical model in the prison system. The language of the medical model is used, but that is all. Perhaps the major difference between then and now is in the numbers of persons incarcerated rather than in terms of any significant differences in philosophy or linguistics. One year after it was opened, the Paris Hôpital Général held about one percent of the population! In the United States today, the proportion of the population incarcerated in penal institutions (including local jails and juvenile institutions) is about one-fifth of one percent.

With this heritage, can we now expect to be able to make any change

5. Graeme R. Newman, "A Theory of Deviance Removal," *British Journal of Sociology* 26, no. 2 (June 1975), pp. 203–217.

6. Paul W. Bamford, *Fighting Ships and Prisons* (Minneapolis: University of Minnesota Press, 1973).

7. Michael Foucault, *Madness and Civilization* (London: Tavistock, 1965), pp. 10–11.

8. Ibid. See note 4, ch. 1, p. 291.

9. Ibid, p. 7.

10. Regulations of Hôpital Général articles XII and XIII, quoted in ibid., note 7, p. 292.

11. Ibid., p. 40.

of direction in the way we treat those defined as "offenders"? Is it true that a society gets the kinds of criminals it deserves? If so, what kinds of societal change may permit us to expect a change in the patterns of crime and what we decide to do about it?

Perhaps an optimistic view may be taken. The Pennsylvania Quakers of the eighteenth century made a very considerable impact upon the design of prisons and the philosophy of the treatment of offenders. Their influence dominated the policy of this country and extended its authority to most of the Western world and even beyond. Are the Quakers of today less influential than those of 200 years ago? Will the reversal of their earlier policy statements be received with as much care and attention as the initial propositions?[12] This is an open question.

SCIENCE AND VALUES

There are few technological problems which today cannot be considered capable of solution if they are capable of description. We are on much less secure ground when we look to morals and values. The anchor points of the value system of the past have been crumbling for two centuries, and now there is no firm basis for our reference of meaning in ethics. There used to be three classes of anchor points which, from time to time, formed coalitions —the political powers concerned with civil and internal issues; the military powers concerned with the security from external threat; the

religious powers. The figures relating to these reference authorities changed with time and with the complexity of civilization but remained fairly consistent in their divisions—the head of the family, the head of the tribe, the king, representing one line; the head of the family, the warriors, the military establishment, representing another; the priests and kings were often in coalition and often in conflict, and the religious leaders formed associations with medicine and magic and related these to the organization of law. The ordinary man (at whatever period of time) was always in need of being saved— saved from wild beasts, from foreign invasion (the warriors would look after that), from breakdown of the social structure (the politicians and kings would look after that), and so on. There were always those ready to play the rōle of the saviors, and all too often it was difficult to discriminate the saviors from the exploiters.

Saviors (or exploiters) experienced no shortage of demand for the services they had to offer. Peddlers of potions, belief merchants, and protection agents, all did good business. When few could forge steel or fashion stone, write or read, make fire or prepare potions, there was a mystery about those who could do so. The mystery, linked with the beliefs in magic (superstitions as we would now say!), provided the anchor points for values and the associated rituals of the populace. Upon whom could they rely if not on these power figures for the expectation of a longer or better life; and if survival was not here, then some promise of hereafter? Even the biblical prophets had to demonstrate their au-

12. It seems fair to characterize the general trend of the recommendations of *Struggle for Justice* (see note 2) as a complete reversal of the policy of rehabilitation and reform previously advocated.

thority by miracles. The miracle-makers and the value-makers (law givers) were often the same. So far as the majority of the population today in this country is concerned, these gods have departed, although, for some, their representatives have considerable authority to pronounce upon moral—or even medical and scientific—questions.

There was a period when the authority of the religious leaders was challenged with some success. The early scientific methodologists were seen as holding out the promise that values could be subject to proofs—that science could save us. Knowledge was power, and power could save. Now we are not so sure. Since 1945 we have had all the power we could possibly want at the disposal of our "warriors." But do we see this as providing more protection? Is survival more certain now than it was even a few decades ago? Most people would answer in the negative. But if we cannot look upward for guidance about values, at least we can look around us. And that is what is currently being done.

EQUITY—STRUCTURING DISCRETION IN DECISION

We are, today, no longer talking about "justice" but rather about "equity"; we are prepared to accept an inevitable, certain arbitrariness in many determinations and policy decisions, but we are not willing to accept capriciousness; we no longer need a firm basis in strong subjective feelings of certainty, because we can deal with the issue of rationality under uncertainty; we may not know where we are going in the end, but we know where we ought to go from here; we are not

sure about how to do good, but we know how to do less harm, and we can insist upon that.

How can we distinguish "equity" from "justice"? It is in the earlier analogy—justice looks up; equity looks around for its reference. The following figure would seem to provide a formula. When we are concerned with "equity," we are making comparisons with others who are "sufficiently similar," and the origin may be no more than arbitrary—we may still be unjust, but at least we will be unjust more equally! Specifically, we "look around" for critiques of our decisions. Justice implies an absolute reference point or "law" to which each individual case is separately referenced, and since each case is, by this means, made to accord with a fixed point, each is made to accord with each other. Thus "justice" includes the idea of "equity" while "equity" does not include the idea of "justice."

By striving for less and by making more modest claims, we may achieve more. We might compare what we do with offenders who are somewhat similar (some collection of information involving classification of, say, the nature of the crime and the prior record[13]). By reference to some concept of law, we may ensure a hierarchy of punishments which is consistent within the bounds of the measurement. We shall not claim to do "right" but to dispose of offenders with the minimum of disparity. We shall hold to our opinions less vigorously and be ready for experiments and changes,

13. See, for example, Don M. Gottfredson et al., "Making Parole Policy Explicit," *Crime and Delinquency*, January 1975, pp. 34–44. The "collective of information" referred to here is, of course, represented by the summation sign in the figure.

FIGURE 1

ILLUSTRATION OF THE DIFFERENCE BETWEEN THE DEFINITION OF
JUSTICE AND OF EQUITY AS USED IN THIS PAPER

JUSTICE

$$LEX$$

$$\uparrow \qquad \uparrow \qquad \uparrow \qquad \uparrow \qquad \uparrow \qquad \uparrow$$
$$x_1 \longleftrightarrow x_2 \longleftrightarrow x_3 \longleftrightarrow x_4 \longleftrightarrow x_5 \longleftrightarrow x_6 \ldots \ldots$$

EQUITY

$$x_1 \longleftrightarrow x_2 \longleftrightarrow x_3 \longleftrightarrow x_4 \longleftrightarrow x_5 \longleftrightarrow x_6 \ldots \ldots$$

$$\rightarrow \sum_{x=1}^{j} \rightarrow LEX$$

and we will listen to challenges made on moral grounds by those outside our profession or expertise.

In the manner suggested, we have separated issues of policy from issues of individual case determinations. Information which is relevant to general policy questions may now be sought and specifically processed and not consist merely of a set of half-remembered individual cases or dramatic precedents. Policy considerations set boundary conditions within which the individual determinations can vary, but these limits are such as to structure discretion rather than destroy it. In practice, for example, this methodology would lead to the establishment of guidelines for sentencing of offenders, but not to fixed mandatory sentences. While, in general, it might be expected that individual determinations were to be made within the guideline limits, there would be provisions for departure outside these, either upward or downward, provided that such departures were supported by arguments and these arguments were regarded as sufficient by at least one other judge. There would seem to be no necessity for all cases to be determined by a panel of judges; indeed this would be dysfunctional

since it would trivialize the procedure. A court district or a state or other convenient politico-juridical unit could determine its own general policy for sentencing in terms of the seriousness of the instant offense and the previous record (adding other factors of mitigation or exaccerbation in these could be agreed within and defended without the judiciary).

PAROLE—AN OPEN POLICY EXAMPLE

The proposed model for sentencing given above is quite similar to that adopted by the United States Board of Paroles (Federal) in 1973. The board based its guidelines on detailed research, then published the policy with the detailed tables. These tables indicate the expected time that an offender with a particular record and kind of criminal background would be detained before release on parole—that is, the period of incarceration. Public comment was invited with respect to the guidelines and to the general policy. Several test cases have been heard in the courts. These have concerned various jurisprudential and constitutional issues of the new policy, including arguments that the guidelines make little, if any, allowance for the idea of rehabilitation.

There are many among those directly concerned with the system as well as informed laymen who still hope that ways may be found to provide efficient treatment for offenders. Some are looking to techniques of conditioning and chemotherapy, while others still believe in token economies, vocational training, group dynamics, or other methods. Your author's personal and considered view is that any treatment which is powerful enough to be effective in modification of the behavior of offenders will be too intrusive to be morally acceptable. The important point of take-off from our present position would seem to be that the concept of "equity" can be quantified and can form the basis for decision rules. This approach seems to be both morally acceptable and technically feasible.

THE FUTURE

Something like prisons will be needed for a long time. Prisons are there because the public demands them. They provide a kind of factory where the product is punishment, and we are the customers, paying a high price through taxation. We are also buying the separation of "them" from "us," at least in terms of reduced risk; but the questions of efficiency and morality remain. Could we, for example, buy a reduced risk more cheaply or with less intrusive constraints on the lives of "them"? If any taxpayer believes that the penal system is helping to "correct" offenders by any means, all the evidence is against him. By any reasonable definition of "treatment," penal systems contain none of it. It would be best if we accepted this as a fact while at the same time accepting that there is a general demand for such institutions.

In the area of criminal justice, the slogans are so easy, the ritualism so entrenched, the thinking so muddled, the data so bad that rational projection of future situations seems hopeless. Crime cannot be dealt with by political slogans, where the "War on Crime" rapidly degenerates into a war on "criminals." Illegal human behavior is as complex as legal human behavior, and yet the former is seen as a simple matter of the intransigence of a minority.

Where criminal justice is likely to go in the next decade seems fairly set by what is currently in the "pipe-line." However, while there have been few significant changes in the last 200 years, it seems that we are now at the threshold of a discontinuity. More of the same will not do, but we may continue to try to do it. That way lies disaster —it will force the discontinuity. If we continue to simplify the problem of crime to the problem of the criminal, we shall certainly make no inroads into the problem of crime. We must give up the belief that we can control crime by increasing penalties or by inventing new forms of punishment, by developing new "treatment" programs, or by community correctional services. More profit might well be derived from (a) research in the study of victims, (b) experimental modifications of the environments in which crimes take place, (c) studies of the decision processes of the criminal justice agencies and personnel, (d) investigation and control of the illicit marketplaces. A large proportion of crime is economic behavior which is defined as illegal; perhaps economists should make more attempts to deal with it.

POLITICS AND A PRESCRIPTION

Our politicians, when faced with a demand to do something about a problem which they consider to be insoluble, do something—they make a law against it! (Shades of primitive incantations: cure by edict!) The practical effect of this is to place in the field of law many problems which, although difficult, might be better resolved in other specialist areas. Could, for example, the drug problem have been better dealt with without the intervention of law, the police, courts, prisons, and the whole machinery of criminal justice?

We must, as a matter of great urgency, examine, unscramble, and assess the technological, medical, scientific, and moral questions in relation to how we define and what we do about "the offender." When this is done, we should be able to see specific kinds of problems to which different and specific kinds of problem-solving methods could be applied: medical problems; economic problems; moral problems and problems which lie in the "cracks between disciplines."

EQUITY OF LIMITED JURISDICTION?

To deter from socially undesirable activities, there must be commensurate punishments. Similarly, there must be incentives toward socially desirable behaviors, and these should be commensurate rewards. Equity is a moral value which informs and should control both rewards and punishments. But if fraud is punished while slick business practices are too highly rewarded, even though the function of law is to control only at the boundaries, it would appear that the concept of equity is violated. There are serious problems of doing justice in an unjust society.

162

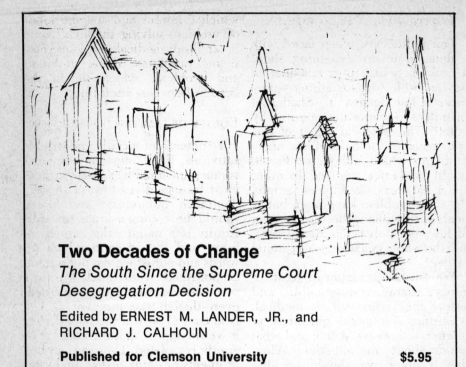

Two Decades of Change
*The South Since the Supreme Court
Desegregation Decision*

Edited by ERNEST M. LANDER, JR., and
RICHARD J. CALHOUN

Published for Clemson University   **$5.95**

America in a Divided World, 1945–1972

Edited by ROBERT H. FERRELL
Cartography by John M. Hollingsworth

In this volume Professor Ferrell completes his documentary
history of the diplomacy of the United States and includes
a composite index to all three volumes. FOUNDATIONS OF
AMERICAN DIPLOMACY, 1775–1872, and AMERICA AS A
WORLD POWER, 1872–1945, are still available.

$9.95

To order any of our books, simply send your check
for the advertised list price to:

University of South Carolina Press
Columbia SC 29208

*The day after we receive your check, we'll mail your
order postpaid book rate.*

162d

Kindly mention THE ANNALS *when writing to advertisers*

Book Department

INTERNATIONAL RELATIONS

ELMER BENDINER. *A Time for Angels: The Tragicomic History of the League of Nations.* Pp. xiv, 441. New York: Alfred A. Knopf, 1975. $12.95.

This book recounts the short unhappy life of the League of Nations. Elmer Bendiner calls it a "tragicomic history" but the story yields few laughs.

As the saying goes, happy lives are pretty much the same; unhappy lives are mostly unique. The 27-year life of the League was depressingly dreary in its own particular way. As necessary if not sufficient conditions for this singularity, there was first of all the fearful legacy of World War I, then the extravagant vision-mongering of President Wilson, next the rising tide of anti-Bolshevist suspicions, next the high tide of aggressive chauvinism, and finally the entrance on the European stage of swaggering dictators like Mussolini and Hitler. All of these circumstances weighed heavily on the fragile life of the League. In the end, they crushed it. High-minded idealism proved no support against the deeds of national self-interest and the contingencies of history.

Bendiner's work draws on many sources—letters, memoirs, reminiscences, newspapers, and League of Nations archives. The author is strongest in presenting the individualizing detail, the representative quotation, the colorful aside in his narrative. The result makes for a vivid, pictorial, personalized, and aphoristic history. It would be unfair to characterize the total value of this book in terms of its memorable anecdotes. Yet striking vignettes appear in every chapter. Desperately fighting for the purity of the League's Covenant in 1919, Wilson suddenly launches into an inspired speech in Paris, one that "left secretaries gasping with admiration, their pencils in their hands, their duties forgotten and hardly a word taken down." While dining on duckling at an unpretentious inn in Thoiry near Geneva, Briand and Stresemann come to an international understanding in 1926. A decade later Danzig Nazi Arthur Greiser delivers a pompous speech before the Council of the League. Afterwards he struts around giving periodic Hitler salutes. When the press laughs, Greiser modifies his last salute with a bent arm and a ridiculously obscene gesture. Finally there is the unforgettable portrait of the admirable diplomat and last Secretary-General of the League, Sean Lester. Loyally tending the League's dying gasps in Geneva, he is invited to San Francisco for the founding of the United Nations Organization. Once in the United States, Lester is barely tolerated and treated like a corpse at a wedding.

In the end, it is the defects of its virtues that limit this book. The narrative text simply overwhelms any opportunities for analysis. What were the social forces, economic interests, ideological bogies that made the League an abortive experiment? Unhappily, problems of this kind are not explored in *A Time for Angels*.

RICHARD M. HUNT
Harvard University
Cambridge
Massachusetts

ROBERT W. JACKMAN. *Politics and Social Equality: A Comparative Analysis*. Pp. xiv, 225. New York: John Wiley & Sons, 1975. $14.95.

The author presents a causal model of cross-national variations in the degree of within-nation social equality as measured by three indicators: one is an index of social insurance program experience, another is an index of social welfare (based on health and nutrition indicators), and the third is a measure of inequality in the distribution of income. The study is based on aggregate data from sixty countries drawn primarily from the *World Handbook of Political and Social Indicators*.

The study begins with an examination of the effect of level of economic development on various indicators of social equality. These results are combined into a relatively simple path model which is elaborated upon in each subsequent chapter. That is, in each chapter several potentially relevant intervening variables are considered and those which do not prove to be spurious are incorporated into the model. In the final path model eight predictors account for sixty percent of the variance in (intersectoral) income inequality.

Several indicators of political structure and stability are considered. A measure of "democratic performance" has significant bivariate effects on social equality, but when level of economic development is controlled, the effects prove to be spurious. Indicators of political stability and political violence are considered and a measure of long-term political stability remains in the final model. Indicators of the strength of

parties of the noncommunist left, of the strength of labor unions, and of ethnolinguistic fractionalization are considered; they prove to have little impact on social equality and all drop out in the final model.

Jackman's book is must reading for those interested in quantitative comparative analysis of political and social inequality. It is one of the most clearly written and well reasoned studies of its type to date. The procedures for an incremental approach to causal model construction are lucidly presented.

The limitations of the study are those which I would expect to be associated with any study which seeks to present a causal model based on cross-national aggregate data to account for social inequality. Serious questions can be raised about the adequacy with which the causal model so constructed captures the essence of the causal processes which mediate the effect of level of economic development on the extent of social inequality. The use of path models for causal analysis based on cross-national aggregate data at the present stage of the art is much more problematic than Jackman would have us believe.

JOHN B. WILLIAMSON
Boston College
Chestnut Hill
Massachusetts

JAMES TURNER JOHNSON. *Ideology, Reason, and the Limitation of War: Religious and Secular Concepts, 1200–1740*. Pp. x, 291. Princeton, N.J.: Princeton University Press, 1975. $12.50.

LOIS G. SCHWOERER. *"No Standing Armies," the Antiarmy Ideology in Seventeenth-Century England*. Pp. x, 210. Baltimore, Md.: The Johns Hopkins University Press, 1975. $10.00.

Professor Johnson explores the interaction of religious and secular thought on the formulation of a just war doctrine and rules for conducting war as they developed between 1200–1740. Those chapters treating medieval theory on these subjects—especially the impact of scholasticism and chivalry—are adequate, but the latter portion of the book seems limited both in scope and in interpretation. Admittedly one commentator considers the work to be "the most significant book on the just war doctrine to be published in recent years," but the reader does wonder if such enthusiasm might be linked to the fact that a Princeton University professor is discussing a Princeton University Press book.

The attitudes toward war are traced from 1200–1740 through the writings of selected authors. So far as Professor Johnson goes the work is thoughtful, but the number of authorities consulted is limited. For example, Professor Johnson's theme as to how a "just war" developed into a "holy war" after the Reformation (although highly provocative) needs further development. One wonders why the treatment of Anglo-Netherlands writings on the subject, vast as they are, were limited pretty much to Hugo Grotius, Francis Bacon, William Ames, and Matthew Sutcliffe. He does draw some excellent material into the notes which should have been woven into the text.

Also irritating is the format of the book. Why appendices are used after each section of a scholarly book to give biographical sketches that could be found in any biographical dictionary or encyclopedia is surprising. Most of the information would be known to the reader of such a work, and, if biographical incidents influenced the theme, surely the text or a footnote would have been more appropriate. Consequently a more lucid and readable result could have been achieved.

Professor Johnson in some instances carries his themes up to the present. He traces past thinking to modern dialogue concerning war and its restraints. Unfortunately it only takes one side to make a war and a number to prevent one. It is a pity that the organization of the book, the limiting of authorities, and in some places the style limit what would have been an excellent book to being just an ordinary one.

Professor Schwoerer's work presents a real contrast with the above. It is well researched, erudite, treats a more limited period, but covers it more thoroughly. Although she perhaps places an over emphasis on the importance of English antimilitarism on English political action, she makes a good case and does much to separate myth from reality in British attitudes towards a standing army. She calls attention with authority and clarity as to how British thinking on matters military affected English constitutional development in the seventeenth century and American thought on similar lines throughout the next hundred years. She has culled the official documents, pamphlet literature, and secondary accounts in a most detailed manner, and the result is an excellent book. One cannot help point out that Edward Russel was Earl of Orford, not Oxford, and that the jacket illustration is an inferior reprint of a work done at least a hundred years earlier and also on deposit at the Folger Shakespeare Library. These are minor points. Her evaluations of contemporary thinking in England as to standing armies as opposed to the militia are interesting contrasts of professional versus amateur and the problem of politics versus civic responsibility.

Professor Schwoerer points out that the motives behind criticism of the army were mixed; principles, partisanship, propaganda, parliamentary tactics, parochialism, and personal advantage all played roles. This is a work by a scholar who knows her materials and how to use them. One is somewhat surprised that there were so few references to Dutch theory on military matters. The jacket itself is based on a Dutch manual of arms, and many Netherlands ideas on war and armies dating at least back to Erasmus were known and published in seventeenth-century England. Nevertheless this is a good book and is a valuable study of antiarmy ideology and its ramifications during the period covered.

JOHN J. MURRAY

Coe College
Cedar Rapids
Iowa

ALVIN Z. RUBINSTEIN, ed. *Soviet and Chinese Influence in the Third World.* Pp. v, 231. New York: Praeger, 1975. $17.50.

John Kenneth Galbraith, when he was ambassador to India, once remarked that he could convince the Indians to do anything they had already made up their minds to do. This collection of papers undertakes the task of measuring the effectiveness of efforts to convince by the Soviet Union and China. Although the papers are generally of high scholarly quality, it is, to say the least, a difficult analytical chore to separate the results of "influence" from mere coincidence of views.

Rubinstein sets the framework— which is frequently ignored by the contributors—in an introductory essay. Among the hypotheses he sets out are (1) influence is apt to be greater when utilization of aid grants is higher—that is, the amount of the announced grant is not the key but the percentage actually committed for use; (2) showcase projects do not produce a climate for long term influence; (3) the political value of economic assistance diminishes over time and the continuation of it often results from a need to counter the presence of a rival; (4) terms of trade, rather than volume, are a better indicator of influence; and (5) failure of the donor country to purchase products of plants built with its assistance leads to friction and diminished influence. The editor also notes that the acquisition and handling of data for the study of influence are "awesome."

The articles cover almost every area of the third world. They range from a less satisfactory historical treatment of Soviet-and-Sino-Indonesian relations to a close study of Indo-Soviet interaction by William Barnds, who has already published a valuable book on Indian relations with the great powers. A useful article by George Ginsburgs looks at the Soviet reaction to Chinese influence in Africa and Latin America, drawing on Soviet sources to illustrate, to an extent, the third hypothesis of Rubinstein mentioned above.

Rubinstein concludes by stating that the studies show that "the influence of the Soviet Union and China on the actual domestic and foreign policy behavior of courted third world countries has been modest," adding that studies of this type are in their "infancy." As much might also be said for studies of American influence in the same areas of the world and when such are done the conclusion that American influence has also been "modest" might well be drawn. The studies also show that what might be called "reverse influence" is at work as the recipient countries draw the great powers (Soviet Union, China or the United States) into local disputes which more often than not conflict with the interests of the great powers themselves.

The studies and the introductory and concluding essays justify Rubinstein's final remark: they do "constitute and advance toward a more accurate understanding of Soviet/Chinese influence in third world countries."

CRAIG BAXTER

Accra
Ghana

DAVID WALL. *The Charity of Nations: The Political Economy of Foreign Aid.* Pp. v, 181. New York: Basic Books, 1973. $7.95.

This is a sensible book about aid. It is so in part because it raises questions and examines issues without the preconception that there are always known or even knowable answers.

The issues are cast in economic terms. Aid comes from taxes collected by governments in rich countries. It may or may not pass through intermediaries (multinational agencies) on the way to foreign peoples through their governments. What are the motivations of aid-giving countries? Up to what point can taxes be collected and used for aid? What is the return or expected return which can be compared to the forgone consumption implied by taxes? These relate to the supply of aid and follow some introductory data and a discussion of their interpretation.

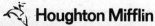
Kindly mention THE ANNALS *when writing to advertisers*

Similarly matters of the demand for aid are analyzed. On a costless basis, demands are near infinite, but there are costs: dependency, distortions, political pay-offs, and the like. Even considering costs, the demand far exceeds the supply and any conceivable supply. This raises the question of *how* to allocate available aid (since use of the market mechanism would make no sense in the aid context) and, secondly, *who* should do the allocating?

If there were means to predict the effectiveness of aid in different national situations, these could be a great help in solving the allocation problem, but regrettably the Rosenstein-Rodan formulation of 1961 (the only formula in the book) is, for empirical and conceptual reasons, no help; nor, for that matter, is the familiar two-gap model. Thus, the answer to the Wall question, "Can there be a scientific basis for determining the allocation of aid?" is NO! (p. 157). Besides the insufficiency of the models (read "the economics of development"), the contributing taxpayers are far from homogeneous in desires and expectations; donor governments are not altogether clear in their decision-making (in general, aid is a miniscule issue for representatives vis-à-vis their electors which gives a bias toward aid reduction). Ambiguities arise, too, in the relationships between recipient governments and their constituents.

All this is refreshing. Consider the opening shot: "Aid" may (may not) lead to "growth" which is only vaguely (and not always equally) related to "development" which may or may not be related to "alliance," "friendship," or "political affinity" which were probably the initial justifications for the aid. We know very little about the functional relationship, if any, between one variable and the next in the series.

The major issues are reviewed from the radical and conservative points of view, from the donor and recipient government points of view, and from various points of view among recipient citizens. Most questions have already been alluded to, but in the chapter on the forms of aid, issues such as "grants versus loans," "multilateralism versus bilateralism" and "programs versus projects" are given particular attention.

The book is a "primer" but only in a very special sense. It is basic, it reads well and simply. But it is not properly an "introduction" to the subject since it lays bare the collective ignorance of economists (particularly) on the matter of induced development. The lay reader probably could be better "introduced" in another way. But the object lesson in humility as a clear and sharp reminder can be of much value to academicians and development practicioners on the donor end and to the growing group of "planners" on the recipient end.

"As a political animal," says Wall (p. 4), "I regard aid as a good thing, the more the better. As an economist by profession I am concerned with seeing that aid is used as efficiently as possible." And thereby starts his tale. . . .

JOHN M. HUNTER
Michigan State University
East Lansing

AFRICA, ASIA AND LATIN AMERICA

SHAHRAM CHUBIN and SEPHR ZABIH. *The Foreign Relations of Iran: A Developing State in a Zone of Great-Power Conflict.* Pp. 378. Berkeley: University of California Press, 1975. $17.50.

A study of the foreign policy of "a small state in a zone of Great-Power conflict" should be timely for American thinking on international relations, particularly because of the growing importance of the Persian Gulf and of oil in world politics. Moreover, a study of Iran's foreign policy helps to dramatize the risks in viewing third world countries in monolithic terms, as certain officials appear prone to do. For here is a nation which, in March of 1974, pledged one billion dollars to the proposed three billion capital fund to help stabilize the balance of payments of both developing and developed countries affected by the oil shortage. Here is the nation to which Pan American Airways turned for a loan to see it through its severest financial crisis. How fantastic to equate it, in its policies and economics, to those of Chad or Bangladesh. Its foreign policy has moved from a period of no alliances with the West in the early 1950s to participation in a Northern Tier of alliances against the Soviet Union to a de facto nonalignment policy within a generally pro-western world outlook. In other words, even this single country has had its diversity and change.

Iran's policies in the Middle East and the world are a product of the Shah's personal ambitions and diplomacy, the gradual transformation of Soviet policy from expansionism to accommodation, and its growing economic and political capacities. The main value of the present study is its effort to delineate these trends and to place Iran under the spotlight of major theoretical writings on foreign policy and decision making. However, while certain theories are cited, they are not pursued throughout the balance of the study. Theory is limited to the beginning and end of the study.

The book provides a portrayal of the shifts and turns in Iran's foreign policy in response to changing great power thrusts in the area and the changing Middle Eastern political scene. The Shah's success from the time he assumed personal responsibility for foreign policy is delineated. His mistakes and the risk that a "brittle authority which, out of caution and anxiety, may conceal its purposes in secrecy" (Seabury's Foreword) are less vigorously explored.

One point deserves special mention: the propositions and hypotheses on decision-making illustrate both their usefulness in focusing issues and the near banality of this approach, for example ". . . where foreign policy is personal, it will reflect the leader's perception and values . . ." (p. 300). More helpful is the practical suggestion that ". . . in its relations with the superpowers, Iran relies on diplomacy; but in its regional and local relations, where it is relatively strong, it prefers to emphasize might."

A more serious question, and one for Middle East specialists to examine, is how does this study relate to the landmark pioneering studies of men such as Ramazani and Lenczowski? Their works are noted in a rather expansive bibliography, but less so in the text as such. If scholarship is to advance from strength to strength, if "scholars are to stand on one another's shoulders," the interconnection between early and later works ought to be fully traced and acknowledged. This is the first calling of those privileged to serve "the university."

KENNETH W. THOMPSON
International Council for Educational
  Development
New York

RICHARD DEACON. *The Chinese Secret Service.* Pp. 523. New York: Taplinger Publishing Co., 1974. $14.95.

With China's re-emergence as a great power, there is an urgent need in the Western world to know its intelligence operations. Unfortunately, little has been published on this subject in the English language. Richard Deacon's book *The Chinese Secret Service* is a timely contribution to our understanding of one of the vital aspects of Chinese politics.

This book is a historical description and analysis of Chinese secret service from about the fourth century B.C. to the present. It deals with both internal security and external espionage in thirty-seven chapters with illustrations. The author selects some particular periods and personalities for detailed treatment, such as Sun Tzu, Empress Wu, the Mongols, Ho Shen, Tsu-hsi, Li Lien-ying, the Boxers, the secret societies, "Two-Gun" Cohen, Abbot Chao Kung, K'ang Sheung and Tai Li. The style of the book is novelistic with many interesting accounts of the chicaneries and adventures of colorful individuals.

The author's attempt to cover more than two thousand years of Chinese secret service activities has necessarily led to superficiality in many parts of the book. His approach is basically episodical and personality-oriented. He has failed to provide the reader with a comprehensive study of the structure and functioning of the Chinese secret service system. Nor has he analyzed its activities in a larger conceptual framework of Chinese government and politics.

The more serious weakness of the book, however, lies in Deacon's many misleading conclusions based on limited evidence. For instance, he maintains that *I Ching* influenced Mao Tse-tung on his transformation of Marxism and Communism into "totally different Maoism." He has grossly exaggerated the importance of Sun Tzu's teachings and *I Ching* in Chinese secret service. It is absurd to say that the main function of the Chinese secret service in the latter part of the 19th century was to recover art treasures although that may have been one of its incidental assignments. It is too far-fetched to link the pornographic Chinese novel *Chin P'ing Mei* to secret service!

The book contains too many irrelevant materials. It reads more like a book on general Chinese history than on Chinese secret service. Although the book has shed no new light on the subject, it has put together many useful data in one convenient volume. It is a welcome addition to the extremely limited literature in this field. There is still a critical need for a definitive work on Chinese secret service.

GEORGE P. JAN
University of Toledo
Ohio

JONATHAN DERRICK. *Africa's Slaves Today*. Pp. 256. New York: Schocken Books, 1975. $13.50.

The impact of the African slave trade has been very great. Somewhere between 70 and 100 million descendants of Black Africans transported in this trade now people areas outside of Africa. There is a vast literature on the Atlantic trade and on its effects in both the New World and Africa. On the other hand, there has been relatively little systematic attempt to bring together information on the extent of the persistence within Africa of social statuses which might be regarded as slavery. In practice this latter job is a difficult matter because it is a diverse set of institutions, and also because slavery is officially proscribed under the legal codes of nearly every country in the world, thus making information difficult to obtain.

Mr. Derrick begins by opting for the formal definitions of slave and slavery contained in the League of Nations Slavery Convention of 1926 and the Supplement of the United Nations of 1956. The heart of this definition is the treatment of a person as another's property. He tries to keep this distinction in his sights but finds himself broadening his view to serf-like statuses, forced labor and castes.

There seem to be two main themes in his survey. The first is an effort to understand the indigenous social orders of African societies which either sanction slave status or generate economic conditions which maintain it. The second theme is the examination of conditions in external areas such as the Arabian Peninsula, or internal areas like Ethiopia or the Republic of South Africa which create a demand for slaves or something close to them.

The issues raised in a subject such as this are very many. The volume of sources which must be controlled is of immense proportions, and the judgment required in interpreting the masses of information is exacting. The author falls a bit short on all scores. By making the decision to examine indigenous social orders he not only raises a key issue, but at the same time takes on an overwhelming task. There are hundreds of indigenous social orders in Africa. Even if all were fully described the task would be formidable. As it is, many are unreported or only partially described, and still the numbers defeat him, for his attention is devoted to only a relatively few of the better known cases. To supplement this he takes an institutional approach to certain well-known customs on a kind of survey basis: bride-price, the relation of pygmies to the farming peoples, Tutsi-Hutu relationships, and so on.

His examination of external and internal demand for cheap labor which generates a continuation of slaving is also too brief. He discusses the persistence of slavery in the Arabian Peninsula and its connection with the pilgrimage to Mecca in a generally interesting but brief fashion. Five chapters are devoted to economic circumstances connected with colonialism: to forced labor or to labor migration which reduce people to near slave status. A final chapter summarizes the findings of the study and discusses the sorts of changes in economic and social conditions which could lead to the disappearance of slavery and related practices.

The study is important and interesting, but the treatment afforded it in a book of only 240 pages is too brief and sketchy to be entirely satisfactory. Mr. Derrick opens far more issues than he can deal with in a scholarly manner in such brief compass. He fails to take full advantage of the enormous increase in original historical publication on the Atlantic slave trade of recent years and his chapter entitled "The Old Slave-Trade" seems thin in view of the substantial contributions of such scholars as Philip Curtin which make the original sources vastly more accessible than they were only a few years ago.

His ethnographic references are generally very good, but far too few to fully achieve his stated goals. His discussions of Liberia, South Africa and Ethiopia are based on too few sources in view of the bodies of literature available.

In sum, this book is either too short or too long: too short to implement its excellent central idea, too long to be simply a statement of that idea and a plan for future research.

EDGAR V. WINANS
University of Washington
Seattle

ROBERT H. DONALDSON. *Soviet Policy toward India: Ideology and Strategy.* Pp. vii, 338. Cambridge, Mass.: Harvard University Press, 1974. $15.00.

This book is a study of the impact of the professed ideological commitments of the Soviet Union on Soviet policy in relation to India. The author concludes that Soviet policy toward India, beginning from the Bolshevik Revolution till date, has been dictated more by the self-interest of the Soviet Union than by considerations of Marxist-Leninist-communist ideology. He seeks to bring out this divergence between theory and Soviet practice with an exhaustive scrutiny of the all-too-frequent and vociferous pronouncements of Soviet leaders and of the writings and commentaries of Soviet specialists on India.

That there is such a divergence, in general, between actual policy on the one hand and the principles supposed to govern it on the other is neither new nor surprising. Indeed, both the superpowers and large countries such as China and India continually face the problem of having to reconcile their policies with their professed ideals and ideologies. Thus the contradictions between American pronouncements on freedom and official U.S. support of dictatorships, between the revolutionary rhetoric of the Chinese and their cynical policies toward genuine struggles of national liberation, or for that matter, between Indian assertions of self-determination and a contrary official policy: these are well known.

The question then arises: how effective and even relevant is this stereotyped analytical framework in evaluating Soviet policy toward India? In other words, is this process governed solely by the expediency of Soviet self-interest? How relevant are other related factors such as, for instance, a pragmatic evaluation by the Soviets of Indian realities?

While it is almost a truism that ideological assertions are not decisive whereas self-interest is dominant in Soviet policy-making and actual policies, the analytical framework seeking to explain these policies in the Indian context must also take account of the gradually evolving response of the Soviet Union to the objective situation in India—a task which the author does not appear to regard as relevant.

It is arguable that for almost three decades until the death of Stalin, this awareness was not a decisive element in

Soviet policy formation toward India. Indeed, the Soviet interest in India during these years was peripheral. Thus, as is documented by the author, both under Lenin and Stalin, the internal and external considerations relating to the survival and consolidation of the Soviet state and the socio-economic transformation of the Soviet economy were paramount elements in Soviet policy formation in general.

At the same time, however, it is possible to argue that, during the Leninist-Stalinist period, the Soviets decided to adopt a low-profile stance in India by reason of certain objective factors on the Indian scene. Through most of the period, the Indian communists remained a disorganized, ineffectual group. Their terrorist activities were effectively put down by the British. Their role in the Indian political struggle was reduced to the adventurism of terrorist-agitators by the broad-based independence movement under Gandhi's leadership with its emphasis on a non-violent strategy. (These details and many more are narrated by the author in a chronological fashion but not effectively integrated into his analytical framework.) Indeed at the Second Congress of the Comintern in July 1920, Lenin, while instructing the motley group of Indian Communists that they support the "bourgeois-liberation movement," said: "the Hindu Communists did not succeed until the present time in establishing a Communist party in their country, and because of this single fact the views of Comrade Roy are to a large extent not well grounded" (p. 10). Perhaps for the same reason, the Soviet policy-makers under Stalin found it difficult to work out a decisive plan of action for the Indian communists.

In the period after Stalin's death, however, the facts seem clearer and it would seem to be certainly fruitful to explore Soviet policy-making in India in terms of the pursuit of Soviet self-interest, in light of, and in response to, changing Indian realities. Such an explanatory framework is more realistic than the author's straight-jacketed one which seeks to explain the process solely in terms of Soviet self-interest without integrating the factors on the Indian political and economic scene into the analysis. Thus, in the context of the policy of peaceful coexistence initiated by Khruschev, the Indo-Soviet rapport began with a realistic assessment by the Soviets of the stability of the Indian political system under Nehru; his left-of-center economic policies with their emphasis on planning and heavy industries (which also satisfied Soviet predilections in this regard); his foreign policy initiatives such as his peace proposals for the resolution of the Korean conflict, the seating of Communist China in the U.N., his active endorsement of the Geneva peace proposals for resolving the Indochina conflict (all of which predate active support by the Soviets to India on issues such as Kashmir and Goa). With the emergence of China as a geophysical factor inimical to the interests of both India and the Soviet Union, the convergence of interest has resulted in a sustained, successful Indo-Soviet relationship.

While the role of ideology in this process, as the author correctly emphasizes, is irrelevant, ideology is not static, anymore than religious dogma. One must keep in view, therefore, the communist tradition of continuous adjustments, refinements and even "enrichment" of the core of Marxist doctrine in response to new objective phenomena—a practice which is more or less absent in the Western democratic tradition. In this process, a good deal of theorizing and revisions of existing dogma take place in response to changing phenomena. In the context of the present book, this is true of writings of Soviet specialists on the emergence of the developing countries and their problems. That is to say, current Soviet commentaries and ideological pronouncements on the problems of developing countries largely proceed from a realistic assessment of the problems of developing countries (for example, their economic and political diversity); and Soviet policy formation, at least in the case of India, has tended to reflect such assessments.

While the book therefore does not quite succeed in being an insightful and useful analysis (as distinct from a description), of Soviet policy towards India, it has a mass of information on the chronology of events in India and the Soviet Union and updates it beyond the Bangla Desh war to the present.

PADMA DESAI
Harvard University
Cambridge
Massachusetts

STEPHEN LYON ENDICOTT. *Diplomacy and Enterprise: British China Policy, 1933–1937.* Pp. xv, 209. Vancouver, Canada: University of British Columbia Press, 1975. $15.00.

The major thesis of this book is that, in the period under study, British East Asian policy underwent a decided shift in emphasis. The Leith-Ross mission, the decision to move the legation to Nanking and to strengthen the commercial counsellor staff, the negotiations for currency and railroad loans represented a more activist policy pursued by the Treasury under the leadership of Neville Chamberlain, then Chancellor of the Exchequer, and Sir Warren Fisher, the permanent undersecretary. The Far Eastern Department of the Foreign Office had favored a more quiescent policy which, while it sought to win Chinese support, abjured any move considered provocative to Japan. To it, the Treasury policies, adopted by the cabinet, smacked too much of outmoded treaty-port diplomacy and involved the risk of intensifying Sino-Japanese hostilities which could only result in the elimination of British interests in China. An even more striking change, Endicott asserts, was that which transpired in Chamberlain's own views. Having been the chief protagonist of a policy of friendship with Japan, designed as a measure of coping with the increasing German threat in Europe, he embarked on a course seemingly in contradiction with this basic strategy.

How to account for these shifts in policy which, in Endicott's view, not only marked a return to the methods of old-style imperialism but also reflected an underestimation of the strength of both Chinese nationalism and Japanese expansionism? The answer, we are told, is to be found in the influence of a China market lobby which wanted the assurance of government support in pursuit of the "vast China market" still deemed available to the entrepreneurially bold and the politically resolute. Composed of such major corporations as Shell-B.P., ICI, Unilever as well as such "old China hands" as Jardine, Matheson and Swire and Sons, its influence was sufficiently powerful to upset the basic strategic and political considerations on which British policy in China had been based.

The sweeping conclusions Endicott attempts to draw are the weakest element of the book. The decisive impact of business influence is asserted but nowhere convincingly demonstrated. Whether or not one accepts the Leninist theory of imperialism, it can not be sustained on the basis of the material presented. For this, the author would need another book. Missing, too, is a view of Britain's China policy from the perspective of her overall foreign-policy considerations. One suspects that this would produce a more complex formulation of the determinants of policy.

The major strength of the book lies in the material presented drawn from official documents, private papers of governmental and business figures, and from interviews. These shed light on conflicts within the government, on the views of some of the leading personalities, and on aspects of decision-making in Britain during this period.

WILLARD H. ELSBREE
Ohio University
Athens

R. D. MALLON AND J. V. SOURROUILLE. *Economic Policymaking in a Conflict Society: The Argentine Case.* Pp. 264. Lawrence, Mass.: Harvard University Press, 1975. $16.00.

The most interesting material found in this account is the compilation of data on income, farm prices and industrial growth. The description of economic trends found in chapters dealing with agriculture, industry and foreign trade are also useful. The discussion of the differential impact of inflation on the distribution of income and the financing of growth was also illuminating. But the authors were not merely seeking to present an economic history of Argentina, of which they are quite knowledgeable, but attempting to diagnose the sources of the ills of Argentina, which they presumed to locate in something described as the policymaking structure which purportedly lacked the flexibility and proper political supports ("coalitions") to fashion a consensual development policy. The authors offer their own recipes. The result is a major disaster: the locus of social conflict is attributed to atavistic irrational behavior rather than to the imperatives inherent in capitalist society: ". . . the psychology of a primitive, tribal society, not of a responsible, pluralistic one." The authors' discussion is full of the empty rhetoric derived from a now discredited modernization theory: "pluralism" is meant to describe a class-divided society; "pragmatism" is the ideology of minor reforms within a capitalist society; "responsible" refers to those who follow prescribed political formulas. Moral imperatives replace scientific analysis of social reality. The effort to describe the "fundamental cause of the semi-stagnation" as the result of policymaking not properly adapted to the conditions of a conflict society is question-begging on the grandest scale: the substantive demands of the major classes which contest power preclude the kinds of "adaptations" that the authors prescribe. The inability of the authors to conceptualize class conflict vitiates their effort to theorize about 'solutions'. The vacuous terminology itself obscures basic issues: the vague "conflict society" stands in place of historically specific class conflict in a dependent capitalist society; "policymakers" and "development strategies" are divorced from the class structure as manifestations of benighted politicians or isolated technocrats. Policy

managers (and the whole state apparatus) are seen as neutral subjects capable of fashioning the most diverse coalitions as if it were all a magic show, despite the fact that the military and police have shown, in recent years, a clear propensity to jail workers and protect property owners. The writers, unhappy with the social-political content of their subject matter, impose vacuous formulas that leave substantive questions unanswered: why does capitalist development generate class polarization and class conflict? It is not adequate to label it a "crisis syndrome" or attribute it to malevolent wills. The spinning off of 'mediative' institutions outside of the current Argentine socio-economic realities is as productive as Alpine yodeling exercises.

JAMES F. PETRAS
State University of New York
Binghamton

ELAINE POTTER. *The Press as Opposition: The Political Role of South African Newspapers.* Pp. 228. Totowa, N.J.: Rowman and Littlefield, 1975. $13.75.

This book is an important and at the same time a limited contribution. It is important because it deals with a significant subject and is a systematic attempt to fill a very real gap, because it has much that is new or brought together in this context for the first time, and because it makes a genuine contribution to the history of South Africa since the victory of the National Party in 1948. Specifically it deals with the twenty years from 1948 to 1968 although the opening chapters provide a brief survey of the development of the press prior to that year. The book is divided into seven chapters entitled "Politics and the Press," "A Brief History of the Press," "The Ownership Structure of the Press," "Who Reads the Newspapers," "Suppression of Opposition," "The Press and Government" and "The Press in Opposition: What the Newspapers Say." It is not unfair to suggest, perhaps, that there is all too little of the last; and there is nothing at all that I can recall concerning journalists and the nature and significance, if any, of their organization. The thesis of the book is stated at the outset and emphasized throughout. It is that between 1948 and 1968 "the English language press became an 'external' opposition, whilst the Afrikaans language press, as an institution within the ranks of government, constituted an 'internal' opposition." The argument takes its point of departure from the political triumph of Afrikaner nationalism which brought about an English-speaking press almost uniformly opposed to the government, its ideology and its party, and closes with the 'verligte-verkrampte' controversy within the Nationalist ranks which produced the government party's first major split. Dr. Potter argues, convincingly enough, that this split came about largely as the result of the ferment generated by the Afrikaans Press. She concludes that the verligte-verkrampte battle "was as much a bid for its [the Cape Nationalist newspaper Die Burger] own ascendancy in the party—and it had suffered a serious falling off in influence under Verwoerd—as a fight against the 'verkramptes'." This, however, was and is a struggle within the framework of Nationalist ideology. The English Press' opposition is not. This, argues Dr. Potter, constitutes treason, "not a fourth estate but a fifth column." She attributes the continuing opposition of the press to a highly independent press ethic (was it so independent before 1948, one wonders?) and the commitment to a different vision of the 'good society'. Why then did the Nationalist government not silence the English-speaking press? She suggests that the main reasons are first, that it is a white press and secondly, that it has never posed a serious threat to Nationalist domination. Moreover, as she carefully points out, not only is the Nationalist government sensitive about its constitutional, legal and parliamentary image abroad; and not only does it succeed in producing an atmosphere of real intimidation by other means; but also, the government is far more concerned with the ideological fervor and conformity of its own Afrikaans-speaking white people than it is with that of the groups outside this community.

The limitations of this book stem from the fact that it never quite escapes either in style or approach from its origins as a doctoral dissertation. It is painstakingly concerned with structural relationships and 'key' questions, one consequence of which is that it rarely makes exciting reading. When it does seek to relate men, motives and events in a rigorous analysis the case is otherwise. Students of contemporary southern Africa will want to read this book.

R. B. BALLINGER
Rhode Island College
Providence

ELLIOTT P. SKINNER. African Urban Life: The Transformation of Ouagadougou. Pp. xii, 487. Princeton, N.J.: Princeton University Press, 1974. $20.00.

Here is a timely and important study. Written by the chairman of the Department of Anthropology at Columbia University and former ambassador to Upper Volta (the first anthropologist to hold such a position), it is a much-needed analysis of African urban life, by an individual who, because of the varying roles he has been able to take in the society he studied and the length of time he has been involved in the area (15 years), is extremely well equipped to provide a balanced view.

The focus is on Ouagadougou, capital of Upper Volta and a municipality located in the heart of the drought-ridden Sahel region of West Africa. Like other Saharan cities its social and material resources are being stretched to the extreme by the intense pressures of incoming desert peoples who are seeking relief from the ravages of drought by migrating to urban centers. Although Skinner's study was not undertaken during the drought period (most of his data were collected in 1964–5), it does provide a valuable social backdrop against which more recent events are being acted out.

This monograph also provides a microcosmic lens through which to project the larger problems of African urbanism. Skinner ably pinpoints two of the more pressing concerns of sub-Saharan municipalities: unemployment and potential class conflict. For one thing, the massive influx of migrants who wish to reside in the more modern sectors of their society, cannot be accommodated in the limited employment market since there are few bureaucratic openings, little industry, and a modest amount of trade and foreign commerce.

For another, Upper Volta has a dearth of natural resources and no seaports for expanding trade, and therefore must rely mainly on agricultural endeavors for internal sources of development capital. Yet agriculturalists now see the powerful urban elite using revenue taken from rural produce to strengthen, not the rural, but the urban infrastructure. Thus the elite is increasingly resented by a growing non-elite sector of agricultural workers and the jobless, both of whom feel their most basic economic needs are being slighted.

Skinner concludes that the rift between elite and non-elite is widening as each sector competes for the slim resources to be found in this nation. The prognosis is that if the now relatively ill-defined class cleavages are allowed to solidify, we can expect to see increasing conflict in urban Africa in the years to come.

SANDRA T. BARNES
University of Pennsylvania
Philadelphia

PETER H. SMITH. *Argentina and the Failure of Democracy: Conflict among Political Elites, 1904–1955.* Pp. 215. Madison: The University of Wisconsin Press, 1974. $12.50.

In *Argentina and the Failure of Democracy*, Peter H. Smith, professor of history at the University of Wisconsin-Madison and author of *Politics and Beef in Argentina* (1969), examines "the formation, duration and decay of democratic rule" (p. xvii) in Argentina by focusing on the Chamber of Deputies. While acknowledging that the Chamber "has rarely initiated and approved legislation over strong presidential opposition" (p. xviii), Smith argues that an analysis of the Chamber can provide important insights into the reasons for the breakdown of Argentine democracy. Specifically, by means of an analysis of 1,712 roll call votes between 1904 and 1955 and a survey of the social background and career patterns of *all* the 1,571 *deputados* who served during the same period, Smith concludes that in the Chamber: (1) the link between social status and party allegiance increased gradually over time, (2) the lines of conflict became increasingly rigid, and (3) party identification was consistently the most significant predictor of voting behavior. The general impression received is of an ever more polarized Chamber.

Most of the analysis of the Chamber is presented in Chapters Two through Five. They are preceded by an introductory chapter that provides an historical overview of Argentina that stresses its late industrializing, export-oriented economy, the autonomy of the army and the growth of the urban working class. In the final chapter, Smith releases himself from the constraints of his data to write a broad, interpretative essay on contemporary Argentine politics. Borrowing from the "crisis approach" to political change developed by the Committee on Comparative Politics of the Social Science Research Council, he contends that Argentina has experienced crises of participation, legitimacy and distribution. The participation crisis of the early 1900s was met by expanding the electorate. The new voters swelled the ranks of the Radical Party which, as a result, decided it no longer had to compromise with other elites. A legitimacy crisis ensued that triggered the 1930 coup. A distribution crisis coincided with the legitimacy crisis and the growth of an ignored urban proletariat, thus paving the way for Perón. Since Perón, "efforts to alleviate one of the crises aggravate one or both of the others" (p. 108). The result is political stalemate.

Argentina and the Failure of Democracy is both methodologically sophisticated and intellectually stimulating. The book constitutes a significant contribution to the literature on Latin American politics. It can be read most profitably by people possessing some knowledge of twentieth-century Argentina.

SUSAN KAUFMAN PURCELL
University of California
Los Angeles

ROBERT F. TURNER. *Vietnamese Communism: Its Origins and Development.* Pp. 517. Stanford, Calif.: Hoover Institution Press, 1975. $14.95.

In spite of its promising title, Robert Turner's book does not answer some basic questions about Vietnamese Communism. What is lacking is an analysis of the relationship between Vietnamese Communism and its social milieu.

In its defense it may be said that the book is a well-written narrative of the fifty-five years since Ho Chi Minh followed the majority of the French Socialist Party into the Third International in 1920. All of the big dates, names and places are in order, and some minor factual errors of other authors are corrected. Vietnamese Communist documentary materials in translation and interviews with defectors are used, although other important primary source material, mainly in Vietnamese, evidently was not examined.

The narrative follows the precedent of conventional wisdom as to choice of topics for emphasis and is suffused with the author's own hostility toward his subject. For example, Turner emphasizes the distinction between the Communists and the "Nationalists." He fails to see that it was nationalism which propelled Vietnamese during the 1920s and 1930s into an alliance with International Communism and cannot digest evidence that "proletarian internationalism" continues to serve Vietnamese national interests. Nor does he recognize that nationalism has organizational as well as ideological implications which the Communists best understood and

most effectively realized in practice. After Turner, the role of nationalism in Vietnamese Communism is still an open question. On the importance of land reform, he observes that before the Resistance ninety-eight percent of the farmers in the North cultivated land they owned, but he neglects to mention his sources also show that extreme parcelization and indebtedness to moneylenders drove a large proportion of these farmers into disadvantageous, unstable tenancy arrangements. Land reform and cooperativization indeed had an abstract severity based on class that is distasteful to liberal sensibilities, but Turner fails to appreciate that, due to the deterioration of traditional patron-client relationships and sharply rising population throughout the colonial period, private ownership could not maintain an equitable distribution of economic security in this precarious agricultural zone. He also imagines the Vietnamese people to have been undifferentiated (for example, generalizations such as "popular dissatisfaction with the Viet Minh" and "The Communists had never been popular in southern Vietnam"), whereas cleavages of class and opinion always have been a key to understanding the Vietnamese Revolution. In general, Turner's study fails to account for how Vietnamese Communism evolved in relation to social forces inside Vietnam and applies evaluative standards drawn from Western experience to a society in which authoritarian, corporate models have been the norm.

WILLIAM S. TURLEY
Southern Illinois University
Carbondale

PETER WORSLEY. *Inside China.* Pp. 270. Totowa, N.J.: Rowman and Littlefield, 1975. $12.50.

Peter Worsley visited China for three weeks in 1972. This book presents direct reporting on his experiences, combined with "prior and subsequent reflection" (p. 19). He is not a China specialist and does not know Chinese. But on his return to England, he says, "I steeped myself in the literature" (p. 21). His personal observations about China are, for the most part, clear and convincing. These observations have value in the difficult and important task we Westerners have of understanding the vast human complex of China and the historic events taking place there.

The strongest part of the book is the discussion of rural communes (Chapter 4 and elsewhere) which Worsley calls "the heart of the matter." On this subject more than any other, his direct reporting combines successfully with other material to produce a generally satisfactory statement of how communes, and their constituent brigades and teams, operate. On other subjects, especially the cities, he provides useful information, and in some of his reflections, especially in the concluding chapter, he makes worthy contributions. The map in the endpapers and the index are valuable features.

But the book has such grave shortcomings that I find it difficult to suggest who might gain from reading all or most of it. Worsley is an anthropologist who has had experience on several continents. He expresses the admirable hope (p. 19) that people will think about China anthropologically, comparing and contrasting China with their own society. But almost nowhere do I find in this book, on careful reading, evidence that Worsley himself has made such a comparison really carefully. He cheats his readers with occasional brief references to Britain that, aside from some telling statistics on prices of certain consumer products (pp. 256–259) and some family expenditure data (p. 229), appear more like ill-informed and offhand slurs on his own people than products of professional anthropological research and analysis.

A second serious weakness is failure to document assertions adequately. The book makes a great many statements and presents many statistics without a single source footnote. There are numerous text references to authors, but not one page citation. Hard information, especially quantitative, about China is at such a premium that Worsley's teasing with unsubstantiated material is unpardonable.

A third grave error is Worsley's failure to restrict his writing to matters on which

he is sufficiently informed. While he is so casual about his own experience that he does not even reveal his full itinerary in China, he touches—at times very badly—subjects and countries not essential to his story. We do not need his views on Tibet. His initial chapter ("Capitalist Asia") is a discredit to a serious scholar. I wish he had put effort instead into making his historical survey of China (Chapter 3, "Stability and Revolt") more solid and balanced.

There is a fourth large problem of this book, but on this reasonable persons may disagree about the worth of Worsley's work. He is a Marxist and he presents more than seems useful, especially for an American audience, on purely Marxist issues, such as disillusioned ex-Communists in Britain who won't believe positive reporting on China (pp. 15–18), and questions like the inevitability of "determinisms, bourgeois and Marxist alike" (page 207 and elsewhere). A Western Marxist should be able to help the rest of us understand China. The way Worsley describes the communes and some other features of Chinese life, as well as some of his reflections, probably gains from his outlook. But he scorns "China-watchers," especially American (pp. 19, 28, 126, 144, 181, but in a different tone, p. 261). Here he makes a mistake if he wants to discuss China with serious students. Unless he intends to write only for other Marxists, he should inform himself on what serious students of China are doing, and relate his remarks to the accumulating corpus of information and interpretation. He might be surprised not only at the information he gains but also at the empathy for China shown by many who are spending their lives studying that unique and hugely important country.

WARREN S. HUNSBERGER
The American University
Washington, D.C.

EUROPE

GLEN BARCLAY. *The Rise and Fall of the New Roman Empire.* Pp. 210. New York: St. Martin's Press, 1975. $16.95.

Italophilia is frequently a warranted and pleasant condition, especially when it relates to the Italian people, their culture or the natural beauty of the land. However, when it is based on Italian politics, domestic or international, it can be a malady. *The Rise and Fall of the New Roman Empire* reads like an Italophile's apology for Italy's foreign policy in the past hundred years.

Author Glen Barclay, a New Zealand historian, indicates that the purpose of his book is to describe the nature of Italian influence in Europe and in Africa from 1890 to 1943. Also, Barclay describes the way the influence was exerted and the consequence of Italian activities for other nations.

Following a discussion of some of Italy's post-*Risorgimento* European activities, Italian efforts to establish the nation as a colonial power in Africa at the end of the Nineteenth Century are reviewed. Italy's maneuvering among the European powers before World War I is then described. Also, its expansionist plans and hunts for glory in the Balkans, the Mediterranean and again in Africa are presented. The questionable conclusion is offered that in the complicated international activities leading up to the world conflict, Italy held the balance in Europe even though she was the weakest of the great powers.

Italy's entry into World War I on the side of the Allies is described as the only course of action open to the nation. The country's war efforts and problems are depicted in such a way as to emphasize mistreatment on the part of the Allies. In fact, the Italian role in the conflagration is made to appear as being decisive for the Allied victory. The peace settlement and Italy's paucity of reward are discussed. Mussolini's rise to power during Italy's post-war difficulties and the role he assumed in foreign affairs seem natural to the author. The Italian dictator acted like De Gaulle in that both leaders upon assuming office had to affirm the importance and authority of their nations to the world. According to Barclay, the real tragedy of the 1930s was that the Western powers failed to recognize that Mussolini, the disruptor of world peace,

was its only available guardian. This is a dubious conclusion on many grounds.

This book covers a great deal of familiar ground and contributes little of original value. The author's speculation about almost victories and critical outcomes of wars dependent in one case on one more torpedo often weaken the picture being portrayed. Italy's role in world politics has frequently been underestimated, but this book does harm to its image because of overstatement.

STEPHEN P. KOFF
Syracuse University
New York

ELLIOT R. GOODMAN. *The Fate of the Atlantic Community.* Pp. xx, 583. New York: Praeger, 1975. $27.50.

Elliot R. Goodman's prodigious effort to research-analyze the fate of the Atlantic Community is worthy of the highest accolades possible. The author brilliantly intertwines the promising declarations by politicians and the authoritative commentaries of scholars, both in Europe and America. His cohesive volume serves as a monumental treatise to the halting successes combined with haunting failures to forge that larger "community" that Goodman hopefully visualizes beyond even the loose "partnership," however defined, that has emerged since World War II.

Goodman's scholarly theories of social and moral community ("human infrastructure"), political institution-building, and security strategies, including planning and decision-making are prudently measured within the prevailing actualities. While DeGaulle was properly characterized as the "disintegrator" of the community complex, particularly his *force de frappe* and his concept, with all its gyrations, towards an "independent continental Europe," Russia included, this reviewer was concerned by the author's neglect of America's actual policies towards Europe's integration beyond the military security dilemmas involved in NATO.

America's singular national interests, global confrontation with the Soviets, including the fiasco in the Vietnam War, certainly confused the Europeans, and infused greater hesitancy towards even the "United Europe," which has to emerge prior to a realistic Atlantic Community.

Goodman's articulation on NATO planning, changing strategic theories, multiple balanced forces, Salt I and II serve as authoritative background for future protected negotiations.

His apt attention to the German Problem, political and security-wise, might have been strengthened by a solid analysis of Willy Brandt's *Ostpolitik*, the initiator of the later detente. Goodman is very suspicious of detente ("fragile and artificial"), due to his perceptions of Soviet imperatives.

The author's economic dimensions, including the pervasive growth and indirect influences of the multinational corporations were superbly interwoven with his major themes; as was his cautious, yet realistic analysis of the emerging North-South relationship.

Perhaps Goodman was confronted by a publication time-factor since he presented only fragmentary insertions of the vital, though ever-shifting Nixon Administration policies, which further exacerbated Europe-American relations.

Yet, as a compendium up to 1970, the author's mosaic of scenarios merits the avid attention of both practitioner and scholar alike as they attempt to diagnose the complexities—of the energy crisis, of economic dislocations, and of the Arab-Israeli protracted conflict—which presently occupy the latent Atlantic Community.

Even the more recent Helsinki (cosmetic) declarations may be more realistically interpreted due to Goodman's brilliant historicity.

ALFRED J. HOTZ
Augustana College
Sioux Falls, S.D.

T. F. LINDSAY and MICHAEL HARRINGTON. *The Conservative Party, 1918–1970.* Pp. viii, 271. New York: St. Martin's Press, 1974. $15.95.

In their preface the authors tell us their aim is to study the development of the Conservative Party since 1918. They have not intended to write a general history of the period; they have intended to write only an extended essay on the subject to amuse their readers and provoke discussion among them. They have, in fact, done far more than arouse their readers' interest for they have illuminated such complex subjects as the roles of the Leader of the party and of the Shadow Cabinet, the relation of the Queen to her Prime Ministers, the impact of coalition governments on party structure, and the interrelations of the Parliamentary party with the constituency party. Both authors are journalists associated with the *Daily Telegraph*, a newspaper regarded as not unfriendly to the Conservative Party. Yet the authors have retained their independence to freely criticize, sometimes harshly, the Conservative leaders and their policies.

In their introduction the authors begin with the proper assertion that the Conservative Party is a coalition; they nevertheless spend much time trying to identify conservatism as an entity. They attempt to identify conservatism with Burke's *Reflections on the French Revolution,* but they would do better to give more attention to Sir Robert Peel's *Tamworth Manifesto* of 1835 in which he sought a new coalition of all social groups with privilege, power, position, and property, including the propertied classes of the recently enfranchised factory towns. Peel's realism, not the romanticism of Burke and Disraeli, provides the best understanding of the modern Conservative Party.

The seventeen chapters of this political history are nearly evenly divided into two periods, the interwar years and the decades since the Second World War. During the 1930s when the Conservatives controlled the Coalition Government, such subjects as the abandonment of the gold standard, the adoption of Imperial preference, and the appeasement of the dictators receive the authors' attention. They regard the election of 1945 as the most important of the present century. This election returned the

Labor Party to office with sufficient power to nationalize major industries and to establish the welfare state. While accepting the social welfare reforms, the Conservatives have opposed the nationalization of industry by taking a position in favor of free enterprise and individual initiative. Over foreign affairs the Party has become deeply divided; like their eminent leader Winston Churchill, they have presided, against their wishes, over the dissolution of the British Empire. Such policies as the abandonment of the Suez Canal, the loss of the African colonies, the independence of India, and the entry into the Common Market have reduced Great Britain to a minor role in world affairs.

RAYMOND G. COWHERD
Lehigh University
Bethlehem
Pennsylvania

GERALD H. MEAKER. *The Revolutionary Left in Spain, 1914–1923.* Pp. viii, 562. Stanford, Calif.: Stanford University Press, 1974. $18.95.

Gerald H. Meaker has written "not a history of the working classes per se, but of the revolutionary movements or elites that contested for supremacy among them." In this work, he has not only given us an incisive study of the leadership of the Spanish Left but also has compared its development with that of the Left in other European countries, notably France, Italy, and Germany. A major objective, admirably carried out, is to pose questions and suggest areas for further study.

Meaker concludes that the Spanish Left, whether Communist, Anarcho-syndicalist, or Socialist, failed, and he sees the failure in the response of the Spanish labor movement to the Russian revolution. Perhaps nowhere else in Europe was the Russian revolution greeted with such enthusiasm as in Spain, but no Leninist party of consequence emerged to lead the Spanish proletariat. Explaining this paradox forms the unifying theme of Meaker's book.

Meaker's approach to his subject is varied. Though his principal concern is ideology, he deals effectively with the economic, social, and institutional framework of early twentieth century Spain. His best methodological tool is prosopography. Through studies of the careers of the most significant leaders, he explores the full range of options open to the Left. These studies take on added significance because we get a glimpse of the early careers of such people as Largo Caballero, Angel Pestaña, and Joaquin Maurín (to name just a few) who played important roles during the Second Republic-Civil War period.

The problem with Meaker's work is that it rests on a false paradox. Meaker contributes significantly to our understanding of the impact of the Russian revolution on the Spanish proletariat, but to assume that this enthusiasm should have led logically to the creation of a strong Leninist party is misleading. Such a development would have been inconsistent with the history of the Spanish working classes. As Meaker has shown, the Spanish Left had no taste for Leninism; the idea of a "dictatorship of the proletariat" was alien and abhorrent to them. Those Spanish leftists who went to Russia came away with the view that the Bolshevik revolution was not the kind of revolution they wanted for Spain. And they rejected the Bolshevik model not because they were "ideologically retarded" or intoxicated with millenarian fantasies, but because they were repulsed by what they saw. The Anarchist and Anarcho-syndicalist delegates to the Comintern were particularly upset by the Bolshevik suppression of the Worker's Soviets. The Spanish Left did not want a revolution that subverted the ends to the means.

We must look elsewhere to explain the failure of the Left to take advantage of the revolutionary atmosphere of 1917–1923. The failure, and Meaker correctly perceives it, is one of leadership. However, this failure lay not in the Left's inability to create a disciplined political party of the Leninist mold, but in its failure to bring about a union between the two potential revolutionary organizations already in existence, the Socialist UGT (Unión General del Trabajo) and the Anarchist CNT (Confederación Nacional del Trabajo). Meaker has focused on the need for a political party to serve as the agent of change, but in Spain, a revolution could only be based on a strong disciplined trade union movement. The typical Spanish worker was a-political, not because of millenarianism, a characteristic which Meaker and other Spanish historians have tended to exaggerate, but because he nurtured a cynicism toward the corrupt political system of the Restoration monarchy, thereby developing a natural distrust of political parties. This cynicism was reflected not only among Anarchists and Anarcho-syndicalists, but also among Socialists. How else can one explain the huge difference in membership between the Socialist UGT and its political arm, the PSOE (Partido Socialista Obrero Español)?

These criticisms notwithstanding, Meaker has made an important contribution to the field of Spanish history. His thorough, absorbing, and provocative account of the Spanish Left during the critical period between 1914 and 1923 will serve for any serious student as an indispensable starting point.

FREDERIC H. ENGEL
La Jolla
California

EDWARD SHORTER and CHARLES TILLY. *Strikes in France, 1830–1968.* Pp. vii, 428. New York: Cambridge University Press, 1974. $27.50.

This is a systematically researched book on a highly specialized theme, the aim of which is to "single out the strike itself as a distinctive form of collective action" and, taking the case of France, to measure how far it has been transformed by industrialization. Strikes became a regular and accepted feature of collective action in Western countries with industrialization in the 19th and 20th centuries. Shorter and Tilly examine the

phenomenon of strikes in France from a variety of standpoints, including their historical development and the importance of variables such as locality, the degree of urbanization, the impact of technology and the kind of industry.

The overriding theme of the book is the role of strikes as a form of political action in the struggle for power to establish workers' rights and political representation. This theme is set in contrast to two alternative interpretations of strike action in France: economic interest and the 'frustration-aggression theory'. The political motive was less evident in the generation from the beginning of the July Monarchy, when the strike was used in an uncoordinated fashion by circles of skilled craftsmen to negotiate a better deal, but with the mass mobilization of workers from the 1880s the strike assumed a direct political purpose. Industrial growth was crucial here both in concentrating workers within certain urban areas and in changing the nature of their organization. Organization is seen as the key to the increase in the incidence of strikes and in the degree of participation in them, while at a later stage they became briefer in duration thus again emphasizing their function in political protest. A further politicizing factor was the role of the state and the nature of labor relations (chapter 2). In the absence of an accepted system of collective bargaining between both sides of industry, the state was viewed by workers' associations as the necessary intermediary. Strikes were therefore employed to force intervention by the government, whose main concern was not so much the suppression of strikes per se as the maintenance of social and political order.

The method used to establish the political argument is the classification of official data (especially statistical reports of the Labor Office) on the some 100,000 strikes that occurred in France between 1830 and 1968. The result is an impressive and exhaustive collection of information, which no doubt explains the conscious decision by the authors to refrain from considering the use of memoirs, interviews, newspaper accounts, court proceedings, correspondence and other archival material (p. 19). This is on reflection a serious defect for it deprives the book of much substantial meaning and also 'color' and accounts for the impression that the authors are laboring their theme of the political strike. The book suffers from too little contextual setting, which should have been presented in an introductory chapter. For instance, the rise of strike action for political ends is not really related to the rise of political socialism (apart from one passing reference to the relevance of this on page 166). More should have been said about the character of different French trade unions, although there is some discussion later of the CGT (pp. 168–71). Finally, there should have been some direct justification for selecting France as the example of an industrialized country.

GEOFFREY PRIDHAM
University of Bristol
England

HAYDEN WHITE. *Metahistory: The Historical Imagination in Nineteenth-Century Europe*. Pp. xii, 448. Baltimore, Md.: Johns Hopkins University Press, 1973. $15.00.

This major work is the outcome of Professor White's continuing interest in contemporary historical theory. Inseparable from this interest are two interrelated intellectual activities: the first, a theoretical examination of the premises of historical knowledge; the second, a moral-practical meditation on the assumptions and attitudes of today's professional historians who have, in his opinion, left history in a state of "theoretical torpor" and made it far more an education in fatalism and cynicism than liberty and revolution. It is in reference to these two dimensions, the theoretical and the practical, that Professor White's *Metahistory* can be reviewed.

Professor White's theoretical intention is bold. He seeks to do nothing other than to transform our understanding of nineteenth century history, and thereby force a reevaluation of contemporary historical writing and theory which, in his opinion, are absolutely dependent on nineteenth century theories and models of history. In particular, Professor White conducts his analysis in relation to the major writings of the nineteenth century master historians—Michelet, Ranke, Tocqueville, and Burckhardt—and the nineteenth century philosophers of history—Hegel, Marx, Nietzsche, and Croce. He believes that a linguistic-stylistic analysis of their writings reveals a common ground of choice upon which they all equally rendered their poetic visions of the past. These choices—categories of historical perception and creation—are in White's terminology: (1) the mode of emplotment (providing overall meaning to the story) which can be either romantic, tragic, comic, or satirical; (2) the mode of argument (interrelating the parts of the story) which can be either formist, mechanistic, organicist, or contextualist; (3) the mode of ideological implication which can be either anarchist, radical, conservative, or liberal. These three essential modes of telling a story and giving it a meaning involve a fourth and necessary choice, that of language. In his most complex discussion of the theory of tropes, White again distinguishes four options in relation to the choice of language; they are metaphor ("essentially representational"), metonymy ("reductionist"), synecdoche ("integrative"), and irony ("negational").

While reading this work one fundamental question persistently arose in my mind. Could not Professor White have written substantially the same expositions and arrived approximately at the same conclusions with a far less encumbered language and complex methodology? More specifically, might he have not primarily analyzed these thinkers, as well as others treated, in reference to that one single question, which in one fashion or another, has dominated all serious nineteenth and twentieth century historians and thinkers alike? That is the question of progress. For surely what these men thought of radical changes of European society and their implications for class, nation, freedom, culture and humanity at large, prefigured, influ-

enced, and largely determined their historical reflections. An analysis based upon this theme — not that different from Professor White's ideological mode — would have the double advantage of relating history in general to the emerging social sciences and the arts (the historical novel in particular), as well as placing historical understanding in comparison with countless nineteenth century religious, moral, aesthetical, political, and purely propagandistic uses of the past.

The suggestion of a certain ahistorical character to Professor White's linguistic-stylistic methodology, which is implicit in the above comments, is given additional weight when it is noted that he has essentially omitted from his discussion of nineteenth century history, and mention of history's broadening encounter with the growing social sciences, radical new means of textual criticism, the discovery of not only new civilizations but the awesome reality of hundreds of millenia of previously unthought pre-history. Inescapably these new realities of nineteenth century consciousness, as well as those brought forth by the rapid, unprecedented, and truly staggering succession of nineteenth century events, profoundly effected the poetic, aesthetic, moral, and other metahistorical visions of past, and the modes by which historians sought to document, shape, and render these visions. In effect, nineteenth century historical theory and practice must first and foremost be understood in relation to the dynamics of nineteenth century consciousness and action. Significantly, the very eight major thinkers whom Professor White chose, have their greatness as historians in large measure because their unique and monumental works constitute not only a reconstruction of things past but an unusual comment on the course of things present.

It is this same ahistorical spirit that mars, in the opinion of this reviewer, the implicit practical-moral impulse of the work. The "theoretical torpor," which he claims is upon the profession, is debatable and the vices which he describes at the heart of the profession (a feigned moral neutrality, the pretense of a scien-

tific objectivity, and a self-serving ironic cast of mind which destroys in embryo all approaches to history which might upset the comfortable mental and material hierarchies of the craft) seem in fact more true of the profession in the early 1950s than early 1970s. In turn, sympathetic reconstructions of Michelet's theme of history as resurrection, Marx's revolution, and Nietzsche's rebellion against history, do not furnish the poetics of new histories. No matter how philosophically conscious and thereby free a twentieth century historian be, he cannot write a comic history of his own times. The very hard tangible fact of the Atomic Bomb, to choose but one irrepressible specific of twentieth century consciousness of so many (for example, the First World War or Italian Fascism), prohibits certain treatments of man's past and suggests that irony, satire, and even tragedy are not equal to describing our times.

For having consistently stressed the importance of events in forming historical consciousness in contrast to the primacy which Professor White attributes to the mind in historical creation, I will undoubtedly be accused of having played that old and tiresome game of academic teeter-totter. But this is an important work, one which will occupy no small place in future discussions of the state of historical theory, and because of this one says what one believes one should, however conventional and common that be. And I, for one, put my weight on that side of the fulcrum which inclines towards the belief that *mind is in rather than above reality; that events, past and present, create interpretations rather than interpretations, past and present, create events.*

JOSEPH AMATO
Southwest Minnesota State College
Marshall

UNITED STATES

LIEF H. CARTER. *The Limits of Order.* Pp. xiii, 206. Lexington, Mass.: Lexington Books, 1974. $15.00.

RICHARD QUINNEY. *Critique of Legal Order: Crime Control in Capitalist*

Society. Pp. ix, 206. Boston, Mass.: Little, Brown & Co., 1974. $7.95.

Professor Carter's book is an excellent case study of an ignored area of the criminal justice system, the office of prosecuting attorney. It fills a major gap in the literature.

Drawing on organization theory, field observations, questionnaires and open-ended interviews, Carter describes a world of uncertainty (Chapters 2–5). The uncertainty arises because ". . . prosecutors possess no accepted body of knowledge that explains: (1) precisely why they punish, (2) when a given punishment is or is not appropriate, (3) how the facts of a case may change as it moves from filing to disposition, and (4) how police, judges, defense attorneys, and the public will react to decisions they make (p. 3).

The most fascinating aspect of this study is that Carter concludes that Americans must accept this uncertainty as necessary for the successful performance of the criminal justice system. A prosecutor's success depends on flexibility and freedom from cumbersome standardization in the disposition of cases.

Turning to the weaknesses of the book, there are frequent lapses into unintelligible jargon. But the major disappointment is Carter's final chapter in which he recommends certain reforms to bring some regularity and predictability in the disposition of cases (Chapter 6). The reader is led to expect a philosophical discussion of certain standards to guide prosecutors in the disposition of cases. This would have been a significant conclusion for an otherwise significant study. Unfortunately, Carter closed with a management manual on how prosecutors can more efficiently run their offices.

Professor Quinney's book, by far the more intellectually stimulating of these two works, is a passionate rejection of the current philosophical assumptions underlying contemporary social science and especially, criminological theory (Chapters 1 and 2). Carter's book is an example of what Quinney detests about contemporary social science.

For Quinney, the overriding emphasis of social science is on the explanation of events and the maintenance of the status quo. "Little attention is devoted to questions about why law exists, whether law is indeed necessary, or what a just sytem would look like" (p. 4).

Quinney offers instead a Marxian perspective. In a capitalist system, law is a tool by which the ruling class — composed of those persons who own and control the means of production — maintains and protects its class interest. The state is not an impartial agency devoted to protecting the rights of its people and providing for their welfare. "In thinking about individual freedom, we tend to overlook the fact that civil liberties are in the hands of a ruling elite, and we do not actually have these rights in practice" (p. 144). Finally, social scientists must understand that the "rates of crime in any state are an indication of the extent to which the ruling class, through its machinery of criminal law, must coerce the rest of the population, thereby preventing any threats to its ability to rule and possess" (p. 52).

One of the best features of this book is that Quinney attempts to document that the state and the law are appendages of the ruling class (Chapters 3 and 4). Through an examination of the social-economic backgrounds of the members of Crime, Riot and Violence Commissions, and the operations of the Law Enforcement Assistance Administration, Quinney challenges non-Marxists to disprove this fundamental tenet of Marxism.

Quinney has written a provocative book. While there is a tendency to overgeneralize, it is certainly not glibly written. The major disappointment is the tendency to employ only an economic explanation of events. The reader wonders how Quinney can write about the origins and control of crime in America and virtually ignore racism.

J. F. HENDERSON
Ohio University
Athens

ROBERT F. DURDEN. *The Dukes of Durham, 1865–1929.* Pp. xi, 295. Durham, N.C.: Duke University Press, 1975. $19.95.

One might be skeptical of this work, whose author and publisher are both from Duke University. But Professor Durden has admirably uncovered previously unknown family records, and produced an engaging, balanced account of Washington Duke and his sons James, the entrepreneur, and Benjamin, the philanthropist.

Although allegedly a *family* history, the book is weaker on the father, whose activity from 1850 to 1880 went largely unrecorded. We learn that he came home from the Civil War angry at the secessionists and determined to build a life selling tobacco. But it was son James who made the fortune, by methods familiar to students of other trusts: rebates and secret favorable rentals, personal generosity but ruthless treatment of recalcitrant partners and competitors, and both vertical and horizontal consolidation. There was also the modern use of cheesecake and athletes in advertising.

Author Durden uses Kolkoesque language when he asserts that "Duke . . . proceeded to rationalize an industry that had been chaotic." But there is evidence that James' ultimate goals included both the elimination of competitors and the amassing of huge profits. The enterprise was worth 50 cents in 1865, about $120,000 when James took it over in 1880, and more than $25 million in 1890 when he created the American Tobacco Company. So great was his power that when the Supreme Court dismantled the trust in 1911, it turned to Duke himself for a reorganization plan.

Meanwhile, Benjamin was supporting a variety of philanthropies. Here the family idiosyncrasies helped. The Dukes were wealthy, aristocratic Republicans among people who were poor Democratic or Populist farmers. Ben therefore gave to blacks as well as whites, and upheld academic freedom on the question of racism, both in disregard to the customs in white supremacist Carolina. On balance, the Dukes seem less distinctly Southern and more like their northern tycoon counterparts. They were perhaps the best examples of Henry Grady's New Southern "Yankee." When Ben fell ill, James took over the philanthropy, particularly by endowing Duke University. Significantly, he did so only after a favorable ruling in a price controversy.

This then is a very worthwhile book. One major stylistic flaw is the repetition of first and middle names. Only rarely does clarity demand such usage in referring to the Dukes, but all characters are repeatedly identified by full names, even in successive paragraphs. Noticeable also by its absence was the most burning question this former cigarette addict can think of: "Why do people smoke?"

WILLIAM T. GENEROUS, JR.
The Choate School
Wallingford
Connecticut

JIM F. HEATH. *Decade of Disillusionment: The Kennedy-Johnson Years.* Pp. xvi, 332. Bloomington: Indiana University Press, 1975. $12.50.

"A disaster," a "decade of disillusionment," a time when "something went wrong." Jim F. Heath's view of the 1960s will find its supporters but even his own evidence suggests that a more favorable reading of the period is possible. As Heath notes in some detail, the folks who gave us Vietnam also discovered the city, brought us medicare, launched a war on poverty, added civil rights measures, and promulgated environmental legislation.

And had Professor Heath ventured out of the mountain tops of Washington with greater frequency, the sweep of the 1960s might have been enlarged. The Vietnamese war, as with all wars, brought with it startling social changes, many of them irreversible, not all of them volitional, and not all of them "a disaster." To ferret out these developments, Heath might have devoted more than belated single paragraphs to women, organized labor, and the consumer culture. Census material would have revealed some dramatic demographic trends. Income shifts, the arrival of Puerto Ricans in large numbers to seaboard cities, the changing profile of the college population, the apotheosis of the conglomerates, and the altered nature of work itself might have been profitably explored.

However, *Decade of Disillusionment* is primarily concerned with political, not social, history. To those who lived through the 1960s, the book will resemble a pleasant visit to old friends and relatives: the principal actors are vividly recalled, the narrative is familiar, and there is nothing that will jar the reader. Heath views the Kennedy-Johnson administrations as part of a lineal continuity reaching back to the New Deal, and he strives at all times for balance. To those whose political coming of age is of more recent vintage (and it is to this group that the book appears to be pitched), *Decade of Disillusionment* will provide a sprightly, solid introduction.

How will the 1960s look when time affords greater perspective? Heath contends that the decade will appear much less vast to readers of the twenty-first century than it does today, and he is undoubtedly correct. Although he sees the decade as more prone to violence than any other since the Civil War, it was probably not more violent than either the 1870s or the 1890s. Americans in 1919 and 1934 also agonized over mass disorder. Vietnam proved traumatic; so have most of America's wars. In the 1960s, bright promises faded, radicalism ultimately took a drubbing, black gains proved ephemeral. For better or worse, these tendencies have also cropped up in the nation's past. Heath's decision not to over-inflate the politics of the 1960s makes excellent sense.

CHARLES H. TROUT
Mount Holyoke College
South Hadley
Massachusetts

THOMAS C. KENNEDY. *Charles A. Beard and American Foreign Policy.* Pp. v, 199. Gainesville: The University of Florida Press, 1975. $8.50.

Since the turn of the century there has been no more controversial historian than Charles A. Beard. Among the recent graduates of the "new left" school of revisionists there may lurk the ingredient for future notoriety, but it is doubtful that any will match the intensity of the debate which has swirled around Charles A. Beard.

Certainly the historical profession has need of isolated examinations of the type resulting in this book. Excessive investigation in reference to such trail-blazing scholars as Harry Elmer Barnes, William A. Williams, Charles C. Tansill and Charles A. Beard is impossible. These men have left a legacy which extends well beyond the foundation of revisionist methodology; they have stimulated, if not polished, the skills of judicious inquiry.

Thomas C. Kennedy's study of Charles A. Beard is the culmination of not quite a decade of research, and rests not upon Beard's published works, guest editorials and book reviews alone, but also upon the bulk of his surviving manuscripts, consisting largely of letters between colleagues and adversaries, correspondence between the author and Beard's family as well as scholars and contemporaries who were privileged to observe the emergence of Beard's theories on and assessments of the nature and ends of American government, in particular the relationship of this government to the conduct of foreign policy and its impact upon the governed.

In constructing his evaluation of Charles A. Beard's journey along that path of scholarship and historical inquisition which made him the foremost critic of United States foreign policy as it related to our entry into both World Wars, the author divides his book along watersheds in Beard's career that are both neat and logical. Of these chronological brackets, the most detailed, and the soundest analysis, is found among those sections tracing Beard's shift from quasi-internationalism to "continentalism." Supplemented with two excellent chapters on American neutrality prior to Pearl Harbor Day and the effect of the Second World War on

Beard's assessment of Franklin D. Roosevelt as war leader, the author delivers a concise portrait of a rather enigmatic, oftentimes contradictory, personality. The figure that emerges is complex and inconsistent; the optimist who believed in progress, the skeptic who was awed more by principles than by men, the anti-imperialist who did not condemn the *idea* of imperialism, the economic determinist who condemned the exportation of our brand of democracy yet commended the Truman Administration for its efforts to alter the political and economic life-style of post-war Japan.

As an overview of the writings of Charles (and Mary) Beard, this book automatically deserves attention. As an objective, and unclouded, assessment of the man's place within the historical community, it warrants acclaim.

CALVIN WARNER HINES
Stephen F. Austin State University
Nacogdoches
Texas

KATHERINE DU PRE LUMPKIN. *The Emancipation of Angelina Grimké.* Pp. xv, 265. Chapel Hill: The University of North Carolina Press, 1974. $11.95.

BELL IRVIN WILEY. *Confederation Women.* Contributions in American History, no. 38. Pp. xiv, 204. London, England: Greenwood Press, 1975. $10.95.

In the past few decades the North American continent has become very conscious of and interested in its beginnings. Perhaps this is partly due to the unquenchable thirst of the mass media—or perhaps to the kudos that comes from unearthing one's past as an "old American" or a "fourth generation Canadian." At any rate we have wisely begun to dip into our short history while we can still talk to the 80 year olds who remember their settler days or the stories of settler grandparents, and can still find precious early letters in the attic.

Not all our pioneers, however, had the time, inclination, or learning to write of their experiences, and many historically priceless documents have been thrown away. Fortunately the women described in these two books were highly educated for their day and lived in the letter writing period. The authors' main source of information comes from their letters and diaries.

Angelina Grimké (1805–1879) and her remarkable older sister Sarah, were surely two of the leading reformers of all times. Angelina's story has been recorded before, but never with such detailed and intimate understanding. Data collected over more than 20 years and a profound identification with the area in which Angelina lived have enabled Lumpkin to describe her life with the same insight that made her earlier autobiography, *The Making of a Southerner*, such an impressive portrayal of Southern socialization. Few escape from their early family training in attitudes and prejudices. But both Lumpkin and Angelina did, and the latter's revolt against the "natural" acceptance of slavery and the "subordinate" position of women is an engrossing story.

Wiley's description of three other women who lived in the same period also gives an enlightening picture of leading Southern women, but seems to lack the intimate knowledge of the situation—and perhaps women—of Lumpkin's. But for once the colonels and generals are relegated to supporting positions in the Civil War, and the "women behind the men" are given their due. It was not the fashion in those days to give white feathers to supposed "slackers," but women did put on a "pout and sulk" campaign to stimulate volunteering, and Wiley describes how the "hand that rocked the cradle" also handed men the guns with which to do battle. Women also gave such practical assistance as smuggling weapons, taking charge of farms and plantations and working in government services and industry. A writer of the time wrote "Hurrah for the ladies! They are the soul of the war."

Three women, Mary Boykin Chestnut (1823–1886), Virginia Tunstall Clay (1825–1915) and Varina Howell Davis

(1826–1906) are each given a chapter which deals in some detail with their lives. The final chapter contains a general summary of Southern women's work for the Lost Cause.

The way in which these women supported the Southern effort could in some ways be compared to the way in which the educated women of India supported their husbands, replaced them when they went to prison, and even joined them in prison during the fight for independence. However, the results of women's first venture outside the home were different in each country. For, whereas the Indian women achieved great recognition and prestige and even high government positions after independence, the Southern women's contribution to the war had little effect in changing their status. In a limited way it launched them into the men's world of work, but it did not give them the vote or other legal benefits. Perhaps the ardent reformer, Angelina Grimké, could accept this more than the other three women, for she had gradually learned by experience just how slowly deeply laid attitudes and patterns change.

AILEEN D. ROSS
McGill University
Montreal
Canada

DUNCAN J. MACLEOD. *Slavery, Race and the American Revolution.* Pp. vi, 249. New York: Cambridge University Press, 1974. $15.95.

The paradox of a libertarian revolution taking place in a slave society without eradicating slavery is one of the thorniest problems with which interpretors of the American Revolution have had to deal. In this book Duncan J. MacLeod, lecturer in American history and fellow of St. Catherine's College, Oxford, demonstrates that the problem is not new. The anomaly of slavery in a free society—in a society, indeed, which flattered itself as being *the* great refuge of freedom—was acutely embarrassing to the men of the late eighteenth century. So long as slavery lasted, Bernard Bailyn argued,

"the burden of proof would lie with its advocates to show why the statement 'all men are created equal' did not mean precisely what it said: *all* men, white or black."

MacLeod has attempted to show how the Americans, especially but not only the southerners, dealt with this paradox. In the northern states where there were comparatively few blacks the abolition of slavery was effected early (though racism persisted in virulent form). In the South the problem was more difficult. Much as they deplored and regretted slavery, Thomas Jefferson and his contemporaries feared far more the consequences of a large free black population, not only on stable society but also on the very republican political institutions.

On the face of it, then, slavery was at odds with the natural right to liberty, and to the men of the first generation of the federal republic a large emancipated black population was to an even greater extent incompatible with the first principles of the American Creed. What, then, to do? Colonization of freedmen in Africa had its proponents, but on neither economic nor humane grounds did this recourse have a lasting popular appeal. Slavery for the indefinite future appeared to be the least of the evils. Once this point of view gained currency, its adherents buttressed it with social, economic, and scientific reinforcements. Racism, not absent in 1750, became far more pronounced during the period between 1790 and 1820.

MacLeod finds much to commend in the writings of Winthrop Jordan, William Freehling, and other historians who have been grappling with racism in early Anglo America, but he disagrees with them on the chronology of the heightening of the anti-Negro prejudice and also with its basic cause. To him the supreme irony lies in the fact that "the first great onslaught on slavery in America was impelled . . . by a belief in universal and natural rights: but it helped to produce a positive racism and an explicit denial of those rights" (p. 184). He may be correct, but it is disturbing to see MacLeod giving short shrift to such factors as changes in economic patterns in his accounting for the growing defense of slavery and racial antagonism. This is, however, a provocative little book and a welcome addition to the literature of slavery and race in the federal republic.

WILLIAM M. DABNEY
University of New Mexico
Albuquerque

THOMAS H. NAYLOR and JAMES CLOT-FELTER. *Strategies for Change in the South.* Pp. 316. Chapel Hill: The University of North Carolina Press, 1975. $14.95.

Thomas H. Naylor and James Clotfelter, employing a rigorous systems analytic framework and devoting particular attention to the economic, educational, and political subsystems, convey to the reader the present state of the South and set forth assorted policy recommendations generally designed to enhance the quality of life in the region. For operational purposes, the authors define the South to include the eleven states of the Old Confederacy along with Oklahoma and Kentucky.

The major and lasting value of this work is one of a descriptive nature. Professors Naylor and Clotfelter portray, and substantiate with appropriate data, the major features of the economic, eductional, and political subsystems of the South, although much of what they note has been written many times before. Once again, we are reminded that many of the inhabitants of the South suffer because of low per capita incomes and that the taxation structure of the region is largely regressive, with an undue emphasis placed on the sales tax as a source of public funds. And again we are told that the South must honestly and forcefully confront and deal with the "burden of race" if it is going to maximize its developmental potential.

Generally, I was rather unimpressed with the assorted policy recommendations advanced by the authors. Most importantly, practically none of these recommendations, such as the plea to institute a guaranteed annual income,

has any unique applicability to the South. Second, some policy recommendations, including that of providing abortions free of charge, lack political feasibility. And finally, from a normative point of view one may well question the wisdom of many of these policy proposals. For instance, the authors advocate the desirability of city-county governmental consolidation despite the fact that recent studies indicate that the benefits of local governmental merger might be far outweighed by the costs involved.

In short, Professors Naylor and Clotfelter in *Strategies for Change in the South* provide a good descriptive overview of the region and much material for discussion. One wishes that the authors had taken more care and thought in formulating their policy recommendations.

NELSON WIKSTROM
Virginia Commonwealth University
Richmond

HART M. NELSEN and ANNE KUSENER NELSEN. *Black Church in the Sixties.* Pp. ix, 172. Lexington: University Press of Kentucky, 1975. $11.50.

The object of this study is to take account of the black church through the decade of the sixties. For Negroes, generally, it was an eventful decade; the black man's chances for education improved and his prospects for advancing in the labor market and for entering the professions had never moved so far in so brief an interval. Over the years, in its own way, the Negro church has been involved. The Nelsens take account of that involvement while considering the future of the black church.

The report accounts for several years of factfinding (one wonders why) and apparently much pondering. Over the past three decades there have been dozens of studies. For their study city, the Nelsens gathered data about the Negro community in and around Bowling Green (approximately 36,000, 1970), Kentucky, which figured as background for the whole study. One becomes quite aware early in his reading that Negro scholars are not of one mind regarding the social worth of the traditional black church, a wholly American creation by Negroes at the common-man social level. Among the Negro scholars there are some, such as E. Franklin Frazier and Charles S. Johnson, who a generation ago called the black church a barrier to the social and cultural advancement of the race. Many intellectual Negroes share that view.

According to the view entertained here, a need for the black church continues. Some who may not agree with the religious behavior of the black church favor its militancy and expect the preacher to speak out. One conclusion should be mentioned: very little emerged to support the idea that religiosity is greater among blacks than among whites. Indeed there are some who consider the folk meetings of the black church as an art form, which presents quite a contrast to the stiffness of a typical white service.

It is likely that many who take up this book will have had no contact with the rural Negro church or the "storefront" church found in most large urban slums. A few paragraphs of description might have served a good purpose. This reviewer is painfully aware of a second lack which is common to many sociological works dealing with the structure, functions and changes of societies: no mention is made, except most indirectly, about the work Negroes live by. This is especially important because here is a people numbered among Rudyard Kipling's "Sons of Martha," the hewers and the carriers. Their numbers are few among the craftsmen and professionals. It is a subject touching the industrial social class system. The three main marks of a social class are level of education, level of income and one's occupation. What is here is good but it does not complete the picture.

NELS ANDERSON
University of New Brunswick
Fredericton, N.B.
Canada

EDWARD C. PAPENFUSE. *In Pursuit of Profit: The Annapolis Merchants in the Era of the American Revolution,* *1763–1805.* Pp. viii, 288. Baltimore, Md.: The Johns Hopkins University Press, 1975. $12.00.

The urbanization of the Chesapeake area has long been discussed in terms of the phenomenal rise of Baltimore. In passing, Annapolis is usually mentioned as a dying, third-rate port, totally overshadowed by its younger and more vigorous neighbor. This book attempts to end this nearly exclusive focus on Baltimore by examining the growth of Annapolis, the contributions of its merchants to the American commercial system, and their later adaptation to the city's decline. Papenfuse succeeds admirably in this goal, but more than that, he has made an important contribution to our understanding of urban development in the Revolutionary era.

Papenfuse begins by tracing the stages of Annapolis's development in the century before the Revolution. Unlike most colonial cities, its growth resulted primarily from its role as a political capital, rather than trade. When governing the colony became a year-round business after 1715, wealthy planters came to Annapolis in growing numbers. Their spending, and the wages they paid their servants, increased demand for imported goods and spurred the city's commercial development. After 1763, merchants took greater initiative in promoting trade, and Annapolis became an important commercial, as well as political, center. The activity of these merchants is the major theme of the book. Papenfuse concentrates primarily on four merchants. Through their activities, first as importers of British goods and later as competitors to British tobacco merchants, these men broke the hold of British middlemen on the American tobacco trade. During the war years, they capitalized on their earlier successes, building up extensive contacts with merchants in other American cities, supplying the continental army, and initiating some trade with France. After the Revolution, however, the problems of recovery from war, competition from Baltimore, and depression in the tobacco trade made it impossible to continue the trade on the same terms as before. By 1790 these merchants had dissolved their final partnership, and it was clear that the city in general was declining in importance. Most merchants, however, remained in the city and successfully adapted to new forms of business activity, most notably establishing one of the country's first agricultural banks.

Papenfuse goes beyond discussing the mercantile activities of the principal businessmen to analyze in detail the career experiences of most of Annapolis's adult men. He was able to trace a remarkably high percentage of the city's residents, and discusses their careers to determine the impact of declining opportunity on the city as a whole. Despite some problems in his method of determining mobility, this section is an admirable attempt to break away from the dependence on the experiences of a few key merchants which usually plagues studies of early American economic development. He has managed to combine analysis of economic change with such social issues as population growth, wealth distribution, and social mobility. As a conseqeunce, Papenfuse has written not merely a book about merchants and commercial development, but a broader study of urban growth and decline which takes into account both the role of the major merchants and the experiences of the rest of the community.

LYNNE E. WITHEY
University of Iowa
Iowa City

AUSTIN RANNEY. *Curing the Mischiefs of Faction: Party Reform in America.* Pp. 234. Berkeley: University of California, 1975. $8.50.

One of the most potentially explosive issues on the American electoral scene is the question of major partisan reform. Since the founding of the Republic, public officials, theorists, civic leaders and authors of high school text books have been ambivalent, at best, about the existence of political parties and their influence upon elections. Most, in resig-

nation, have decided that forcible elimination of parties would be both costly and dangerous. Rather, partisanship must be carefully regulated and controlled so that its excesses may be checked and minimized.

Austin Ranney, professor of political science at the University of Wisconsin and a member of the Democratic Party's recent commission on Party Structure and Delegate Selection (the "McGovern-Fraser Commission"), has produced a literate and readable study of the history and politics of party reform. In fact, the volume had its genesis in the author's "Jefferson Memorial Lectures" delivered at the University of California, Berkeley in 1973. Ranney's matter-of-fact, conversational style and his frequent, dry humor belie this genesis.

In addition to his style, Ranney's writing has a second important quality. He is able to take relatively "common-sense"—and not necessarily original—propositions and make of them edifying, valuable arguments. This is accomplished through a piercing realism and a profound understanding of the sociopolitical context within which events occur. Thus, while the author spends much time on issues of a constitutional or legal nature, he never loses sight of the fact that one's theoretical perspectives regarding partisanship are invariably colored by one's own partisan affiliations.

Equally, Ranney has no illusions about party reform. He is fully aware that the rules of national party commissions, state laws that regulate local parties and judicial decisions (or their lack) do not occur in a vacuum. Ranney often paraphrases the words of contemporary students of party reform who have claimed: "Changing the rules changes the game." The arena in which the game is played, it may further be added, also influences the stakes and the manner in which it is played. It is interesting in this regard that neither the Supreme Court nor the Congress have taken active roles in party reform. Unfortunately, Ranney does not pursue this issue.

The author also spends considerable time on recent Democratic Party reforms as they manifested themselves at the 1972 Democratic Convention. He meticulously presents both the views which blame the 1972 Democratic Presidential debacle on the "new politics" and those which claim that no relationship between party reforms and the Nixon landslide exists. He particularly concentrates on the controversial guidelines of the McGovern-Fraser commission requiring delegations to the national conventions to include representation of "minority groups, women, and young persons in reasonable relationship to their presence in the population." Equally descriptive is Ranney's analysis of the conflicts surrounding the seating of the California and Illinois delegations and the concomitant alienation of some of the most powerful of party regulars.

In sum, *Curing the Mischiefs of Faction* is a valuable and articulate essay dealing with the problems of partisan reform in America from several perspectives. The depth of its analysis is enhanced and punctuated by its brevity and fluency. Ranney has given us an interesting work which will serve the specialist and novice alike.

DAVID J. SCHNALL
Staten Island Community College
The City University of New York

DAVID J. SCHNALL. *Ethnicity and Suburban Local Politics.* Pp. vi, 168. New York: Praeger, 1975. $15.00.

The major thrust of this book is to explore empirically the relationship between ethnicity and political attitudes and behavior. Ethnicity is defined as religious affiliation, and, for Catholics, perceived national origins. Political interest and participation, views toward local and broader issues, and, especially, vote choice for candidates for local and national office in 1972 are the political variables analyzed. The site of the study is Ramapo, a suburb near New York City.

Contrary to expectations, the overall impact of ethnic factors on political orientations in this suburban arena is not overwhelming. Religious identification

has some bearing on group similarity in candidate preference and in organizing attitudes toward local issues, but there is little trace of an impress upon voting for candidates of one's ethnic group, or feelings about national issues, or rates of political interest and participation. Even where a relationship between religion and political behavior or outlook is found, it pales in comparison with the effect of other variables. For instance, religious affiliation falters as a direct means of structuring vote preference when compared to the influence of racial attitudes and, primarily, party identification. Through utilization, however, of a form of causal modeling, religion appears to play an indirect role in influencing vote choice.

On the positive side, this book presents a solid piece of empirical research in the area—ethnicity and suburban politics—that has generally been given short shrift in the social science literature. The findings uncover a number of important political themes including the diversity and salience of politics in suburbs, and the relative unimportance of ethnic orientations in influencing political views and action at least in the suburban context studied.

Conversely, there are some limitations to this book, a point that the author cogently acknowledges in the concluding chapter. The analysis is very descriptive, with not enough attention paid to the theoretical underpinnings of the information uncovered. The research design is too narrow to answer fully the questions raised about the import of ethnicity in suburban political environments. To elaborate: First, the number of ethnic groups studied is small, covering three generic religions and three national origins (Italian, Irish, and German) only in the case of Catholics. Perhaps this limited ethnic breakdown is a true reflection of the suburb investigated. Even so, this suggests a second problem with the research design, namely only one political arena is analyzed. To facilitate comparisons, and thus to expand knowledge, future ethnic research should cover a multitude of groups in varied locales. Prime consideration in the choice of research sites should be given to the overall ethnic make-up, the political history and governmental structures in the area, and the cultural milieu surrounding the ethnic. Finally, in surveying ethnicity attention must be given to developing questions that tap the salience and intensity of ethnic factors to the respondent. Very little effort was exerted in this study along this last line.

Withal, even given its shortcomings, this book is a welcomed contribution to those concerned with systematic empirical analysis of the importance of ethnicity on political behavior.

JAMES W. LAMARE

The University of Texas
El Paso

LOUIS SEAGULL. *Southern Republicanism*. Pp. iii, 186. New York: John Wiley & Sons, 1975. $5.95.

Since Kevin Phillips' brazen exposition of Nixon's Southern strategy six years ago, the academic community has awaited a more objective prospectus on the Southern party system. Will Southern Democracy outlive its aging Congressional delegation? Will the influx of blacks into Democratic party councils drive the white majority to Republicanism? Will the in-migration of Northerners to the "Sun Belt" reinforce Republican conservatism?

Professor Seagull gives us that objectivity. His general finding is well-supported—that the white-collar sector in the South has adopted the Republican banner, and that the region is converging on the "New Deal alignment" which has long dominated the rest of the nation's politics. The strongest sections of the book are the vignettes he offers of competitive campaigning in the South. He shows us the successful marketing of not-too-lily-white Republicanism by Bo Calloway and Winthrop Rockefeller, as well as the Democratic fratricide that propelled Bill Brock to the House in 1962 and Jesse Helms to the Senate ten years later.

The book's statistical model, however, has serious flaws. By using election totals

(from 1944 to 1972), Seagull relies on ecological reasoning: that the behavior of a socio-economic group can be identified with the behavior of the counties where it is concentrated. The fallacy is most apparent in his treatment of the black belt, which he finds "unstable" terrain for toryism. Seagull echoes Key's finding from the days when Southern blacks simply did not vote—that as the proportion black increases, so does (to borrow Seagull's euphemism) "the traditional antipathy to the politics of desegregation." Seagull mentions that the instability might be related to the increasing number of voting blacks. (When he "controls" for this possibility by throwing "proportion black *and* registered" into the regression, he hides a reference to multicollinearity in the footnotes.)

Paired with realignment is electoral expansion. While "para-racial issues" (bussing, crime, employment discrimination) remain salient to the Southern white, they also confuse and cross-pressure him, conflicting with Southern economic progressivism. It is not surprising that preliminary studies of both the 1972 and 1974 elections show Southern white turnout falling, while black participation steadily rises. Black mayors in Richmond, Raleigh, and Atlanta suggest that white-collar Republicanism is the losing side, now more than ever. While Seagull treats the emergent black vote in the South only peripherally, its significance is not lost on Southern politicians. When the white and black Democratic parties in Mississippi finally merged this summer, one of their first orders of business was an "affirmative action plan" to recruit and organize minority voters.

More important than the "critical elections" Seagull finds are the crises which gave the South two-race, if not two-party, politics. The abolition of the rural white primary in 1960, the seating of the Freedom Party in Atlantic City, and the passage of the Voting Rights Act: all placed an enormous strain on the Southern political system whose aftershocks are still being felt. A study of the dramatic changes recently wrought on Southern attitudes and voting behavior must include more qualitative history and survey data (less convenient than election statistics, but much more powerful). For that, we're still waiting.

SCOTT RAFFERTY
Princeton University
Princeton, N.J.

SOCIOLOGY

JOAN ABRAMSON. *The Invisible Woman: Discrimination in the Academic Profession.* Pp. 248. Washington, D.C.: Jossey-Bass, 1975. $12.50.

BENJAMIN R. BARBER. *Liberating Feminism.* Pp. 153. New York: Seabury Press, 1975. $6.95.

MELVILLE CURRELL. *Political Woman.* Pp. 201. Totowa, N.J.: Rowman & Littlefield, 1974. $15.00.

Women's inequality in today's society is the theme taken by three scholarly and dispassionate authors. Barber and Currell are political scientists; Abramson is a journalist and university teacher who recounts her own personal experience and some useful knowledge that grew out of it. Abramson and Currell, both women, describe things as they are; Barber ends with a suggested utopia. Barber's book is charming; the others are clear and factual.

In *Liberating Feminism*, Barber examines and eschews both extreme positions regarding women's nature. Nature is taken to mean female vulnerability, hormonal passivity, historical dependency. The naturalists insist that we are sexual animals driven by forces society can only disguise: woman equals a womb. Therefore, we really cannot do anything about it, nor should we want to. The liberationists argue that femininity and sexual differentiation are incompatible with equality. Therefore, women must deny sexuality and become creatures of their own volition. Barber argues that neither natural slavery nor liberated androgyny has a viable solution: people are not animals or gods, but precisely in between. Equality is a social and political condition, prescribing modes of treating men and women, not describing comparative identities. Equality will come out of the "just polity," which allows personhood within mutuality of the sexes.

Barber's eloquent felicity of phrase yields gems such as "A liberated woman . . . can take untroubled pleasure in the complimentary rituals by which men open doors before them—as long as the doors are held open, not shut, and lead into polling booths and executive suites as well as kitchens and nurseries" (p. 116). This is all very nice, but the female reader feels compelled to ask, "Who will give us this just polity?" Not likely the men interested in preserving male dominance or those oblivious of the fact that they hold most of the power and tend to make most of the decisions.

The "power problem" is addressed in Currell's *Political Woman*. In sharp contrast to Barber's philosophical analysis, Currell deals with facts and empirically derived analysis concerning the role of women in the British Parliament and of those who stood for election. An important theme in women's self-reported motivation for entering British political life is "helping" others and gaining enabling power. In actuality, as politicians move towards the source of power, the number of women declines drastically. Typically, women are placed in human problems endeavors, such as education and welfare, not in decision-making or executive positions affecting Britain *vis-à-vis* other governments in the world.

Currell's data show that women's gains since the new interest in liberation are highly illusory. Discrimination within the scope of her study seems to be more at the level of selection of candidates than elsewhere. With some of the same concern as Barber, Currell warns that our thinking about liberation is characterized by a confusion between *equality* and *identity* of men and women.

The Invisible Woman at a large American university, Joan Abramson attests to the apparent futility of struggle with the dominant male power structure. This talented journalist and popular teacher was "put off," "put down," and, finally,

The people's choice.

Students and professors agree. For substance, for style... you just can't top Deutsch and Morlan.

POLITICS AND GOVERNMENT
How People Decide Their Fate, Second Edition
Karl W. Deutsch, Harvard University
624 pages/1974/$11.50
Instructor's Manual

AMERICAN GOVERNMENT
Policy and Process, Second Edition
Robert L. Morlan, University of
Redlands
460 pages/paper/1975/$8.50
Instructor's Manual

CAPITOL, COURTHOUSE AND CITY HALL
**Readings in American State and
Local Politics and Government
Fourth Edition**
Edited by Robert L. Morlan, University
of Redlands
329 pages/paper/1972/$8.25

For adoption consideration, request examination copies
from your regional Houghton Mifflin office.

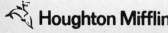

Houghton Mifflin Atlanta, GA 30324   Dallas, TX 75235   Geneva, IL 60134
Hopewell, NJ 08525   Palo Alto, CA 94304   Boston, MA 02107

Kindly mention THE ANNALS *when writing to advertisers*

New & Recent Titles

INTRODUCTION TO CRIMINAL JUSTICE

Donald J. Newman, *School of Criminal Justice, SUNY, Albany*

A comprehensive overview of the criminal justice system that blends legal and sociological aspects, stresses formal law, and shows how the system of crime control works. Focus is on routine functioning of police, traditional tasks of prosecutors, judges and the standard correctional bureaucracies, and *how* the system operates.

507 pages/1975/$12.95

A complete self-instructional course . . .
SURVEY OF THE CRIMINAL JUSTICE PROCESS

Hugh Nugent, J.D.

Twenty-four lessons on twelve audio cassettes cover the basic criminal justice process from enactment of a statute through arrest, trial, appeal and correction. Taped lessons are integrated with a student workbook. *Inquiries invited concerning free two-week preview.*

12 audio cassettes, workbook/$187.50

CRIME AND JUSTICE ADMINISTRATION

Alvin W. Cohn, *Administration of Justice Service*

A brief, non-technical overview of crime causation and the criminal justice system, including concepts, practices, problems, and programs associated with criminology and criminal justice administration in contemporary America.

236 pages/February 1976

POLICE-COMMUNITY RELATIONS
Images, Roles, Realities

Edited by Emilio Viano, *American University, and* Alvin W. Cohn, *Administration of Justice Service*

A collection of important articles focusing on day-to-day problems of policing the community. Content is balanced between articles from journals and material from public sources.

552 pages/paperbound and clothbound/February 1976

"put out." In her book, Abramson relates her personal experience with discrimination; debunks myths of women's lower productiveness and professional dedication; evaluates available outside agencies for helpfulness; and offers some concluding advice to women academics and male administrators.

Figures employed by Abramson indicate that women faculty earn three-fifths of the salary of their male counterparts and that although women are popular as instructors (32 percent), only 8 percent are full professors—with most of these holding that rank in all-female departments. The term "quality" for women means that they are the best in the country; for men, that they meet some, not necessarily all, of the written requirements. The same behavioral characteristics (such as 'aggressiveness) are rewardable for men and punishable for women. Noting that "rights are never passively conferred . . . they are actively taken" (p. 220), Abramson predicts that redress for women faculty is possible only through the courts (group action) and political clout (for example, block voting). In contrast to expectations for a "just polity" (which failed even when attempted by Plato), Abramson and Currell answer Barber with the argument: women will have equality when they gain their fair share of power.

BARBARA W. VAN DER VEUR
Ohio University
Athens

T. B. BOTTOMORE. *Sociology as Social Criticism*. Pp. 219. New York: Pantheon Books, 1974. $10.00.

During the present sparse intellectual period of overwhelming dogmatic allegiance to either functionalism or conflict theory, T. B. Bottomore has consistently maintained one of the few truly 'critical' sociological voices. Although Professor Bottomore soundly rejects Parsonian social interpretations, he conversely projects a healthy skepticism toward theorists who merely desire a strict reaffirmation of 19th century Marxist polemics in a postindustrial era. Fundamentally, Bottomore is a sociologist without parameters—moreover, his impartial palette usually appears uniquely imbued with refreshing hues. Unfortunately, in this latest three-part book of previously published essays, the author's thematic schemes seem to have faded somewhat as a consequence of repeated application.

Part One of *Sociology as Social Criticism*—entitled "Social Theories" —savagely disputes Parsonian functionalism, the 'end of ideology' proposition, and A. W. Gouldner's 'crisis contingency' throughout a series of well-reasoned articles. While these essays exhibit an admirable degree of coherence, few of Bottomore's disparaging remarks are new—for example, most sociologists are probably familiar with the author's contention that the past decade of political unrest dealt a serious empirical blow to the 'end of ideology' argument of S. M. Lipset, Daniel Bell, and Raymond Aron. Similarly, in this opening section of the book, the author's criticisms of Gouldner and Parsons are not particularly earth-shattering.

Parts Two and Three of the monograph—respectively entitled "Class and Elites" and "Social Movements and Political Action"—correspondingly offer a rather mundane commentary on the development of a critical sociology. In this portion of the book, Bottomore's major assertions include the following: (1) conflict and stability are both important societal characteristics; (2) social classes are still viable elements in a postindustrial age; and (3) critical sociologists should strive to promote political awareness. Although these insights may seem profound to the sociological novice, any specialist who has sustained even a slight degree of disciplinary cognizance must be well-acquainted with such themes.

Bottomore's analysis does have a few formidable moments, most notably in the essay entitled "The Political Context of Technology." Here, the author perceptively suggests that technologically oriented social scientists are often masking some weakness in theoretical comprehension with their mechanistic paradigms. Granted several such enlightening comments penetrate the text, a copious quantity of mediocre statements must still be waded through to occasionally derive these incisive gems.

Ultimately, however, the problems evinced in *Sociology as Social Criticism* are typical of the difficulties incurred in many other current social scientific monographs. In an age of 'fast food' sociology—where the insatiable consumption of concepts promptly transforms yesterday's smorgasbord into today's hash—the author's intuitive 1969 essays seem rather tedious in their 1974 format. Nevertheless, even an outdated and uninspired treatise by the consistently critical Bottomore constitutes superior sociology when compared with most other contemporary theoretical manuscripts authored by narrow dogmatic Marxists and functionalists.

RICHARD A. WRIGHT
Indiana University
Bloomington

ABNER COHEN. *Two Dimensional Man: An Essay on the Anthropology of Power and Symbolism in Complex Society*. Pp. vii, 156. Berkeley: University of California Press, 1974. $8.50.

The principal message of this little book is that symbolic action is alive and well in modern society and that it can be shown to perform functions there not unlike those which are familiar to readers of anthropological reports on primitive societies. The author maintains that groups in modern societies utilize symbols associated with kinship, friendship, and ritual to further their economic and political interests. *Two Dimensional Man*, therefore, is an additional indication of a salutary revision in social scientific thinking which in the past (See, for example, Marcuse's *One Dimensional Man*) has tended to see modern society primarily as a stripped down world organized on the basis of formal contracts, dominated by a secular rationality, and filled with alienated people. This message may be more startling to

political scientists and economists than to social anthropologists and sociologists who are beginning to take it for granted.

What is more intriguing in this book is a series of case studies of interest groups (some of them based on the author's own field work) in developing and developed societies which are prevented by structural circumstances from establishing themselves as formal associations and which use various informal mechanisms for maintaining or furthering their power. The kinds of groups considered are ethnic, such as the Ibo in Ibadan, Nigeria, elite, such as the City men of London, religious, such as the Tijaniya of the Ibadan Hausa, secret ritualistic, such as the Freemasonry of the Creoles of Sierra Leone, and "cousinhoods," such as the Anglo-Jewish gentry. These case studies illustrate the author's theoretical points, but they are neither extensive nor intensive enough to constitute a contribution in themselves.

If not the message nor the case studies, what is the significant contribution of this book? The theory, which Cohen lays out in textbook fashion, is familiar to those who have read Gluckman, his associates, and descendents. The reminder in the last chapter, particularly, to use manageable, empirically related concepts (in this instance, "power groups" instead of "social classes") is perhaps timely, but it isn't particularly engaging. The author's indication in the preface that the book is addressed to students of the behavioral sciences generally who might profit from an "exploration of the possibilities of a systematic study of the dynamic interdependence between power relationships and the symbolic order in complex society" may provide the justification for publication of this book. The language is simple and straightforward. Even with its pedestrian style this book could find a broad audience which can profit from its solidly based "generalist" approach. But one still wonders whether a primer on the subject was needed.

DENNISON NASH
University of Connecticut
Storrs

LYNN A. CURTIS. *Criminal Violence: National Patterns and Behavior.* Pp. xx, 231. Lexington, Mass.: Lexington Books, 1974. $15.00.

Gradually we learn how to think about crime. For all these centuries during which the attention of reasoning men has been given to the topic, we have relied on the imaginations of law-givers, judges, philosophers, and, latterly, social scientists. As rational men, they have put themselves in the place of the abstracted criminal and explained what would motivate them to the commission of an offense or deter them from it. Law and policy have always depended heavily on such speculations. Because a rational man would not commit murder ·if he thought he would be hanged as punishment, we impose capital punishment for the protection of society. A felicific calculus can be proposed by a Bentham entirely without data to test it, and be regarded throughout the succeeding centuries as a fundamental contribution to thought about crime. Contemporary economists who should know better will grumble their way through accumulations of obviously suspect data and emerge with propositions about deterrence and crime control which resound with an authority which they seldom claim for conclusions in their own domain.

The culture of national commissions has begun to change all that. President Johnson was accused of finessing decisions he did not wish to make by referring them to the nation's thinkers, preferably on an interdisciplinary basis. His instincts were correct; there was little that the President or the Federal government could do about crime, but social scientists, given some money, could pile up facts which had never been assembled in one place before. Out of this tortuously lengthy process, we are provided with the wherewithal for replacing a priori speculation with empirically grounded thought.

The National Commission on the Causes and Prevention of Violence was the most productive of the Johnsonian soundings of American criminogenetics. This slim but dense volume is its latest assay of our country's most persistent affliction. Its author, a diligent exponent of the Pennsylvania school of criminology, has brought together the findings of a national survey of the incidence and character of the four violent felonies — murder, rape, robbery and aggravated assault. Ten percent samples of the 1967 arrest reports of seventeen cities were drawn, coded and tabulated. Out of this formidable process, Curtis has assembled findings related to the demographics of violence, the interpersonal relationships which occasion it, the motives, the victim's part in precipitating these offenses, and the weapons chosen to carry them out. For what he considered to be good measure, he has included a wide selection of foreign comparisons drawn from various exotic sources, ranging from obvious Canadian experience to data on violence in the Igbo and Gusii tribes of Africa.

Curtis explicitly limits the purposes of this report to the provision of baseline data, the determination of convergence in violent behavior systems, and the description of national and regional patterns "with an eye to . . . policy and theoretical implications." His presentation is a puzzle. We are provided with tables which exhaustively compare violence in the aggregated seventeen cities of this country with data from Israel, Scotland, the USSR, and Ghana, among many other locales. Except on the issue of gun control, where the American tolerance of hand-guns results in stark contrast with the volume and nature of violence in other countries, these comparisons are not particularly interesting. What are we to make out of a finding that in the seventeen U.S. cities 10.9 percent of the homicides were motivated by "robbery, theft, gain, sexual attack, or other crime," whereas these motives were operative in only seven percent of the homicides committed by Western Jews in Israel, and by 10 percent of the homicides in Uganda? The opportunity to consider American inter-city differences in detail has been frittered away by cross-cultural distractions which cannot add to an understanding of our own problem. Nowhere in this volume does Curtis really make possible the promised study of national and regional patterns. The data on the seventeen cities are consistently lumped together, as though American urban life is as homogeneous as that of an African tribe.

There is one exception to Dr. Curtis' predilection for aggregated analysis. In a chapter on spatial distribution of violence, he has applied the advanced concept of isopleth study to the data of five of his seventeen cities. This technique, borrowed from geographers, provides a means for expressing the density of criminal events in contour lines produced by data of equal incidence, much like the isotherms and isobars of the meteorologists. The procedure is difficult, expensive, but useful in establishing the natural contours of crime rather than relying on the comparison of arbitrarily established census tracts, and city or county boundaries. Out of this part of the study, Curtis emerges with the finding that the black poor are disproportionately more violent than the white poor in the vast concentrations of Chicago and Philadelphia, but not in the smaller ghettoes of Boston, San Francisco and Atlanta. To Curtis, this suggests the hypothesis that the rates of black violence increase with the size of the black population, an idea well worth further study. Whether a simpler methodology might have produced the same tentative finding opens another perplexity which cannot be settled here.

This report is a splendid opportunity sadly missed. There is much for the social policy-maker to cogitate about, especially as to the web of factors associated with violence, and such cogitations will surely help to bring the formulation of criminal policy down to the empirical earth. But the lesson for criminologists interested in influencing the country's laws is to be faithful to their own data before engaging in flirtations with the data of others.

JOSEPH P. CONRAD
The Academy for Contemporary
   Problems
Columbus
Ohio

LEWIS S. FEUER. *Ideology and the Ideologists.* Pp. 220. New York: Harper & Row, 1975. $14.00.

Much of the history of sociology has been a struggle to escape from ideological trappings and establish a scientific discipline on par with the traditional sciences. In the tradition of the "father of sociology," Auguste Comte, "objectivity" in social inquiry was a major ideal from the outset. Before the 1960s, most professional sociologists felt the discipline had achieved solid scientific standing. However, political events in the "turbulent 60s" brought not just sociology, but all science, up for critical scrutiny. In the demystification of science which followed, several scholars advanced cogent new perspectives. A representative work was Thomas Kuhn's *Structure of Scientific Revolutions*, which suggested that all scientific "truths" are subject to revision, if not outright rejection, as social conditions change. In other words, factual knowledge is a subjective social creation— molded by the specific socio-historical circumstances.

Lewis Feuer's essay, *Ideology and the Ideologists*, is an attempt to discredit this new challenge to the immutability of scientific truth. Though his essay is introduced as one in a series of "Explorations in Interpretive Sociology," Feuer dispenses with the expected sociological analysis and writes a polemic against what he sees as a "revival of ideology."

He attempts to answer five questions central to an analysis of ideology: (1) Is there a pattern to the rise and fall of ideology? (2) How can changes in ideological fashion be explained? (3) Why are young intellectuals so drawn to ideology? (4) What are some characteristics of intellectuals? (5) Has ideology contributed to rationality in society?

These are important questions for students of political thought and for those interested in the "sociology of knowledge." The latter focuses on the relationship between thought ("truths") and social conditions. Unfortunately, Feuer's essay fails to fulfill the promise of the questions he raises.

Displaying formidable scholarship in the process, Feuer attributes three common "ingredients" to all ideologies: (1) An "invariant myth" concerned with the liberation of some oppressed group ("The Mosaic Myth"); (2) a compound of philosophical tenets which fluctuate between ideological extremes ("Law of Wings"); and (3) an historically chosen people to lead the society. Feuer argues that the application of these components of ideology to society has a denigrating effect since the ideologist ". . . seeking to identify with a lowlier group, to find some higher organum of truth, invariably casts aside some of his civilized, or bourgeois, or white rationality."

Feuer finds each new generation of intellectuals a contemptible lot. Drawing on an imposing kitbag of psychoanalytic tools—highly unbecoming for a sociologist—he finds younger intellectuals drawn to the ideological mode as a result of flawed psyches. Guilt, regression, masochism, sadism, impulse to rejection, death wishes, and infantile modes of consciousness are but a few of the epithets applied. He claims that all ideologists, but particularly the younger generation, are overtly authoritarian, anti-truth, anti-science, and antisemitic. Feuer sees them as conformists of marginal intellect who use catchwords, perpetrate myths, and have a tendency to "regress to primitivism." By middle-age, however, Feuer finds the once-young firebrands typically shunning their ideologies in more noble pursuits, such as science.

Feuer is convinced that these ideologists/intellectuals have a uniformly pernicious—and sometimes downright monstrous—impact on society. Dis-

tinguishing between "intellectuals" and ideologists on the one hand, and "men of intellect" and scientists/scholars on the other, he concludes that until the former put away ideology in favor of detached scientific analysis, civilization will have one more burden to bear.

This essay should not be mistaken for a piece of social-scientific analysis. In fact, the essay is a caricature of objectivity in being a polemic against ideologists. Feuer does not seem to see the irony of his attempt, but besides this, the essay has serious flaws. Firstly, he selects data to support the case against ideology and its architects; secondly, he could just as readily have substantiated many rival interpretations, sometimes with greater plausibility; thirdly, he makes many controversial assertions without the courtesy of documentation or discussion. Some border on the absurd—for example, ". . . America has been a country singularly lacking in ideology."

Throughout the essay, Feuer shows no understanding of relativism—that is, that knowledge is a social creation and that even the hardest scientific fact is based on a set of mutable presuppositions. Since objective social conditions form the "structure" within which science must operate for each historical epoch and since prevalent values, in turn, shape social conditions, it follows that value-free science is a logical and practical impossibility.

In advocating noncritical detachment as the ideal role for "men of intellect," Feuer ignores the historical consequences of such a stance. In the name of scientific detachment, "rational" men too often stand passively by while the generals and corporate managers use the products—for example, napalm, mustard gas, thalidomide—to terrorize, maim and murder. The men creating these macabre products certainly meet Feuer's criteria of rationality and objectivity; what they conspicuously lack is compassion and human empathy. And until we can evolve social institutions based on a humanistic value hierarchy,

Feuer's image of the "scientist as savior" will be just another ideology.

THOMAS J. RICE
Denison University
Granville
Ohio

CLIFFORD GEERTZ, ed. *Myth, Symbol, and Culture*. Pp. ix, 227. New York: W. W. Norton, 1974. $8.50.

Anthropology has always acknowledged close identity with the humanities through its deep concern with linguistic recording and analysis, oral literature (folklore and myth), primitive art, ritual and religion. Nineteenth century anthropologists often drew on the classical tradition for illustrative parallels, as in Sir James Frazer's *The Golden Bough*. Interpretation of myth and religion was largely done in terms of putative psychological reactions of hypothetical prehistoric primitives, universalized to all mankind and ordered upon a theoretical framework of evolutionary progression. In the first two-thirds of the present century, however, anthropologists and classicists all but lost touch with each other as social evolutionary theory fell into disfavor among non-Marxist anthropologists and natural science empiricism came to dominate their interests. Yet, in the past several decades there has been a burgeoning of anthropological concern with the symbolic expression of values and beliefs as factors in the creation, acceptance, and maintenance of meaningful ways of life, essential to individual motivation and the survival of societies. The discovery of possible "natural orders" in structural linguistics has heightened enthusiasm for the search for "deep" structures in social systems—a search which may best be facilitated by working through their symbolic transformations in various cultural systems.

Clifford Geertz has been the leading figure in the United States in exploring and demonstrating how symbol systems (especially, religious) express a human denial of the chaos in life experience, and how they clothe conceptions of a general order with a pervasive aura of reality which comes to dominate the moods and motivations of men and women.

The present volume is the outgrowth of an effort to draw a group of social scientists and humanists together, not for an "integration of the social sciences and the humanities," but for an experimental juxtaposition of creative minds working on common problems with contrasting methods.

The product is a collection of generally brilliant essays, expounding intellectual analyses of a variety of interesting phenomena, all thrusting toward a truly deep—hence fuller—understanding of complex but standardized human activities.

The anthropologists Geertz, Fernandez, and Douglas each take an ethnographic complex as an empirical behavioral starting point. The lead article by Geertz offers a fascinating prototype in method and exposition in revelation of the rich cultural significance to be unfolded in so seemingly simple a thing as the traditional Balinese cockfight. Fernandez uses Asturian animal metaphors as a springboard from which to launch a probe into the cultural uses of metaphor to enhance understanding of one's universe by cross-referencing domains of experience. Mary Douglas moves from an anthropological analysis of British eating "foibles" to a structural explanation of Hebraic food abominations.

Of the five essays authored by humanistic scholars, that by Steven Marcus on the transformation from young man to the matured Charles Dickens, which unfolded in the writing of the *Pickwick Papers*, will probably strike most readers as the most intriguing. Yet, there is much beauty and interest to be found in R. A. Brower's, "Visual and Verbal Translation of Myth: Neptune in Virgil, Rubens, and Dryden," while the Manuels' (Frank and Fritzie) natural history of the idea of Paradise traces the formal expression of the Western World's yearning for the transformation of imperfect reality into the ideal perfection of the mythic state of being.

This is a book in which not a single statistic is cited. It deals throughout with transformations, but not the transformation of social phenomena into numbers; its authors play no games of scientism. They are virtuosos of classical scholarship at its best, richly learned, imaginative and creative thinkers who deal not with the obvious, and who write with an almost overpowering elegance.

E. ADAMSON HOEBEL
University of Minnesota
Minneapolis

ANDREW M. GREELEY. *Ethnicity in the United States: A Preliminary Reconnaissance.* Pp. 347. New York: John Wiley & Sons, 1974. $14.95.

NATHAN GLAZER and DANIEL P. MOYNIHAN, eds. *Ethnicity: Theory and Experience.* Pp. 531. Cambridge, Mass.: Harvard University Press, 1975. $15.00.

The old argument of whether culturally diverse societies such as the United States have assimilationist or persisting pluralist tendencies is currently undergoing a revival in a refurbished suit of clothes called ethnicity. Andrew M. Greeley's contribution takes the form of sociological science, involving mostly statistical analysis of opinion derived from interviewing descendants of American immigrants. The Glazer and Moynihan work is a collection of sixteen impressionistically oriented papers by different authors, and the editors announce it as the beginnings of a world theory of ethnicity.

Both works are composed of inchoate material unworthy of publication in book form. Greeley's suffers from the multiplicity of persons and occasions from which the material derives. Chapter titles announce what is not found in the chapters. According to the index, a definition of ethnicity should first appear on page thirty-five. It does not. Greeley questions, rightfully, Marx's concept of class conflict, but after several casual sentences, he drops this fundamental issue entirely. The prose in Glazer and

Moynihan's work suffers from flabbiness. In one essay, the author states: "Historically, all who have lived beyond the pale of Chinese civilization tended to assume that the Chinese were blessed with a homogeneous culture and a common racial stock. The Chinese themselves, in their reverence for their ancestors and their reference to their multitudes as being of the 'old hundred surnames' seemed to stress their biological rites. As knowledge of China grew, foreigners began to discover that behind the Chinese posture to the world there were in fact important internal divisions." The author means, I take it, that foreigners are beginning to learn that the Chinese nation lacks a homogeneous culture and a common racial stock.

The books are difficult to summarize because of their varying styles and substance. Setting aside the innumerable definitions of ethnicity, ethnics, and ethnic groups, the argument brought forward, in gross terms, seems to be that ethnicity comprises the bonds of kinship generated by shared traits. These traits, which include common language, religion, and national origin, are distinguishable from other ties, like those of class or profession. Ethnicity provides a basis for classifying individuals into ethnic groups. Presumably, blacks as well as whites are classifiable as ethnics. One also notes that ethnicity establishes not only self-identity, but also the adversary. Furthermore, ethnics employ their groupings as a means of pursuing common interests and the resultant conflict is rising. Finally, the growth of ethnic consciousness is fostered by the breakdown in traditional social structures and by the politicization of decisions affecting community life. The evidence points to the persistence of cultural diversity; thus the assimilationist theory loses credence. In sum, while the ethnic experts talk around the nature of ethnicity and fail to reach a definition, they all agree that the trend is important and rising.

I cannot speak for the world, but in the United States no serious conflict exists among white ethnic groups. The conflict lies between white workers and black workers (or, more precisely, those claiming to be their spokesmen) and between the Wasp-Jewish upper-class intellectuals who manage the society's zeitgeist and the Roman-Eastern Catholic intellectuals unacceptable for entrance into the club on their own cultural terms. These two sets of recognized spokesmen have had their way, but at the price of destruction of urban life.

Moreover, I suspect that assimilation will occur in the long run, not because of integrationist policies, but in spite of them. The homogenization of tastes by corporate propaganda, the decline over generations of the cultural distinctions attributable to differences in national origin, the American work technology that decreases social snobbery by creating different sets of technicians with claims to prestige, and the decline in income disparity will increase assimilation and, probably, boredom.

JOSEPH ANTONIO RAFFAELE
Drexel University
Philadelphia
Pennsylvania

HAROLD R. ISAACS. *Idols of the Tribe: Group Identity and Political Change.* Pp. x, 242. New York: Harold R. Isaacs, 1975. $10.95.

This book makes a strong argument for the relationship between personality dynamics and large group political activity. Unconscious drives motivate group identity and consequently political change. Referring frequently to an exceptionally wide range of information from biblical sources to classical and contemporary events, philology, psychology, political science and comparative religion, the author arrives at his conclusions by citing persuasive relationships.

Neither the central concept nor the use of supporting data is new to those interested in group dynamics. That behavior is motivated by internal drives, whether one considers them "primordeal" (or learned) is certainly not original; the author mentions his rela-

tionship to affiliation theories proposed by Freud, Erikson, Shills and Geertz.

His major construct rests upon an acceptance of two needs considered as instinctual: the need for group affiliation and the need for self-esteem. Everyone, consciously or unconsciously, identifies with a basic group. Even when we struggle against a relationship this avoidance is balanced by something more attractive. Humans cannot deny this instinctual need for affinity.

Any one individual's self-esteem reflects an identification with a particular group. High levels of personal self-esteem are proportionate to such status as the group possesses in the social and political area. Groups are identified through shared symbols of communality. These may be sharing a common religion, common historical experiences at the hands of a majority group, shared racial characteristics or common ethnic and national identification. Acting much like Jung's "complexes" the very intensity of the need for identity attracts clusters of these elements into representative social and political alliances. They make for cohesive forces and encourage shared perceptions of self.

On a larger scale, if we accept the world as a combination of interrelated entities forming a balanced configuration, any change in the parts demands a change in the whole. Groups through experience, or changed social and economic circumstances, who find their status no longer consistent with reality, will force a reorganization of political relationships. Evidence of this is suggested by Black Americans, Malays in the Philippines, North African Jews in Israel and numerous others. These minorities are not willing to accept an accustomed political and social status and its accompanying demeaning level of self-esteem. Political upheavals follow.

Utilizing a Gestalt approach, the author does make a brief gesture in the direction of locating instinctual needs within the configuration of the neurological system. He is more successful in treating his concepts politically and historically.

This book is more historical than scientifically experimental in approach. The wealth of references and the creative matching of psychodynamics with contemporary and historical episodes produce an informative view which encourages much insightful learning. It heuristically suggests the possibility of predicting future group behavior if suitable instruments for measuring levels of basic group identity and reflected self-esteem can be devised and recorded for comparison purposes. The record of cross-cultural research in various disciplines attests to many previous attempts with, to date, only minor success.

The author's intellectual search for the roots of the drive for affiliation and its consequences sympathetically reflects his own humanism. It makes for a rewarding survey and is highly recommended.

I. R. STUART
Herbert H. Lehman College
City University of New York

PAUL LERMAN. *Community Treatment and Social Control: A Critical Analysis of Juvenile Correction Policy.* Pp. v, 253. Chicago, Ill.: The University of Chicago Press, 1975. $12.50.

Among the many myths to which both laymen and academicians adhere is the one that our efforts at correcting youthful deviance have progressed. Rather than reflecting a "spirit of revenge and restraint," treatment of youthful offenders is assumed to be characterized by attempts to reform and reintegrate them. Paul Lerman's study suggests that there are major discrepancies between what we believe to be the case; what our goals are with respect to treating youthful offenders; and reality.

This study focuses on an effort of the State of California to implement a community treatment project (CTP) as an alternative to institutionalization of presumably miscreant youth. Because this program became a model for correctional authorities across the United States, assessment of outcome is of practical significance. Lerman provides us with a detailed analysis and evaluation of the results of the experiment and some suggestions for alternative correctional policies.

The project was designed to compare control youth (who spent an average of 8 months in an institution) with experimentals (who were placed in communities). Because the time period during which the program operated was extended it is difficult to determine whether or not the experiment would have been successful, overall, but the author holds that if the original plan had been adhered to it might have at least been a fiscal success. As it was it proved neither a fiscal nor correctional success.

A detailed analysis of data derived from research reports and other documents demonstrates that what is supposed to be treatment is really social control; that the behavior of the adult agents who process youth changes more than the behavior of their charges; that the discretionary choices allowed these agents leads to broad definitions of deviance, including much arbitrariness; and that participation in the system creates more deviance. These are but some of the findings of this study which, this reviewer feels, ought to be a model for evaluation research.

Lerman has demonstrated that thoughtful conceptualization and careful, painstaking analysis can provide us with unequivocal directives for social problems policy. Social scientists in general and sociologists, in particular, have reason to take pride in this work.

EPHRAIM H. MIZRUCHI
Maxwell Policy Center on Aging
Syracuse University
New York

GEORGE HARWOOD PHILLIPS. *Chiefs and Challengers: Indian Resistance and Cooperation in Southern California.* Pp. xi, 225. Berkeley: University of California Press, 1975. $10.95.

WINTHROP YINGER. *Cesar Chavez: The Rhetoric of Nonviolence.* Pp. 143. Hicksville, N.Y.: Exposition Press, 1975. $6.50.

George H. Phillips' book traces the complicated inter-relations among Indians, Californios, Americans, and Mormons in mid-19th century Southern California. Not many people were involved. San Diego and Los Angeles were isolated white enclaves then. The Mexican grant *rancheros* were few and more ominous in the imaginations of the Anglos and themselves than in reality. The Indians were of unfabled tribes: Cahuillas, Cupeños, and Luiseños. And the dramatic climax of the story is a pretty smalltime raid on a Colorado River ferry and a few sheepmen in 1851.

If its subject is not grandiose, however, *Chiefs and Challengers* is easily among the very best books recently published in the area of Native American Studies. This field was contrived because of academic neglect or dismissal of Indians as little more than environmental impediments. Unfortunately, it has dissipated, following "Black Studies," "Women's Studies," and other political disciplines into a morass of sentimentalism. Its literature is divided about evenly between white liberal self-flagellations and the reminiscences of wise, kindly, and hearty, albeit often phoney, old chiefs. This book, on the contrary, portrays the Indians as flesh and blood human beings, of all things. And, therefore, as fit subjects for close and critical scrutiny.

Elementary? Yes, but also unusual in a field cluttered with junk. What Professor Phillips has done is to write good history rather than to patronize and pander. The result is an account which is, in part genuinely from an Indian perspective, a sort of study which is valid and sorely needed. Within a sound sociological framework, the author has provided an account of cultural confrontation which deserves a wide readership.

Descendants of these same Southern California tribes were possibly among the field laborers who formed Cesar Chavez's National Farm Workers Association in 1965. Some may have been in the crowd at Delano that cheered him when, on March 10, 1968, Chavez ended the 25-day fast that brought his movement international attention and much valuable support.

Winthrop Yinger's book is a line-by-line, word-by-word exegesis of the brief (485-word) statement which was read for the debilitated Chavez on that day. The author is surely correct in viewing the fascinating character of Chavez as the heart of the early farm workers' movement. He is also right in his premise that this document is central to understanding that remarkable man. Chavez's simple humility, his mystical and pious Mexican Catholicism, and an integrity that remains unblemished after a decade of probing and provocation by the determined (and often dirty) California agribusiness establishment make him *un Santo* to whom one reacts with the same astonishment with which the citizens of Assisi greeted their crazy Francis.

But Reverend Yinger asserts that Chavez shrewdly calculates his rhetoric, easily as it may come to him. This might well be true (for all that it means). But, as with other aspects of the book, the author merely states his point and proves nothing, while carrying on endlessly in trivialities. Slim as the book is, it is too long. It belabors the obvious page upon page, beating every little pointlet to death and then propping the poor corpse up for another flail or two. There is little here which has not been said better and more briefly in several of the books listed in the bibliography which is, incidentally, an excellent list, well worth a few of the interested scholar's dimes at the xerox machine.

JOSEPH R. CONLIN
California State University
Chico

DAN SAKALL and ALAN HARRINGTON. *Love and Evil: From a Probation Officer's Casebook.* Pp. ix, 372. Boston, Mass.: Little, Brown & Co., 1974. $8.95.

Here is one of the rare books of this genre which, once begun, is hard to put down. It consists essentially of short biographies of murderers, would-be murderers, drug addicts, prostitutes, sex offenders, robbers, speed freaks, and others awaiting trial. All of these persons appeared before Dan Sakall, Senior Deputy Adult Probation Officer, Arizona State Superior Court, Tucson, Arizona, and it was his function to try to work out some sort of solution to their mixed-up lives. This book, authored by him and Alan Harrington, deals sympathetically and in detail with each of the individuals —whether a seemingly well-off sales executive who twice attempts to murder his three-year-old stepdaughter for $30,000 insurance, a mother who assists in the rape of her eleven-year-old daughter, a beautiful girl hooked on heroin and trapped by a series of bad checks, a killer who murders solely because people are there, or a boy who attempts to kill a couple of Federal narcotic agents after they got the goods on his friend. These and other fascinating personalities all come to life in this book.

Intertwined with the stories of these lives is a brief biography of Sakall, who grew up along with nine other children as the son of a sadistic brutal father, but a selfless, loving, kind mother. From the age of five he worked long hours on the family farm picking potato bugs and tomato worms. If he missed any of these bugs—and he did because of bad eyesight—he would get a beating. He did do well in school and tried to escape his hard life through religion and social work. Perhaps, as he suggests, the severity of his life helped him to understand those with whom he had to deal. The contrast between those involved with the law and his own background makes the book even more intriguing as the reader wonders why Sakall did not succumb.

Toward the end of the book there is a thought-provoking chapter called "Toward a New Probation." Because the authors believe that criminal law in the United States as now carried on under a legal adversary system has become deeply harmful to all concerned, they recommend that instead of a system of dominance which breeds hatred an attempt be made to enhance a person's esteem in the eyes of his neighbors and contemporaries as well as his own. At present, the whole court system is

humiliating to the individual brought to trial and corrupting to those who participate in plea bargaining and the games played with people's lives.

All who are interested in criminal justice in the United States will profit from a careful reading of this thought-stimulating account of how one man tried to understand what happens to the personalities of the offenders for whom he must make recommendations to the court.

H. ASHLEY WEEKS
Isle of Springs
Maine

ROBERT STEVENS and ROSEMARY STEVENS. *Welfare Medicine in America: A Case Study of Medicaid.* Pp. xxi, 386. New York: The Free Press, 1974. No price.

This is an important book for everyone concerned about national health policy. It is essentially a social history—the first comprehensive review of the development, administration and impact of America's largest and deepest involvement in welfare medical care. Stevens and Stevens undertook their study on the strong hunch that government is irrevocably committed to even greater involvement in health care, and that Medicaid, therefore, constitutes a "remarkable instructive museum for those who must plan for the future" (p. xx).

The study's structure is based on background chapters on the competing American traditions of social insurance and public assistance. It then shows how the incompatibilities of these traditions were woven into Medicaid—via its legislative predecessor, the Kerr-Mills Act of 1960. The meat of the book is a detailed analysis of federal-state implementation, particularly in New York and California. How the meaning of legislation is modified by local interpretation is an important theme.

But the larger question raised is about the original intent and meaning of Medicaid itself. Not only was the initial legislation unclear as to its goals (as well as to whether potentially conflicting goals could be resolved), but the first eight years of Medicaid were marked by continuing confusion in the states growing out of the basic ambiguity which it encompassed, between a medical care program and a public assistance program.

In reconstructing their history, this lawyer and public health specialist team has incidentally provided a useful guide to the maze of federal and state programs, debates, and quite importantly, the literature. Much of the latter is buried in rather hard to get hearings, special reports, unpublished papers and occasional newsletters; all of it is referenced here, in over a thousand footnotes.

The social policy field is in desperate need of just this kind of synthesis and evaluation of large scale, federal policies. While there has been much talk in recent years about evaluation of smaller scale programs, the assessment of broad policies over relatively long periods has tended to be neglected. This case study fills just such a need, and furnishes an excellent example of how good policy evaluation can be done.

Unfortunately, from what is known about the reading habits of overworked decision makers, probably very few of those who could profit most will find the time to go through this scholarly volume. A compressed version, aimed at a more general audience, would find a wide and appreciative readership.

FREDERICK R. EISELE
The Pennsylvania State University
University Park

ECONOMICS

KAREN DAVIS. National Health Insurance: Benefits, Costs and Consequences. Pp. xiii, 182. Washington, D.C.: The Brookings Institution, 1975. $8.95.

This is the essential text to start with in understanding and analyzing various approaches to national health insurance in the United States. The book is timely, well-organized, clear; data collection has been impressive and yet unobtrusive;

the book is short, full of helpful tables and figures, well indexed, and reasonably priced. The analysis is understandable to the layman and helpful to the academic. All the information is in one place, and here is the place.

The eight chapters are concerned with goals, basic issues and a comparison of the seven major proposals introduced in Congress as of 1974. The goals include general access to medical care, elimination of financial hardship in receiving care and limiting the rise in health care costs. The Congressional proposals are compared relative to: population covered, range of medical benefits, direct patient payments, total costs, impact on employers, cost to individuals by income class, effect on private insurance companies, role of state governments, and methods of payment to providers. Quality of care is conspicuous in its absence from the list.

Some data Ms. Davis has collected which are not generally exposed in Congressional hearings and debate are: tax subsidies for medical care deductions currently result in an annual loss of six billion dollars in federal tax revenues; less than forty percent of the poor in the labor force have even limited private health insurance, and only eleven percent have insurance for non-hospital services; over a billion dollars of marketing costs could be saved by federal administration of a national health insurance program; and, in 1970, over four million Americans had out-of-pocket medical expenses in excess of $1,000— half this number were in families with incomes of less than $10,000 per year.

Ms. Davis' own recommendations for national health insurance are: comprehensive benefits for all Americans; direct patient payments with deductibles and coinsurance, up to $1,000 per year with no payment by the poor and a sliding scale of payment by the near-poor; financing by a combination of general revenues and a tax on payroll and unearned income; administration by the federal government; doctors to accept the allowable charge as full payment for their services, and financial incentives to increase access for minorities and rural residents. My own preference would have been for a full length explanation, rather than a three-page listing of contents, of the "Davis" bill, its benefits, costs and consequences — but, of course, this was not the purpose of this excellent new book.

ANTHONY R. KOVNER
International Union, UAW
Solidarity House
Detroit
Michigan

JOSEPH A. PECHMAN and P. MICHAEL TIMPANE, eds. *Work Incentives and Income Guarantees: The New Jersey Negative Income Tax Experiment.* Pp. 232. Washington, D.C.: The Brookings Institution, 1975. $9.95. Paperbound, $3.50.

In 1965 R. Sargent Shriver, then director of the Office of Economic Opportunity (OEO), began toying with the idea of a negative income tax as a long-run possibility for improving the traditional welfare system. The election of 1966 produced a Congress relatively hostile to the OEO and the Great Society programs. Many questioned that a program which gave income for no work, would in fact encourage people to work; there were even some who believed that such programs might *discourage* some recipients from working. But the faithful—those who favored a negative income tax—received a grant of $8,000,000 from the OEO to study the impact of such a program. In the application for the grant, the OEO, with its high standards of ethical behavior, insisted that the programs be described as "work incentives" rather than as "negative income tax."

The first fourteen months of the grant were spent in planning. It was decided that the funds should be divided with one-third going to the income recipients and the other two-thirds to the research effort. Four years were spent in the actual operation of the experiment; the final sixteen months, in the analysis of the data collected and the production of a final report consisting of four volumes

released in 1973 and 1974 by the Department of Health, Education, and Welfare.

In April of 1974, the Brookings Panel on Social Experimentation held a two-day conference of economists, sociologists, political scientists, and research administrators from the Brookings Institution to review the findings of the official report and to draw lessons from it regarding income maintenance policy and social experimentation in the future. This book, the second in the Brookings series of Studies in Social Experimentation, is the result of that conference. It is a record of how the experiment came about, and of its operational design. It examines the influence of the experimental negative income tax on the labor supply and includes a critical evaluation of the experiment and its findings.

The supporters of the program have not given up. They read into the findings that recipients of such assistance do not reduce their work effort *very* much, and that if Congressmen and the public in general understood what the evidence shows, they too would favor such a program. Another appraisal, however, stresses that the study does not show what the effects of a permanent negative income tax would be, and that the experiment tells "little about the impact on labor supply or the increase in transfer cost that would be associated with the adoption of a negative income tax." The researchers all agree, however, that there is need for further research.

KENNETH L. TREFFTZS
University of Southern California
Los Angeles

LEONARD S. RUBINOWITZ. *Low-Income Housing: Suburban Strategies.* Pp. vii, 323. Cambridge, Mass.: Ballinger, 1974. $13.50.

Opening up the suburbs to low income families is among the hardier of current causes. It flowered in the Civil Rights era of the 1960s, took some bad lumps during the first Nixon Administration and shriveled under heat from environmentalists who may or may not have cared for or from whom the environment was to be protected. More recently, as severe slumps recurred in construction and evidence mounted about the economic costs of environmental protection, major segments of the business community— real estate organizations in particular— have begun to challenge suburban land development restrictions so that the poor-people-in-the-suburbs movement has picked up fellow travelers, hope and steam.

In the United States you cannot have a movement without taking on a batallion of lawyers. Lawyers cannot function without a suitable bag of tricks—cases, decisions, statutes, subparagraphs or punctuation marks sieved from the gargantuan record of our times. This book is essentially a manual for attorneys engaged in promoting a particular movement. Things being as they are, it is at the same time a manual for the other attorneys who are engaged in checking this movement. It is sufficiently well put together to be readable and informative for those of us who are on the sidelines paying the freight.

The book describes recent legal events relating to suburban exclusion of low-income housing, beginning at the county level, then at the regional or metropolitan level, next at the state and finally at the federal level. This is preceded by accounts of exclusionary techniques practiced by suburban communities—mainly zoning-out apartments and smaller sized home lots; the author makes it clear that legal attacks on exclusionary devices are not feasible at the local government level. "Most suburban jurisdictions will keep doing their best to keep out housing for low- and moderate-income people," he says (page 48). "It is up to county and regional bodies, states, and the federal government to reverse this pattern." He does not gloss over the fact that most suburbanites went to the suburbs to avoid low- and moderate-income neighbors. The philosophy is that the law is greater than the life-style, or in his own words, "Legal action does not require a broad base of political support" (page 260).

So girded he begins with a tale of the Fairfax, Virginia, County ordinance in 1971 requiring developers to include at least six low-income and 15 moderate-income dwellings among every one hundred new homes built. This ordinance was nullified on constitutional grounds because it appeared to be a "taking" of the developer's property. That legal issue has not been fully tested, however; in many other situations described later in the book similar "formula" allocations of building permits have been somewhat more successful.

An alternative to court decisions or legislative actions mandating low-income housing in suburban areas is the "carrot and stick" method. It is within the power of federal agencies to withhold funds for sewer construction, parks and so on if a particular suburban community fails to promise not to exclude low-income housing. State governments, now largely in control of federal housing subsidy funds, are in a position to make similar bargains. The federal revenue sharing program requires recipient communities to show compliance with a whole litany of national community development objectives, though the language, the procedure and the application of this requirement are still very loose.

The book is straightforward. It was written to help a cause. It is competent in that good case references are provided in support of the techniques and strategies for advancing this cause. It is weak and misleading, however, with respect to that item so much ignored by the legal mind—evidence. The author asserts, no doubt from conviction, that "it is both right and necessary that housing be made available in the suburbs for people with low and moderate incomes" (p. 1). Maybe it isn't. If it isn't then perhaps courtroom techniques and legislative actions to make this come about will do the larger community more harm than good. If it can be shown in court to be counter-productive or unnecessary then the court may overrule the legal bag of tricks.

The era of litigated movements is

already giving way to the age of the trade-off. We cannot have a perfectly serene environment without reducing our consumption of other things. We don't know how to curb inflation without raising unemployment. We have to make choices, strike a balance or discover ways to have our cake and eat it too. Mostly we order our priorities, and this requires being more explicit about what we really hope to accomplish. It is not at all clear what social pay-off will result from economic integration of the suburbs.

If the attraction of the suburbs is that poor people don't live there, the movement to integrate suburbs economically is surely fatuous. If the object is simply egalitarian, then we may find ourselves subsidizing middle-income families who feel like moving to a neighborhood where houses start at $200,000. If low-income families do find housing in the affluent suburbs, where will they shop? Shall we use our bag of tricks to integrate I. Magnin and J. C. Penney's?

The fact is that a metropolitan region consists of distinguishable chunks of land, just as a side of beef includes several different cuts. Choice cuts of beef or land, can be sold for more, and that helps to keep the price of less choice cuts low. It is not very sensible to mandate T-bone steak for everyone—or bottom round, to say nothing of soup bone or tripe. What is to be gained by mandating economic integration of the suburbs?

The author argues briefly in Chapter 1 that there is a metropolitan mismatch of jobs and housing—low-income jobs are shifting outside the central city while high-income jobs are predominantly in the urban core, resulting in unnecessary cross-commuting. There are adequate numbers to make a superficial case for suburban integration on this ground. The flaws in the argument are ignored, and they are major. The obvious, but impractical remedy of having the rich and poor simply switch residences (or jobs) would save gasoline but it would hardly result in economic integration. In fact, suburbanites have more or less consciously elected to bear higher commuting costs in exchange for the less expensive land

and the particular amenities of the suburbs. Middle-income suburbanites cannot afford the land that central city low-income families occupy. More to the point, really, is the fact that blue-collar occupations which drift away from central cities do not disperse like dust on the whole suburban landscape. They cluster in particular outskirts. Gradually some suburban districts become identified with blue-collar employment as middle-income residents move away from encroaching industry. It is a selective and long-run process. It is not helped by busting the zoning ordinance in junior executive-land forty miles away. It may be accelerated by flogging the lower-middle income suburbanite who happens to own an obsolescent home in the direction that industrial plants have decided to move; but that may not seem entirely fair. An opposing attorney, or even a consultant, might start talking about "equal protection."

The author of this book clearly believes that the law ought not be subservient to political sentiment. We are beginning to learn, however, that law cannot prevail against reality. It is true that low-income housing is scarce in American suburbs. Why this is so, and what follows from it is far from clear. Courtroom techniques don't help us answer these basic questions. *Low-Income Housing: Suburban Strategies* is a workmanlike examination of legal techniques, undoubtedly valuable to those who are involved pro or con in the movement to which it relates. It is useful beyond that because it exposes the shallowness of a simply legalistic approach to an important community issue.

WALLACE F. SMITH
University of California
Berkeley

DAVID SECKLER. *Thorstein Veblen and the Institutionalists: A Study in the Social Philosophy of Economics.* Pp. x, 160. Boulder: Colorado Associated University Press, 1975. $10.00.

There is a real need for a book making Veblen more understandable to social scientists today, but unfortunately this is not the book. The author believes that Veblen's eclecticism sprang from an inability to find a comfortable ideological stance on the key issue of free will versus determinism. "Forced from humanism, unable to accept either historicism or behaviorism, Veblen fled into obscurantism; that is one of his secrets" (p. 85).

No one will deny his stature as a leading American obscurantist, but the question remains of just what Veblen was trying to accomplish. The author believes that during the highly productive years between 1898 and 1909 Veblen was "preoccupied with matters of methodology" (p. 52). Upon this dubious premise he constructs a humanist Veblen who uses the instincts of workmanship and idle curiosity as a basis for universal human nature and a behavioralist Veblen who explains time-specific institutions and thought patterns in relation to the economic base of a given society.

I prefer to view this dichotomy from another standpoint. Veblen was preoccupied with two tasks—an anthropological study of a culture in which he himself was an unassimilated immigrant offspring and a refutation of the subjective utility theories of what is now known as neoclassical economics. Veblen the critic rebelled at the determinism of the economic models of others while adopting a functionalist anthropological viewpoint on particular institutions and their need to mesh in a stable social system.

The achievement of Veblen as a social scientist is submerged by tying him too closely to his early training as a philosopher and especially by the labored effort to find a parallel between Veblen's humanistic side and the economic individualism of Hayek, von Mises, and Robbins. Lord Robbins supervised the dissertation upon which this book is based and wrote a brief foreword laying out the supposed parallel: in both systems of thought "collective social phenomena are traced back to individual motivation with mind as an operative entity" (p. x). That describes the humanistic side of almost everyone.

The book is filled out with a description of the influence of the German historical school on the founders of the American Economic Association and with rather lackluster chapters on the other two-thirds of the institutionalist triumvirate—Wesley C. Mitchell and John R. Commons. But it is Veblen that the book is about, and the final chapter uses Popper's distinction between refutable "scientific" theories and irrefutable "philosophic" theories to place Veblen's work firmly in the latter category. Veblen, like Freud, is thus banished from the scientific pantheon. Veblen's explanation sketches may indeed be irrefutable, but they are also something more than mere satire in showing that a deeper significance lurks behind seemingly innocuous social observances. If that's social philosophy, then there's a need for more of it today.

WILLIAM G. WHITNEY
University of Pennsylvania
Philadelphia

PAUL TAUBMAN and TERENCE WALES. *Higher Education and Earnings: College as an Investment and a Screening Device.* Pp. xvii, 302. New York: McGraw-Hill, 1974. $17.50.

The Taubman and Wales study, prepared for the Carnegie Commission on Higher Education and the National Bureau of Economic Research, is based on the results of a 1969 follow-up survey of a large number of male volunteers to the Army Air Corps who had to pass the Aviation Cadet Qualifying Test during World War II. The data base included information about physical and mental abilities, education, earnings, and employment.

The book is organized in such a way that the research hypotheses and results are presented in nine fairly short chapters and the problems associated with research methods are presented in twelve self-contained appendixes. The appendixes cover such topics as problems in measuring education; estimation of the mean income for the open-ended class; response bias, test scores, and factor analysis; and estimation of private and social costs of higher education. Mainly because of its organization, the Taubman and Wales work should be of interest to a wide audience and not limited to the economics profession. Taubman and Wales present most of the economic theory behind their analyses in Chapter 2, "The Human-Capital Approach to Higher Education." That chapter is concise, with economic concepts simply and clearly explained.

Part of their work is devoted to four different measured rates of private return to higher education: before tax and after tax for both a deflated and a non-deflated rate of return. Their estimated rates of return range from a low 1.4 percent after tax-deflated return for the Ph.D. degree to a high 15.0 percent after tax-non-deflated return for "some college." The private costs used in their model were forgone earnings plus expenses for tuition and other college related items. The researchers also estimated social rates of return for a half-dozen or so different educational categories. Because this reviewer does not believe that this is the appropriate forum to comment on what should or should not be included in measuring social costs, suffice it to say that the cost Taubman and Wales used in calculating the social rate of return was forgone earnings set at three-quarters of the earnings of high-school graduates plus the resource cost per student in higher education. Their deflated social rate of return for the entire sample was 10.5 percent for "some college" and 1.7 percent for the Ph.D. degree.

As the title of the book indicates, Taubman and Wales also look at education as a screening device, which they define as a person being excluded from an occupation in which he would have higher earnings but is excluded because of the lack of educational attainment. Taubman and Wales find that a substantial part of differential earnings results from the screening phenomenon rather than education per se.

This reviewer would have preferred a summary chapter that highlighted all the many findings and also related these findings to policy issues that local, state, and federal governments must continually solve. The authors did not include a summary chapter, nor did they say much about education policy.

In summary, this is a well written and researched book that is a welcome addition to the literature.

MARY A. HOLMAN
The George Washington University
Washington, D.C.

OTHER BOOKS

ABELSON, PHILIP H. *Energy for Tomorrow.* Pp. v, 78. Seattle: University of Washington, 1975. $5.95. Paperbound, $2.50.

ABRAHAM, HENRY J. *The Judicial Process: An Introductory Analysis of the Courts of the United States, England, and France.* 3rd ed. Pp. v, 543. New York: Oxford University Press, 1975. $12.95. Paperbound, $5.95.

ADAMS, M. IAN. *Three Authors of Alienation: Bombal, Onetti, Darpentier.* Pp. 128. Austin: University of Texas Press, 1975. $8.50.

ADIE, W. A. C. *Oil, Politics, and Seapower: The Indian Ocean Vortex.* Pp. v, 98. New York: Crane, Russak & Co., 1975. $4.95. Paperbound, $2.95.

ADLER, NORMAN M. and BLANCHE DAVIS BLANK. *Political Clubs in New York.* Pp. v, 275. New York: Praeger, 1975. No price.

ALBORNOZ, NICOLÁS SÁNCHEZ. *The Population of Latin America: A History.* Pp. 317. Berkeley: University of California, 1975. $3.95. Paperbound.

ALLEN, HARRY E. and CLIFFORD E. SIMONSEN. *Corrections in America: An Introduction.* Criminal Justice Series. Pp. vii, 555. Beverly Hills, Calif.: Glencoe Press, 1975. $12.95.

ALLEN, ROBERT L. *Reluctant Reformers: Racism and Social Reform Movements in the United States.* Pp. 347. New York: Doubleday, 1975. $3.50. Paperbound.

ALLISON, LINCOLN. *Environmental Planning: A Political and Philosophical Analysis.* Studies in Political Science. Pp. 134. Totowa, N.J.: Rowman and Littlefield, 1975. $8.50.

AMANN, PETER H. *Revolution and Mass Democracy: The Paris Club Movement in 1848.* Pp. xii, 370. Princeton, N.J.: Princeton University, 1975. $14.50.

Amnesty International Report on Torture. Pp. 285. New York: Farrar, Straus and Giroux, 1975. $3.45. Paperbound.

ANDERSON, B. L., ed. *Capital Accumulation in the Industrial Revolution*. Pp. v, 212. Totowa, N.J.: Rowman and Littlefield, 1975. $8.00.

ANDERSON, GRACE M. *Networks of Contact: The Portuguese and Toronto*. Pp. ii. 194. Ontario, Ca.: Wilfrid Lauier University, 1974. No price.

ANDERSON, JAMES E. *Public Policy-Making*. Pp. vii, 178. New York: Praeger, 1975. $8.50. Paperbound, $3.95.

ARKHURST, FREDERICK S., ed. *U.S. Policy toward Africa*. Pp. v, 259. New York: Praeger, 1975. $6.95. Paperbound.

The Arms Trade Registers. A SIPRI Monograph. Pp. v, 176. Cambridge, Mass.: MIT Press, 1974. No price.

ARONOWITZ, STANLEY. *Food, Shelter and the American Dream*. Pp. 188. New York: Seabury Press, 1974. $7.95.

AXINN, JUNE and HERMAN LEVIN. *Social Welfare: A History of the American Response to Need*. Pp. vii, 319. New York: Dodd, Mead & Co., 1975. $6.95. Paperbound.

BALL, GEORGE W., ed. *Global Companies: The Political Economy of World Business*. Pp. vii, 179. Englewood Cliffs, N.J.: Prentice-Hall, 1975. No price.

BANKS, ARTHUR S., ed. *Political Handbook of the World: 1975*. Pp. viii, 491. New York: McGraw-Hill, 1975. $19.95.

BARBER, SOTIRIOS A. *The Constitution and the Delegation of Congressional Power*. Pp. 153. Chicago, Ill.: University of Chicago, 1975. $12.00.

BARKER, LUCIUS J. and TWILEY W. BARKER, JR., eds. *Civil Liberties and the Constitution*. 2nd ed. Pp. iii, 474. Englewood Cliffs, N.J.: Prentice-Hall, 1975. $14.95. Paperbound, $8.75.

BARNARD, T. C. *Cromwellian Ireland: English Government and Reform in Ireland, 1649–1660*. Oxford Historical Monographs. Pp. viii, 349. New York: Oxford University Press, 1975. $29.00.

BARRETT, NANCY SMITH. *The Theory of Macroeconomic Policy*. 2nd ed. Pp. v, 483. Englewood Cliffs, N.J.: Prentice-Hall, 1975. $12.95.

BAXTER, WILLIAM F. *People or Penquins: The Case for Optimal Pollution*. Pp. 110. New York: Columbia University Press, 1974. $5.95. Paperbound, $1.95.

BELOFF, MAX and VIVIAN VALE, eds. *American Political Institutions in the 1970s*. Pp. 194. Totowa, N.J.: Rowman and Littlefield, 1975. $19.50.

BERKIN, CAROL. *Jonathan Sewall: Odyssey of an American Loyalist*. Pp. 200. New York: Columbia University Press, 1974. $10.95.

BLECHMAN, BARRY M. *The Control of Naval Armaments*. Pp. vii, 100. Washington, D.C.: Brookings Institution, 1975. $2.50. Paperbound.

BLECHMAN, BARRY M., EDWARD M. GRAMLICH and ROBERT W. HARTMAN. *Setting National Priorities: The 1976 Budget*. Pp. vii, 243. Washington, D.C.: Brookings Institution, 1975. $3.95. Paperbound.

BLOCH, MARC. *Slavery and Serfdom in the Middle Ages*. Pp. 290. Berkeley: University of California Press, 1975. $17.50.

BLOLAND, HARLAND G. and SUE M. BLOLAND. *American Learned Societies in Transition*. Pp. xv, 130. New York: McGraw-Hill, 1974. $6.95.

BLUMBERG, PHILLIP I. *The Megacorporation in American Society: The Scope of Corporate Power*. Pp. x, 188. Englewood Cliffs, N.J.: Prentice-Hall, 1975. $9.95. Paperbound, $5.95.

BOSERUP, ANDERS and ANDREW MACK. *War without Weapons: Non-violence in National Defense*. Pp. 194. New York: Schocken Books, 1975. $6.50. Paperbound, $2.95.

BOXER, C. R. *Women in Iberian Expansion Overseas, 1415–1815: Some Facts, Fancies and Personalities*. Pp. 142. New York: Oxford University Press, 1975. $12.75.

BRAEMAN, JOHN, ROBERT H. BREMNER and DAVID BRODY. *The New Deal*. Vols. I and II. Pp. x, 775. Columbus: Ohio State University, 1975. $30.00 per set.

BRAND, JACK. *Local Government Reform in England*. Pp. 176. Hamden, Conn.: Archon Books, 1974. $10.00.

BRODY, BARUCH. *Abortion and the Sanctity of Human Life: A Philosophical View*. Pp. 162. Lawrence, Mass.: MIT Press, 1975. $8.95.

BROWNING, EDGAR K. *Redistribution and the Welfare System*. Pp. 131. Washington, D.C.: American Enterprise Institute for Public Policy Research, 1975. $3.00. Paperbound.

BURGHARDT, ANDREW F., ed. *Development Regions in the Soviet Union, Eastern Europe, and Canada*. Pp. v, 192. New York: Praeger, 1975. No price.

BYRD, JACK, JR. *Operations Research Models for Public Administration*. Pp. vii, 276. Lexington, Mass.: Lexington Books, 1975. $18.50.

CALIFANO, JOSEPH A., JR. *A Presidential Nation*. Pp. 338. New York: W. W. Norton, 1975. $9.95.

CANTOR, ROBERT D. *Voting Behavior and Presidential Elections*. Pp. 139. Itasca, Ill.: F. E. Peacock, 1975. $3.50. Paperbound.

CATANESE, ANTHONY JAMES. *Planners and Local Politics: Impossible Dreams*. Pp. 192.

Beverly Hills, Calif.: Sage, 1974. $10.00. Paperbound, $6.00.

CHANG, CHUN-SHU, ed. *The Making of China: Main Themes in Premodern Chinese History*. Pp. vii, 347. Englewood Cliffs, N.J.: Prentice-Hall, 1975. $14.95. Paperbound, $6.95.

CHATTERJEE, PARTHA. *Arms, Alliances and Stability*. Pp. ix, 292. New York: Halsted, 1975. $19.75.

CHIN, FRANK et al. *Aiiieeeee: An Anthology of Asian-American Writers*. Pp. 320. New York: Doubleday, 1975. $3.95. Paperbound.

CLOWARD, RICHARD A. and FRANCES FOX PIVEN. *The Politics of Turmoil: Poverty, Race, and the Urban Crises*. Pp. v, 365. New York: Vintage, 1975. $2.95. Paperbound.

COATES, DAVID. *The Labour Party and the Struggle for Socialism*. Pp. v, 257. New York: Cambridge University Press, 1975. $14.95. Paperbound, $5.95.

COBB, ROGER W. and CHARLES D. ELDER. *Participation in American Politics: The Dynamics of Agenda-Building*. Pp. v, 182. Baltimore, Md.: Johns Hopkins University, 1975. $3.95. Paperbound.

Congressional Quarterly's Washington Information Directory, 1975–76. Pp. v, 829. New York: Quadrangle, 1975. $7.95. Paperbound.

CONROY, HILARY. *The Japanese Seizure of Korea, 1868–1910: A Study of Realism and Idealism in International Relations*. Pp. 532. Philadelphia: University of Pennsylvania Press, 1974. $5.45. Paperbound.

COULOUMBIS, THEODORE A. and SALLIE M. HICKS, eds. *U.S. Foreign Policy Toward Greece and Cyprus: The Clash of Principle and Pragmatism*. Pp. 161. Washington, D.C.: The Center for Mediterranean Studies, 1975. No price.

CURTIS, MICHAEL et al., eds. *The Palestinians: People, History, Politics*. Pp. v, 277. New Brunswick, N.J.: Transaction Books, 1975. $4.95. Paperbound.

CUSHMAN, ROBERT F. *Cases in Constitutional Law*. 4th ed. Pp. viii, 732. Englewood Cliffs, N.J.: Prentice-Hall, 1975. $15.95.

DANNHAUSER, WERNER J. *Nietzsche's View of Socrates*. Pp. 283. Ithaca, N.Y.: Cornell University Press, 1974. $15.00.

DE CARLO, JULIA E. and CONSTANT A. MADON. *Innovations in Education for the Seventies: Selected Readings*. Pp. viii, 276. New York: Behavioral Publications, 1975. $9.95. Paperbound, $4.95.

DeCROW, KAREN. *Sexist Justice*. Pp. 363. New York: Vintage, 1975. $2.95. Paperbound.

DE SOLA POOL, ITHIEL et al. *The Prestige Press: A Comparative Study of Political Symbols*. Pp. v, 359. Cambridge, Mass.: MIT Press, 1970. $3.95. Paperbound.

DESPERT, J. LOUISE. *The Inner Voices of Children*. Pp. 162. New York: Brunner/Mazel, 1975. $4.95. Paperbound.

DIAL, O. E. and EDWARD M. GOLDBERG. *Privacy, Security, and Computers: Guidelines for Municipal and Other Public Information Systems*. Pp. v, 169. New York: Praeger, 1975. $14.00.

DIBBLE, VERNON K. *The Legacy of Albion Small*. Pp. vii, 255. Chicago, Ill.: University of Chicago, 1975. $15.00.

DINNERSTEIN, LEONARD and KENNETH T. JACKSON, eds. *American Vistas: 1607–1877*. 2nd ed. Pp. vii, 289. New York: Oxford University Press, 1975. $2.95. Paperbound.

DINNERSTEIN, LEONARD and KENNETH T. JACKSON, eds. *American Vistas: 1877 to the Present*. 2nd ed. Pp. vii, 401. New York: Oxford University Press, 1975. $3.50. Paperbound.

DOWNS, ANTHONY. *Opening Up the Suburbs: An Urban Strategy for America*. Pp. vi, 219. New Haven, Conn.: Yale University Press, 1973. $2.95. Paperbound.

DOWNS, JAMES F. *Cultures in Crisis*. 2nd ed. Pp. iv, 237. Beverly Hills, Calif.: Glencoe Press, 1975. $4.95. Paperbound.

DUKE, RICHARD D. *Gaming: The Future's Language*. Pp. iv, 223. New York: Halsted Press, 1975. $12.50.

DUMONT, RENE. *Utopia or Else*. Pp. 180. New York: Universe Books, 1975. $8.50.

DUTTON, BERTHA P. *Indians of the American Southwest*. Pp. xi, 298. Englewood Cliffs, N.J.: Prentice-Hall, 1975. $14.95.

EKSTEINS, MODRIS. *The Limits of Reason: The German Democratic Press and the Collapse of Weimar Democracy*. Oxford Historical Monographs. Pp. vii, 337. New York: Oxford University Press, 1975. $22.50.

EL-AYOUTY, YASSIN, ed. *The Organization of African Unity after Ten Years*. Pp. vi, 262. New York: Praeger, 1975. $18.50.

ENDICOTT, JOHN E. *Japan's Nuclear Option: Political, Technical, and Strategic Factors*. Pp. vii, 289. New York: Praeger, 1975. $20.00.

EVANS, JOHN G. *The Environment of Early Man in the British Isles*. Pp. 234. Berkeley: University of California Press, 1975. $12.95.

FERGUSON, JOHN. *Utopias of the Classical World*. Pp. 228. Ithaca, N.Y.: Cornell University Press, 1975. $11.50.

FINN, R. WELLDON. *Domesday Book: A Guide*. Pp. ix, 109. Totowa, N.J.: Rowman and Littlefield, 1975. $8.00.

FITZGERALD, JACK D. and STEVEN M. COX. *Unraveling Social Science: A Primer on Perspectives, Methods, and Statistics*. Pp. v, 180. Chicago, Ill.: Rand McNally, 1975. No price.

FIZDALE, RUTH. *Social Agency Structure and Accountability*. Pp. 231. Fair Lawn, N.J.: R. E. Burdick, 1975. $9.75.

FLEXNER, ELEANOR. *Century of Struggle: The Woman's Rights Movement in the United States*. Revised Edition. Pp. viii, 405. Lawrence, Mass.: Harvard University Press, 1975. $15.00.

FLOORE, FRANCES BERKELEY. *The Bread of the Oppressed: An American Woman's Experiences in War-Disrupted Countries*. Pp. 292. Hicksville, N.Y.: Exposition Press, 1975. $10.00.

FONTAINE, ROGER W. *Brazil and the United States: Toward a Maturing Relationship*. Pp. 127. Washington, D.C.: American Enterprise Institute for Public Policy Research, 1974. $3.00. Paperbound.

Foreign Relations of the United States, 1949: The Far East and Australia. Vol. VII. Pp. iii, 600. Washington, D.C.: U.S. Government Printing Office, 1975. $8.75.

Foreign Relations of the United States, 1949: The United Nations; the Western Hemisphere. Vol. II. Pp. iv, 827. Washington, D.C.: U.S. Government Printing Office, 1975. $10.40.

Foreign Relations of the United States, 1949: Western Europe. Vol. IV. Pp. iii, 878. Washington, D.C.: U.S. Government Printing Office, 1975. $11.15.

FRIEDLANDER, WALTER A. *International Social Welfare*. Pp. v, 230. Englewood Cliffs, N.J.: Prentice-Hall, 1975. $9.95.

FRIEDMAN, LEWIS B. *Budgeting Municipal Expenditures: A Study in Comparative Policy Making*. Pp. vi, 249. New York: Praeger, 1975. $17.50.

FUSTER, F. THOMAS, ed. *Education, Income, and Human Behavior*. Pp. xi, 437. New York: McGraw-Hill, 1975. $17.50.

GALTUNO, JOHAN. *A Structural Theory of Revolutions*. Pp. 78. The Netherlands: Rotterdam University Press, 1974. $17.50. Paperbound.

GAMBINO, RICHARD. *Blood of My Blood: The Dilemma of the Italian-Americans*. Pp. 388. New York: Doubleday, 1975. $3.50. Paperbound.

GAMSON, WILLIAM A. *The Strategy of Social Protest*. Pp. ix, 217. Homewood, Ill.: Dorsey Press, 1975. $5.95. Paperbound.

GANDHI, INDIRA. *Indira Gandhi: Speeches and Writings*. Pp. 221. New York: Harper & Row, 1975. $10.00.

GARAN, D. G. *The Key to the Sciences of Man: The "Impossible" Relativity of Value Reactions*. Pp. ix, 561. New York: Philosophical Library, 1975. $10.00.

GARRETT, CLARKE. *Respectable Folly: Millenarians and the French Revolution in France and England*. Pp. x, 237. Baltimore, Md.: Johns Hopkins University, 1975. $10.00.

GIAP, VO NGUYEN. *Unforgettable Months and Years*. Pp. 103. Ithaca, N.Y.: Cornell University, 1975. $6.50. Paperbound.

GIBNEY, FRANK. *Japan: The Fragile Super Power*. Pp. 347. New York: W. W. Norton, 1975. $10.00.

GILBERT, MARTIN. *Atlas of the Arab-Israeli Conflict*. Pp. 101. New York: Macmillan, 1975. $6.95.

GINZBERG, ELI and ALICE M. YOHALEM, eds. *The University Medical Center and the Metropolis*. Pp. v, 175. New York: Josia Macy, Jr. Foundation, 1974. $10.00.

GOURÉ, LEON and MORRIS ROTHENBERG. *Soviet Penetration of Latin America*. Monographs in International Affairs. Pp. iii, 204. Coral Gables, Fla.: University of Miami, 1975. No price.

GREEN, ROSE BASILE. *Primo Vino*. Pp. 83. Cranbury, N.J.: A. S. Barnes, 1975. $4.95.

GREENE, FRED. *Stresses in U.S.-Japanese Security Relations*. Pp. vii, 110. Washington, D.C.: Brookings Institution, 1975. $2.50. Paperbound.

GRELE, RONALD, ed. *Envelopes of Sound: Six Practitioners Discuss the Method and Practice of Oral History and Testimony*. Pp. viii, 154. Chicago, Ill.: Precedent Publishers, 1975. $7.50.

GRILLI, ENZO R. *The Future for Hard Fibers and Competition from Synthetics*. Pp. ix, 108. Baltimore, Md.: Johns Hopkins University, 1975. $5.00. Paperbound.

GUNNEMAN, JON P., ed. *The Nation-State and Transnational Corporations in Conflict: With Special Reference to Latin America*. Pp. v, 242. New York: Praeger, 1975. $17.50.

HALL, RICHARD H. *Occupations and the Social Structure*. 2nd ed. Pp. vii, 382. Englewood Cliffs, N.J.: Prentice-Hall, 1975. $10.50.

HAN, SUNGJOO. *The Failure of Democracy in South Korea*. Pp. 251. Berkeley: University of California, 1975. $10.00.

HANCE, WILLIAM A. *The Geography of Modern Africa*. Fully Revised, 2nd ed. Pp. x, 657. New York: Columbia University Press, 1975. $17.50.

HANCOCK, ROGER N. *Twentieth Century Ethics*. Pp. vi, 240. New York: Columbia University Press, 1974. $10.00.

HANIFI, M. JAMIL. *Islam and the Transformation of Culture.* Pp. x, 182. New York: Asia Publishing House, 1975. $8.95.

HARRIS, CHAUNCY D. *Guide to Geographical Bibliographies and Reference Works in Russian or on the Soviet Union.* Pp. xviii, 478. Chicago: University of Illinois, 1975. $5.00. Paperbound.

HARVEY, EDWARD B. *Industrial Society: Structures, Roles, and Relations.* Pp. ix, 417. Homewood, Ill.: Dorsey Press, 1975. $13.95.

HEILBRONER, ROBERT L. and LESTER C. THUROW. *Understanding Macroeconomics.* 5th ed. Pp. iii, 314. Englewood Cliffs, N.J.: Prentice-Hall, 1975. $5.95. Paperbound.

HEILBRONER, ROBERT L. and LESTER C. THUROW. *Understanding Microeconomics.* 3rd ed. Pp. v, 280. Englewood Cliffs, N.J.: Prentice-Hall, 1975. $5.95. Paperbound.

HOARE, QUINTIN, ed. *Early Writings: Karl Marx.* Pp. 449. New York: Random House, 1975. $4.95. Paperbound.

HODGETTS, J. E. and O. P. DWIVEDI. *Provincial Governments as Employers: A Survey of Public Personnel Administration in Canada's Provinces.* Pp. xi, 216. Montreal, Ca.: McGill-Queen's University Press, 1974. $13.50. Paperbound, $6.00.

HOLLER, FREDERICK L. *Information Sources of Political Science.* Five Volume Set. Santa Barbara, Calif.: American Bibliographical Center, 1975. $24.50 per set. Paperbound.

HOLLICK, ANN L. and ROBERT OSGOOD. *New Era of Ocean Politics.* Pp. v, 131. Baltimore, Md.: Johns Hopkins University, 1975. $8.00. Paperbound, $2.75.

HOLT, JOHN BRADSHAW. *German Agricultural Policy, 1918–1934.* Pp. vi, 240. New York: Russell & Russell, 1975. $14.00.

HOWE, FLORENCE, ed. *Women and the Power to Change.* The Carnegie Commission on Higher Education. Pp. xiii, 182. New York: McGraw-Hill, 1975. $7.95.

HOWLEY, DENNIS C. *The United Nations and the Palestinians.* Pp. 165. New York: Exposition Press, 1975. $8.50.

INCIARDI, JAMES A. *Careers in Crime.* Pp. vii, 252. Chicago, Ill.: Rand McNally, 1975. $3.95. Paperbound.

ISRAEL, J. I. *Race, Class and Politics in Colonial Mexico, 1610–1670.* Oxford Historical Monographs. Pp. viii, 305. New York: Oxford University Press, 1975. $25.75.

JAFFA, HARRY V. *The Conditions of Freedom: Essays in Political Philosophy.* Pp. vii, 280. Baltimore, Md.: Johns Hopkins University, 1975. $12.50.

JELAVICH, BARBARA. *The Hapsburg Empire in European Affairs, 1814–1918.* Pp. vii, 190. Hamden, Conn.: Archon Books, 1974. $7.50.

JONES, PETER, ed. *The International Yearbook of Foreign Policy Analysis.* Vol. I. Pp. 213. New York: Halsted Press, 1974. $17.95.

KAGEN, DONALD. *Problems in Ancient History.* Vol. I. 2nd ed. Pp. v, 480. New York: Macmillan, 1975. $5.95. Paperbound.

KAGEN, RICHARD I. *Students and Society in Early Modern Spain.* Pp. xii, 278. Baltimore, Md.: Johns Hopkins University Press, 1975. $13.50.

KAMMEYER, KENNETH C. W. *Population Studies: Selected Essays and Research.* 2nd ed. Pp. v, 509. Chicago, Ill.: Rand McNally, 1975. $5.95. Paperbound.

KARLEN, HARVEY M. *The Pattern of American Government.* 2nd ed. Pp. viii, 496. Beverly Hills, Calif.: Glencoe Press, 1975. $7.95. Paperbound.

KELLEY, ROBERT. *The Sounds of Controversy: Crucial Arguments in the American Past.* Pp. v, 569. Vols. I and II. Englewood Cliffs, N.J.: Prentice-Hall, 1975. $5.95 each. Paperbound.

KENNEY, DAVID, JACK R. VAN DER SLIK and SAMUEL J. PERNACCIARO. *Roll Call! Patterns of Voting in the Sixth Illinois Constitutional Convention.* Pp. ix, 85. Urbana: University of Illinois, 1975. $3.45. Paperbound.

KERKVLIET, BENEDICT J., ed. *Political Change in the Philippines: Studies of Local Politics Preceding Martial Law.* Pp. v, 261. Honolulu: University of Hawaii Press, 1974. No price.

KILEFF, C. and W. C. PENDLETON. *Urban Man in Southern Africa.* Pp. 254. Signal Mountain, Tenn.: Mambo Press, 1975. No price.

KING, KENNETH, ed. *Ras Makonnen Pan-Africanism from Within.* Pp. v, 293. New York: Oxford University Press, 1975. $13.75.

KINSBRUNER, JAY. *Chile.* Pp. xii, 176. New York: Harper & Row, 1974. $13.00. Paperbound, $3.45.

KIRKEMP, RONALD B. *An Introduction to International Law.* Pp. ix, 235. Totowa, N.J.: Littlefield, Adams, 1975. $3.95. Paperbound.

KOMANOFF, CHARLES et al. *The Price of Power: Electric Utilities and the Environment.* Edited by Joanna Underwood. Pp. 151. Lawrence, Mass.: MIT Press, 1975. $18.50. Paperbound.

KONING, HANS. *The Almost World.* Pp. 213. New York: Monthly Review Press, 1975. $2.95. Paperbound.

KORR, CHARLES P. *Cromwell and the New Model Foreign Policy*. Pp. 282. Berkeley: University of California, 1975. $12.50.

KOSINSKI, LESZEK A. and R. MANSELL PROTHERO, eds. *People on the Move: Studies on Internal Migration*. Pp. 393. New York: Barnes & Noble, 1975. $29.00. Paperbound, $14.50.

KOSS, STEPHEN. *Nonconformity in Modern British Politics*. Pp. 263. Hamden, Conn.: Archon Books, 1975. $14.50.

KRISBERG, BARRY. *Crime and Privilege: Toward a New Criminology*. Pp. vii, 181. Englewood Cliffs, N.J.: Prentice-Hall, 1975. $8.95. Paperbound, $3.45.

KUNKEL, JOHN H. *Behavior, Social Problems, and Change: A Social Learning Approach*. Pp. v, 213. Englewood Cliffs, N.J.: Prentice-Hall, 1975. $9.95.

KUSHNER, HOWARD I. *Conflict on the Northwest Coast: American Russian Rivalry in the Pacific Northwest, 1790–1867*. Contributions in American History, no. 41. Pp. xii, 227. Westport, Conn.: Greenwood Press, 1975. No price.

LACH, DONALD F. and EDMUND S. WEHRLE. *International Politics in East Asia since World War II*. Pp. v, 388. New York: Praeger, 1975. $7.95. Paperbound.

LAMONT, WILLIAM and SYBIL OLDFIELD, eds. *Politics, Religion and Literature in the Seventeenth Century*. Pp. vi, 248. Totowa, N.J.: Rowman and Littlefield, 1975. $12.50. Paperbound, $6.75.

LANGER, WILLIAM L. et al., eds. *Western Civilization: Prehistory to the Peace of Utrecht*. Vol. I. 2nd ed. Pp. v, 526. New York: Harper & Row, 1975. $7.95. Paperbound.

LANGER, WILLIAM L. et al., eds. *Western Civilization: The Expansion of Empire to Europe in the Modern World*. Vol. II. 2nd ed. Pp. v, 485. New York: Harper & Row, 1975. $7.95. Paperbound.

LANGFORD, PAUL. *The Excise Crisis: Society and Politics in the Age of Walpole*. Pp. 187. New York: Oxford University Press, 1975. $17.00.

LAPCHICK, RICHARD E. *The Politics of Race and International Sport: The Case of South Africa*. Studies in Human Rights, no. 1. Pp. xxx, 268. Westport, Conn.: Greenwood Press, 1975. $13.95.

LAQUEUR, WALTER and GEORGE L. MOSSE, eds. *Historians in Politics*. Pp. 250. Beverly Hills, Calif.: Sage, 1974. $12.50. Paperbound, $6.00.

LEACH, RICHARD H. and TIMOTHY B. O'ROURKE. *Dimensions of State and Urban Policy Making*. Pp. v, 418. New York: Macmillan, 1975. $6.95. Paperbound.

LEGGATT, TIMOTHY, ed. *Sociological Theory and Survey Research: Institutional Change and Social Policy in Great Britain*. Pp. 336. Beverly Hills, Calif.: Sage, 1975. $17.50.

LENCZOWSKI, GEORGE, ed. *Political Elites in the Middle East*. Pp. 227. Washington, D.C.: American Enterprise Institute for Public Policy Research, 1975. $9.50. Paperbound, $3.50.

LEVITAN, SAR A., WILLIAM B. JOHNSTON and ROBERT TAGGART. *Minorities in the United States: Problems, Progress, and Prospects*. Pp. 106. Washington, D.C.: Public Affairs Press, 1975. $3.50. Paperbound.

LEWIS, BERNARD. *History: Remembered, Recovered, Invented*. Pp. vii, 111. Princeton, N.J.: Princeton University Press, 1975. $6.95.

LEYMORE, VARDA LANGHOLZ. *The Hidden Myth: Structure and Symbolism in Advertising*. Pp. 208. New York: Basic Books, 1975. $10.00.

LOOMIS, CHARLES P. and INGEBORG PAULUS. *Karl Marx: His Life and Teachings*. Pp. x, 169. East Lansing: Michigan State University, 1974. $8.50.

MACLACHLAN, COLIN M. *Criminal Justice in Eighteenth Century Mexico: A Study of the Tribunal of the Acordada*. Pp. 153. Berkeley: University of California, 1975. $9.00.

MALLET DU PAN, JACQUES. *Considerations on the Nature of the French Revolution*. Pp. viii, 113. New York: Howard Fertig, 1975. $11.75.

MANHEIM, JAROL B. *The Politics Within: A Primer in Political Attitudes and Behavior*. Pp. vii, 145. Englewood Cliffs, N.J.: Prentice-Hall, 1975. $6.95. Paperbound, $3.95.

MANN, DALE. *Policy Decision-Making in Education: An Introduction to Calculation and Control*. Pp. vii, 210. New York: Teachers College Press, 1975. $12.95. Paperbound, $6.95.

MARCUS, STEVEN. *Engels, Manchester and the Working Class*. Pp. viii, 271. New York: Vintage, 1975. No price. Paperbound.

MASSIALAS, BYRON G., NANCY F. SPRAGUE and JOSEPH B. HURST. *Social Issues through Inquiry: Coping in an Age of Crises*. Pp. xi, 243. Englewood Cliffs, N.J.: Prentice-Hall, 1975. $5.95. Paperbound.

MATHEWSON, KENT, ed. *The Regionalist Papers: Toward Metropolitan Unity*. Pp. iii, 284. Detroit, Mich.: Metropolitan Fund, 1974. $8.75. Paperbound.

MATRAS, JUDAH. *Social Inequality, Stratification, and Mobility*. Pp. v, 434. Englewood Cliffs, N.J.: Prentice-Hall, 1975. $11.95.

MAYNE, RICHARD, ed. *The New Atlantic Challenge*. Pp. 376. New York: Halsted Press, 1975. $17.95.

MCEWEN, WILLIAM J. *Changing Rural Society: A Study of Communities in Bolivia.* Pp. vii, 463. New York: Oxford University Press, 1975. $15.95. Paperbound, $7.95.

MCKIBBIN, ROSS. *The Evolution of the Labour Party, 1910–1924.* Pp. xi, 261. New York: Oxford University Press, 1975. $18.50.

MCLEAN, DONALD B. *The Plumber's Kitchen: The Secret Story of American Spy Weapons.* Pp. iii, 282. Wickenburg, Ariz.: Normount Technical Publications, 1975. $12.95. Paperbound.

MCNALL, SCOTT G. *Career of a Radical Rightist: A Study in Failure.* Pp. 202. Port Washington, N.Y.: Kennikat Press, 1975. $12.50.

MELANSON, PHILIP H. *Political Science and Political Knowledge.* Pp. iii, 183. Washington, D.C.: Public Affairs Press, 1975. $4.50. Paperbound.

MICHELMAN, CHERRY. *The Black Sash of South Africa.* Pp. viii, 198. New York: Oxford University Press, 1975. $18.75.

MILAZZO, MATTEO J. *The Chetnik Movement & The Yugoslav Resistance.* Pp. vii, 208. Baltimore, Md.: Johns Hopkins University, 1975. $12.00.

MILIUTIN, N. A. *Scotsgorod: The Problem of Building Socialist Cities.* Pp. 143. Cambridge, Mass.: MIT Press, 1975. No price.

MILLETT, JOHN D. *Politics and Higher Education.* Pp. x, 147. University: University of Alabama Press, 1975. $6.00. Paperbound, $2.95.

MITCHELL, B. R. *European Historical Statistics, 1750–1970.* Pp. v, 827. New York: Columbia University Press, 1975. $50.00.

MOORE, J. M. *Aristotle and Xenophon on Democracy and Oligarchy.* Pp. 320. Berkeley: University of California, 1975. $12.50. Paperbound, $3.85.

MOORE, JOHN NORTON, ed. *The Arab-Israeli Conflict.* 3 vols. Pp. vi, 3508. Princeton, N.J.: Princeton University Press, 1975. $95.00 per set.

MORPHET, EDGAR L., ROE L. JOHNS and THEODORE L. RELLER. *Educational Organization and Administration: Concepts, Practices, and Issues.* 3rd ed. Pp. v, 566. Englewood Cliffs, N.J.: Prentice-Hall, 1975. $6.95. Paperbound, $2.75.

MOSES, JOEL C. *Regional Party Leadership and Policy-Making in the USSR.* Pp. v, 263. New York: Praeger, 1974. $18.50.

MOSKIVICHOV, L. N. *The End of Ideology Theory: Illusions and Reality.* Pp. 191. Chicago, Ill.: IMPUBS, 1975. $2.25.

MOYNIHAN, DANIEL P. *Coping: On the Practice of Government.* Pp. 430. New York: Vintage, 1975. $4.95. Paperbound.

MUELLER, PETER G. and DOUGLAS A. ROSS. *China and Japan: Emerging Global Powers.* Pp. v, 218. New York: Praeger, 1975. $5.95. Paperbound.

MUNDEL, MARVIN E. *Measuring and Enhancing the Productivity of Service and Government Organizations.* Pp. 296. New York: UNIPUB, 1975. $19.75.

MUSCHAMP, HERBERT. *File under Architecture.* Pp. 117. Lawrence, Mass.: MIT Press, 1975. $10.95.

MYERS, CHARLES A. *Computers in Knowledge-Based Fields.* Pp. viii, 136. Cambridge, Mass.: MIT Press, 1970. $2.45. Paperbound.

NAGEL, STUART S., ed. *Policy Studies and the Social Sciences.* Pp. vii, 315. Lexington, Mass.: Lexington Books, 1975. $19.00.

NAKHLEH, EMILE A. *Arab-American Relations in the Persian Gulf.* Pp. 82. Washington, D.C.: American Enterprise Institute for Public Policy Research, 1975. $3.00. Paperbound.

NEMEC, LUDVIK. *The Czechoslovak Heresy and Schism: The Emergence of a National Czechoslovak Church.* Pp. 78. Philadelphia, Pa.: American Philosophical Society, 1975. $6.00. Paperbound.

Never Too Old to Learn. Pp. i, 109. New York: Academy for Educational Development, 1974. $5.00. Paperbound.

NIEZING, JOHAN. *Urban Guerilla.* Pp. 149. The Netherlands: Rotterdam University Press, 1974. $28.40. Paperbound.

NORTHEDGE, F. S., ed. *The Foreign Politics of the Powers.* Pp. 388. New York: Free Press, 1975. $12.00. Paperbound, $4.95.

NORTHRUP, HERBERT R. and HOWARD G. FOSTER. *Open Shop Construction. Industrial Research Unit.* Major Studies, no. 54. Pp. iii, 400. Philadelphia: University of Pennsylvania, 1975. No price.

The Nuclear Age. A SIPRI Monograph. Pp. v, 148. Cambridge, Mass.: MIT Press, 1975. No price.

O'TOOLE, GEORGE. *The Assassination Tapes: An Electronic Probe into the Murder of John F. Kennedy and the Dallas Coverup.* Pp. 257. New York: Penthouse Press, 1975. $8.95.

PARRY, V. J. and M. E. YAPP, eds. *War, Technology and Society in the Middle East.* Pp. vi, 448. New York: Oxford University Press, 1975. $19.75.

PATTERSON, K. DAVID. *The Northern Gabon Coast to 1875.* Oxford Studies in African Affairs. Pp. viii, 167. New York: Oxford University Press, 1975. $13.25.

PEARSON, CHARLES S. *International Marine Environment Policy.* Pp. vii, 127. Baltimore, Md.: Johns Hopkins University, 1975. $9.00. Paperbound, $2.65.

PENNIMAN, HOWARD R. *Britain at the Polls: The Parliamentary Elections of 1974.* Pp. 256. Washington, D.C.: American Enterprise Institute for Public Policy Research, 1975. $3.00. Paperbound.

POLMAR, NORMAN. *Soviet Naval Power: Challenge for the 1970s.* Revised edition. Pp. vii, 129. New York: Crane, Russak & Co., 1974. $5.95. Paperbound, $2.95.

POMPER, GERALD. *Voters' Choice: Varieties of American Electoral Behavior.* Pp. vii, 259. New York: Dodd Mead, 1975. $10.00.

POUND, ROSCOE. *Criminal Justice in America.* Pp. 226. New York: De Capo Press, 1975. $3.45. Paperbound.

PRANGER, ROBERT J. and DALE R. TAHTINEN. *Nuclear Threat in the Middle East.* Pp. 57. Washington, D.C.: American Enterprise Institute for Public Policy Research, 1975. $3.00. Paperbound.

PRESSMAN, HOPE HUGHES. *A New Resource for Welfare Reform: The Poor Themselves.* Pp. 122. Berkeley: University of California, 1975. No price.

PRESTON, LEE E. and JAMES E. POST. *Private Management and Public Policy: The Principle of Public Responsibility.* Pp. vii, 157. Englewood Cliffs, N.J.: Prentice-Hall, 1975. $8.95. Paperbound, $5.95.

PRICE, ROGER, ed. *1848 in France.* Pp. 192. Ithaca, N.Y.: Cornell University Press, 1975. $8.95. Paperbound, $2.95.

PRINGLE, MIA KELLMER. *The Needs of Children.* Pp. 192. New York: Schocken Books, 1975. $8.00. Paperbound, $2.95.

PULLANILLY, CYRIAC K. *Caesar Baronius: Counter-Reformation Historian.* Pp. 236. Notre Dame. Ind.: University of Notre Dame, 1975. $12.95.

PUTT, WILLIAM D., ed. *How to Start Your Own Business.* Pp. x, 259. Cambridge, Mass.: MIT Press, 1974. $9.95.

A Psychiatric Glossary. Pp. 156. Washington, D.C.: American Psychiatric Association, 1975. $3.00. Paperbound.

QUESTER, GEORGE H., ed. *Sea Power in the 1970s.* Pp. v, 248. Cambridge, Mass.: Dunellen, 1975. $15.00.

RANSEL, DAVID L. *The Politics of Catherinian Russia: The Panin Party.* Pp. vii, 327. New Haven, Conn.: Yale University Press, 1975. $17.50.

READ, DONALD A. and SIDNEY B. SIMON, eds. *Humanistic Education Sourcebook.* Pp. vi, 482. Englewood Cliffs, N.J.: Prentice-Hall, 1975. $10.95. Paperbound, $6.95.

REARDON, JOHN J. *Edmund Randolph: A Biography.* Pp. vii, 517. New York: Macmillan, 1975. $17.50.

RECORD, JEFFREY. *U.S. Nuclear Weapons in Europe: Issues and Alternatives.* Pp. 70. Washington, D.C.: The Brookings Institution, 1974. $2.50. Paperbound.

RIVLIN, ALICE M. and P. MICHAEL TIMPANE, eds. *Planned Variation in Education: Should We Give Up or Try Harder?* Pp. vii, 184. Washington, D.C.: Brookings Institution, 1975. $9.95. Paperbound, $3.50.

ROBBINS, RICHARD G., JR. *Famine in Russia, 1891–1892.* Pp. 262. New York: Columbia University Press, 1975. $12.50.

ROBERTS, DICK. *Capitalism in Crisis.* Pp. 128. New York: Pathfinder Press, 1975. $6.00. Paperbound, $1.95.

ROCK, DAVID, ed. *Argentina in the Twentieth Century.* Pp. vii, 230. Pittsburgh, Pa.: University of Pittsburgh, 1975. $14.50.

ROGGE, O. JOHN. *Why Men Confess.* Pp. 249. New York: Da Capo Press, 1975. $3.95. Paperbound.

RONDINELLI, DENNIS A. *Urban and Regional Development Planning: Policy and Administration.* Pp. 272. Ithaca, N.Y.: Cornell University Press, 1975. $12.50.

ROSENBERG, MARIE BAROVIC and LEN V. BERGSTROM, eds. *Women and Society: A Critical Review of the Literature with a Selected Annotated Bibliography.* Pp. 360. Beverly Hills, Calif.: Sage, 1975. $17.50.

ROWAN, ROY. *The Four Days of Mayaquez.* Pp. 224. New York: W. W. Norton, 1975. $7.95.

RUBIN, STANLEY. *Medieval English Medicine.* Pp. 232. New York: Barnes & Noble, 1975. $15.00.

RUBIN, VERA and RICHARD P. SCHAEDEL, eds. *The Haitian Potential: Research and Resources of Haiti.* Pp. vii, 284. New York: Columbia University, 1975. $15.00.

RUTLAND, ROBERT A., ed. *The Papers of James Madison.* Vol. IX. Pp. vii, 447. Chicago, Ill.: University of Chicago Press, 1975. $18.50.

RYAN, JOSEPH A., ed. *White Ethnics: Life in Working-Class America.* Pp. 184. Englewood Cliffs, N.J.: Prentice-Hall, 1973. No price.

SAFFELL, DAVID C. *The Politics of American National Government.* 2nd ed. Pp. v, 487. Cambridge, Mass.: Winthrop, 1975. $6.95. Paperbound.

SAID, ABDUL A. and LUIZ R. SIMMONS, eds. *The New Sovereigns: Multinational Corporations as World Powers.* Pp. v, 186. Englewood Cliffs, N.J.: Prentice-Hall, 1975. $16.50. Paperbound, $8.50.

SARGENT, LYMAN TOWER. *Contemporary Political Ideologies*. 3rd ed. Pp. ix, 177. Homewood, Ill.: Dorsey Press, 1975. $3.95. Paperbound.

SARKESIAN, SAM C., ed. *Revolutionary Guerilla Warfare*. Pp. viii, 623. Chicago, Ill.: Precedent Publishers, 1975. $13.95.

SARTRE, JEAN PAUL. *Between Existentialism and Marxism*. Pp. 302. New York: Pantheon, 1975. $10.00.

SAUER, CARL ORTWIN. *Sixteenth Century North America*. Pp. 323. Berkeley: University of California, 1975. $4.95. Paperbound.

SCALLY, ROBERT J. *The Origins of the Lloyd George Coalition: The Politics of Social Imperialism, 1900–1918*. Pp. xi, 416. Princeton, N.J.: Princeton University Press, 1975. $19.50.

SCHADT, ARMIN L. *A Counterfeit Reality: The Education of Post-Faustian Man*. Pp. 98. North Quincy, Mass.: Christopher Publishing, 1975. $5.95.

SCHAFER, STEPHEN, MARY S. KNUDTEN and RICHARD D. KNUDTEN. *Social Problems in a Changing Society: Issues and Deviances*. Pp. vii, 262. Englewood Cliffs, N.J.: Prentice-Hall, 1975. $8.95. Paperbound.

SCHROEDER, W. WIDICK et al. *Suburban Religion*. Pp. iii, 266. Chicago. Ill.: Center for the Scientific Study of Religion, 1974. $9.95. Paperbound, $5.95.

SCHUBERT, GLENDON. *Human Jurisprudence: Public Law as Political Science*. Pp. x, 394. Honolulu: University of Hawaii Press, 1975. $15.00.

SCHULZ, JAMES et al. *Providing Adequate Retirement Income*. Pp. xv, 330. Hanover, N.H.: University Press of New England, 1975. $15.00.

SCHWARTZ, DAVID C. and SANDRA KENYON SCHWARTZ, eds. *New Directions in Political Socialization*. Pp. v, 340. New York: Free Press, 1975. $12.95.

SCHWENINGER, MARK. *Prophecy of Mark*. Pp. 45. Hicksville, N.Y.: Exposition Press, 1975. $4.00.

SELIGMAN, LESTER G. et al. *Patterns of Recruitment: A State Chooses its Lawmakers*. Pp. 269. Chicago, Ill.: Rand McNally, 1974. No price.

SENN, ALFRED ERICH. *Diplomacy and Revolution: The Soviet Mission to Switzerland, 1918*. Pp. ix, 221. Notre Dame, Ind.: University of Notre Dame, 1974. $9.95.

SHAPIRO, MARTIN and ROCCO J. TRESOLINI. *American Constitutional Law*. 4th ed. Pp. ix, 779. New York: Macmillan, 1975. $13.95.

SIK, JANG YOUNG. *Econometric Model Building: A Comparative Study of Simultaneous Equation Systems*. Pp. 170. Seoul, Korea: Yonsei University Press, 1973. No price.

SIMPSON, GEORGE and JOHN MILTON YINGER, eds. *American Indians and American Life*. Pp. v, 173. New York: Russell & Russell, 1975. $15.00.

SKAGGS, DAVID CURTIS. *Roots of Maryland Democracy, 1753–1776*. Pp. xi, 253. Westport, Conn.: Greenwood, 1973. $12.00.

SMITH, DAVID HORTON. *Voluntary Action Research: 1974*. Pp. vii, 323. Lexington, Mass.: Lexington Books, 1974. $20.00.

SMITH, GADDIS. *Britain's Clandestine Submarines, 1914–1915*. Pp. 155. Hamden, Conn.: Archon Books, 1975. $7.50.

SMITH, REBECCA M. *Klemer's Marriage and Family Relationships*. 2nd ed. Pp. vi, 424. New York: Harper & Row, 1975. $11.95.

SMITH, WALLACE F. *Urban Development: The Process and the Problems*. Pp. 399. Berkeley: University of California, 1975. $14.75.

SMOLKA, RICHARD G. *Registering Voters by Mail: The Maryland and New Jersey Experience*. Pp. 85. Washington, D.C.: American Enterprise Institute for Public Policy Research, 1975. $3.00. Paperbound.

SOCARIDES, CHARLES W. *Beyond Sexual Freedom*. Pp. 180. New York: Quadrangle, 1975. $7.95.

SOKOLOVSKIY, V. D. *Soviet Military Strategy*. Edited by Harriet Fast Scott. 3rd ed. Pp. vii, 494. New York: Crane, Russak & Co., 1975. $17.50.

SOWELL, THOMAS. *Classical Economics Reconsidered*. Pp. 152. Princeton, N.J.: Princeton University Press, 1974. $9.00.

STARRATT, PATRICIA E. *The Natural Gas Shortage and the Congress*. Pp. 68. Washington, D.C.: American Enterprise Institute for Public Policy Research, 1974. $3.00. Paperbound.

STAVRIANOS, L. S. *Man's Past and Present: A Global History*. 2nd ed. Pp. vii, 593. Englewood Cliffs, N.J.: Prentice-Hall, 1975. $9.95. Paperbound.

STEDMAN, MURRAY S., JR. *Urban Politics*. 2nd ed. Pp. iv, 358. Cambridge, Mass.: Winthrop, 1975. $8.95. Paperbound, $6.95.

STEGGERT, FRANK X. *Community Action Groups and City Government*. Pp. vi, 105. Cambridge, Mass.: Ballinger, 1975. No price.

STEPHAN, JOHN J. *The Kuril Islands: Russo-Japanese Frontiers in the Pacific*. Pp. viii, 279. New York: Oxford University Press, 1975. $20.00.

STERN, FREDERICK MARTIN. *Life and Liberty: A Return to First Principles*. Pp. v, 212, New York: Thomas Y. Crowell, 1975. $7.95.

STOESSINGER, JOHN G. *The United Nations and the Superpowers: China, Russia, and America.* Pp. xi, 216. New York: Random House, 1973. $3.50. Paperbound.

STRAUSS, LEO. *The Argument and the Action of Plato's Laws.* Pp. v, 186. Chicago, Ill.: University of Chicago, 1975. $10.75.

STROMBERG, ROLAND N. *European Intellectual History since 1789.* 2nd ed. Pp. viii, 361. Englewood Cliffs, N.J.: Prentice-Hall, 1975. $6.50. Paperbound.

STUMPF, HARRY P. *Community Politics and Legal Services: The Other Side of the Law.* Pp. 314. Beverly Hills, Calif.: Sage, 1975. $15.00.

SUDMAN, SEYMOUR and NORMAN M. BRADBURN. *Response Effects in Surveys: A Review and Synthesis.* Pp. v, 257. Chicago, Ill.: Aldine-Atherton, 1974. $11.50.

SUNDERLAND, LANE V. *Obscenity: The Court, the Congress and the President's Commission.* Pp. 127. Washington, D.C.: American Enterprise Institute for Public Policy Research, 1975. $3.00. Paperbound.

SZASZ, THOMAS. *Ceremonial Chemistry: The Ritual Persecution of Drugs, Addicts, and Pushers.* Pp. 240. New York: Doubleday, 1975. $2.95. Paperbound.

THIEBLOT, ARMAND J., JR. *The Davis-Bacon Act.* Pp. iii, 239. Philadelphia: University of Pennsylvania Press, 1975. No price.

THOMIS, MALCOLM I. *The Town Labourer and the Industrial Revolution.* Pp. 247. New York: Barnes & Noble, 1975. $11.00.

TILLION, GERMAINE. *Ravenshruck: An Eyewitness Account of a Women's Concentration Camp.* Pp. 280. New York: Doubleday, 1975. $2.95. Paperbound.

TIMKO, MICHAEL, ed. *Twenty Nine Short Stories: An Introductory Anthology.* Pp. 415. New York: Random House, 1975. $4.95. Paperbound.

TÖKÉS, RUDOLF L., ed. *Dissent in the USSR: Politics, Ideology, and People.* Pp. ix, 453. Baltimore, Md.: Johns Hopkins University, 1975. $15.00.

TREZISE, PHILIP H. *The Atlantic Connection: Prospects, Problems and Policies.* Pp. 100. Washington, D.C.: Brookings Institution, 1975. $2.50. Paperbound.

TROW, MARTIN, ed. *Teachers and Students.* The Carnegie Commission on Higher Education. Pp. xiii, 419. New York: McGraw-Hill, 1975. $17.50.

UDRY, J. RICHARD and EARL F. HUYCK. *The Demographic Evaluation of Domestic Family Planning Programs.* Pp. v, 119. Cambridge, Mass.: Ballinger, 1975. No price.

ULLMANN, WALTER. *Law and Politics in the Middle Ages.* Pp. 320. Ithaca, N.Y.: Cornell University Press, 1975. $15.00.

The Virginia Supreme Court: An Institutional and Political Analysis. Pp. x, 188. Charlottesville: University of Virginia, 1975. No price.

VOGEL, EZRA F., ed. *Modern Japanese Organization and Decision-Making.* Pp. 370. Berkeley: University of California, $4.95. Paperbound.

VOLKMER, WALTER E. *American Government: Brief Edition.* Pp. 622. Englewood Cliffs, N.J.: Prentice-Hall, 1975. $7.95. Paperbound.

WADSWORTH, JAMES W., JR. *The Gentleman from New York.* Pp. xi, 457. Syracuse, N.Y.: Syracuse University Press, 1975. $17.50.

WALKER, LESLIE J. *The Discourses of Niccolo Machiavelli.* Vols. I and II. Pp. vii, 988. Boston, Mass.: Routledge & Kegan Paul, 1975. $46.95 per set.

WALTON, HANES, JR. *Black Republicans: The Politics of the Black and Tans.* Pp. 217. Metuchen, N.J.: Scarecrow Press, 1975. $8.00.

WEBSTER, BRUCE. *Scotland from the Eleventh Century to 1603.* Pp. 239. Ithaca, N.Y.: Cornell University Press, 1975. $12.50.

WEBSTER, MURRAY, JR. *Actions and Actors. Principles of Social Psychology.* Pp. ix, 481. Cambridge, Mass.: Winthrop, 1975. $12.95.

WEIDENBAUM, MURRAY L. *The Economics of Peacetime Defense.* Pp. v, 193. New York: Praeger, 1974. $15.00.

WEISS, ROBERT S. *Loneliness: The Experience of Emotional and Social Isolation.* Pp. x, 236. Cambridge, Mass.: MIT Press, 1973. $6.95. Paperbound.

WENDELL, CHARLES. *The Evolution of the Egyptian National Image: From its Origins to Ahmad Lutfi al-Sayyid.* Pp. 352. Berkeley: University of California, 1973. $17.50.

WHITE, WILLIAM D. *U.S. Tactical Air Power: Missions, Forces, and Costs.* Pp. 121. Washington, D.C.: The Brookings Institution, 1974. $2.50. Paperbound.

WILBER, GEORGE L., ed. *Poverty: A New Perspective.* Pp. vii, 196. Lexington: University of Kentucky, 1975. $13.50.

WILKIE, JAMES W. *Measuring Land Reform: Supplement to the Statistical Abstract of Latin America.* Pp. 165. Los Angeles: University of California: 1974. No price.

WILSON, DON W. *Governor Charles Robinson of Kansas.* Pp. vii, 214. Lawrence: University of Kansas, 1975. $11.00.

WOLL, PETER. *Public Policy.* Pp. v, 264. Cambridge, Mass.: Winthrop, 1974. $8.95. Paperbound, $5.95.

WOLL, PETER and ROBERT H. BINSTOCK. *America's Political System.* 2nd ed. Pp. v, 612. New York: Random House, 1975. $8.95. Paperbound.

YAZAWA, MELVIN, ed. *Representative Government and the Revolution: The Maryland Constitutional Crisis of 1787.* Pp. vii, 187. Baltimore, Md.: Johns Hopkins University Press, 1975. $10.00.

YOUNG, KEN, ed. *Essays on the Study of Urban Politics.* Pp. viii, 208. Hamden, Conn.: Archon Books, 1975. $15.00.

ZECKHAUSER, RICHARD et al. *Benefit-Cost & Policy Analysis 1974.* Pp. viii, 514. Chicago, Ill.: Aldine-Atherton, 1975. $27.50.

ZUCKER, STANLEY. *Ludwig Bamberger: German Liberal Politician and Social Critic, 1823–1899.* Pp. ix, 343. Pittsburgh, Pa.: University of Pittsburgh Press, 1975. $14.95.

INDEX

INDEX